THE CAMBRIDGE COMPANION TO
EARLY MODERN WOMEN'S WRITING

Featuring the most frequently taught female writers and texts of the early modern period, this *Companion* introduces the reader to the range, complexity, historical importance and aesthetic merit of women's writing in Britain from 1500 to 1700. Presenting key textual, historical and methodological information, the volume exemplifies new and diverse approaches to the study of women's writing. The book is clearly divided into three sections, covering: how women learned to write and how their work was circulated or published; how and what women wrote in the places and spaces in which they lived, worked, socialized and worshipped; and the different kinds of writing women produced, from poetry, drama and fiction to letters, diaries and political prose. This structure makes the volume readily adaptable to course usage. The *Companion* is enhanced by an introduction that lays out crucial framework and critical issues, and by chronologies that situate women's writings alongside political and cultural events.

Laura Lunger Knoppers is Professor of English at Pennsylvania State University. She has published widely on seventeenth-century British literature, visual culture, politics and religion, particularly on the works of John Milton. Her books include *Historicizing Milton: Spectacle, Power, and Poetry in Restoration England* (1994) and *Constructing Cromwell: Ceremony, Portrait, and Print, 1645–1661* (2000). She has served as President of the Milton Society of America and as elected member of the Seventeenth-Century Literature Division, Modern Language Society of America.

D0722991

THE CAMBRIDGE COMPANION TO

EARLY MODERN WOMEN'S WRITING

EDITED BY
LAURA LUNGER KNOPPERS
Pennsylvania State University

CAMBRIDGE
UNIVERSITY PRESS

CAMBRIDGE UNIVERSITY PRESS
Cambridge, New York, Melbourne, Madrid, Cape Town, Singapore, São Paulo, Delhi

Cambridge University Press
The Edinburgh Building, Cambridge CB2 8RU, UK

Published in the United States of America by Cambridge University Press, New York

www.cambridge.org
Information on this title: www.cambridge.org/9780521712422

© Cambridge University Press 2009

First published 2009

Printed in the United Kingdom at the University Press, Cambridge

A catalogue record for this publication is available from the British Library

Library of Congress Cataloguing in Publication data
The Cambridge companion to early modern women's writing / [edited by]
Laura Knoppers.
p.   cm. – (Cambridge companions to literature)
ISBN 978-0-521-88527-0
1. English literature–Early modern, 1500–1700–History and criticism.   2. English
literature–Women authors–History and criticism.   3. English literature–Women authors.
4. Women and literature–Great Britain–History–16th century.   5. Women and literature–
Great Britain–History–17th century.   I. Knoppers, Laura Lunger.   II. Title.   III. Series.
PR113.C36 2009
820.9′9287′09031–dc22
2009025736

ISBN 978-0-521-88527-0 hardback
ISBN 978-0-521-71242-2 paperback

CONTENTS

CONTENTS

ILLUSTRATIONS

CONTRIBUTORS

CAROLINE BOWDEN, Queen Mary, University of London

KAREN BRITLAND, University of Wisconsin, Madison

VICTORIA E. BURKE, University of Ottawa

DANIELLE CLARKE, University College Dublin

ELIZABETH CLARKE, University of Warwick

JAMES DAYBELL, University of Plymouth

FRANCES E. DOLAN, University of California, Davis

MARY E. FISSELL, Johns Hopkins University

HILARY HINDS, Lancaster University

DEREK HUGHES, University of Aberdeen

LAURA LUNGER KNOPPERS, Pennsylvania State University

LORI HUMPHREY NEWCOMB, University of Illinois at Urbana-Champaign

MARCY L. NORTH, Pennsylvania State University

EDITH SNOOK, University of New Brunswick

MARTA STRAZNICKY, Queen's University, Ontario

WENDY WALL, Northwestern University

HELEN WILCOX, Bangor University, Wales

HEATHER WOLFE, Folger Shakespeare Library

SUSANNE WOODS, Wheaton College (MA), Emerita, and
University of Miami

RAMONA WRAY, Queen's University Belfast

ACKNOWLEDGEMENTS

Many hands have contributed to the making of this volume. At Penn State, I have benefited from a supportive and collegial Renaissance group. I am particularly grateful for early suggestions on the proposal and for sage advice throughout the process from Patrick Cheney. Garrett Sullivan offered cheerful encouragement, and Marcy North not only contributed a chapter, but provided a sounding board at crucial points. Doctoral student Nicole Jacobs gave insightful feedback on the proposal. Giuseppina Iacono was an efficient and conscientious research assistant for this project, ably helping with copy-editing and with the compilation of the Chronologies. Students in my spring 2008 undergraduate and graduate courses on women writers also helped to shape the project in valuable ways.

Librarians have been gracious and attentive in providing resources for this Companion. I am particularly grateful for the generosity of Folger Shakespeare Library Head of Reference, Georgianna Ziegler, and Curator of Manuscripts, Heather Wolfe (also a contributor to this volume), who shared their expertise and facilitated my access to Esther Inglis manuscripts. Many of our volume's images are taken from the Folger collection, and we are indebted to the Folger Photography Department for their efficiency and courtesy. Houghton Library, Harvard University, made it possible for us to publish the cover image of Inglis for the first time.

It has been a great pleasure to work with Cambridge University Press. Four anonymous readers provided remarkably detailed and constructive reports which have refined and strengthened this project. Sarah Stanton has been a superb editor, enthusiastic from the beginning, wise in advice, amazingly prompt and helpful. I am also grateful to my husband, Gary, for his invariable encouragement and for kindly bearing with me on those days when my interest in early modern households took precedence over the work in my own.

Finally, the nineteen scholars whose essays appear in this Companion have not only contributed fine chapters based on their remarkably wide expertise but have been responsive, collegial and enthusiastic throughout the publication process. It has been a privilege to work with old friends and to make new ones in the completion of this volume.

CHRONOLOGIES

Dates are given new style, with the year taken to begin on 1 January.

Events and women's texts

1509	Henry VIII becomes King, marries Catherine of Aragon	
1517	Martin Luther's Wittenberg Theses: beginning of the Reformation in Europe	
1521		Christine de Pisan, *Boke of the Cyte of Ladyes*, published in English
1530		Devonshire Manuscript, *c.* 1530s–40s; contains hands of Mary Shelton, Mary Fitzroy and Margaret Douglas
1533	Henry divorces Catherine of Aragon, marries Anne Boleyn	
1534	Henry breaks with Rome; Act of Supremacy declares him head of the Church of England	
1536	Execution of Anne Boleyn; Henry marries Jane Seymour; Henry closes English monasteries and convents and confiscates their properties (1536–40)	
1540	Henry marries Anne of Cleves; marriage annulled; Henry marries Catherine Howard	
1542	Catherine Howard executed	
1543	Henry marries Catherine Parr	
1544		Elizabeth Tudor (later Queen of England), trans., *Miroir de l'âme pécheresse* (Marguerite de Navarre)
1545		Catherine Parr, *Prayers or Meditacions* Elizabeth Tudor (later Queen of England), trans., Catherine Parr, *Prayers or Meditacions* (into Latin, French and Italian)

1546	Anne Askew burnt at Smithfield for heresy	Anne Askew, *The First Examinacion of Anne Askewe*
1547	Death of Henry VIII; his young son Edward VI becomes King and institutes further Protestant reforms	Anne Askew, *The Lattre Examinacion of Anne Askewe*
1548		Mary Tudor (later Queen of England), translation of Erasmus included in the first volume of *Paraphrase of Erasmus upon the Newe Testamente*
1549	Act of Uniformity imposes first Book of Common Prayer	
1550		Jane Lumley, trans., *Iphigeneia at Aulis* (Euripides)
1551	Geneva (English) translation of the Bible	
1553	Death of Edward VI; Mary I becomes Queen, returns England to Catholicism	
1554	'Marian' (Protestant) exiles flee to Calvinist Geneva; execution of Lady Jane Grey (Protestant contender for the English throne); Queen Mary marries Catholic monarch, Philip of Spain	Lady Jane Grey, *An Epistle of the Lady Jane*
1558	Death of Queen Mary; Elizabeth I becomes Queen, returns England to Protestantism	
1559	Elizabeth crowned in January. Acts of Supremacy and Uniformity	
1560		Anne Lok (or Locke), trans., *Sermons of John Calvin*
1563	Thirty-nine Articles set out the doctrine of the Church of England	John Foxe, *Actes and Monuments* (Book of Martyrs) includes testimony of Anne Askew
1567		Isabella Whitney, *The Copy of a Letter to her Unconstant Lover*
1568	Imprisonment of Mary, Queen of Scots; infant Prince James proclaimed King James VI of Scotland	
1570	Pope excommunicates Elizabeth	
1573		Isabella Whitney, *A Sweet Nosgay, or pleasant Posye*
1574		Elizabeth Tyrwhit, *Morning and Evening Prayer*
1576	First theatre opens in London	
1577–80	Francis Drake sails around the world	

1578		Margaret Tyler, trans., *The Mirrour of Princely Deedes and Knighthood* (Diego Ortúñez de Calahorra)
1580	Parliament passes series of Acts against practice of Catholicism	Elizabeth I, trans., *A Godly Meditation of the Soule* (Marguerite de Navarre)
1582		Thomas Bentley, *The Monument of Matrones* (includes women's writing)
1587	Mary, Queen of Scots, executed (potential Catholic rival to Elizabeth)	
1588	Defeat of the Spanish Armada seen as providential victory of Protestantism over Catholic threat	
1589		Anne Dowriche, *The French Historie*
1590		Mary Sidney Herbert, *Psalmes* (1590s)
1591		Katherine Stubbes's last words recorded in Philip Stubbes's *A Crystall Glasse, for Christian Women*
1592		Mary Sidney Herbert, trans., *A Discourse of Life and Death* (Philippe de Mornay) and *Antonius: A Tragedie* (Robert Garnier), published together
1593	Theatres closed in London because of the plague	
1598		Elizabeth Cary, trans., 'The Mirror of the Worlde' (Abraham Ortelius)
1599		Margaret Hoby, diary (1599–1605)
1600	East India Company is founded	Ann Bowyer's miscellany (compiled *c.* 1600–10); Mary Sidney Herbert, 'Triumph of Death' (Petrarch)
1601	Earl of Essex, former royal favourite, executed after failed rebellion against Queen Elizabeth	Esther Inglis, calligrapher, *Octonaries* (Antoine de la Roche Chandieu)
1602		Alice Egerton writes an entertainment for Queen Elizabeth's visit to Harefield; Mary Sidney Herbert, *A Poetical Rhapsody*
1603	Death of Elizabeth; James VI of Scotland becomes James I, first Stuart King of England; Queen Consort, Anna of Denmark	Anne Clifford, diaries (1603–76) Elizabeth Melvill, *Ane Godlie Dreame* (in Scots dialect)
1604		Elinor Fettiplace, recipe book; Elizabeth Grymeston, *Miscelanea* (several further editions); Elizabeth Melvill, *A Godlie Dreame*

1605	Discovery of Catholic Gunpowder Plot to blow up Parliament and the King; Francis Bacon's *Advancement of Learning* calls for new science	
		Esther Inglis, calligrapher, *Argumenta in Librum Psalmorum Davidis*
1607	Virginia Company sends expedition to the New World, founds Jamestown (first successful British colony in America)	
1610	Galileo's astronomical discoveries are published	Sarah Longe, recipe book (*c.* 1610)
1611	King James (Authorized) Bible	Aemilia Lanyer, *Salve Deus Rex Judaeorum*
1612		Lady Mary Percy, trans., *Abridgment of Christian Perfection* (Achilles Galliardi); Queen Elizabeth's prayers included in Thomas Sorocold's *Supplications of Saints*
1613	Marriage of Elizabeth Stuart, daughter of James I and Queen Anna, to Frederick the Elector Palatine	Elizabeth Cary, *Tragedie of Mariam*
1616		Dorothy Leigh, *The Mothers Blessing*
1617	Frederick takes the throne of Bohemia	Rachel Speght, *A Mouzell for Melastomus*; Lady Grace Mildmay, 'Lady Mildmay's Meditations'; 'Esther Sowernam', *Esther Hath Hang'd Haman*, in response to Joseph Swetnam's *The Araignment of Lewd, Idle, Froward, and Unconstant Women* (1615); Constantia Munda, *The Worming of a Madde Dogge*, in response to Swetnam
1618	Rebellion of the Protestant estates of Bohemia against the Holy Roman Empire begins the Thirty Years' War on the Continent; execution of Sir Walter Ralegh on charges of treason	
1620	The *Mayflower* lands at Cape Cod, Massachusetts, with English colonists; signing of the Mayflower Compact; founding of Plymouth Colony.	Lady Mary Wroth, 'Love's Victory'; *Swetnam, the Woman-hater, Arraigned by Women,* anonymously published in response to Joseph Swetnam
1621		Rachel Speght, *Mortalities Memorandum*; Lady Mary Wroth, *The Countesse of Mountgomeries Urania*
1622		Elizabeth Clinton, *The Countesse of Lincolnes Nurserie*

1624	War with Spain	Esther Inglis, calligrapher, *Emblemes Chrestiens* (Georgette de Montenay); Elizabeth Jocelin, *The Mothers Legacie to her Unborne Childe*
1625	Death of James I; Charles I becomes King; marriage of Charles I and French Catholic princess, Henrietta Maria	Lady Brilliana Harley, letters (1625–43)
1626		Mary Baumfylde, book of medical and cookery recipes
1627	War with France (1627–8)	Elizabeth Cary, *The History of the Life, Reign, and Death of Edward II* (published 1680); Ez. W., *Answer of a Mother unto hir Seduced Sonnes Letter*
1628	Petition of Right presented to Charles I by Parliament; George Villiers, Duke of Buckingham and royal favourite, is assassinated; William Harvey publishes his discovery of the circulation of the blood	Rachael Fane, exercise book
1629	Charles I begins eleven years (1629–40) of 'Personal Rule' without Parliament	
1630		Elizabeth Cary, trans., *The Reply of the Most Illustrious Cardinall of Perron* (Jacques Davy du Perron); Constance Fowler, manuscript miscellany (compiled *c.* 1630–60); Lady Diana Primrose, *A Chaine of Pearle*; M.R., *The Mothers Counsell*
1631		Lady Anne Southwell, miscellany, compilation, *c.* 1631–6
1632		Martha Moulsworth, 'The Memorandum of Martha Moulsworth, Widdowe'; Prudentiana Deacon [pseudonym], trans., *Delicious Entertainments of the Soule* (attributed to Dame Agnes More)
1633	William Laud becomes Archbishop of Canterbury	
1634		Jane Owen, *An Antidote against Purgatory*; Alice Sutcliffe, *Meditations of Man's Mortalitie*
1637	Star Chamber Decree tightens up regulation of print	Mary Fage, *Fames Roule*
1639	First Bishops' War (between England and Scotland); convening and dissolution of Short Parliament	Anonymous, *The Ladies Cabinet Opened*

1640	Second Bishops' War; Long Parliament is convened	Elizabeth Isham, diary (compiled *c.* 1640s, in part retrospective); Mary Granville and Anne Granville Dewes, cookery and medicinal recipes (*c.* 1640–*c.* 1750); Mary Tattle-well and Joan Hit-him-home, *The Womens Sharpe Revenge*
1641	Parliamentary Act abolishing Star Chamber; collapse of censorship regulations; Parliament draws up a list of grievances against the monarch, 'The Grand Remonstrance'; Irish rebellion; execution of Thomas Wentworth, Earl of Strafford and close royal adviser, on charges of treason	Katherine Chidley, *The Justification of the Independant Churches of Christ*; Lady Eleanor (Davies) Douglas, *Appeale to the High Court of Parliament*
1642	Outbreak of civil war between King and Parliament (August); public theatres closed (September)	
1643	Abolition of episcopacy	*The Midwives Petition*
1644		Anna Hume, trans., *Triumphs of Love, Chastitie, Death* (Petrarch), published in Edinburgh
1645	Execution of William Laud, Archbishop of Canterbury	Lucy Cary and her siblings Mary and Patrick write their mother's, Elizabeth Cary's (1585–1639), biography, *Lady Falkland: Her Life* (written 1645–9, published 1861); sisters Elizabeth (Cavendish) Egerton and Jane (Cavendish) Cheyne, 'The Concealed Fancies'; Lady Hester Pulter, 'Poems Breathed Forth by the Noble Hadassas' and 'The Unfortunate Florinda' (incomplete), brought together between 1645–65; Elizabeth Richardson, *A Ladies Legacie to her Daughters*
1646	Charles surrenders to the Scots; first civil war ends with surrender of royalist Oxford	
1647		Sarah Wight, *The Exceeding Riches of Grace* (transcribed and published by Henry Jessey)
1648	Second civil war; Scots intervene on behalf of the King	John Bale, Protestant printer in Wesel, publishes Queen Elizabeth's translation of Marguerite de Navarre's *Miroir de l'âme pécheresse*
1649	Trial and execution of Charles I by beheading outside Whitehall (January); establishment of a republic in England; massacres at Drogheda	Elizabeth Poole, *A Prophesie Touching the Death of King Charles*

	and Wexford (parliamentary victory in Ireland)	
1650	Victory of Oliver Cromwell's army against the Scots at Dunbar	Anne Bradstreet, *The Tenth Muse Lately Sprung up in America, or Severall Poems* (unauthorized publication in London); Katherine Brown, medical and cookery recipes (*c.* 1650–*c.* 1662); Anne Conway begins her correspondence with the Cambridge Platonist, Henry More
1651	Oliver Cromwell's victory over (future) Charles II at Worcester	Mary Cary, *The Little Horns Doom & Downfall* and *A New and More Exact Mappe*; Anna Weamys, *Continuation of Sir Philip Sidney's 'Arcadia'*
1652	First Anglo-Dutch War (1652–4)	Mary Carey, 'Written by me at the death of my 4th sonne and 5th Child Perigrene Payler'; Dorothy Osborne and William Temple begin their clandestine correspondence (1652–4); *Eliza's Babes: Or the Virgins-Offering*
1653	Cromwell dissolves Parliament (April); 'Nominated' Parliament (July–December); Oliver Cromwell becomes Lord Protector of England (December)	Jane Buckhurst, cookery book; Margaret Cavendish, *Poems and Fancies* and *Philosophical Fancies*; An Collins, *Divine Songs and Meditacions*; Elizabeth Grey, *A Choice Manual of Rare and Select Secrets*
1654		Mary Blaithwaite, *The Complaint of Mary Blaithwaite Widdow*; Anna Trapnel, *The Cry of a Stone*; *Anna Trapnel's Report and Plea*; *A Legacy for Saints*; and *Strange and Wonderful Newes from White-Hall*
1655	Capture of Jamaica	*The Queens Closet Opened* (attributed to Henrietta Maria); Hester Biddle, *Wo to thee City of Oxford* and *Wo to thee Town of Cambridge*; Lady Grace Mildmay's grandson, Sir Francis Fane, compiles a commonplace book with some of her advice (1655–6); Aletheia Talbot, *Natura Exenterata;* Margaret Cavendish, *The Worlds Olio* and *Philosophical and Physical Opinions*
1656		Margaret Cavendish, *A True Relation of My Birth, Breeding and Life* and *Natures Pictures*; Margaret Fell Fox, *A Testimonie of the Touch-stone;* Anne Gargill, *A Warning to all the*

		World; Dorothy Waugh, 'A Relation Concerning Dorothy Waugh's Cruel Usage by the Mayor of Carlisle', in *The Lambs Defence Against Lyes*
1657		Mary Howgill, *A Remarkable Letter of Mary Howgill to Oliver Cromwell, called Protector*
1658	Death of Oliver Cromwell; his eldest son, Richard, is named Protector	Anne Venn, *A Wise Virgins Lamp Burning*
1659	Protectorate breaks down	Susanna Parr, *Susanna's Apologie Against the Elders*
1660	Convention Parliament; Stuart monarchy restored; Charles II returns to England; public theatre made legal again; women actors introduced to the stage	Mrs Carlyon, book of medical recipes; Mary Roper, 'The Sacred Historie', 1660s (probable author)
1661	Robert Boyle's *The Sceptical Chemist* makes ground-breaking advances in chemistry	
1662	Quaker Act requires Oath of Allegiance to the King; Act of Uniformity requires the use of the Book of Common Prayer and Episcopal ordination of all ministers; Licensing Act imposes print regulation and restrictions; The Royal Society (a scientific organization) is chartered; marriage of Charles II and Portuguese princess, Catherine of Braganza	Margaret Cavendish, *Plays* (originally written in the 1650s; new edition 1668); Katharine Evans and Sarah Cheevers, *Short Relation of Some of the Cruel Sufferings*; Elizabeth Delaval, meditations (1662–71)
1663		Mary Carleton, *The Case of Madam Mary Carleton*; Katherine Philips, trans., *The Death of Pompey* (Pierre Corneille), performed in Dublin and published in London
1664	Conventicle Act outlaws meetings outside of the Church of England; Margaret Fell imprisoned (1664–8) for Quaker activity	Margaret Cavendish, *Sociable Letters and Philosophical Letters: or, Modest Reflections upon some Opinions in Natural Philosophy*; Katherine Philips, *Poems by the incomparable Mrs. K. P.* (unauthorized publication)
1665	Great Plague in London; second Anglo-Dutch War (1665–7); Robert Hooke's *Micrographia* illustrates the natural world as discovered through the microscope	Anne Bankes, Lady Borlase, book of medical recipes; Lucy Hutchinson, 'Memoirs of the Life of Colonel Hutchinson' (*c.* 1665–71)

1666	Great Fire of London destroys most of the old city	Margaret Cavendish, *The Description of a New World, Called the Blazing World*, appended to *Observations upon Experimental Philosophy*; Margaret Fell Fox, *Women's Speaking Justified*; Mary Rich, diary (1666–77)
1667	Margaret Cavendish visits the Royal Society; Dutch fleet burns English ships and sails up the Medway; Treaty of Breda ends war with the Dutch	
1668		Katherine Philips, trans., *Horace*; Alice Thornton, 'Remembrances' (*c.* 1668);
1669		Frances Boothby, *Marcelia, or, The Treacherous Friend a Tragicomedy*, performed
1670	Formation of Hudson's Bay Company; Treaty of Dover in which Charles II secretly promises to aid Catholic France against the Dutch and to convert publicly (at some unspecified future time) to Catholicism in exchange for French subsidies	Aphra Behn, *The Forc'd Marriage*, performed; Frances Boothby, *Marcelia, or, The Treacherous Friend a Tragicomedy*, performed; Sarah Davy, *Heaven Realized*; Elizabeth Polwhele, 'The Faithfull Virgins', probably performed
1671–3		Julia Palmer composes 200 devotional poems
1671		Mary Rich, 'Memoir'; Theodosia Alleine, *The Life and Death of that Excellent Minister of Christ Mr. Joseph Alleine*; Aphra Behn, *The Amorous Prince*, performed and published; Elizabeth Polwhele, *The Frolicks, or, The Lawyer Cheated*, possibly performed; Jane Sharp, *The Midwives Book*
1672	Charles II's Declaration of Indulgence permits Nonconformist and (private) Catholic worship; Royal Africa Company established; third Anglo-Dutch War (1672 4)	
1673	Parliament forces withdrawal of Declaration of Indulgence; Test Act passed; Catholics and Protestant Dissenters are prohibited from holding public office; James, Duke of York, marries Catholic Princess Mary of Modena	Bathsua Makin, *Essay to Revive the Antient Education of Gentlewomen*; Aphra Behn, *The Dutch Lover*; Sarah Cowper, 'The Medley'; Hannah Woolley (or Wolley), *The Gentlewomans Companion* (authorship disputed)
1674		Susanna Packe, cookery book
1675	Metacom's (King Philip's) War breaks out in New England	Hannah Woolley (Wolley), *The Accomplisht Ladys Delight*

1676		Aphra Behn, *Abdelazer*, performed (published 1677); Lady Ann Fanshawe, 'Memoirs'; Anne Wentworth, *A True Account*
1677		Aphra Behn, *The Rover*; Lady Anne Halkett, 'Memoirs' (1677–8); Anne Wentworth, *A Vindication of Anne Wentworth*; Hannah Woolley (Wolley), *The Compleat Servant Maid*
1678	Titus Oates fabricates a 'Popish Plot' by Catholics to kill Charles II.	Aphra Behn, *Sir Patient Fancy*, performed and published; Anne Bradstreet, *Several Poems*
1679	During the 'Exclusion Crisis' (1679–81), Parliament attempts to exclude the Catholic James, Duke of York, from succession to the throne; formation of Whig and Tory political parties	Aphra Behn, *The Young King*, performed (published 1683) and *The Feign'd Curtizans*, performed and published; Lucy Hutchinson, first five cantos of *Order and Disorder* published anonymously
1680	Margaret Clark executed for arson and theft; Elizabeth Cellier found guilty of libel for publishing *Malice Defeated*	Margaret Clark, *The True Confession of Margret Clark*; Elizabeth Cellier, *Malice Defeated, or, A Brief Relation of the Accusation and Deliverance of Elizabeth Cellier*; Elizabeth Cary, *The History of the Life, Reign, and Death of Edward II* and *The History of the Most Unfortunate Prince King Edward II*, published posthumously
1681–2		Aphra Behn, *The City-Heiress*, performed during 1681–2 season (and then published)
1681	William Penn receives a royal charter to establish Pennsylvania	Aphra Behn, *The Second Part of The Rover*, performed and published
1682		Elizabeth Percy, Countess of Northumberland, *Meditations and Prayers*; Mary Rowlandson, *A True History of the Captivity and Restoration of Mrs. Mary Rowlandson* (published first in Cambridge, Massachusetts, as *The Soveraignty and Goodness of God*)
1683	Rye House plot to assassinate Charles II is foiled	
1684		Aphra Behn, *Love-Letters Between a Noble-man and his Sister* (three parts, 1684–7) and *Poems on Several Occasions*; Elizabeth Fowler, cookery book

1685	Death of Charles II and accession of James II (a Roman Catholic); failed rebellion of James, Duke of Monmouth, illegitimate son of Charles II and Protestant favourite	
1687	Isaac Newton publishes work laying the foundations of modern physics	
1688	Birth of James Francis Stuart, Prince of Wales, raises fears of permanent Catholic succession	Aphra Behn, *Oroonoko, or The Royal Slave*; Mary Carleton, *The Case of Mary Carleton*
1688–9	'Glorious Revolution'; flight and deposition of James II; accession of William (of Orange), now William III, and Mary (daughter of James II)	
1689	Passage of the Bill of Rights and Toleration Act; Nine Years War (1689–97)	Aphra Behn, *The Widdow Ranter*, performed posthumously (published 1690)
1691		Mary Astell, *A Serious Proposal to the Ladies*
1693		Catharine Trotter, *The Adventures of a Young Lady*; [Catharine Trotter], *Letters of Love and Gallantry. And Several Other Subjects. All written by Ladies. Vol. 1*
1694	Mary II dies of smallpox; William rules alone	[Catharine Trotter], *Letters of Love and Gallantry, and Several Other Subjects. Vol. 11 Written by Ladies*
1695–6		'Ariadne', *She Ventures and He Wins*, performed (published 1696); Delarivier Manley, *The Lost Lover*, performed (published 1696); Mary Pix, *Ibrahim, The Thirteenth Emperour of the Turks*, performed (published 1696); Catharine Trotter, adaptation of Behn's *Agnes de Castro*, performed (published 1696)
1696	Passage of Navigation Acts that limit all colonial trade to English-built vessels	Aphra Behn, *The Younger Brother*, edited by Charles Gildon, performed; Delarivier Manley, *The Royal Mischief*, performed and published; Mary Pix, *Ibrahim*, and *The Spanish Wives*, performed and published; Elizabeth Singer Rowe, *Poems on Several Occasions Written by Philomela*
1697		Katherine Philips' letters to Sir Charles Cotterell published posthumously as 'Letters by the late Celebrated Mrs Katherine Philips' in *Familiar Letters*

1700		Susannah Centlivre, *The Perjur'd Husband*, performed and published; Mary Pix, *The Beau Defeated*, published; Catharine Trotter, *Love at a Loss*, performed
1701	Act of Settlement establishes Hanoverian succession (away from the 'Jacobite' line of the exiled Stuart King James and his Catholic son and heir)	
1702	Death of William III; accession of Queen Anne (last Stuart monarch)	
1705		Delarivier Manley, *Secret History of Queen Zarah*; Katherine Philips' letters to Sir Charles Cotterell published posthumously by Bernard Lintot as *Letters from Orinda to Poliarchus*
1707	Act of Union unites Scotland and England, which become 'Great Britain'	
1709		Delarivier Manley, *New Atalantis* (2 vols.)
1712		Elizabeth Freke, *Miscellany* (1712–14)

Writers' lives

Catherine Parr, Queen Consort of Henry VIII	1512–48
Mary Tudor, Queen of England and Ireland	1516–58
Anne Askew	1521–46
Anne Lok (or Locke)	*c.* 1530– before 1607
Elizabeth Tudor, Queen of England and Ireland	1533–1603
Lady Jane Grey	1537–54
Lady Jane Lumley	1537–78
Lady Grace Mildmay	*c.* 1552–1620
Margaret Tyler	*fl.* 1558–78
Lady Alice Egerton	1559–1637
Mary Sidney Herbert, Countess of Pembroke	1561–1621
Elizabeth Grymeston	*c.* 1563–1601/4
Isabella Whitney	*fl.* 1566–73
Aemilia Lanyer	1569–1645
Lady Mary Percy	1570–1642
Lady Elinor Fettiplace	1570–after 1647

Katherine Stubbes	1570/1–90
Lady Margaret Hoby	1570/1–1633
Esther Inglis	1571–1624
Elizabeth Clinton, Countess of Lincoln	c. 1574–1630
Lady Anne Southwell	c. 1574–1636
Elizabeth Richardson, Baroness of Cramond	1576/7–1651
Martha Moulsworth	1577–1646
Elizabeth Grey, Countess of Kent	1582–1651
Elizabeth Melvill, Lady Colville of Culros	c. 1582–1640 or later
Aletheia Talbot, Countess of Arundel, Surrey and Norfolk	c. 1582–1654
Elizabeth Cary, Viscountess Falkland	1585–1639
Lady Mary (Sidney) Wroth	1587–1651/3
Anne Dowriche	fl. 1589, d. 1613 or later
Lady Eleanor (Davies) Douglas	1590–1652
Lady Anne Clifford, Countess of Pembroke, Dorset and Montgomery	1590–1676
Lady Hester Pulter	1595/6–1678
Elizabeth Jocelin	1596–1624
Rachel Speght	1597–after 1630
Lady Brilliana Harley	c. 1600–43
Bathsua Makin	1600–75 or later
Elizabeth Isham	1609–54
Sarah Cheevers	c. 1608–64?
Mary Carey	c. 1609–80 or later
Anne Bradstreet	1612/13–72
Lady Rachael Fane	1613–80
Margaret Fell Fox	1614–1702
Kathcrine Chidley	fl. 1616–53
Dorothy Leigh	d. in or before 1616
Katharine Evans	c. 1618–92
Lucy Hutchinson	1620–81
Mary Cary	1620/1–53
Lady Jane (Cavendish) Cheyne	1620/1–69
Elizabeth Poole	c. 1622–68 or later
Hannah Woolley (or Wolley)	c. 1622–74 or later

Margaret (Lucas) Cavendish, Duchess of Newcastle	1623–73
Lady Anne Halkett	1623–99
Alice Sutcliffe	*fl.* 1624–34
Mary Rich, Countess of Warwick	1624–78
Anne Gargill	*c.* 1625–59 or later
Lady Ann Fanshawe	1625–80
Lady Elizabeth (Cavendish) Egerton Brackley, Countess of Bridgewater	1626–63
Alice (Wandesford) Thornton	1626–1707
Anne Venn	*c.* 1627–54
Dorothy Osborne, later Lady Temple	1627–95
Anne Wentworth	1629/30–93?
Hester Biddle	1629/30–97
Sarah Wight	1631–d. unknown
Anne Conway, Viscountess Conway and Killultagh	1631–79
Katherine Philips	1632–64
Constance Fowler	m. 1634–d. 1664
Dorothy Waugh	*c.* 1636–66?
Mary Fage	*fl.* 1637
Mary Rowlandson	*c.* 1637–1711
Aphra Behn	*c.* 1640–89
Jane Sharp	*fl.* 1641–71
Anna Trapnel	*fl.* 1642–60
Mary Carleton	1642–73
Elizabeth Freke	1642–1714
Anna Hume	*fl.* 1644
Sarah Cowper	1644–1720
Lady Elizabeth Delaval	1648–1717
Anna Weamys	*fl.* 1650–1
Susanna Parr	*fl.* 1650–9
Elizabeth Polwhele	1651?–91?
An Collins	*fl.* 1653
Theodosia Alleine	*fl.* 1654–77
Julia Palmer	*fl.* 1664–73
Mary Pix	1666–1709
Mary Astell	1666–1731

Elizabeth Cellier	1668–88
Frances Boothby	*fl.* 1669–70
Susannah Centlivre	1669?–1723
Delarivier Manley	*c.* 1670–1724
Elizabeth Singer Rowe	1674–1737
Catharine Trotter	1674– 1749

LAURA LUNGER KNOPPERS

Introduction: critical framework and issues

Esther Inglis's oval-framed portrait of herself wearing a wide-brimmed hat and a falling ruff, holding a quill pen and standing behind a table upon which is an ink pot, a small open book and a large sheet of paper, gives a striking visual image of an early modern woman writing (figure 1). The tiny pen-and-ink portrait (45 mm × 31 mm) with a stippled background and leafy frame, is pasted on to the verso of the title page of a 1601 *Octonaries upon the Vanitie and Inconstancie of the World*, one of nearly sixty calligraphic bound manuscripts produced by Inglis and given, in hopes of remuneration, to various noble and royal figures in Scotland, England and France.¹ Raised in Scotland, Inglis was the daughter of French Huguenot (Protestant) refugees who settled in Edinburgh and ran a French school. An accomplished calligrapher, Inglis wrote in often minute letters in a dazzling range of scripts: roman, italic, gothic, mirror writing, broken writing and other ornamental hands. Her texts are manuscript copies (sometimes translations) of printed texts – the Geneva Bible (most often Psalms or Proverbs) or the pious verse of French Huguenot writers – illuminated with flowers or sprays of flowers, birds, butterflies and other insects, squirrels, frogs and snails.²

The pen-and-ink portrait, on either side of which Inglis has written her name in roman majuscule letters, is one of nearly two dozen self-portraits with which Inglis distinctively marks her scribal copying. This example, dated 1624, updates the attire of Inglis's earliest ink self-portraits in which she is shown at her work of writing, wearing an elaborately detailed dress and a conical hat with flowing veil, within an oval frame decorated with fruit and architectural scrolls. The 1624 portrait is modelled on a self-portrait of French Protestant and emblematist Georgette de Montenay, showing how the female calligrapher linked herself to an earlier female writer and artist.³ Like Montenay, Inglis stands behind a table with the implements of writing; but she has changed Montenay's bejewelled French court dress

Figure 1. Pen-and-ink self-portrait (1624) pasted on to title page, verso. Esther Inglis, *Octonaries upon the Vanitie and Inconstancie of the World*, 1601. Folger Shakespeare Library MS v.a.91, fol. 1v.

into traditional sixteenth-century Scottish countrywoman's attire. Four tiny colour self-portraits of Inglis are also known. In one striking example from Houghton Library, Harvard University (cover image), an elaborately decorated green oval wreath and the inscription 'ESTHER INGLIS ANNO 1607' frame a three-quarters-length portrait of Inglis on a brilliant blue background. Wearing a small, low-crowned black hat, a large white ruff and a black dress with a long, pointed bodice and full skirt, Inglis stands behind a red-coloured table; her right hand holds a quill pen and her left hand is placed upon an open book.[4]

The visual self-presentation is not the only means by which Inglis represents herself as a writing woman in her calligraphic manuscripts.[5] In contrast to the usual anonymity of scribal copying, Inglis affixes her name to the title pages of her works, such as the lavish title page of a second (1607) Folger copy of the *Octonaries* (figure 2). Here, the title, scripted to imitate print and surrounded with a naturalistic watercolour border of pansies, red roses, butterflies and a bird on a gold background, asserts (in rather uncertain spelling) that the *Octonaries* are 'WRITIN AND LIMD BE ME ESTHER INGLIS THE XXIII, DECEMB: 1607'. Inglis, of course, needed to identify herself clearly as the 'writer' of her texts if the aim of reward from the recipients to whom they were directed was to be realized.

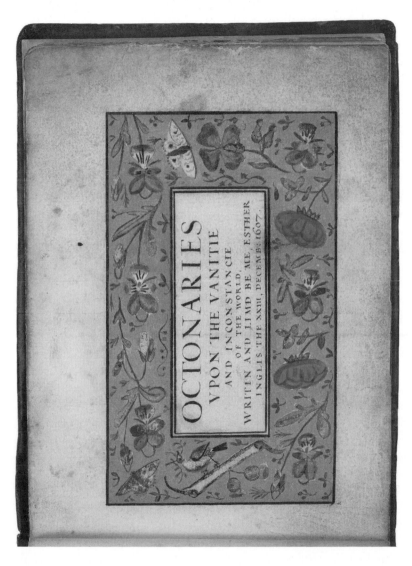

Figure 2. Title page, Esther Inglis, *Octonaries upon the Vanitie and Inconstancie of the World*, 1607. Folger Shakespeare Library MS v.a.92, fol. 1.

Enclosed commendatory verses also correlate with dedications to hoped-for patrons to sketch various figures of Inglis. The 1607 Folger *Octonaries* contains no visual portrait, but a portrait of Inglis is sketched in two commendatory verses by G.D. that follow the title page and dedication. The first, an anagram on Esther Inglis's name ('RESISTING HEL'), begins:

> RESISTING HEL, thou shalt the heav'ns obtaine
> Devils are afray'd of such as them resist
> Draw neere to God, he will draw neere againe
> And compass thee about with armyes blest   (fol. 4)

The second poem, a sonnet 'TO THE ONLY PARAGON, AND matchles Mistresse of the golden Pen. ESTHER INGLIS', contrasts Inglis's work to the 'mightie Monuments' raised by men: 'But thou glore of thy sexe, and mirakill to men | Dost purches to thy self immortell prayse and fame | By draughts inimitable, of thy unmatched Pen' (fol. 5).

Similarly, Inglis uses the conventions of the dedication to shape her self-image in her texts. In a dedication to 'Lord Peter' (John, 1st Baron Petre) in a New York Public Library 1609 copy of the *Octonaries* (Spencer Collection, French MS. 14), Inglis asserts that the 'labours of my pen and pensill' have been found 'very gratious and acceptable' to some of the 'highest and nobils of this land' as well as to 'sundrie of the Peers of this Realme as to the Kings Ma:ᵗⁱᵉ and to the Prince his Grace' (fol. 2). Rather than de-emphasizing her gender, Inglis asks Lord Petre to give her bound manuscript 'sum secret corner in your Ho[nour's] cabinet and so much the rather because it is the handy work of a woman' (fol. 2). In another example, the lavish 1624 *Emblemes Chrestiens* (British Library, Royal MS. 17.D.xvi), copied from Georgette de Montenay and dedicated to Prince Charles, Inglis aligns herself with biblical type, desiring 'to cast my Myte into the Treasurye, as that poore widowe did, whom our Saviour commended … respecting rather yᵉ affection of the giver, then the quantitie of the gift' (fol. 4). In approaching Prince Charles, Inglis casts aside the 'shamefastnesse and feare (which commonlie accompaneis our sexe)', drawing on the prince's 'douce and sweet inclination' to recover 'the Spirit of ane Amazon Lady' (fol. 4). Her elaborately crafted manuscript is the product of 'two yeeres labours of the small cunning, that my tottering right ☞, now being in the age of fiftie three yeeres, might affoord' (fol. 4). This was, in fact, her last volume, as Inglis died later that year.

What can Inglis's self-portraits and her calligraphic self-representations tell us about women's writing in early modern Britain? For all of the demurrals in her dedications, Inglis is not only a model craftswoman but a shrewd player in patronage networks and a remarkable early instance of a woman who writes professionally, exemplifying considerable creativity and ingenuity even while negotiating class boundaries and gender constrictions. The ongoing intersections of manuscript and print can be seen as Inglis not only imitates printed script but copies and reworks actual title pages, borders, ornaments and emblems. Inglis's trilingual work (Latin, French, and English) reminds us of the complexities of literacy (of both reading and writing) in this period, as well as of the need to look at women writers placed beyond London, or even England. Her selection and transcription of biblical and devotional texts show not only the importance of religion in this period, but the symbiosis of reading and writing. Inglis's working collaboration with her clergyman husband, Bartholomew Kello, and the multiple facets of her work – transcription and translation, visual and verbal self-portraits, a compendium of scripts, *trompe-l'oeil* floral borders and even embroidered velvet bindings – show the complexities of early modern women's authorship. Finally, Inglis's tiny, beautifully executed calligraphic manuscripts are not only fascinating cultural artefacts but stunning aesthetic objects. Esther Inglis's work is one striking example of the range and richness of the writing of early modern women, writing that rewards the interest of students and scholars alike.

The scholarly field

The study of early modern women writers has become a major, thriving field in the past twenty-five years. As recently as 1980, women had little representation on Renaissance course reading lists or in such volumes as the *Norton Anthology of English Literature*; nor were primary writings (manuscript or print) by women easily accessible. Few critical books were devoted primarily, much less exclusively, to the study of women. As is well known, this situation has been transformed, for both teaching and scholarship. A survey of university and college websites in the United States and the United Kingdom shows that courses on Renaissance women are widely taught at both the undergraduate and graduate level and that British Literature survey courses typically include attention to early women. Dissertations and first books on early women writers abound, as do edited collections of essays on particular themes or topics. Brown University Women Writers Online, and Early English Books Online have made printed texts by women accessible to a degree unimaginable even ten years ago.[6] The British Perdita project has produced an online database guide to more than five hundred manuscript compilations in collections from around the world.[7] Such book series as Oxford University Press's 'Women Writers in English, 1350–1850' and Ashgate's two series 'The Early Modern Englishwoman: A Facsimile Library of Essential Works' and 'The Early Modern Englishwoman

1500–1700: Contemporary Editions' have made editions of women's texts more broadly available. An array of good anthologies can also now be found for classroom use.

The academic field of early modern women's writing has also seen important theoretical shifts that continue to reshape and invigorate scholarship. Recent scholars have challenged or refined the essentialist assumptions of early work that took a largely biographical approach to women's writing and operated under an implicitly or explicitly evolutionary framework.[8] That is, scholars of early modern women's writing now stress the materiality of gendered writing, the importance of including manuscript as well as printed texts, collaborative as well as single 'authored' texts, and women's writings on a diverse range of non-literary, domestic and religious subjects, including those not explicitly treating female or feminist concerns.[9]

Developments within the broader field of early modern studies have also proved relevant and fruitful for consideration of early modern women's writing. A flourishing of work on manuscript culture, scribal publication and coterie verse has provided new information and new methodologies for scholars attending to a comprehensive range of women's writing.[10] Similarly, work on book history has called attention to the book as material object in shifting technologies of manuscript and print, to the role of the printing house in shaping the meaning of the text, and to the significance of such textual elements as typography and title-page format.[11] Work on the history of reading has dismantled binaries of reading/writing and of private/public and has highlighted the spectrum of literacies, the construction of subjectivity and the role that early owners and readers played in completing the publication process.[12] Studies of the British Atlantic world by historians and literary scholars have prompted scholars of early modern women's writing to move beyond London and England to consider writing in Wales, Scotland, Ireland and British America.[13]

Building upon these recent scholarly developments, this *Companion* offers nineteen original essays written by an international team of leading scholars on the rich and varied materials, sites and genres of women's writing in Britain in the sixteenth and seventeenth centuries. In offering basic historical, methodological and textual information for upper-level undergraduates, graduate students and scholars, these essays exemplify new and exciting approaches to the study of women's writing. The contributors consider but also move beyond *belles lettres* and single authors, offering diverse contexts for and new juxtapositions of texts and writers. Following the frequently tripartite structure of the *Companion* series, this volume gives attention to the materiality of writing, to the spaces and places in which women typically wrote and to the manifold genres of women's writing.

Part One, 'Material matters', considers the physical materials of women's writing. These range from writing implements (quill pen and ink) and writing manuals to women's texts in various forms: from manuscript miscellanies to tiny duodecimo pamphlets to elaborate folio print volumes. Also explored are the ways in which women participated in writing as readers, compilers and book owners and as primary and secondary authors. Part Two focuses on the places and spaces in which women wrote. These include domestic spaces such as the prayer closet, the kitchen, the sickroom and the birthing room, but also places outside the home such as the royal courts, the law courts, theatres, church buildings and educational sites. Part Three explores the diverse genres and forms of writing. These involve not fixed rules but flexible rubrics and guidelines which women appropriate, revise and transform in composing letters, translations, autobiographical accounts, political and religious prose, fiction, poetry and drama.

The tripartite structure of this *Companion* highlights the collaborative, context-generated nature of much of early modern women's writing, challenging notions of 'autonomous' authorship and a canon based on individualistic authors and biographies. This structure also allows contributors to give focused attention to manuscript compilation and circulation and to a wide, historically appropriate range of literary and non-literary genres. At the same time, the tripartite organization of the volume allows for fruitful exchange and cross-reference between chapters and should provide the maximum flexibility for teachers to correlate reading assignments on their favourite texts with the generic rubrics.

Historiography and literary history

What do we mean by 'early modern'? Why this framework in considering women's writing of the sixteenth and seventeenth centuries? That the humanist learning of the Renaissance was available to only a tiny minority of high-placed women, and indeed brought ideology and practices that could diminish women's status, makes the 'Renaissance' a problematic category for women, as Joan Kelly-Gadol some time ago argued.[14] 'Early modern', then, can offer a more capacious and flexible rubric. While the dates shift somewhat depending on subject (politics, economics, religion, culture) and region, 'early modern', roughly 1500–1700, indicates a period of transition in politics, religion, society and the state, usually taken to include the rise (however uneven) of religious diversity, the printing press, capitalism, the centralized and imperial nation state, science and individualism. In Britain (see Chronologies), this period saw the Tudor and Stuart monarchies, the mid-seventeenth-century civil wars, regicide and republic, the restoration of the Stuart monarchy and the 'Glorious Revolution' of 1688–9. Closely related to state politics are developments in the church: Henry VIII's break with Rome, and the ongoing impulse for further reformation in radical Protestantism, eventuating in the radical sectarianism of the civil war period and legally defined dissent after 1660. The history of the book develops in this period in England, from the introduction of the printing press by William Caxton in 1476, to considerable increase in printed books (albeit with manuscript production and circulation still continuing), and a flourishing of men's – and women's – print with the breakdown of censorship in the civil war period. Changes in medicine and science transformed the way in which many people viewed the microcosm of the human body and the macrocosm of the world. The sixteenth and seventeenth centuries were also an age of discovery and empire-building linked with national identity. Yet while religious identity, political participation and print moved towards recognizably 'modern forms', this period also retained distinctly 'early' modes, including constrictive gender roles for women that interacted with prescriptions of class, religion and politics.

Early modern women's writing challenges as much as it follows traditional historical and literary historical frameworks. Women's writing can be explored in relation to male-authored texts, as part of expanding the canon. At the same time, scholars of women's writing have questioned assumptions underlying the idea of the canon itself, while others have sought to define a women's literary history. Did early modern women view themselves as *women* writers? Is the category of women's writing a historical one? Traditional literary historical periods only in part attend to women's writing in such genres as narrative and lyric poetry, drama, fictional and non-fictional prose. And attending to non-literary genres moves women's writing even further outside of the traditional literary historical rubrics.

Yet tools and methods of literary analysis – examination of formalist qualities, of voice, speaker, theme, plot, character, imagery, metaphor and language – can be fruitfully deployed to analyse a wide range of women's texts. Women's drama – on or off the public stage – makes use of structural features, metrical form and coded language. Women's texts make aesthetic claims on our attention, and examining literary forms alongside other wide-ranging genres should enhance rather than detract from our sense of these women's rhetorical and formal writing skills.

Women in history: issues and debates

Who were the women writing these texts? Important early studies of women's writing – in the early modern period and elsewhere – focused on the work of recovery, of bringing women's voices into the canon, or of challenging the whole idea of the canon itself. Such work has been critiqued as essentialist, and more theoretical studies now point to the plurality and instability of the category of 'woman'. With a focus on gender in history, we can move away from both essentializing and deconstruction of identity, grounding our work in historical particulars that include – among other factors – biography and women's life-writing. One crucial analytical tool with which we approach the writing of early modern women, then, is that of gender: the socially constructed roles, behaviour and activities that a given society considers appropriate for men and women, based on perceptions of biological sex.[15] While the normative economy of gender in the sixteenth and seventeenth centuries was based on hierarchy, with the male as superior, the social constructions of gender were not simply binary and static. Rather, gender roles were constructed, modified and reinforced – and sometimes challenged – in religious, scientific, medical, political, legal and literary discourses and practices: including the writing of early modern women.

The women whose writing we consider in this volume were royalist and parliamentarian; noble, aristocratic, middling class and of humble social origins; Catholic, Episcopal, Quaker and Baptist; Whig and Tory; married, single, separated and widowed; daughters, wives, mothers, sisters and grandmothers. They varied in belief and religious practice; in age and political affiliation; in degree of education and accomplishment. Some received humanist educations, while others were taught only rudimentary literacy skills. They lived in London and in Dublin, in Edinburgh and in Boston, Massachusetts, in Essex and in Oxford. 'Women', then, in this volume are understood not as monolithic but as configured in various familial, political, religious and social networks that included men and in which gender was only one important factor, along with class, religion and politics.

Gendered literacies, authorship and the materials of writing

How did these early modern women learn to write? How can variable literacies best be recovered? How can book history and aspects of the material text help us reconstruct women's reading and writing? What does authorship mean in the early modern period and particularly for women?

First, how did early modern women learn to write, given both gender and class constraints? As Caroline Bowden's chapter in this volume makes clear, lack of formal educational institutions for girls did not prevent many early modern women from acquiring – and enhancing – their literacy (reading and writing) skills. Bowden shows that informal education for girls occurred in multiple spaces and ways; in the early modern period, as today, once a basic level of competence in writing literacy was achieved, use and incentive for use continued to enhance such literacy, even outside formal structures of education.

The materials of writing can be reconstructed from writing manuals and extant copy-books. As Heather Wolfe explains in this volume, writing women used three main handwriting scripts – italic, secretary and mixed (later called round) – deploying different scripts on different occasions, and exemplifying different degrees of reading and writing literacy. Even the methods of writing were perhaps more complex than we might expect: so that 'writing' a letter (as James Daybell shows) could involve dictation, following a set model, autographing oneself or some combination of these.

Writing was also linked with reading. As Edith Snook explores, signs of reading left by women in the margins of their books and in their letters, diaries and commonplace books indicate how reading generated creative links among readers and writers, how women made texts personally relevant as they copied them and how commonplacing, like writing in the margins of a book, provided the ground on which to become an author.

Throughout the early modern period, manuscript and printed forms co-existed and intersected. Like their male counterparts, many women preferred manuscript writing and (sometimes) circulation for their letters, diaries, journals, recipe books, religious and devotional writing, and miscellanies. Compiling manuscript miscellanies was an activity that lay between reading and writing, as Victoria Burke shows, and such miscellanies can help us understand how early modern women read as well as wrote. Miscellanies (as Burke argues) also broaden our ideas of authorship, including composite authorship and creative transcription, alteration, and response to texts in verse and prose.

Authorship in the early modern period was not only single but collective and collaborative. The statistics for women's printed writing seem bleak – only 42 first editions between 1601–40 accounting for ½ of 1 per cent of published texts, and 112 new editions by women in the publishing boom of 1641–50 or 1.2 per cent.[16] But, as Marcy North illustrates in this volume, simply counting first editions of single-authored works underestimates the presence and visibility of women's printed texts. Texts might gain attention because of the high rank or notoriety of the author; popular texts such as mother's advice books or recipe (receipt) books could be reprinted more than a dozen times; printing in folio rather than smaller formats brought additional notice; and secondary authorship or authorship of dedications or female-voiced poems also enhanced the place of women's writing in printed texts. A more historically apposite view of women's writing, then, attends not only to the many forms of manuscript writing but to various kinds of print authorship.

Place, space and gender

Where did early modern women write? In thinking about space and women's writing, we need both to challenge and to move beyond binaries of public and private, domestic and political spheres. While early feminist studies saw women's confinement to the home (especially in and after the nineteenth century) as a sign of disempowerment and subordination, scholars now recognize that the domestic in the early modern period was not simply familial or 'private', but a place of work and business as well as of family and social networks and patronage.[17] Both experienced and imagined, material and ideological, space not only reflected but constructed gender relations in this period.[18] Architectural spaces within the household as well as such places as the royal courts, churches and law courts generated and shaped women's writing.

Educational spaces for girls, as Caroline Bowden suggests in this volume, were often found within the household, moving outside the humanist classroom (from which girls were largely excluded) into domestic education, enhanced in the everyday work of household business, receipts and financial transactions. Although woman's best place was said to be in the home, the early modern household, as Wendy Wall explores, was a space of considerable authority, anxiety and fantasy for its residents. 'Writing' in the household, as Wall argues, can be construed very broadly, including such activities as cookery, carving and needlework. Women's writing about health, healing and the body, as Mary Fissell explains, was characteristic of three domestic healing spaces: the closet, the birthing room and the sickroom. Such spaces produced writing in the forms of the recipe book, autobiography and female-authored midwifery manuals.

Devotional spaces, as Elizabeth Clarke explains in this volume, included not only the sanctuaries of the Church of England, but also the imagined spaces from which women critiqued the church in radical and unforeseen ways. Clarke shows how religious buildings for early modern women were imbued with the politics of state and of gender: many preferred the devotional spaces of their own mind to any physical place, and constructed for themselves in their own writing imaginative locations in which they could be confident in their relationships with God. As Karen Britland demonstrates, the royal courts also shaped women's writing: Elizabeth I, with her superb education, translated and wrote within the court; whilst Aemilia Lanyer and the Catholic convert Elizabeth Cary, more precariously placed, used their writing to seek court patronage. Finally, the spaces of the law courts, as Frances Dolan explains, recorded and mediated women's voices in depositions and briefs, making assessment of women's voices as they were raised in early modern law courts particularly challenging. As Dolan suggests, the law courts afforded different opportunities and challenges to women as litigants and defendants, and their everyday struggles, as well as such better-known cases as Anne Clifford or Elizabeth Cary, add valuable new texts to be explored as 'women's writing'.

Form, genre and subject

What did early modern women write? Early modern women drew upon and engaged the traditional literary genres of lyric or narrative poetry, drama and fictional prose. They also wrote in a much wider range of texts (that circulated in print or manuscript). A full understanding of genre or form for early modern women's writing must develop a capacious sense of the literary, and recognize the value of employing literary tools to analyse a wide range of genres. Our study of genre moves, broadly, from manuscript and non-literary forms to literary and print genres and more recognizably modern forms of authorship: commercial and print.

Some of the earliest women's writing in this period took the often-neglected form of translation. Translation, as Danielle Clarke argues, placed women at the heart of textual production: raising issues of authorship, and of the relation between translation, manuscript and print culture. Whilst translation was clearly envisaged as a means by which virtue might be inculcated in women, the consequences of placing women at the heart of an activity central to rhetorical culture were, as Clarke shows, less predictable. Much of early modern women's writing occurred outside of literary genres. One important and pervasive form is the letter. As James Daybell explains, women dictated letters or wrote them themselves; they wrote to family, friends, lovers, patrons and mentors; their letters served personal, social, business, political and religious purposes. Much writing also took the form of life-writing. As Ramona Wray shows, early modern women scripted the self within the familiar structures of diary and memoir, as well as in less familiar forms such as the conversion narrative, prison account, prophecy, biography and legal deposition. Religious writing, dominant for both men and women in this period, took on, as Hilary Hinds explains, a visible and polemical (and often printed) form in the middle decades of the seventeenth century, as an extraordinary profusion of prophetic and religious writings by English women accompanied the tumult of civil war and revolution.

The sixteenth and seventeenth centuries in Britain also show women appropriating and expanding traditional literary genres. As Helen Wilcox explores in this volume, women writing in the first-person form of lyric verse deployed inherited forms with technical virtuosity and imagination; the subjects of women's lyric encompassed not only earthly love and spiritual devotion (drawn from the sonnet tradition and the Psalms), but also social discourse, science, philosophy and even topography. Similarly, as Susanne Woods shows, early modern women's narrative poetry – from Elizabeth Melvill's dreams of a bright angel to Aemilia Lanyer's representation of Christ's passion to Lucy Hutchinson's epic rewriting of Genesis – appropriated and transformed received literary forms of tragedy, biblical and historical narrative, and epic.

We likewise find women writing in various dramatic modes in the sixteenth and seventeenth centuries. Although before the 1660s, women did not write for the commercial stage in England, they nonetheless, as Marta Straznicky explains, translated or wrote dramas for household performance that also circulated in manuscript or, less often, targeted an educated public of play-readers. These ranged from inventive translations stemming from the humanist education that some girls did receive at home (e.g. Jane Lumley) to dramatic uses of the pastoral reflecting on personal, court or political matters (Lady Mary Wroth) to the lavishly printed plays of Margaret Cavendish. After the Restoration, as Derek Hughes shows, women became more active and visible in stage or public drama, in the new roles of actress, playwright and businesswoman. Women translated plays staged in Dublin and in London; and they contributed to the full generic range of Restoration public drama – not only the familiar witty and urbane sex comedies, but also tragicomedies and fully fledged tragedies. As Hughes demonstrates, the work of the most prominent female dramatist, Aphra Behn, reflected the shifting tastes and economic, political and courtly circumstances of the 1670s and 1680s.

Finally, despite cultural suspicions of fiction, especially in the feminized form of romance, early modern women, as Lori Humphrey Newcomb argues, moved deftly from reading to writing prose fiction in the years preceding the full-fledged formation of the English novel. While prefacing their work with disclaimers of topicality, women nonetheless used the seemingly escapist genre of romance to comment obliquely on personal, social or political circumstances, using romance stories of exile, separation and reunion to shadow national narratives of civil war, exile and eventual restoration.

Feminism and its discontents

From who, how, where and what, we come, finally, to the question of why women wrote. In the classroom, the answer might sometimes be assumed even before the question is asked: women wrote out of a feminist or proto-feminist discontent with gendered constraints in the family, society, church and state. Yet much writing by early modern women does not take up feminist concerns per se. Indeed, many early modern women writers voice overt support for gender and class hierarchies. Such a finding can cause a different kind of discontent: in the classroom. What are the various stated intentions and purposes of women's writing? How can we contextualize these within a historical framework, while nonetheless being attentive to questions of gender? How can we best attend to and account for the complex 'double-voicing' of early modern women's texts, as they embody dominant cultural prescripts and yet voice individual identity and dissent?[19]

Early modern women's motives for writing indeed have to do with gender, but also with politics, religion, class, ethnicity and simply practical affairs. Women wrote as part of household management: producing culinary or medical recipes, business receipts, monetary transactions and other records. They wrote letters as part of family, religious, social and political networks. They wrote to defend themselves and their reputations, whether in legal contexts or in various domestic forms of life-writing. They wrote for devotional purposes, to forge a place of worship or to track, order and construct a confessional self. They also wrote for professional gain, whether in popular print or for the stage. They wrote to become literary 'authors', in dialogue and sometimes in competition with male – and female – predecessors and literary traditions.

The question of why early modern women wrote is linked to the question of audience. These women wrote for themselves; they wrote before a divine audience; they wrote on behalf of and to their husbands, children, sisters, brothers and friends; they wrote to potential patrons and political allies; they wrote (whether explicitly or not) to a larger political or religious community, and even to the nation as a whole.

And, as such multiple purposes and audiences show, early modern women, even when not overtly addressing 'feminist' issues and the welfare of women in broad terms, nonetheless constructed gendered identities and exercised agency in ways that can relate to modern feminist concerns. Letters, commonplace books, miscellanies, autobiography, translations, religious writing, poetry, prose and drama can offer a broad lens on gender relations in this period. Early modern women found multiple ways of writing and of circulating their work. Active participants in gender politics, these women writers gained agency within the institutional structures of family and society, church and state, law court and royal court.

The complex purposes and 'double-voicing' of early modern women's writing can be seen as, in conclusion, we return briefly to our Scottish calligrapher and miniaturist, Esther Inglis. We saw that in Inglis's manuscripts, her visual self-portraits were a kind of self-writing variously paralleled and extended by title pages, dedications and commendatory verse. In her 1624 pen-and-ink portrait (figure 1), we noticed that Inglis depicts herself with paper and book and with pen in hand. But Inglis is poised not to begin but rather to *resume* her writing, since the paper before her is already inscribed with a motto that recurs (in two basic forms) in her visual self-portraits: 'de dieu le bien, de moy le rien' (from God the good, from me nothing) and 'De l'Eternel le bien, de Moi le mal ou rien' (from the Eternal the good, from me bad or nothing). Is Inglis's apparent denial of her art in elaborately illuminated artistic manuscripts a simple contradiction? A sign of an oppressed woman gaining agency only through negating the self? We should first note that Inglis's female model, Georgette de Montenay, also inscribed a motto in her self-portraits: 'O plume en la main non vaine' (O pen in my hand not vain). Yet Inglis is not simply self-deprecatory while Montenay is self-assertive. Rather, both women draw upon the fervent Protestant view that the value of all human endeavour (including writing) comes not from the self but in relation to God. Inglis's pen is worthy not despite but because of the modesty, or rather, the piety that she shows. Gender, class, politics, religion and aesthetic concerns all inextricably intertwine in the tiny pen-and-ink self-portrait of Inglis, as throughout her exquisite calligraphic works. And these same factors inform women's writing in Britain throughout the sixteenth and seventeenth centuries. To that rich and diverse body of writing, we now turn.

NOTES

1. The *Octonaries* (eight-line moralistic verses) are translated from *Octonaires sur la Vanité et Inconstance du Monde* by French Huguenot minister Antoine de la Roche Chandieu. This Folger copy, given its faded and water-damaged condition, its dual French and English verses, and its lack of a dedication, seems to have been retained by Inglis as a master copy. Inglis made at least eight additional copies of the *Octonaries*, each dedicated and given to a different hoped-for patron. On the manuscripts and on Inglis's biography see A. H. Scott-Elliott and Elspeth Yeo, 'Calligraphic Manuscripts of Esther Inglis (1571–1624): A Catalogue', *The Papers of the Bibliographic Society of America* 84 (1990), 11–86; and 'Inglis', *Oxford Dictionary of National Biography*. On Inglis's gift-giving as motivated by Protestant impulse, see Georgianna Ziegler, ' "More than

Feminine Boldness": The Gift Books of Esther Inglis', in Mary E. Burke, *et al.* (eds.), *Women, Writing, and the Reproduction of Culture in Tudor and Stuart Britain* (Syracuse, NY: Syracuse University Press, 2000), pp. 19–37.

2. On the transcription of printed books back into manuscript, see H. R. Woudhuysen, *Sir Philip Sidney and the Circulation of Manuscripts 1580–1640* (Oxford: Clarendon Press, 1996), on Inglis, p. 98; and Peter Beal, *In Praise of Scribes: Manuscripts and their Makers in Seventeenth-Century England* (Oxford: Clarendon Press, 1998), on Inglis, p. 14, n. 65.

3. The source portrait appears in Georgette de Montenay, *Emblèmes ou Devises Chrestiennes* (Lyons, 1571). Inglis probably used the later, 1584 Zurich edition. See Georgianna Ziegler, 'Hand-Ma[i]de Books: The Manuscripts of Esther Inglis, Early-Modern Precursors of the Artists' Book', in Peter Beal and Margaret J. M. Ezell (eds.), *English Manuscript Studies*, vol. IX (London: British Library, 2000), p. 86, n. 17; Ziegler, 'Devising a Queen: Elizabeth Stuart's Representation in the Emblematic Tradition', *Emblematica: An Interdisciplinary Journal for Emblem Studies* 14 (2005), 167–76; and Patricia Demers, *Women's Writing in English: Early Modern England* (Toronto: University of Toronto Press, 2005), pp. 146–7.

4. The portrait, measuring 75 x 85 mm, is from *Argumenta in Librum Psalmorum Davidis* (1606), Houghton Library, Harvard MS Typ 212, fol. 9v.

5. For consideration of how Inglis appropriates the conventions of both presentation manuscripts and print culture to construct an authorial self, see Susan Frye, 'Materializing Authorship in Esther Inglis's Books', *Journal of Medieval and Early Modern Studies* 32 (2002), 469–91.

6. See Brown Women Writers: www.wwp.brown.edu/.

7. See the Perdita project: www.warwick.ac.uk/english/perdita/html/.

8. See, for instance, Danielle Clarke and Elizabeth Clarke (eds.), *'This Double Voice': Gendered Writing in Early Modern England* (Basingstoke: Palgrave Macmillan, 2000).

9. See, for example, Margaret J. M. Ezell, *Writing Women's Literary History* (Baltimore and London: Johns Hopkins University Press, 1993); and Ezell, 'The Laughing Tortoise: Speculations on Manuscript Sources and Women's Book History', *English Literary Renaissance* 38.2 (2008), 331–55.

10. Harold Love, *Scribal Publication in Seventeenth-Century England* (Oxford: Clarendon Press, 1993); Arthur Marotti, *Manuscript, Print, and the English Renaissance* (Ithaca, NY: Cornell University Press, 1995). See also Victoria Burke's chapter in this volume.

11. Margaret J. M. Ezell, *Social Authorship and the Advent of Print* (Baltimore and London: Johns Hopkins University Press, 1999). See also Marcy North's chapter in this volume.

12. Heidi Brayman Hackel, *Reading Material in Early Modern England: Print, Gender, and Literacy* (Cambridge: Cambridge University Press, 2005). See also Edith Snook's chapter in this volume.

13. David Armitage and Michael J. Braddick (eds.), *The British Atlantic World, 1500–1800* (Basingstoke: Palgrave, 2002). See Kate Chedgzoy, *Women's Writing in the British Atlantic World: Memory, Place and History, 1550–1700* (Cambridge: Cambridge University Press, 2007).

14. Joan Kelly-Gadol, 'Did Women Have a Renaissance?', in Renate Bridenthal and Claudia Koonz (eds.), *Becoming Visible: Women in European History* (Boston: Houghton Mifflin, 1977), pp. 137–64.

15. Joan Scott, 'Gender: A Useful Category of Historical Analysis', *The American Historical Review* 91.5 (1986), 1053–75; Kathleen Canning, *Gender History in Practice: Historical Perspectives on Bodies, Class, and Citizenship* (Ithaca and London: Cornell University Press, 2006), especially chapter 1.

16. See Patricia Crawford, 'Women's Published Writings 1600–1700', in Mary Prior (ed.), *Women in English Society 1500–1800* (London and New York: Routledge, 1985), pp. 211–82 (265–6).

17. See Helen Hills, 'Theorizing the Relationship between Architecture and Gender in Early Modern Europe', in Hills (ed.), *Architecture and the Politics of Gender in Early Modern Europe* (Aldershot: Ashgate, 2003), pp. 3–22.

18. On social space, see Henri Lefebvre, *The Production of Space*, trans. D. Nicholson-Smith (Oxford: Basil Blackwell, 1991).

19. On 'double-voicing', see Elaine Showalter, 'Feminist Criticism in the Wilderness', in Elizabeth Abel (ed.), *Writing and Sexual Difference* (Chicago: University of Chicago Press, 1982), pp. 31–5.

PART ONE

Material matters

I

HEATHER WOLFE

Women's handwriting

The advent of printed writing manuals in England at the end of the sixteenth century transformed the way that children and adults learned to write. Also known as copy-books, these manuals consisted of sets of printed woodcuts or engravings of exemplar alphabets and sentences designed specifically for imitation. Learning was democratized, limited only by the ability to obtain a copy-book and basic writing supplies. Between 1570 and 1700, at least sixty different writing masters published well over 115 separate editions of copy-books (many other editions no longer survive). Jean de Beau Chesne, a French Huguenot emigrant, and John Baildon, an English writing master, compiled the first copy-book for an English audience, *A booke containing divers sortes of hands, as well the English as French secretarie with the Italian, Roman, chancelry & court hands* (London, 1570).[1] Martin Billingsley's *The Pen's Excellencie or the Secretaries Delighte* (London, 1618) is the first surviving new copy-book of the seventeenth century.[2] The writing master and engraver *extraordinaire* Edward Cocker (d. 1675) came on to the scene in 1652 and dominated the copy-book market until 1700.

Early modern England was unique among European countries in having numerous scripts in simultaneous usage: secretary, Roman, Italian (italic), various legal scripts and mixed (later formalized into 'round hand' from which our modern cursive is derived). The penman John Davies of Hereford bemoaned this situation in *The writing schoolemaster* (1631): 'There is no kingdome but ours that have any more hands in ordinary use as their naturall hand ... ours hath (well neare) as many hands as courts of record, and they so strange and different too, that very few of our own people know or can read them' (B2v). Secretary, an angular script with gothic features, was the hand most widely used by Elizabethan and Jacobean Englishmen, 'the onely usuall hand of England, for dispatching of all manner of businesses', according to Billingsley (*The Pen's Excellencie*, C2r). The most 'usuall hand' for Englishwomen was a script that combined features of both Roman and italic.

Roman, developed in late fourteenth-century Italy, was based on the ninth-century Carolingian minuscule script, which in turn was an imitation of the simple and elegant letter forms of classical Greece and Rome that survived on monuments and buildings. Roman letters were upright and circular with spaces between each letter. Or as one writing manual describes it: 'It will conduce much to the exact symmetry and beauty of the Roman Hand, to consider its dependencies on the form of a Circle, as the Italian on that of an Oval ... It is not proper for the Letters thereof to joyn.'[3] Similarly, William Panke's *Most Breefe, Easie and Plaine Receite for Faire Writing* (London, 1591) describes the Roman hand as 'most usually written unjoyned & commendable ... observe but a reasonable distance in the setting of your letters ... For joyning of the letters wil be (in a learner) a cause of close writing, which in a Roman hand is not tollerable' (A7v). In *The new invention, intituled, calligraphia: or, the arte of faire writing* (St Andrews, 1622), David Browne refers to 'the universall ROMANE Character' (¶¶7r), while Billingsley calls it a 'hand of great account, and of much use in this Realme, especially in the *Universities*' (*The Pen's Excellencie*, C2v).[4] The popularity of the roman hand was solidified by the printer Aldus Manutius, who turned it into a typeface in the sixteenth century.

Its cousin, Italian, according to Billingsley, is 'not much different from *Roman*, but in manner and forme, of much incongruity thereunto', 'a most excellent and curious *hand*, and to be written with singular command of hand', 'of late is growne very usuall' (*The Pen's Excellencie*, C3r). Italian, or italic, was often described as a cursive hand based on the shape of an ellipsis or oval, with joined letters that sloped to the right, and many letter forms that could be formed with minimal pen lifts (and were thus faster to write). In *The writing schoolemaster*, Davies correctly foresaw the reasons why italic would eventually overtake secretary in England:

> The *Italian* hand therefore (of any forrain Character) I chiefly commend; nay, I preferre it farre before our English secretaries of either kinde, in respect of the generalitie of the use: for alas, out of this kingdome there is no use of our secretary hand, more then that in *France* or *Holland* ... The *Italian* every where in the Christian world is in frequent use, and all our letters of State to forrain parts and Princes, are usually written in that hand, at least as neare as our English secretaries and clarks can perform it therein. This is the character that shewes most boldnesse, freenesse, and bravery of the hand; and who hath this hand at command, may command with facility all other usefull hands.
>
> (B2v)

While some English masters were careful to distinguish between italic (and Italian) and Roman, others referred to scripts inconsistently or conflated or confused their definitions. In *The schoole of faire writing* (London, 1591), Peter Bales contends that 'no one hand requireth more cunning and skill in the joyning thereof, then the Romane or Italian hand' but then notes, in contrast to other masters, that '[t]he letters also especially of the Romane hand must so lincke and joyne one into another, and one out of another, as in no hande more' (D4v). In *The guide to pen-man-ship* (London, 1664), Edward Cocker describes '*Italick Hand*' as being 'betwixt a *Roman* and *Italian*. Which in regard it is a Hand Generally known and most easie to attain, we recommend it to the imitation of Women kind' (C1r). The 'Cursary or *Running Mixt Hand*' is either a mixture of Roman and italic, or roman, italic and secretary (C2r), while the '*Swift Running-Hand*' is 'Composed of *Roman* and *Italian*' (C2v). Cocker's 'Roman hand' is not 'the slow disjoyn'd old fashion'd *Roman*, but a hand more according to the present time, and more fit for any manner of businesse wherein such a hand can be useful' (D1v). The engraved alphabets and proverbs representing these hands do not always reflect his subtle distinctions. Ambrose Heal provides an apt assessment of the ambiguous descriptions: 'towards the end of the sixteenth century the Italian writing-masters ceased to exert a direct influence outside their own country, though the description "Italian" is retained to describe any condensed and strongly inclined script with long looped ascenders and full descenders'.[5]

Learning to write

Girls usually learned to write, if they learned at all, at the age of seven, after learning how to read and embroider. They might be taught at home or in a relative's household, by family members, tutors, governesses, or writing masters or mistresses. Elizabeth I learned to write from her French tutor, Jean de Bellemaine, and her Latin and Greek tutor, Roger Ascham. James I's daughter Elizabeth learned to write from Beau Chesne. Elizabeth Cary, Viscountess Falkland, probably learned to write from Davies, who also tutored Elizabeth Baskerville, Elizabeth Dutton and Anne Tracy.[6] Grace Mildmay (1552–1620) records in her autobiography that her governess 'would sett me to cipher with my penn ... & sometymes set me to wryte a supposed letter to this or that body concerning such & such things'.[7] In the 1580s, Jane Tutoft sent her daughter to the household of her cousin, Nathaniel Bacon, imploring him in a bold round secretary hand to 'let hyr lern to wryt & to rede & to cast acount & to wash & to bru & to backe & to dres meat & drink & so I trust she shal prove a great good huswyf' (Folger MS L.d.603). Anne Murray, Lady Halkett (b. 1623), recalls in her memoirs that at the age of seven she had no fewer than eight tutors, for languages, music, dancing, writing and needlework. Margaret Cavendish (b. 1623) remembers being tutored in singing, dancing, music, reading, writing and needlework.[8]

Women were one of the many intended audiences for copy-books, along with children preparing to enter grammar school (for which the ability to write was usually a prerequisite) and unschooled adults. Beau Chesne dedicated the printed copy-book, *La Clef de L'Escriture laquelle ouvre le chemin à la jeunesse, pour bien apprendre à escrire la vraye lettre Françoyse & Italique* (London, c. 1593), to three sisters, Ladies Mary, Elizabeth and Aletheia Talbot, citing the 'vertuous zeale which I perceive doth move the desire of your fine and daintie pennes to surmount even the best in skill and nimblenesse of well writing' (*ij). He also created a French manuscript copy-book for James I's daughter, Elizabeth.[9] Elizabeth Percy, Lucy Percy and Lucy Stanley (along with Henry Percy and 'Henry Northumberland') added their names to a sixteenth-century French manuscript copy-book, *La manière de bien choisir tailler et tenir La Plume*.[10] Theophila Hackett practised her signature in a copy of Beau Chesne and Baildon's *A book containing divers sortes of handes* (1570); Anne Roane (along with John Roane) inscribed her name in secretary hand (c. 1630–40) in a copy of Billingsley's *The Pen's Excellencie*; Elizabeth Baldwin (along with 'Richard Baldwyn') signed her name in four different styles (compared to her brother's seven) on the front endleaf of a copy of Richard Gething's *Calligraphotechnia* (1619); a 1657 copy of Cocker's *Arts Glory, Or The pen-man's treasurie* is inscribed 'Anne Licoris / Her Booke / November ye 29th / 1664' and 'John Lycoris His Booke'.[11]

In addition to copy-books, manuscript exercise books also provide insight into the learning process. Ann Bowyer created a copy-book (c. 1600–10) with exemplars taken directly from Beau Chesne and Baildon's italic and Roman models, which were then copied out repeatedly by another member of her family.[12] Rachael Fane's teenage exercise book (c. 1628) includes copies of moral distichs in a secretary hand. Mary Evelyn's teenage exercise book (1649) contains exemplars and copies of proverbs and couplets in Latin and English, in a variety of italic hands, with most pages and sometimes each line initialled or signed by her.[13] On single sheets of paper, Elizabeth Meynell copied the exemplar sentence 'Those power well wishers who are better willing' nineteen times, and, in 1689, Anna FitzWilliam copied the exemplar sentence 'Beautie will fade when sicknes doth invade' eleven times.[14]

Before the dissolution of the monasteries, girls might learn to write from nuns in convent schools; beginning in the early seventeenth century,

English recusant girls could be taught at newly founded English monastic communities on the Continent. If the local school statutes permitted girls, they might attend one of the free elementary schools which taught reading and writing in preparation for grammar school. One such free elementary school was run by a woman, Lady Elizabeth Periam, in Henley, in 1609.[15] Another option was boarding schools. A boarding school in Windsor in the first part of the seventeenth century charged £16 per girl per year, for 'dyett, lodging, washeing, and teacheing them to worke [embroider], reading, writing, and danceing', with an extra charge for instruction in singing, the viol, virginals or lute.[16] In the second half of the seventeenth century, many more schools run for and by women included writing in their curriculum, including schools run by Mrs Parnell Amye (*fl.* 1648) in Manchester, Mrs Foster (*fl.* 1639) in Chislet, Kent, Mrs Isley (*fl.* 1620) in Westerham, Kent, and Mrs Frend (*fl.* 1628), Mrs Perwich (*fl.* 1643) and Mrs Playford (*fl.* 1679), all in London.[17]

The first free writing school which explicitly included girls was at Waitby. A 1692 Waitby statute decreed that the master was to 'teach the Children of the Inhabitants ... both boys and girls, in Latin or English, both writing and arithmetic'. It is likely that the famous free writing school at Christ's Hospital, founded by Dame Ramsay *c.* 1577, taught writing to girls before the earliest published reference in 1710, when 'the girles shall noe longer goe to the Writing School to learn to write but that some conveniency shall be made in their own school for their writing, and that the Writing Master shall send his servant to instruct them at such hours as shall be thought most convenient'.[18]

In addition to these free writing schools, there were smaller private writing schools that charged tuition, as well as private tutors who offered their services. Some teachers used trade cards or broadsides to advertise their services, such as the writing mistress Elizabeth Penniston, whose *c.* 1690 trading card states: 'At the Maidens Writing-School ... Young Ladies and Gentlemen Are taught the Arts of Fair Writing Arithmetick and True Spelling of English by Eliz: Penniston Daughter to Mr. Tho. Topham a late Eminent Writing Mr. of this City. Such as please may be taught at their Habitations'.[19] Elizabeth Beane, 'Mistress in the Art of Writing', had at least three students whom she guided in the production of exuberantly written and illustrated arithmetic exercise books: Sarah Cole in 1685 (figure 3), Mary Serjant in 1688 and Anna Dowe in 1689.[20] The title pages to these manuscripts include impressive command-of-hand figures (each made with a single stroke), popular among writing masters and students in the second half of the seventeenth century.

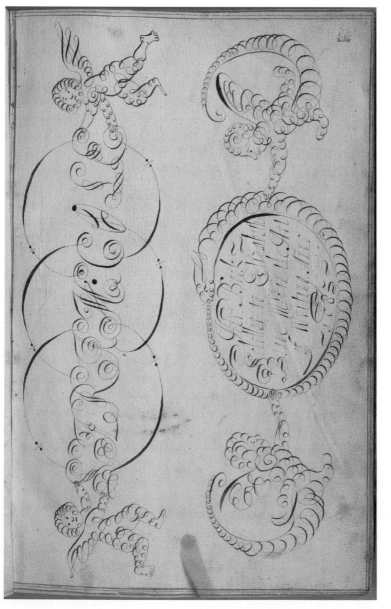

Figure 3. Title page, Sarah Cole's arithmetic exercise book, 1685: 'SARAH COLE Her Book Scholler to Elizabeth Beane Mistress in the Art of Writing Anno 1685'. Folger Shakespeare Library MS v.b.292.

A women's style of handwriting? Theory and practice

The early modern debate over whether women should learn to write was a lively one. Echoing a common argument, Daniel Tuvil's *Asylum Veneris, Or a Sanctuary for Ladies* (London, 1616), notes that girls were often prevented from learning to write on the grounds that the pen betrays 'Virgine Chastitie ... by venting foorth those amarous Passions, that are incident to hotter bloods' (p. 88). Tuvil recounts this argument to deride it, since if women were barred the pen, then they should equally be barred the needle, which could be used to embroider illicit messages. As late as 1638, Jacques du Bosc's *The Secretary of Ladies* accused men who doubted the propriety of allowing women to write of being motivated by 'ignorance or envy': 'if there bee any who cannot yet consent that Gentlewomen should write, I assure my selfe this book will convert them' (A6r–v).

Billingsley devotes over a page of his manual to the practical reasons why women should learn to write, criticizing the opinions of any who would bar women from writing as 'utterly lame' and indefensible: 'Suffer me not to give connivence to that ungrounded opinion of many, who affirme *Writing* to bee altogether unnecessary for women.' Navigating the paperwork of widowhood was a chief consideration: 'The practice of this Art is so necessary for women ... that no woman surviving her husband, and who hath an estate left her, ought to be without the use thereof.' Memory-assistance was another: 'if any Art be commendable in a woman ... it is this of *Writing*; whereby they, commonly having not the best memories (especially concerning matters of moment) may commit many worthy and excellent things to Writing, which may occasionally minister unto them matter of much solace'. And, no less important, Billingsley emphasizes the benefits of wives being able to communicate privately with their husbands 'in either of their absences' (*The Pen's Excellencie*, C1v–C2v).

The script most typically recommended for women, and which eventually came to be thought of as a woman's hand, was Roman. According to Billingsley, Roman was:

> the easiest hand that is written with Pen, and to bee taught in the shortest time: Therefore it is usually taught to women, for as much as they (having not the patience to take any great paines, besides phantasticall and humorsome) must bee taught that which they may instantly learne; otherwise they are uncertaine of their proceedings, because their minds are (upon light occasion) easily drawne from the first resolution. (C2v–C3r)

'Phantasticall' and 'humorsome', women were thought best suited to the relative ease of the Roman hand. However, Davies's *The writing schoolemaster* criticizes the ignorance of his fellow writing masters for teaching women the 'dull set Romane' script, which wearied men and women alike because of the time-consuming pen lifts after every letter. Davies expresses concern that Roman could be detrimental to the creative powers of female writers because they risked forgetting their 'inventions' before setting them down, just as he has himself, 'when I am about any such businesse my self, I am fain to neglect the fairenesse of my hand, for the freenesse of it to help my memory'. In contrast, both the cursive secretary and italic scripts, with their connective strokes between letter forms, were 'useful, lively, gracefull and ready'. Because 'women naturally have as much facility in joyning, and are as nimble handed in all manuall qualities' as men, they should be taught the italic hand (B2r). Richard Mulcaster's *Positions* (London, 1581) advises that 'it were better for them to have use of their pen, for the good that comes by it, then to wish they had it, when the default is felt', and therefore women should be taught to write italic 'faire and swiftly' (pp. 177–8). Cocker's *The guide to pen-man-ship* states that 'italick hand' is used by scholars, most gentlemen, merchants, and is 'of excellent use for Women, which they may imitate with facility, and write with dexterity'. By way of encouragement, he boasts: 'I have taught a Maid to write this Hand very well in one Afternoon, that never writ a Letter before' (D1v).

Despite the fact that Davies champions the teaching of cursive scripts (secretary and italic) to women, his preference for italic over secretary is clear: 'Never saw I yet a woman that could write our English secretary hand lively, though the *Romane* or *Italian* handsomly: because they naturally lack strength in their hand to perform those full strokes, and (as it were) to bruise a letter as men do.' Davies contrasts the way Italians hold their pens (they write italic with a 'light and easie pulse') with how the French, Dutch and English hold theirs, in order to write 'more solid and substantiall hands' (*The writing schoolemaster*, A1v). Perhaps this is behind Lord George Carew's comment in 1624 that Lady Ralegh's handwriting style is 'rounde and quicke, which in women may be excused'.[21]

In early modern England, men and women were subjected to similar writing exercises, which English writing masters based on the recommendations of Quintilian, Erasmus and continental writing masters. William Kempe's *Education of Children in Learning* (London, 1588) instructs the teacher to show the student how to hold the pen, form the letters proportionally, and then join the letters by 'drawing the Pen upon the figures of shadowed letters, then of writing without shadowed letters by imitating a Copie, lastly, of writing without a Copie' (F3v). Similarly, John Brinsley's chapter on writing in *Ludus Literarius, or, the grammar schoole* (London, 1612) suggests that the youngest children learn by having their hands guided and by tracing letter forms 'with a peece of chawke vpon a board, or table, or with a peece of blacke lead upon a paper' (F2r). For particularly troublesome letters, students should practice in 'voyde' spaces in their book, or on 'waste paper' (F3r), and mistakes in black lead could be erased with 'the crums of new wheate bread' (G4r). Like Brinsley, John Davies recommends tracing copy-book letters with a dry (inkless) pen, 'the better to acquaint his hand with their shape and draught' (*The writing schoolemaster*, A2r). Some copy-books helpfully broke letter forms into individual strokes and stroke families, as well as showing how various combinations of letters were joined. Cocker claimed that if one learned italic *o*, *i* and long *s* first, one would know all the basic strokes for forming the rest of the alphabet, since joining *o* and *i* makes *a*, the top of a long *s* and *o* make *b*, and so on (*The guide to pen-man-ship*, D1v). Writing on pre-ruled paper was advised by various masters so that students learned to write letters of the same size in a straight line, between two guide lines. Students could use a 'ruling pen' (or dry quill) to create the lines, and then draw the body of each letter within them. Brinsley recommended that students practise writing for an hour a day, preferably at one p.m. when 'commonly their hands are warmest and nimblest'. Their letters should only be considered good if 'no difference can bee found betweene it and the copie letter' (*Ludus Literarius*, E4v) in terms of height, size and width. Good handwriting consisted not only of good letter forms, but also of good joins, minimal botching and straight lines. To this end, the schoolmistress in the anonymous *The Wit of a Woman* (1604) goads a female student: 'What have you written? looke you, a faire maide, and make such foule blottes, and not a streight line?'[22]

Early modern writing manuals casually perpetuated familiar stereotypes about women's flighty and weaker nature in order to explain why Italian hands might be more suited than secretary to women writers. The truth was that writing was laborious, messy and tiring for both genders. In addition to a quill (typically from the first four flight feathers of a goose) and a pen knife, one needed ink, paper and either pounce, sandarac or Calais sand (to prepare the paper for writing if it were too 'spongy' and to dry the ink on the page). Feathers needed to be cleaned, hardened and their shafts trimmed before at least five or six cuts were made with a pen knife to create the nib (small nib and long slit for italic; broader nib for secretary). A student had to learn how to make ink and hold the pen, how much pressure to exert, how to reshape the nib and how to avoid 'botching' (sloppy corrections). Almost all female-compiled receipt books from the seventeenth century include one or more time-intensive recipes for making black ink out of rainwater (or beer, wine or vinegar), gall nuts and copperas (iron sulphate or vitriol) (figure 4). Erect posture and writing on a sloped flat surface had a profound effect on the quality of writing and flow of ink. In *The writing scholemaster*

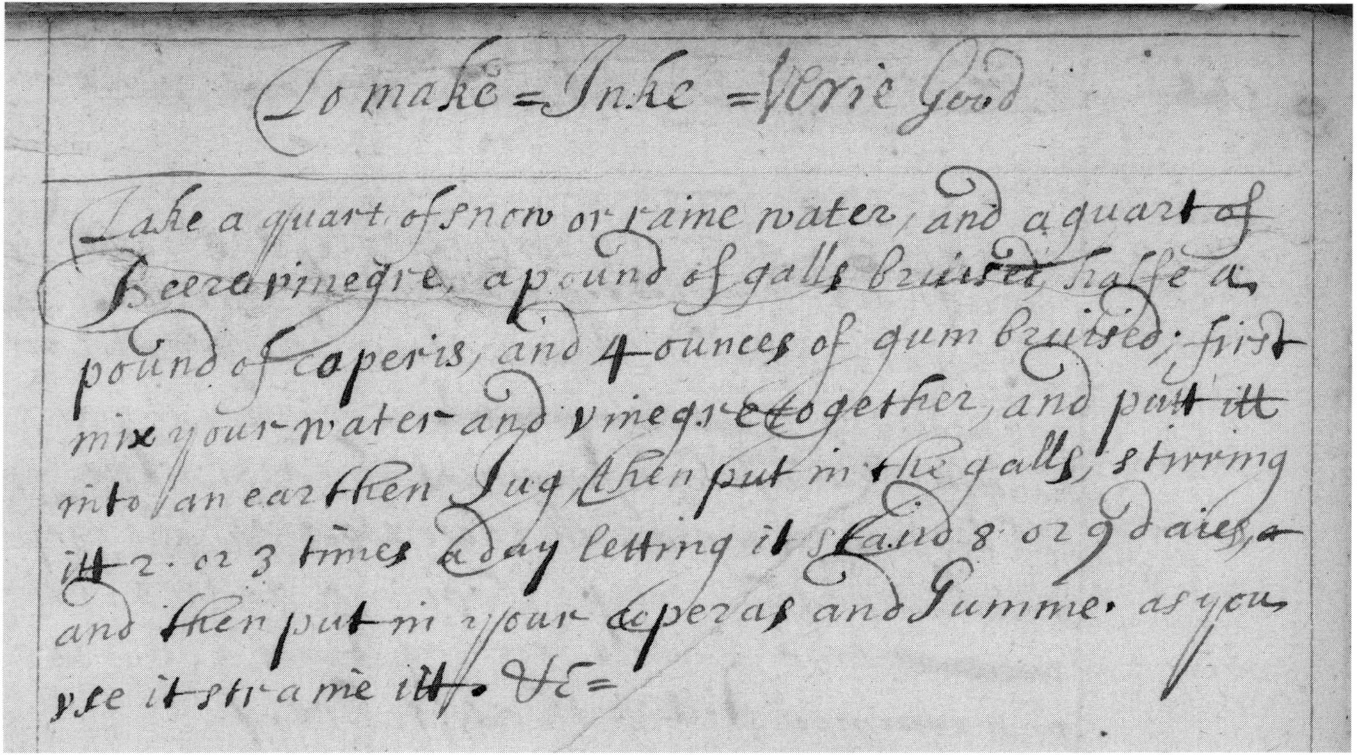
To make = Inke = Verie Good
Take a quart of snow or raine water, and a quart of
Beere vinegre, a pound of galls bruised, halfe a
pound of coperis, and 4 ounces of gum bruised; first
mix your water and vinegre together, and putt itt
into an earthen Jug then put in the galls, stirring
itt 2. or 3 times a day letting it stand 8. or 9 daies,
and then put in your coperas and Gumme. as you
vse it straine itt. &c=

Figure 4. Example of a round hand. Ink recipe, Anne (Granville) Dewes's receipt book, *c.* 1640– *c.* 1750. Folger Shakespeare Library MS v.a.430, fol. 42. Transcription: To make = Inke = Verie Good. Take a quart of snow or raine water, and a quart of Beere vinegre, a pound of galls bruised, halfe a pound of coperis, and 4 ounces of gum bruised; first mix your water and vinegre together, and putt itt into an earthen Jug, then put in the galls, stirring itt 2. or 3. times a day letting it stand 8 or 9 daies, and then put in your coperas and Gumme. As you vse it straine itt. &c=

(London, 1590), Bales recommends that in order to avoid fatigue and injury the quill should be held 'softly in your hande, with no more strength than is needfull: for by griping the penne over hard, you shall wearie both your fingers, your hand, and your wryst' (Q3r). Further, stooping could impair one's health, as could the position of one's head: 'tourne not your head too much aside, nor bend it downe too lowe, for avoyding of wearines and paine' (Q4r). Cocker mentions that 'young Practitioners are not strong enough to perform' the body strokes of certain capital letters (*The guide to Pen-man-ship*, D1r).

Not surprisingly, excuses for poor writing and complaints of aching heads or hands (often because of gout, but also perhaps a form of repetitive stress injury) were not uncommon. The Countess of Shrewsbury explains in 1592 that her son is writing on her behalf 'for feare of bringing great payne to my hed', while her husband similarly notes in 1580: 'I … am at this present so trobled with paine and stifnes in my hand that I cannot write my self.'[23] Dorothy Bacon describes the causes of her 'ell wrytten lettar' (written in a bold secretary hand) thus: 'my penn is naught, my eyncke worse, and my inwensyon [invention] worst of all'.[24] Even Elizabeth I acknowledges her 'skribled Lines' in the postscript of a letter to James VI/I (Folger MS x.d.397). In 1619, Lady Anne (Bacon) Townshend adds a postscript to a letter to her son Sir Roger Townshend, written in a legible italic hand but with crooked lines and numerous corrections, 'I wish you might reade my scriblinge?' (Folger MS L.d.595). John Winthrop, future Governor of Massachusetts, similarly describes his wife's 'scribbling hand'.[25] Many men and women had 'scribbled' hands simply because they were inexperienced; others, because they wrote in haste; others, because their ink was too thick, their paper too rough, their quill too worn or because of temporary physical or mental weakness.

Thousands of surviving examples of early modern women's hands represent an array of unique styles which show expressivity, liveliness, creativity and artistic expression in their proportion, slant and size. It is difficult to generalize about early modern women's handwriting since the range and style of scripts evolved so dramatically in the period, narrowing eventually into a single hand, the round hand, used by men and women alike. Also, men and women frequently used different scripts, or different levels of formality of the same script, for different occasions: to show deference, to write rapidly, to write in Latin, or to sign one's name, for example. That being said, the majority of women between roughly 1550 and 1650 used a non-cursive italic script, which in addition to being the script recommended by many writing masters, was the script used by queens, princesses and noblewomen. In addition to being easier to learn than secretary, it was fashionable,

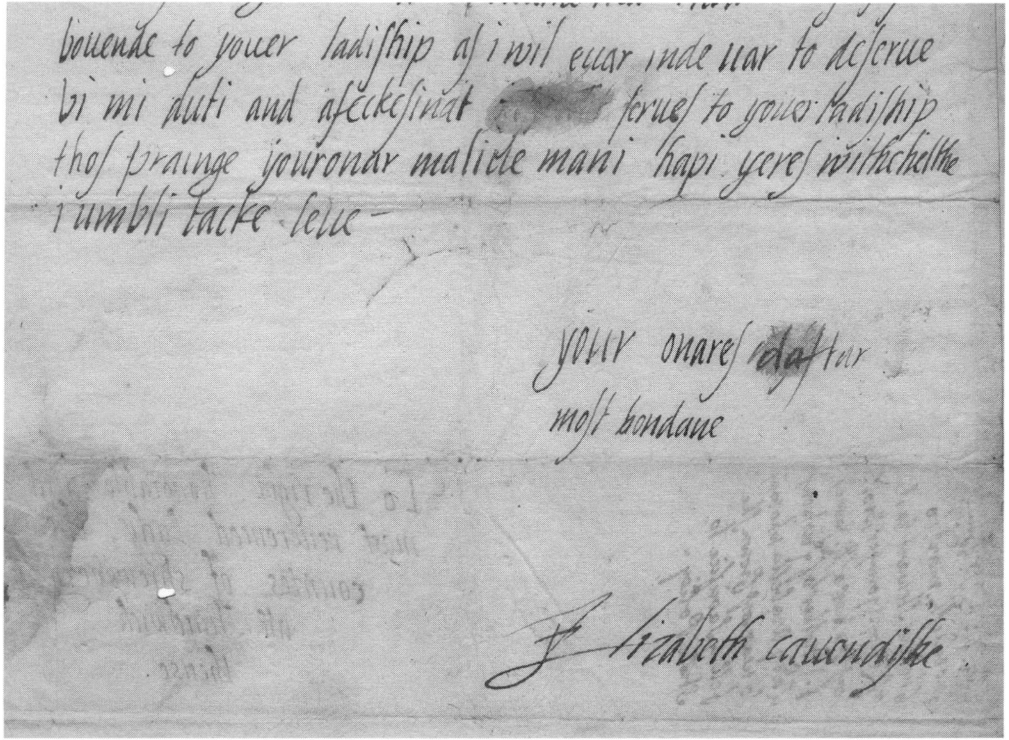

Figure 5. Example of an italic hand. Detail, autograph letter signed, from Elizabeth (Cavendish) Stuart, Countess of Lennox, to Elizabeth, Countess of Shrewsbury [before October 1574]. Folger Shakespeare Library MS x.d.428 (50).

Transcription: ... bouende to youer ladiship as i wil euar inde uar to deserue bi mi duti and afeckesinat serues to youer ladiship thos prainge your onar maliue mani hapi yeres with helthe I umbli tacke leue – your onares daftar most bondane Elizabeth cauendishe [... bound to your ladyship as I will ever endeavour to deserve by my duty and affectionate service to your ladyship. Thus praying your honor may live many happy years with health, I humbly take leave. Your honor's daughter most bounden, Elizabeth Cavendish] modern and beautiful, signifying a humanist and refined background. Mary, Queen of Scots, educated in France, was the first monarch of Scotland to write in a non-cursive italic hand. Queen Elizabeth and her half-siblings, Mary and Edward, were taught to write it exclusively, as was Lady Jane Grey.[26] Elizabeth maintained a formal hand with serifed letter forms for inscriptions but adopted a faster, looser and more eclectic unserifed style for letters, which one of her court secretaries identified as her 'running hand'.[27] Figure 5 exemplifies a typical non-cursive running italic hand, lacking serifs and other ornamentation. While the letter forms suggest an emphasis on economy and speed, the unusual orthography and the lack of majuscule (capital) letters also suggest a lack of training. This form of informal unjoined italic script does not appear in writing manuals.

Non-cursive semi-formal italic (testeggiata ('headed') style), which is the most typical style of women's handwriting 1550–1650, could take many shapes and forms. Figure 6 is a *c.* 1608 unpractised, upright, angular hand with an abundance of pen lifts, disproportionately elongated ascenders and awkwardly formed letters such as *a, e, n* and *r.* Figure 7, *c.* 1609/10, is more rounded, fluid, sloped and playful. The writer adds curled finials to her *k,* spurred flourishes to her *f,* terminal *e* and *s* and initial *c,* a loop in the middle of her *w* and a looped tail to her *y.* Both examples show typical 'bulbed' or 'clubbed' serifs on certain letter forms (see the tops of the *b, d, f, h, k, l* and long *s*) and a similar use of ligatures for certain letter combinations (see *st* in 'sister' in figure 6; *ck* in 'Eseckes', *ch* in 'muche', *st* in 'rest' in figure 7). Bulbed serifs were formed by making hooks at the tops of ascenders which then filled with ink as the writer made a downstroke. Lobes on letters such as *p* were sometimes open at the bottom (see figure 7) and sometimes at the top (see figure 6). A comparison of letter forms used by both writers in words and phrases such as *you, and, weare/were, kindest/kindly, I rest, my mother* reveals a range of other differences.

Both before and after English writing manuals began identifying the italic and Roman script as female scripts, women used secretary. French tutors and Continental writing manuals undoubtedly had an influence: Lodovico Curione's *La Notomia delle Cancellaresche corsive* (Rome, 1588) includes a plate of secretary labelled 'lettre qui escrivent les dames de France'. Henry VIII's mother, Elizabeth of York, and at least five of his wives – Catherine of Aragon, Anne Boleyn, Jane Seymour, Anne of Cleves and Catherine Parr (who also wrote italic) – used secretary hand, along with Elizabeth I's nurse, Lady Margaret Bryan, and her governess, Katharine Ashley.[28] Caroline Bowden notes that eight of the fifty-three women who signed their own names in a book recording gifts from the Queen to her Privy Chamber wrote in secretary or a mixed hand.[29] Grace Mildmay (1552–1620) wrote her autobiography

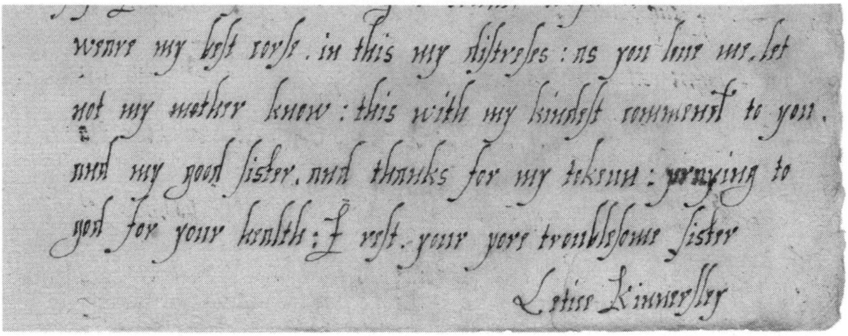

Figure 6. Example of an italic hand. Detail, autograph letter signed, from Lettice Kinnersley to Walter Bagot, 14 September 1608[?]. Folger Shakespeare Library MS L.a.598.

Transcription: ... weare my best corse, in this my distreses: as you loue me, let not my mother know: this with my kindest commendations to you and my good sister, and thanks for my tokenn: praying to god for your health: I rest your pore troublesome sister Letice Kinnersley [... were my best course, in this my distresses. As you love me, let not my mother know. This with my kindest commendations to you and my good sister, and thanks for my token. Praying to god for your health, I rest, your poor troublesome sister, Letice Kinnersley]

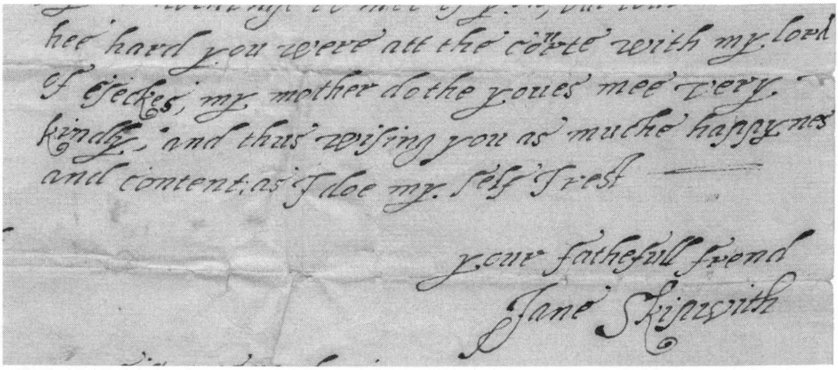

Figure 7. Example of an italic hand. Detail, autograph letter signed, from Jane (Skipwith), Lady Throckmorton to Lewis Bagot, 24 March 1609/10. Folger Shakespeare Library MS L.a.851.

Transcription: ... hee hard you were att the courte with my lord of Eseckes, my mother dothe youes mee very kindly, and thus wising you as muche happynes and content; as I doe my self I rest your fathefull frend Jane Skipwith [... he heard you were at the Court with my Lord of Essex. My mother doth use me very kindly. And thus wishing you as much happiness and content as I do myself, I rest your faithful friend, Jane Skipwith] in an italic hand but made corrections and revisions in a secretary hand, and the surviving educational notebooks of her granddaughter, Rachael Fane (1613?–80), show that she was taught both secretary and italic.[30] In 1574, Mercy Harvey concocted a complicated scheme for a married nobleman to send letters *to* her that appeared, on the address leaf, to be *from* her (to her brother), by inscribing 'To mie loving brother, Mr. G.H.' on the address leaf 'in a small raggid secretary hand'.[31] Indeed, as shown in this example from calligrapher and miniaturist Esther Inglis (discussed in the Introduction to this volume), secretary *could* be identified as a woman's hand (scc figure 8).

Elizabeth Cary and at least six of her children, Anne, Mary, Lucy, Elizabeth, Patrick and Lucius, all had cursive mixed hands with very few pen lifts, suggesting that the children were taught by their mother or each other, since this level of cursiveness was unusual in the first half of the seventeenth century.[32] The prophet Eleanor Davies was another early adopter of the cursive hand, while later in the century, Dorothy Osborne, Lucy Hutchinson, Lady Hester Pulter and Lydia DuGard all wrote in confident cursive italic hands.[33] These cursive hands represent the mastery of a skill deemed difficult for women: 'joining' letters with diagonal hairline strokes formed with the edge or corner of the pen's nib. The banished queen turned schoolmistress in Richard Brome's play *The Queen and the Concubine* (1635) criticizes one of her students for prematurely attempting joining: 'No child you must not Joyn-hand yet: you must your letters and your minums better first.'[34] Indeed, joining was usually cited as the most difficult aspect of writing, and writing masters had varying opinions as to which italic letters could be joined to each other and which letters could be formed in one, two or three strokes.

Conclusion

Writing masters were naturally sceptical about the aesthetic ramifications of mixing scripts. Browne advised against it: 'Yet there be some who intermingle Secretarie letters in words of Romane writ, & Romane letters in words of Secretarie writ: they may mix their Dishes together as they please, but I will holde mine severall' (*The new invention*, B8v). Billingsley's *A coppie booke containing varietie of examples* (London, 1668) advised using 'maturity of Judgement' and common sense when it came to mixing scripts: 'for it were ridiculous for a man to croud into a hand naturally perpendicular (as our Set Secretary is) the Letters of another consisting of oblique or slanting lines, as the *Roman* and *Italian* hands do' (A2v).

But any initial discomfort from writing masters seeking to preserve the purity and separation of individual scripts was soon replaced by the very practical concerns of legibility and speed. Italic and secretary evolved into

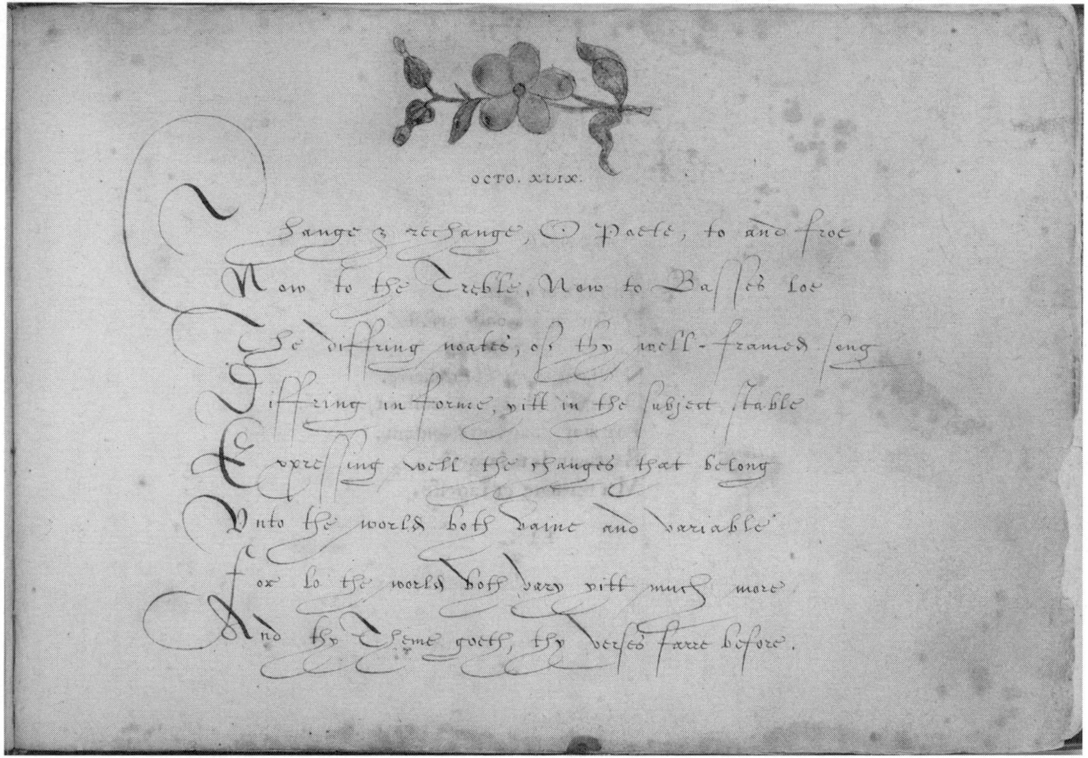

Figure 8. Example of a secretary hand. Octonary 49, Esther Inglis, *Octonaries upon the Vanitie and Inconstancie of the World*, 1601. Folger Shakespeare Library MS v.a.91, fol. 50r.

Transcription: Change & rechange, O Poete, to and froe / Now to the Treble, Now to Basses loe / The diffring noates, of thy well-framed song / Diffring in forme, yitt in the subject stable / Expressing well the changes that belong / Vnto the world both vaine and variable / For lo the world both vary yitt much more / And thy Theme goeth, thy verses farre before.

eclectic individual mixes, which rapidly evolved into a more uniform 'round' hand, a cursive script with linking loops and rounded letter forms that is a precursor to modern handwriting. By the end of the seventeenth century, most men and women had adopted the round hand. Secretary, Roman and italic hands continued to be reproduced in writing manuals, but appear to have been viewed as 'novelty' hands rather than useful scripts. The new hands of the late sixteenth century became the antiquated hands of the late seventeenth century. They were learned for the purpose of reading old documents, rather than creating new ones.

NOTES

1. This was followed by *A newe booke of copies* (London, 1574), *A new booke, containing all sortes of handes* (London, 1590), William Panke's *Most Breefe, Easie and Plaine Receite for Faire Writing* (London, 1591) and Peter Bales's testy rejoinder, *The schoole of faire writing* (London, 1591). No copies are known to survive of two other manuals, Christopher Gower's *The way to fayre wrytinge* (1587) and George Penn's *A methode to teach to wryte* (1589).
2. Other new writing manuals soon followed: Richard Gething's *Calligraphotechnia or The art of faire writing sett forth* (London, 1619), John Davies's *The writing schoolemaster* (London, 1620?; 1631), David Browne's *The new invention, intituled, calligraphia: or, the arte of faire writing* (St Andrews, 1622), and William Comley's *A new copy-booke of all the most usuall English hands* (London, 1622).
3. Martin Billingsley, *A coppie booke* [1668], A3v (STC 3061).
4. In contrast, Davies (B2r) and Cocker (Wing C4838, D1v) cite the universality of the italic hand.
5. Ambrose Heal, *English Writing Masters* (Cambridge: Cambridge University Press, 1931), p. xxx.
6. H. R. Woudhuysen, *Sir Philip Sidney and the Circulation of Manuscripts, 1558–1640* (Oxford: Clarendon Press, 1996), p. 38.
7. Helen Ostovich and Elizabeth Sauer (eds.), *Reading Early Modern Women: An Anthology of Texts in Manuscript and Print, 1550–1700* (New York and London: Routledge, 2004), p. 254.
8. Jerome de Groot, '"Euery one teacheth after thyr owne fantasie": French Language Instruction', in Kate Moncrief and Kate McPherson (eds.), *Performing Pedagogy: Gender and Instruction in Early Modern England* (Aldershot: Ashgate, forthcoming, 2010). I am grateful to Jerome de Groot for sharing his essay with me prior to publication.
9. Newberry Library, Wing MS ZW 639 .B382.
10. 'Duke of Northumberland at Alnwick', *Historical Manuscripts Commission*, 3rd Report, Appendix (1872), p. 114.
11. Hackett: Bodleian, Douce B6 75, G2; Roane: Bodleian, Antiq.e.E.1618.2, last page of preface; Baldwin: British Library, C.79.b.16; Licoris: Newberry Library, Wing ZP 645 .C632, in Eve Rachele Sanders, *Gender and Literacy on Stage in Early Modern England* (Cambridge: Cambridge University Press, 1998), frontispiece.

12. Victoria E. Burke, 'Ann Bowyer's Commonplace Book (Bodleian Library Ashmole MS 51): Reading and Writing Among the Middling Sort', *Early Modern Literary Studies* 6.3 (January 2001), 1.12 [url: http://purl.oclc.org/emls/06–3/burkbowy.html]. See also Burke's discussion of Bowyer in chapter 3 of this volume.

13. British Library, Add MS 78437. The copy-book was probably made by Evelyn's husband's scribe and librarian, Richard Hoare, whose name appears on fol. 12.

14. Ampleforth Abbey, SS289v2; Bonham's catalogue, 22 March 2004, lot 677.

15. Herbert C. Schulz, 'The Teaching of Handwriting in Tudor and Stuart Times', *Huntington Library Quarterly* 6.4 (1943), 396.

16. Folger MS L.e.[644]. See Laetitia Yeandle, 'A School for Girls in Windsor', *Medieval and Renaissance Drama in England* 17 (2005), 272–7.

17. Schulz, 'The Teaching of Handwriting', p. 425. See also Caroline Bowden's chapter on women's education in this volume.

18. Schulz, 'The Teaching of Handwriting', p. 408.

19. Reproduced in Heal, *English Writing Masters*, p. 84.

20. Folger MS v.b.292; Yale, Beinecke, Osborn Shelves MS fb.98; Sotheby's, 27 March 1972, lot 23.

21. Alexander Grosart (ed.), *The Lismore Papers*, series 2, vol. III (Printed for private circulation, 1888), p. 105.

22. Bianca F.-C. Calabresi, ' "You sow, Ile read": Letters and Literacies in Early Modern Samplers', in Heidi Brayman Hackel and Catherine E. Kelly (eds.), *Reading Women: Literacy, Authorship, and Culture in the Atlantic World, 1500–1800* (Philadelphia: University of Pennsylvania Press, 2008), p. 94.

23. British Library, Lansdowne MS 71, fol. 2; Folger MS x.d.428 (104).

24. Jane Key (ed.), 'Letters and Will of Lady Dorothy Bacon, 1597–1629', *Norfolk Record Society* 56 (1993), 87.

25. Sanders, *Gender and Literacy*, p. 226.

26. See Alfred Fairbank and Berthold Wolpe (eds.), *Renaissance Handwriting* (London: Faber and Faber, 1960), plates 25, 28, 29, 33.

27. Janel Mueller and Leah S. Marcus (eds.), *Elizabeth I: Autograph Compositions and Foreign Language Originals* (Chicago and London: University of Chicago Press, 2003), p. xvii.

28. *Ibid.*, p. xiv. For examples of the hands of Elizabeth of York and Anne of Cleves, see Arthur Schwarz, *Vivat Rex!* (New York: Grolier Club, 2009), pp. 57, 190.

29. Caroline Bowden, 'Women as Intermediaries: An Example of the Use of Literacy in the Late Sixteenth and Early Seventeenth Centuries', *History of Education* 22.3 (1993), 223.

30. Ostovich and Sauer, *Reading Early Modern Women*, pp. 254, 74.

31. Sanders, *Gender and Literacy*, p. 166.

32. For reproductions of these hands see Heather Wolfe, 'The Scribal Hands and Dating of *Lady Falkland: Her Life*', *English Manuscript Studies* 11 (2000), 192–202 and Ostovich and Sauer, *Reading Early Modern Women*, pp. 142, 216.

33. For reproductions of these hands see Ostovich and Sauer, *Reading Early Modern Women*, pp. 142, 216, 228, 284, 302.

34. Calabresi, '"You sow, Ile read"', p. 95.

READING LIST

Beal, Peter. *A Dictionary of English Manuscript Terminology, 1450–2000*. Oxford: Oxford University Press, 2008.

Beal, Peter and Margaret J. M. Ezell (eds.). *English Manuscript Studies, 1100–1700: Writings by Early Modern Women*. Vol. IX. London: British Library, 2000.

Burke, Victoria E. and Jonathan Gibson (eds.). *Early Modern Women's Manuscript Writing: Selected Papers from the Trinity/Trent Colloquium*. Aldershot and Burlington: Ashgate, 2004.

Fairbank, Alfred and Berthold Wolpe. *Renaissance Handwriting: An Anthology of Italic Scripts*. London: Faber and Faber, 1960.

Marshall, Hilary. *Palaeography for Family and Local Historians*. Chichester: Phillimore, 2004.

Millman, Jill Seal and Gillian Wright (eds.). *Early Modern Women's Manuscript Poetry*. Manchester and New York: Manchester University Press, 2005.

Osley, A.S. (ed.). *Scribes and Sources: Handbook of the Chancery Hand in the Sixteenth Century*. Boston: David R. Godine, 1980.

Ostovich, Helen, and Elizabeth Sauer (eds.). *Reading Early Modern Women: An Anthology of Texts in Manuscript and Print, 1550–1700*. New York and London: Routledge, 2004.

Whalley, Joyce Irene. *English Handwriting, 1540–1853: An Illustrated Survey Based on Material in the National Art Library, Victoria and Albert Museum*. London: Her Majesty's Stationery Office, 1969.

2

EDITH SNOOK

Reading women

Reading was a vital way for early modern women to engage with the culture of early modern Britain. As a socially stratified skill, learned first with print, then handwriting and finally Latin, reading could be attempted with the particular literacy skills available to individuals. Reading was charged with instilling religious doctrine and political ideology, even as it could become an agent of social change. In both print and manuscript culture, reading modulated with social, technological and economic shifts in textual production and circulation. Undertaken in silence and aloud, reading had private and public dimensions, psychological and cultural consequences and a physiology. It was also a deeply gendered activity, not because women necessarily read in ways essentially different from men, but because access to education and wealth, along with the belief that women's bodies and minds were designed by God for a domestic life, informed how, why and what women read.

Evidence of women's reading is somewhat elusive. Because women were much less likely than men to create marginalia, it is difficult to trace their reading practices in the way that Lisa Jardine and Anthony Grafton, William Sherman, and Kevin Sharpe have done with Gabriel Harvey, John Dee and William Drake.[1] This problem of evidence characterizes the study of all non-élite readers, although the moral value accorded female silence created an especially feminine reluctance to annotate books. A book's margins were not necessarily a private space, since books were often shared, and women did not tend to assume that they had the authority to render a comment. Even more, women were less likely than men to be literate. David Cressy argues that in seventeenth-century England only about 10 per cent of women were able to sign their names, about the same rate as the most illiterate group of men.[2] Yet more people could read than could write, as Margaret Spufford demonstrates using the evidence of book publication, the dominant pedagogical practice of teaching reading before writing and the wide availability of teachers.[3] That said, the activities of female readers who could not write remain largely invisible to us because they left little trace, with the result that evidence is slanted towards middling- and upper-class women.

Wealth and access to education affected who might learn to read, but the meanings that readers contrived were the labours of one mind, or several working together. Roger Chartier argues that these meanings were neither totally determined nor totally free, for readers' methods and understanding were swayed by authorial strategies of writing, obedience to learned rules and the imitation of models.[4] English women's reading was further constrained by gender. For instance, Richard Brathwait's early modern conduct book recommends reading to all women but construes it as a fortification of female sexuality that ensures the chastity of virgins and the faithfulness of wives. To this end, Brathwait enjoins women to follow a curriculum of the Bible, the church fathers, Plato, Seneca and Cicero, in translation.[5] Such prescriptions are common and visible in the evidence that we have of women's reading, in the kinds of books that women read and in the way that they comment on their reading material – or fail to comment, for female reading is typically construed as a passive activity. Women are not to critique books but imbibe them, reading only what is wholly edifying so they will remain pure. Whatever their class, women should not follow the learned example of Erasmus's Christian prince in reading critically to pull jewels from proverbial dung heaps. Such dictates not only proscribe particular books and forms of knowledge – including romances, love poetry and plays – but define the very process of female learning as an act of obedience. Mary Evelyn, in a 1672 letter to her son's tutor, seemingly accepts such constraints when she writes that 'Women were not born to read authors and censure the learned, to compare lives and judge of virtues, to give rules of morality, and sacrifice to the Muses'; moreover, she adds, 'We are willing to acknowledge all time borrowed from family duties is misspent'. Still, Evelyn assesses Donne's reputation and offers a witty and informed critique of John Dryden's *The Siege of Grenada* (more commonly, *The Conquest of Granada*).[6] Women's reading often negotiates thus between conformity to gendered models of reading and creativity in understanding texts as intellectually, spiritually and socially significant. The remainder of this chapter will look at existing marginalia and then at other forms of evidence of women's reading, including life-writing (biographies, autobiographies, letters and meditations that remained unpublished in the seventeenth century) and printed texts in more literary forms, such as maternal advice books, poetry and romance. Although these forms do not exhibit the work of reading as directly as do marginalia and miscellanies (Victoria Burke discusses the latter in this volume), they do register how women thought about the materials, methods and reasons for reading.

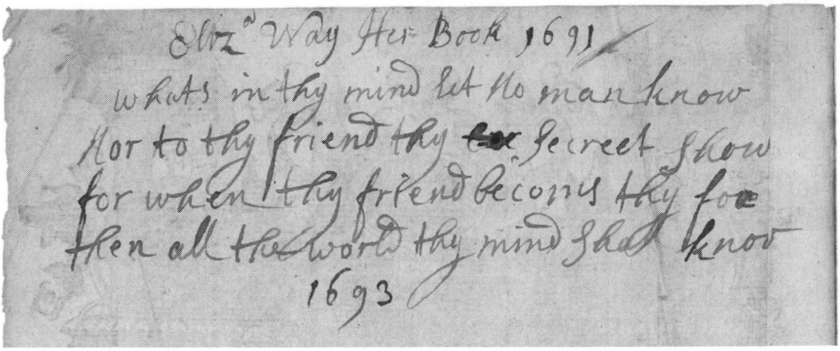
Eliz^{a} Way Her Book 1691
whats in thy mind let no man know
Nor to thy friend thy secreet show
for when thy friend becoms thy foe
then all the world thy mind shall know
1693

Figure 9. Elizabeth Way, ownership signature and inscription. Detail, title page verso, *Sermons of Master John Calvin, Upon the Booke of Job. Translated out of French by Arthur Golding* [London, 1574]. Folger Shakespeare Library STC 4445 Copy 1.

Despite the lack of encouragement for active reading, early modern women did write in their books. By far the most common annotations are names, inscribed as signs of ownership. These often take the form used by Elizabeth Way in her 1574 folio volume of the *Sermons of Master John Calvin, Upon the Booke of Job*, translated by Arthur Golding: 'Eliz^{a} Way Her Book 1691' (figure 9). Inscriptions also record births, baptisms, deaths and the presentation of the book as a gift, and margins and blank pages are utilized for writing practice and accounts.[7] Some marks are more extensive, but most still evade making textual commentary. Elizabeth Way, for instance, adds under her name:

> Whats in thy mind let no man know
> Nor to thy friend thy secret show
> for when thy friend becoms thy foe
> then all the world thy mind shall know
> 1693

In other blank spaces in the volume, two meditative poems quote and rearrange emblems from Francis Quarles's *Emblems*, while another poem – a meditation on Psalm 42 autographed in 1727 – may be an original composition. Such inscriptions say little about how Way understood Calvin's sermons, but the verse's stress on securing one's inward life must inform her willingness to annotate. The rewriting of Quarles and the Psalm shows how reading produces writing. Neither Calvin's printed book nor Quarles's emblems nor the Bible are deferentially treated but offer a place and a language to compose moral principles and spiritual attitudes, even where others might see them. Otherwise, we know of only a few women who used marginalia to comment directly on their reading. Margaret Hoby records in her diary that she writes 'notes in my bible of the chapter' (p. 146), while Frances Wolfreston wrote brief comments in Shakerley Marmion's play *A Fine Companion* (1633).[8] Most substantially, Anne Clifford and her amanuenses wrote in several of her books, making marginalia another form through which Clifford demonstrated her keen interest in her family's history.[9]

Domesticity was central to how women construed reading, for the household provided its space, rationale and schedule. Not to be underestimated, domesticity resulted in a diverse array of reading practices – dialectical, sociable, spiritual, intellectual, emotional, practical and politically engaged – with a variety of religio-political positions. The diary of Lady Margaret (Dakins) Hoby (1570/1–1633) records her daily activities, primarily at Hackness Hall in Yorkshire, between 1599 and 1605. Surviving as British Library Egerton MS 2614, the diary provides, at least in the first years, detailed notes on how reading, both solitary and communal, structures Hoby's devotional life. Mary Ellen Lamb focuses on the diary's psychological dimensions and argues that it illustrates 'another form of the Reformation subject', whose interiority 'remains relational even in the private act of solitary reading'.[10] As a reader, Margaret Hoby is also engaged in spiritual combat which requires an active way of knowing. Her personal reading practice assumes a public and political significance that is not defined simply by obedience. Alone and with her servants, Hoby reads Foxe's Book of Martyrs, a polemical Protestant tome, while also reading Catholic books ('the principles of poperie out of one of their owne bookes' and 'a popeshe booke' (p. 83)) with her chaplain, Mr Rhodes. A dialectical approach to reading is evident, too, in Hoby's approach to controversies within the Church of England over ecclesiastical governance and Christ's harrowing of hell. In this vein, Mr Rhodes reads her 'Mr Cartwright and the Bushoppe of Canterberies booke' (p. 56). This is probably one of Thomas Cartwright's replies to John Whitgift, Archbishop of Canterbury, printed in 1573, 1575 and 1577. Cartwright and Whitgift demand that their readers judge their arguments, know the opposing position and desire to seek truth. Cartwright states in his preface to the 1573 *A replye to an answere made of M. Doctor Whitgifte Against the admonition to the Parliament* that he had wanted to reprint the Bishop's words to show that he was not misrepresenting them, a tactic Whitgift used in his *An Answere to a Certen Libel intituled An Admonition to Parliament* (1572). Although Cartwright claims to be unable to follow suit for economic reasons, he provides page references to the Bishop's works in all of his replies.

Lady Hoby is within the bounds of appropriate female reading, for she reads religious books in a domestic context, even having a minister guide her interpretations. Yet their willingness together to tender debate has political results. When her books demand an active dialectical method, whether she is listening to Mr Rhodes or reading herself, Hoby's reading disrupts gender hierarchies. When reading Catholic books, she can neither imbibe nor obey. Her search for truth, moreover, leads her to conclude that 'the title of Lord Archbusshopes are Unlawful'. Questioning the Scriptural basis for episcopacy with 'peace of Conscience' (p. 141), she questions the foundations of English government. Despite the emphasis on Bible reading, Protestant England had a long-standing fear of just such varieties of meanings, particularly amongst female and lower-class readers. The martyr Anne Askew could signal her resistance to Henry VIII's church simply by going to the Lincoln minster to peruse a bible because a 1543 law forbade women to read the Bible publicly; gentle and noble women could read by themselves, but not to others, so they could influence no one. By Hoby's time, the apprehension remained if the law did not. The Bible was a discourse of truth, providing its readers with a mantle of authority, which Hoby assumes, for she commutes her style of reading into action, not by publishing, but by reading and discussing books and sermons with her household and her neighbours.

Other female writers venerated reading as an inheritance to pass on to their children and used their own reading as a justification for writing. Literate mothers were, after all, often first responsible for teaching children to read. Dorothy Leigh's frequently reprinted maternal advice book, *The Mothers Blessing* (1616), urges her sons to instruct all members of their household to read and to refuse to be a witness at a baptism unless the child will be taught to read. The autobiographical writings of Grace (Sharington), Lady Mildmay (*c.* 1552–1620), entitled in manuscript form 'Lady Mildmay's Meditations', comprise an autobiography and spiritual meditations, now preserved at the Northamptonshire Central Library.[11] Both commence with reading lists, the autobiography by recommending to her daughter, Mary (Mildmay) Fane, and her children the Bible, Foxe's *Actes and Monuments* (or Book of Martyrs), English histories, law and classical philosophy; the meditations, addressed to Mary, commend the Bible, Musculus's *Common Places*, Foxe's *Actes and Monuments*, Thomas à Kempis's *The Imitation of Christ* and Mildmay's own meditations, a curriculum that, but for the last item, is identical to that taught by her own mother, Lady Sharington, who 'thought it ever dangerous to suffer young people to read or study books wherein was good and evil mingled together' ('Lady Mildmay's Meditations', pp. 23–4, 28, 70–1). More of Lady Mildmay's maternal advice appears in Folger MS v.a.180, a commonplace book compiled *c.* 1655/6 by her grandson, Sir Francis Fane (a younger son of Mary Fane and Francis Fane, 1st Earl of

Westmoreland) for his son Henry. It collects advice to various offspring by Lady Mildmay, Mary (Neville) Fane, Baroness Le Dispencer (the 1st Earl's mother), Mary Fane, Countess of Westmoreland, and male family members. Bible reading is a persistent theme. For the Countess of Westmoreland, not only does reading animate a love of virtue, but heeding advice confers legitimacy. Those who neglect their ancestors' lessons, 'are not ligitimate heires; but as bastard plants shall take noe deep roote'; by them the family will be destroyed (fol.13). For Lady Mildmay and the Fane/Mildmay family, reading should incline the reader to civic and moral virtue and so produce social stability grounded upon venerable families and the Protestant faith. Despite the domestic context, maternal advice on the topic of reading becomes a charge to the spiritual quality of public life.

Like Lady Mildmay, Lady Anne Clifford, the Countess of Pembroke, Dorset and Montgomery (1590–1676), had to fight for her paternal inheritance. Her diaries, written within and against a context of legal conflict over this land, create such a rich picture of her reading that Clifford has become one of the central figures in the history of early modern reading.[12] 'The Great Picture', a triptych commissioned by Clifford, provides visual evidence of that reading. The painting marks her wealth in all its details, from clothing, to musical instruments, to drapery, to libraries, and figures Clifford as a wise, baronial landowner and office holder. Bordered by family crests, the central panel of 'The Great Picture' focuses on Clifford's parents (the Countess and Earl of Cumberland) and her deceased brothers. The left panel represents Anne Clifford at the age of fifteen when she was disinherited by her father, while the right shows her at fifty-six when she finally came into possession of her patrimony. Each panel also contains lengthy scrolls which detail Clifford's life, and altogether some fifty-one books, their titles clearly marked. The shelves above the head of the young Anne illustrate her reading in English and translated European literature, philosophy, theology, devotion, history, architecture and geography. The older Anne Clifford rests her hand on Pierre Charron's *Book of Wisdom* and the Bible, whilst the books on the shelves above her head are in disarray, as if in constant use (figure 10).[13]

For the more mature Clifford, books and literacy are a mode of government, a bequest, not just to her own children, but also to her tenants and servants. Julie Crawford argues that Clifford approached the state as 'a mixed rather than absolutist monarchy' and engaged its competing sites of power; for William Sherman, libraries were one of these sites, collected to be useful to the state.[14] By representing her library, Clifford translates her reading into a form of matriarchal governance, grounded in her wisdom and invested in literacy. As Baroness Clifford, she repaired churches,

Figure 10. Right-hand panel from 'The Great Picture' depicting Lady Anne Clifford, Countess of Dorset, Pembroke and Montgomery (1590–1676) in middle age, 1646 (oil on canvas) by Jan van Belcamp (1610–53) (attr.).

built almshouses and restored her five castles, but improving her estates also included cultivating the literacy of their inhabitants. In 1664, Clifford gave lands 'for the maintenance of a parson qualified to read praiers & the Homilies of the Church of England & to teach the Children of the Dale to write and read English'.[15] In 1665, she paid 'for Little Bookes to give to Boyes in the Howses': three popular devotional manuals – Lewis Bayly's *Practice of Piety*, Michael Sparke's *Crums of Comfort* and Nicholas Themylthorpe's *A Posie of Godly Prayers* – as well as *The Mothers Blessing*, likely Dorothy Leigh's maternal advice book, which had been reprinted most recently in 1663.[16] In 1673, Clifford purchased to give away fifty-five books of devotion by John Rawlet, minister of Kirkby Stephen (1673–82), a town in Cumbria near Pendragon, one of Clifford's castles.[17] The books must have been either Rawlet's *A Treatise of Sacramental Covenanting*, an explanation of the Church of England's doctrines on the sacraments, or *An Explication of the Creed, the Ten Commandments, and the Lord's Prayer with the Addition of Some Forms of Prayer* (1672). Both works were designed for the poor. The Bishop of Carlisle's funeral sermon on Clifford reports that such purchases were habitual in her household; Clifford, he says, bought different books of devotion four times a year and allowed her servants to choose one that they did not already own.[18] In taking responsibility for the literacy of her tenants and servants, Anne Clifford extends maternal instruction through her role as a baroness, quite explicitly so in the gift of *The Mothers Blessing*. At least in part, her efforts seem designed to inculcate loyalty to the doctrines of the English church, and so to facilitate order in the years after the civil war and Restoration.

These women illustrate Christopher Haigh's point that 'Protestants were readers; that was what their leaders expected, and that was how their enemies identified them'.[19] But despite the rhetoric, Catholic women were not apathetic about books. Frances Dolan and Heather Wolfe have explored the personal and social reading practices of Catholic women in domestic and conventual life.[20] The authors of the biography of Elizabeth (Tanfield) Cary, Viscountess Falkland (1586–1639), *Lady Falkland: Her Life*, preserved in manuscript in the Archives Départementales du Nord in Lille, France, detail the prelude to and consequences of Lady Falkland's 1626 conversion to Catholicism.[21] They use their mother's 'bent to reading' to configure that conversion as a spiritual necessity. Complicating what we have seen of the important role of mothers as teachers of reading, this narrative positions Cary's mother and mother-in-law as hindrances to her love of reading, the former forbidding her candles and the latter confining her to her chamber and taking away all her books (pp. 108–9). According to her biographers, the Viscountess herself is linguistically skilled and widely read (pp. 105–6, 212–13). Young Elizabeth Tanfield received from her supportive father a copy of Calvin's *Institutes of Christian Religion,* 'against which she made so many objections, and found in him so many contradictions, and with all of them she still went to her father, that he sayd: this girle hath a spirit averse from Calvin' (p. 108). By the time she was twenty, reading had confirmed Cary's doubt of the Protestant religion. Richard Hooker's *Of the Laws of Ecclesiastical Polity* 'left her hanging in the aire', and she learned that Saint Augustine, much admired by her and by seventeenth-century Protestants, was actually a Catholic (pp. 110–11). Only when Cary has been confined to her house by King Charles I after her conversion does she receive her first Catholic book of devotion (p. 134). By cataloguing her reading, the narrative insists that Cary converts not because Catholic books and priests have moulded her pliable, feminine mind but because Protestant books have left her unconvinced of the verity of their doctrines. Like Margaret Hoby, Elizabeth Cary has a dialectical reading practice: 'she did allways continue with leave to read protestant controvertists' (p. 213). For Cary's children, however, their mother's method justifies the very faith Hoby saw as a threat to the nation.

Although the primary focus of female reading was religious prose, women did read other types of books. In her poem *Salve Deus Rex Judaeorum* (1611), Aemilia Lanyer represents as her readers nine of her most illustrious female contemporaries, including Queen Anna, Margaret Clifford, then Dowager Countess of Cumberland, and Anne Clifford, then Countess of Dorset. Lanyer models in print a method of reading that justifies her poetry and recuperates female sexuality by employing it as a ground for gaining knowledge about Christ.[22] The correspondence of Anne (Finch) Conway, Viscountess Conway and Killultagh (1631–79) – much of it in British Library Additional MSS 23213–6 – also testifies to a reading practice that extends beyond religious prose. Conway's letters, particularly those exchanged with the Cambridge scholar Henry More, demonstrate that she is a reader of science, philosophy and medicine.[23] Medical reading enabled Conway to have a degree of control in her own healthcare and was undertaken by many women, judging by the large number of surviving manuscript recipe collections.[24] In his correspondence with Conway, More recommends books and answers questions. The balance of power is not all More's, however, for if he is a scholarly man with access to institutional knowledge, Conway is a viscountess with the social power of class and connections. Here, as in Lanyer's verse, the practices of reading and patronage overlap. Conway is the patroness of two of More's works, but even beyond this, they develop a gendered version of the servant/master relationship that Lisa Jardine and William Sherman identify: the scholar serves a politically involved public figure by selecting texts to be read in preparation for action.[25] More and Conway adapt this form to more private ends, as More serves the Viscountess as an intermediary between Ireland, where she resided much of the time, and Cambridge University, which did not admit women. More sends her books as a form of service. As More explains on his shipment of his *A Modest Enquiry into the Mystery of Iniquity* (1664), 'though I can not come in person to wayt upon your Ladiship, yett I have sent my Substitute, a copy of my late book, which whyle your Ladiship reades, you converse with the best part of me, my minde and understanding' (*Conway Letters*, p. 228). Like Anne Clifford, the Viscountess Conway reads companionably with a servant, and like Margaret Hoby, she reads with a learned man who lends his conversation to her substantial intellectual life.

Finally, despite cultural censure, women did read romances, a form that is discussed further in Lori Humphrey Newcomb's chapter in this volume. Margaret Tyler (*fl.* 1558–78) defends women's reading of romances in her preface to her translation, *The Mirrour of Princely Deedes and Knighthood* (1578). Printed in 1621 and continued in manuscript, *The Countess of Montgomeries Urania* by Lady Mary Wroth (1587?–1651/3) uses the genre of romance to reflect on many facets of reading, of letters, poems, romances and women's writing.[26] The courtship letters of Dorothy Osborne (1627–95), written to William Temple between 1652 and 1654 (British Library Additional MS 33975), are replete with the discussion and exchange of romances; romances provided a means for Osborne to elicit Temple's views on love and offer her own.[27] Lady Elizabeth (Livingston) Delaval (1648?–1717), on the other hand, repents of her romance reading. In her meditations on her life between 1656 and 1671 (Bodleian Library Rawlinson MS D.78), Delaval insists that her romance reading had numerous ill effects, including introducing her to thoughts of love, making her proud, inducing disobedience to her governess and keeping her from useful learning and 'reading so many chaptier's in the French Bible and so many in the English one'.[28] Delaval's turn against romances is not simply acquiescence to conventional morality. Their influence remains, for as Margaret J. M. Ezell argues, romances provide a plot and language to structure her own courtships.[29] The rejection also marks the development of a class-based ethic of reading. For Delaval, romances were a component of an intrigue with a servant, and she comes to disapprove of secrets with servants, not just for herself and Mistress Carter, but for her aunt, Lady Stanhope, who socializes privately with her former chambermaid (*Meditations*, p. 64). In this context, romance reading was eroding class and social authority. As a result of such reading, not only has Delaval disrespected her teacher and elders, but the maid has had the opportunity to sway her mistress to Presbyterianism and to undermine the class-based household order by using intimacy with her mistress to have no one loved more than herself (pp. 33, 30). Delaval concludes that when a mistress reads with servants, the books should be the Gospels and the Psalms, books that affirm her authority within that reading circle (p. 117). For the mistress, there is appropriate privacy in a 'love of solitude' for prayer and Bible reading (pp. 62, 63), but that reading must be guided by books by learned men, 'rather then trust to my own interpretations' (p. 117). The romance puts at stake the very structures of society, and Delaval's rejection of the form confirms not only the intellectual governance of learned men – a feature common to vilifications of romance – but also the authority of class, which elevates gentlewomen over their maids.

In the reading of early modern women, there was often public policy. Hierarchical structures of gender and class affected whether or not early modern women could read at all, as well as the kinds of books they read and the authority and confidence with which they did it. Frances Dolan argues that reading and writing could even be detrimental to women when it was associated with illegality and violence and used as a mechanism of social control.[30] Certainly mistresses who read to their servants or taught them to read were often concerned with maintaining social order. But for some women, reading could also provide a means to reconstruct that order. Reading alone and with others allowed early modern women to engage questions of theology, philosophy and science, usually deemed to be outside the female purview, and to think in ways that challenged gender hierarchies. Even when women did not write publicly about reading as Dorothy Leigh, Aemilia Lanyer and Mary Wroth did, mothers and mistresses could influence the reading and faith practices in their households and parishes. Women's choices of reading material for themselves and others materialized beliefs about a social order based on class, religion or gender. Even the method of reading could be political, whether in valuing conformity or endorsing debate. Women's reading may not be about the building of female community, as we might like, but reading and writing about it were critical in women's struggle for social authority in early modern Britain.

NOTES

1. Lisa Jardine and Anthony Grafton, '"Studied for Action": How Gabriel Harvey Read His Livy', *Past and Present* 129 (1990), 75–6; William Sherman, *John Dee: The Politics of Reading and Writing in the English Renaissance* (Amherst: University of Massachusetts Press, 1995); Kevin Sharpe, *Reading Revolutions: The Politics of Reading in Early Modern England* (New Haven, CT: Yale University Press, 2000).

2. David Cressy, *Literacy and the Social Order* (Cambridge: Cambridge University Press, 1980), pp. 41, 118–28.
3. Margaret Spufford, *Small Books and Pleasant Histories* (Athens: University of Georgia Press, 1981). See also Suzanne W. Hull, *Chaste, Silent and Obedient: English Books for Women, 1475–1640* (San Marino, CA: Huntington Library, 1982).
4. Roger Chartier, *The Order of Books*, trans. Lydia G. Cochrane (Cambridge: Polity Press, 1994), p. 23.
5. Richard Brathwait, *The English Gentlewoman* (London, 1631), pp. 184–7.
6. Mary Evelyn, 'Letters of Mrs. Evelyn', in *Diary and Correspondence of John Evelyn*, vol. IV (London, 1863), pp. 10, 25–6, 31.
7. See Edith Snook, *Women, Reading, and the Cultural Politics of Early Modern England* (Aldershot: Ashgate, 2005), pp.16–21; Heidi Brayman Hackel, *Reading Material in Early Modern England* (Cambridge: Cambridge University Press, 2005), pp. 214–21.
8. All references to Hoby's diary are to *The Private Life of an Elizabethan Lady: The Diary of Lady Margaret Hoby 1599–1605*, ed. Joanna Moody (Stroud: Sutton, 1998); William Sherman, 'What Did Renaissance Readers Write in their Books?', in Jennifer Andersen and Elizabeth Sauer (eds.), *Books and Readers in Early Modern England* (Philadelphia: University of Pennsylvania, 2002), p. 126.
9. Stephen Orgel, 'Marginal Maternity: Reading Lady Anne Clifford's *A Mirror for Magistrates*', in Douglas A. Brooks (ed.), *Printing and Parenting in Early Modern England* (Aldershot: Ashgate, 2003), pp. 267–89; Hackel, *Reading Material*, pp. 222–40. On Jane Grey's marginalia, as well as her printed works, see Edith Snook, 'Jane Grey, "Manful" Combat, and the Female Reader in Early Modern England', *Renaissance and Reformation/Renaissance et Réforme* (forthcoming).
10. Mary Ellen Lamb, 'Margaret Hoby's Diary: Women's Reading Practices and the Gendering of the Reformation Subject', in Sigrid King (ed.), *Pilgrimage for Love: Essays in Early Modern Literature in Honor of Josephine A. Roberts* (Tempe, AZ: Arizona Center for Medieval and Renaissance Studies, 1999), p. 86.
11. Linda Pollock (ed.), *With Faith and Physic: The Life of a Tudor Gentlewoman 1552–1620* (London: Collins and Brown, 1993).
12. See Hackel, *Reading Material*, and Orgel, 'Marginal Maternity', as well as Mary Ellen Lamb, 'The Agency of the Split Subject: Lady Anne Clifford and the Uses of Reading', *English Literary Renaissance* 22 (1992), 347–68.
13. G. C. Williamson, *Lady Anne Clifford*, 2nd edn (East Ardsley: S. R. Publishers, 1967), pp. 334–45, 489–507.
14. Julie Crawford, 'The Case of Lady Anne Clifford; Or, Did Women Have a Mixed Monarchy?', *PMLA* 121.5 (2006), 1682–9; Sherman, *John Dee*, p. 38.
15. *The Diaries of Lady Anne Clifford*, ed. D. J. H. Clifford (Stroud: Sutton, 1990), p. 169.
16. *Lady Anne's Account Book for 1665 and 1667–1668*, Hothfield Manuscripts WD/Hoth/A988/17, in *The Papers of Lady Anne Clifford* (East Ardsley: Microform Academic Publishers, 1999).
17. Williamson, *Lady Anne Clifford*, p. 510.

18. Lord Edward, Bishop of Carlisle, *A Sermon Preached at the Funeral of the Right Honorable Anne Countess of Pembroke, Dorset, and Montgomery* (London, 1677), pp. 33–4.

19. Christopher Haigh, *English Reformations: Religion, Politics, and Society under the Tudors* (New York: Oxford University Press, 1993), p. 194.

20. Frances E. Dolan, 'Reading, Work and Catholic Women's Biographies', *English Literary Renaissance* 33.3 (2003), 328–57; Heather Wolfe, 'Reading Bells and Loose Papers: Reading and Writing Practices of the English Benedictine Nuns of Cambrai and Paris', in Victoria E. Burke and Jonathan Gibson (eds.), *Early Modern Women's Manuscript Writing* (Aldershot: Ashgate, 2004), pp. 135–56.

21. Wolfe argues that the biography was written between 1645 and 1649 by Cary's daughter, Lucy, the main scribe, and by her siblings Mary and Patrick, who supplemented and altered the narrative. Heather Wolfe, 'Introduction' and 'Textual Introduction', *Elizabeth Cary Lady Falkland: Life and Letters,* ed. Heather Wolfe (Cambridge: Renaissance Texts from Manuscript; Tempe, AZ: Arizona Center for Medieval and Renaissance Studies, 2001), pp. 45, 59–69, 86–9. All references are to this edition.

22. Jacqueline Pearson, 'Women Writers and Women Readers: The Case of Aemilia Lanyer', in Kate Chedgzoy, Melanie Hansen and Suzanne Trill (eds.), *Voicing Women: Gender and Sexuality in Early Modern Writing* (Keele, Staffordshire: Keele University Press, 1996), pp. 5–54; Snook, *Women, Reading*, pp. 115–35.

23. *The Conway Letters*, ed. Marjorie Hope Nicolson, rev. edn Sarah Hutton (Oxford: Clarendon Press, 1992).

24. For more on reading practical books, see Elizabeth Tebeaux, 'Women and Technical Writing, 1475–1700', in Lynette Hunter and Sarah Hutton (eds.), *Women, Science and Medicine 1500–1700* (Stroud: Sutton, 1997), pp. 29–62.

25. Lisa Jardine and William Sherman, 'Pragmatic Readers: Knowledge Transactions and Scholarly Services in Late Elizabethan England', in Anthony Fletcher and Peter Roberts (eds.), *Religion, Culture and Society in Early Modern Britain* (Cambridge: Cambridge University Press, 1994), pp. 102–24.

26. Mary Ellen Lamb, 'Women Readers in Mary Wroth's *Urania*', in Naomi J. Miller and Gary Waller (eds.), *Reading Mary Wroth* (Knoxville: University of Tennessee Press, 1991), pp. 210–27.

27. Carrie Hintz, *An Audience of One: Dorothy Osborne's Letters to Sir William Temple, 1652–54* (Toronto: University of Toronto Press, 2005), pp. 64–86.

28. *The Meditations of Lady Elizabeth Delaval*, ed. Douglas G. Greene, vol. 190, The Publications of the Surtees Society (Gateshead: Northumberland Press, 1978), pp. 29, 30.

29. Margaret J. M. Ezell, 'Elizabeth Delaval's Spiritual Heroine: Thoughts on Redefining Manuscript Texts by Early Women Writers', *English Manuscript Studies 1100–1700* 6 (1992), 216–37.

30. Frances E. Dolan, 'Reading, Writing, and Other Crimes', in Valerie Traub, M. Lindsey Kaplan and Dympna Callaghan (eds.), *Feminist Readings of Early Modern Culture* (Cambridge: Cambridge University Press, 1996), pp. 143–4.

READING LIST

Daybell, James. '"I wold wyshe my doings myght be … secret": Privacy and the Social Practices of Reading Women's Letters in Sixteenth-Century England'. In Jane Couchman and Ann Crabb (eds.), *Women's Letters Across Europe, 1400–1700*. Aldershot: Ashgate, 2005, pp. 143–61.

Ferguson, Margaret. *Dido's Daughters: Literacy, Gender, and Empire in Early Modern England and France*. Chicago: University of Chicago Press, 2003.

Hackel, Heidi Brayman and Catherine E. Kelly (eds). *Reading Women: Literacy, Authorship, and Culture in the Atlantic World, 1500–1800*. Philadelphia: University of Pennsylvania Press, 2007.

Sanders, Eve Rachele and Margaret W. Ferguson (eds.). *Literacies in Early Modern England*. Special Issue of *Critical Survey* 14.1 (2002).

Sharpe, Kevin and Steven N. Zwicker (eds.). *Reading, Society and Politics in Early Modern England*. Cambridge: Cambridge University Press, 2003.

3

VICTORIA E. BURKE

Manuscript miscellanies

In her manuscript miscellany, Ann Bowyer writes 'weomenkind ar man's woe', followed by 'o man wee weomen ar kind' (Bodleian Library MS Ashmole 51, fol. 4r). Directly beneath this is the rhyming couplet: 'Explod that S & giue y^r wom^{e}n dew / Then you shall find our sentenc is most trew.' The large initials 'F:B' in the right margin could apply to both passages, raising several questions. Did a person (a family member?) with the initials F. B. write these lines, which Ann Bowyer later transcribed? Did the writer or scribe of these lines wish to engage playfully (or more seriously) with an anagram disparaging to women? Such lines demonstrate the potential interactive nature of manuscript compilation in the period, as readers and writers could transcribe, respond to and even alter what they chose to include in their own compilations.

During the early modern period, much literary activity took place in handwritten form. One of the most valuable records we have of manuscript culture is the manuscript miscellany, each one a unique collection of writing culled from a number of sources. Often these miscellanies contained verse, sometimes identifiable as having been copied from printed sources, sometimes known to have circulated in some kind of manuscript transmission, sometimes unknown in any other versions. But these manuscript miscellanies can be difficult to characterize, since material in prose of all types (from sermons to personal records to material gleaned from historical sources) is also often found in their pages. Since the 1980s, the manuscript culture of the early modern period has become an important area of study.[1] More recently, women's participation in this significant literary system has become an expanding field.[2]

In the recent past, manuscript miscellanies have been used by textual editors, alongside other more conventional sources such as presentation manuscripts of an author's work, to help establish authoritative canons of known writers.[3] Now miscellanies are also appreciated for the ways in which they demonstrate exactly how their compilers interacted with literary culture. Compiling is an activity that lies somewhere between the processes of reading and writing: not only can these sources offer unparalleled access to what early modern people read, but they can also help show the myriad ways in which they read. As Edith Snook's chapter in this volume makes clear, the history of reading is a flourishing scholarly topic, one which manuscript miscellanies in particular can help illuminate because of the traces apparent in them of compilers' reading and writing practices. Two models which might be particularly useful for this kind of evidence are the theories that reading can be seen as poaching (in Michel de Certeau's formulation) or appropriation (Roger Chartier).[4]

Michel de Certeau has argued that reading is not a passive act, but rather that 'readers are travellers; they move across lands belonging to someone else, like nomads poaching their way across fields they did not write, despoiling the wealth of Egypt to enjoy it themselves' (*The Practice of Everyday Life*, p. 174). He then contrasts writing with reading: writing accumulates and reproduces itself, while reading loses what it obtains due to the erosion of time. The work of compiling partakes of both of these activities. Roger Chartier also explores what exactly it is that readers do, calling it 'labour' and 'appropriation' ('Texts, Printing, Readings', pp. 156–7). He points out that readers make 'highly distinct uses' of the same text. Chartier cites the worried preface to a 1507 tragicomedy by Fernando de Rojas, in which the author fears that one of the ways people will read his text is by retaining only the 'pleasantries and proverbs', the 'easily memorized formulas' (pp. 154–5). Well might Rojas have worried: the commonplace method learned in schools advocated the ruthless extracting of sententious sayings from works of literature, and arranging them under alphabetical headings. But, as Chartier points out, the cultural appropriation involved in reading allows the reader autonomy in the face of forces which try to circumscribe her responses (pp. 171–3).

Miscellanies remind us that the category of 'author' in this period was not fixed. In the sixteenth century the modern notion of an author as the force which governed a text had not yet crystallized since 'authorship was just one of many conventions controlling the reception of written works'.[5] As fundamentally social forms, manuscripts invite us to consider categories such as composite authorship and social authorship.[6] Claudia Limbert and John O'Neill have argued that a poem in the Katherine Philips canon entitled 'Advice to Virgins' and beginning, 'A marry[d] state affords but little Ease / The best of husbands are so hard to please', was unfinished on her death. Another, unknown poet completed it, and then the poem circulated unattributed in manuscript. Limbert and O'Neill have termed this kind of collaboration, between writers not consciously writing together, composite authorship.

In Margaret Ezell's conception of social authorship, a manuscript was a medium for social exchange. Citing the example of the Tixall circle of poets, Ezell notes that the social function of authorship becomes apparent through the exchange of verse across a number of manuscripts (*Social Authorship*, pp. 25–8). The Tixall manuscripts include Constance Fowler's miscellany (Huntington Library MS HM 904), her brother Herbert Aston's miscellany (Beinecke Library MS Osborn Shelves b.4), and at least three more compilations from the family, discovered by Arthur Clifford in the nineteenth century and now lost.[7] In this system a reader does not merely consume but also produces literature, 'editing, correcting, or copying the text and extending its circulation of readers' (Ezell, *Social Authorship*, p. 40).

Attributions in a miscellany should often be approached with caution. An obviously incorrect name cited as the author of a poem can indicate the person who transcribed it or perhaps a chain of circulation: the compiler may have received the poem from the person whose name she is citing. Henry King's popular elegy on his wife, 'An Exequy', was transcribed into Anne Southwell's miscellany (Folger Shakespeare Library MS v.b.198, fol. 21v)[8] under the heading, 'An Elegie Writen by Mr Barnard brother to M^{res} Jernegan y^t dyed at Acton', demonstrating that the poem was used to commemorate another untimely death, this time in a local family. Attributions can sometimes be coded, penetrable only to insiders, such as in Constance Fowler's miscellany (Huntington Library MS HM 904), which uses initials and sometimes ciphers to identify writers such as her brother, Herbert Aston.

When a work is anonymous, many different factors may be in play. The author's name might have been known to the compiler, or to the group from which the compiler obtained the poem, and so it was not seen as necessary to note it. Indeed, the absence of a name could initially have been a marker of privilege which is since lost due to the poem's subsequent wider circulation. Marcy North distinguishes various functions of 'coterie anonymity': 'a fashionable stance, a record of discretion, or a game of ciphers and pseudonyms'.[9] As scholars of women's writing, we can have a special interest in individual anonymous poems demonstrably written by women. Evelyn Newlyn proposes a number of criteria for discerning women's voices in anonymity including identifying manuscripts with a higher potential for containing women's work because of provenance, history or a known link with a woman; noting material matters such as collation, palaeography and layout; and employing specific criteria when analysing individual poems, which include the use of certain themes (such as a desire for virginity).[10] A large number of anonymous poems appear in the Maitland Quarto Manuscript (Cambridge, Magdalene College, Pepys Library MS 1408), linked on the first folio with the date 1586 and the name Marie Maitland.[11] Nearly half of the manuscript's approximately ninety-five Scottish poems were written by Sir Richard Maitland of Lethington, Marie's father. Among the other poets identified in the volume are Alexander Montgomerie, and brothers Thomas and Robert Hudson, members of the so-called Castalian band of poets at the court of James VI. Marie Maitland's role in the quarto volume is uncertain, but she may have been its scribe, either partially or wholly (the two main styles of script may belong to one hand). Maitland is commemorated as a poet by two poems (numbers 69 and 85 in Craigie's edition), but no poems are attributed to her (Newlyn, 'A Methodology', pp. 92–4).

Another courtly manuscript containing a large number of anonymous poems is the sixteenth-century Devonshire Manuscript (British Library MS Additional 17492), a miscellany of early Tudor verse and medieval extracts dating from the 1530s and 1540s.[12] Even though the poetry of Thomas Wyatt dominates the volume, very few ascriptions to him appear in its pages, suggesting that anonymity functioned as a marker of insider information. North notes that only about twenty-four poems in this volume are attributed, leaving more than 150 anonymous items (*The Anonymous Renaissance*, p. 161). Elizabeth Heale observes that many of the poems participate in a kind of social exchange in which women (or female-voiced replies) were key.[13] This is apparent perhaps most visibly in the final section of the manuscript (fols. 89v–92r), which contains extracts from Thynne's 1532 edition of Chaucer's works.[14] These medieval extracts from Chaucer, Hoccleve (translating Christine de Pisan) and Richard Roos for the most part take up positions common in the debate on the virtue or vice of women, with misogynist lines appearing alongside apparently female-voiced retorts. This section of the manuscript demonstrates perfectly how excerpted texts could be re-formed into new works by compilers, particularly in the case of a translation from Ovid's *Remedia Amoris* (fol. 90r). The scribe has chosen to emend one of the lines from 'The cursydnesse yet and disceyte of women' to 'the faythfulnes yet and prayse of women', effectively reversing its meaning.[15]

In his manuscript, Robert Overton appropriated poetry to commemorate his wife Ann, something he termed 'applicatory Poetry'.[16] Overton took a number of poems by Katherine Philips, a Royalist who conformed to the Church of England, and adapted them to sanctify his republican Puritan wife. Rather than write original verse, Overton sought to celebrate his wife with 'this blushinge tribute of a borrowed muse', which David Norbrook notes is a passage adapted from Katherine Philips (in which Overton changed 'artless' to 'borrowed'), who was herself adapting Donne ('"This blushinge tribute"', pp. 232, 237 and 265 n. 22). Poetry in miscellanies could thus be appropriated by men and women of different political and religious casts.

Readers and compilers not only transcribed material into their manuscripts, choosing faithful reproduction or active engagement, or something between the two: they also contributed their own verse. 'Compiler poetry' is the term that Arthur Marotti has suggested for verse composed by the owners or transcribers of manuscript miscellanies (*Manuscript, Print*, pp. 171–208). Marotti cites a number of cases of compilers who respond to the material they are transcribing by imitating it, thus contributing their own verse in a 'shared literary language', and potentially affiliating themselves with the notion of upper-class ownership of poetic texts (pp. 181 and 196). Compiler poetry may attest to the aspirational function of some of these manuscripts. Active engagement in the form of answer poetry is also extant in miscellanies, sometimes evidence of a kind of poetic competition on similar themes (pp. 159–71). One famous verse exchange between Lady Mary Wroth and Edward Denny, Baron of Waltham found its way into several miscellanies. Denny objected to Wroth's thinly disguised depiction of his family in her prose romance *Urania* and wrote a scathing verse attack. Wroth answered Denny's critiques point by point. She also rewrote his concluding exhortation, 'Work o th' Workes leave idle bookes alone / For wise and worthyer women have writte none', as 'Take this then now lett railing rimes alone / For wise and worthier men have written none.'[17]

In Constance Fowler's miscellany (Huntington Library MS HM 904), we can further see the dynamics of answer poetry in action. After a long section of blank leaves (fols. 53r–135v), Fowler has transcribed Lady Dorothy Shirley's 'of uncon[s]tancy', in which the speaker berates an unnamed man for disdaining her after claiming that he loved her. The erstwhile lover responds with an extended, and rather metaphysical, image of a mirror: when he looked into the mirror he thought he saw her face looking out, seeing her as 'another selfe' (fol. 137r). But when he went away, other men looked in the glass, causing her reflection to mirror their laughs and smiles, leaving no impression of the speaker. A later answer poem is much more complimentary: Katherine Thimelby wrote 'upon the LD saying KT could be sad in her company', to which the addressee, Lady Dorothy Shirley, responded with 'The L.D. ansure' (fols. 158r–159r, see figure 11 for fol. 158v). In Thimelby's poem, the speaker laments that her exterior appearance could suggest sadness, when she is instead full of joy at being in Shirley's presence. Shirley's answer follows immediately, charmingly suggesting that her own misreading of Thimelby's face is like that of 'dull witts' (fol. 158v) who do not understand 'curious lines that's drawne by Art and skill' (fol. 159r). Fowler has transcribed answer poems at the beginning and end of a section of the

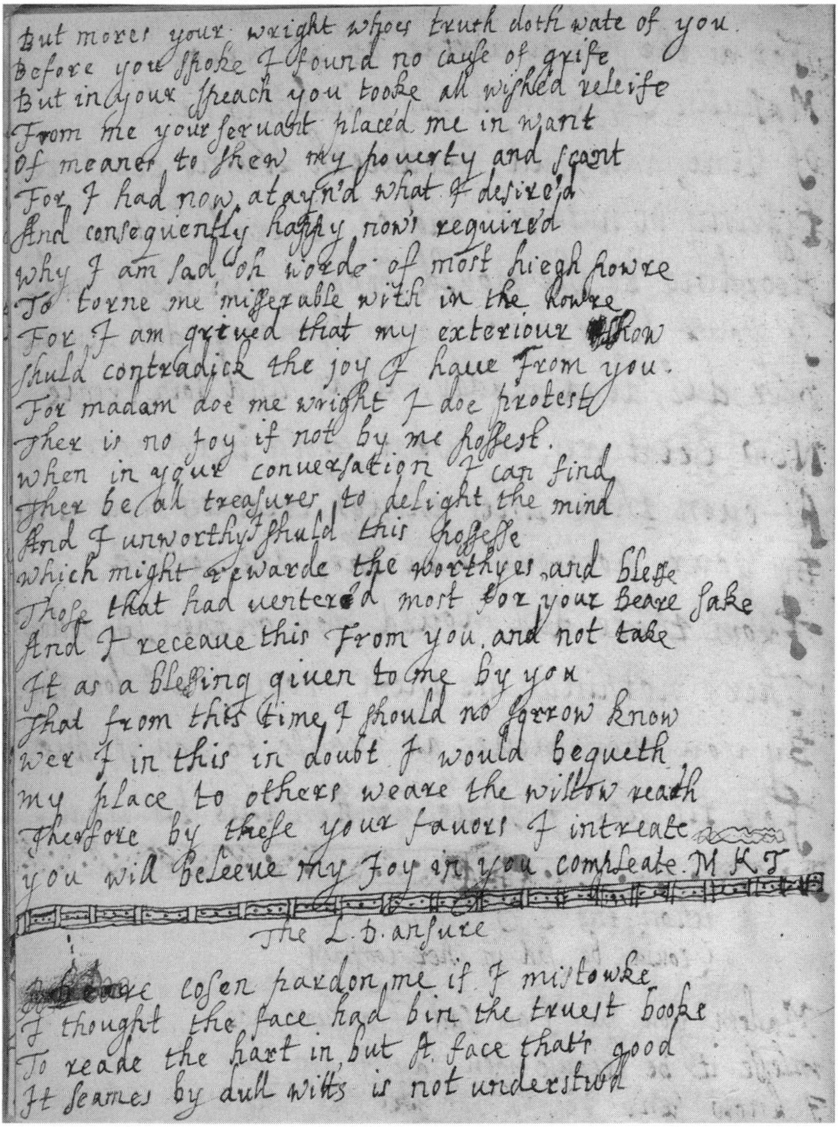

But mores your wright whoes truth doth wate of you
Before you spoke I found no cause of grife
But in your speach you tooke all wished releife
From me your seruant placed me in want
Of meaner to shew my pouerty and scant
For I had now, atayn'd what I desire'd
And consequently happy now required
why I am sad, oh worde of most hiegh howre
To torne me misserable with in the howre
For I am grieved that my exterioure show
shuld contradick the joy I haue From you.
For madam doe me wright I doe protest
Ther is no joy if not by me possest.
when in your conuersation I can find
Ther be all treasures to delight the mind
And I unworthy shuld this possesse
which might rewarde the worthyes, and blesse
Those that had uentered most for your Beare sake
And I receaue this From you, and not take
It as a blessing giuen to me by you
That from this time I should no sorrow know
wer I in this in doubt I would bequeth
my place to others weare the willow reath
Therfore by these your fanors I intreate
you will beleeue my Joy in you compleate. M K T

The L. D. ansure

receaue cosen pardon me if I mistowke
I thought the face had bin the truest booke
To reade the hart in but A face that's good
It seames by dull witts is not understood

Figure 11. Answer poetry in Constance Fowler, Manuscript Miscellany. Huntington Library MS HM 904, fol. 158v.

manuscript (fols. 159v–182r are blank), framing her circle's literary activities with particularly interactive poetry.

It is also important to consider the ways in which texts circulated in manuscript. Jason Scott-Warren's notion of networks (open-ended, loosely defined communities circulating material to other groups) suggests how widely manuscript material could be transmitted.[18] Personal miscellanies rarely record the precise circumstances in which items were transcribed; instead they are 'points of transit within networks of copying'.[19] Communal identities could be forged in many different ways ('institutions, localities, or kin groups') and overlap and movement between communities was constant (Scott-Warren, 'Reconstructing Manuscript Networks', p. 33). Exactly how and where a reader obtained a text can be puzzling, as in the case of Ann Bowyer.

Bodleian Library MS Ashmole 51 is a manuscript compiled by two main hands, one of which is Bowyer's. We can pinpoint her identity because she had a famous son, the antiquary Elias Ashmole, who preserved her manuscript. The daughter of a draper from Coventry and later the wife of a saddler from Lichfield, Bowyer can be located among the middling classes of the early seventeenth century, reminding us that manuscript culture was not always the preserve of the upper classes. Bowyer's manuscript, containing sententious rhyming couplets, six poems, an inscription from a gravestone, notes on colours and handwriting exercises, allows us a glimpse into the educational opportunities available to a young woman in the Midlands. Bowyer's favourite authors were Drayton, Spenser and Chaucer. Fol. 7r (figure 12) provides a glimpse into the compilation practices of Bowyer and her co-compiler. The top third of the page contains eight rhyming couplets in two columns, suggesting a self-contained poem. But a closer look reveals that these couplets are largely unrelated moral *sententiae*, probably grouped together because they have all been extracted from cantos two, three and four of Drayton's *The Barons Warres*. The bottom two-thirds of the page comprise a version of Donne's 'A Valediction: forbidding mourning'. Bowyer's contribution stops in stanza three, halfway through the third line, and the second main hand of the manuscript continues, indicating with a small drawing of a hand that the poem continues in the second column. The inclusion of this poem in a manuscript that is so obviously indebted to printed works is significant, since Donne's poem was not printed until 1633, long after the likely date of the compilation of this manuscript. Where exactly Bowyer would have obtained this example of coterie verse is uncertain, but the choice of Donne is not surprising since the manuscript circulation of his verse was extensive. On the previous leaf, fol. 6r, Bowyer has transcribed a heavily altered version of another popular poem transmitted primarily in manuscript, 'The

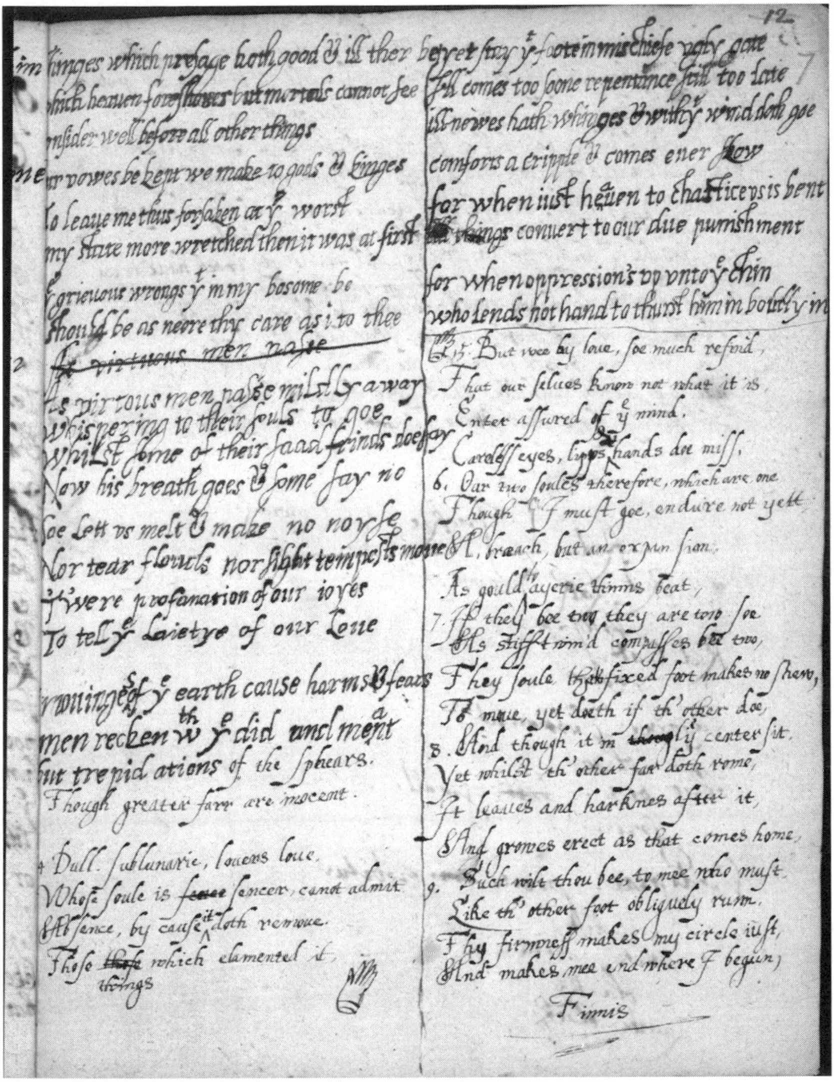

Figure 12. Extracts from Drayton and a Donne poem in Ann Bowyer, Manuscript Miscellany. Bodleian Library MS Ashmole 51, fol. 7r.

Lie', usually attributed to Sir Walter Ralegh. This miscellany shows us a non-élite compiler extracting proverbial wisdom from printed texts and engaging with popular manuscript verse.

Miscellanies were compiled by women in a variety of contexts, including the court, the family, particular religious and political circles and even, to some extent, the universities. The Scottish Maitland Quarto (Pepys Library MS 1408) contains verse by the courtier Richard Maitland and by court poets favoured by James VI. The Devonshire manuscript (British Library MS Add. 17492) of the court of Henry VIII shows women collecting and responding to verse in aristocratic and royal settings. Though scribal hands dominate, prominent women from the court of Henry VIII also added their hands to the volume: Mary Shelton (Anne Boleyn's cousin), Mary Fitzroy (sister of the poet Henry Howard, Earl of Surrey) and, in particular, Margaret Douglas (the King's niece).[20] The lines attributed to 'T. H.' or Thomas Howard, dramatically record the doomed love affair of Howard and Margaret Douglas, imprisoned in the Tower of London (where Howard was to die) for their impolitic marriage (fols. 26r–30r; Heale, 'Women and the Courtly Love Lyric', pp. 304–5). Given its illustrious courtly links, it may be surprising to note the haphazard nature of the miscellany, which includes some twenty hands and spans a number of years. Nearly half of the leaves have been left blank, often marking separations between groupings of poems.[21] The manuscript was not used sequentially, giving it the appearance of an autograph album.

Ann Bowyer's family, much more modest in social status than the courtly contacts of Marie Maitland and the women of the Devonshire manuscript, seems nonetheless to have provided educational opportunities for Ann and possibly a sibling, who practised handwriting exercises on the final pages of the volume (Bodleian Library MS Ashmole 51). The family was also an enabling space for Elizabeth Lyttelton, whose father Sir Thomas Browne helped feed her intellectual life. Cambridge University Library MS Additional 8460 is a miscellany of verse and prose compiled primarily by Lyttelton in at least two main phases, given slight differences in her penmanship. Several of the writers found in Lyttelton's miscellany might have been included because they were known to her family, including Dr Edward Reynolds (a friend of Sir Thomas Browne's), Thomas Flatman (whose cousin knew Browne) and John Wilmot, Earl of Rochester (Lyttelton's brother, Edward Browne, was Rochester's physician during his last illness). Other items in the miscellany demonstrate Lyttleton's own reading of printed and manuscript texts. The three poems or verse extracts on the death of Queen Elizabeth that appear on page 8, for instance, were printed in Thomas Heywood's *The life and death of Queene Elizabeth* (1639) on sigs. C5v, C6r and C7r.

One manuscript, Bodleian Library MS Rawlinson poet. 153, contains these three items on fol. 8v,[22] suggesting that Lyttelton was not unique in grouping these items together, or indeed that she might have copied this grouping of extracts from a manuscript source. Later in this manuscript (p. 80 reversed), Lyttelton includes the first stanza of an epitaph on Queen Elizabeth which appeared in this printed volume on sig. C8r. Heywood's poem is itself a reworking of William Browne's 'On the Countess Dowager of Pembroke', an epitaph on Mary Sidney, reminding us of the textual malleability of works that appeared in miscellanies.[23] Lyttelton's version differs somewhat from the printed Heywood text, indicating that a reader (whether Lyttelton herself or a previous transcriber) wished to alter the terms of praise for the subject of the poem.

Anne Southwell similarly enjoyed a domestic relationship that allowed her writing to flourish, as her extant miscellany indicates. Folger Shakespeare Library MS v.b.198 is a folio volume which contains a variety of poetry, prose and memoranda of a domestic nature. Southwell's original verse on the ten commandments comprises over a third of the volume's contents; other autograph poetry, much of it in a scribal hand, encompasses religious lyrics, elegies, epitaphs, dialogues, verse epistles, songs and sonnets. Transcribed verse by other poets also appears in the miscellany. Southwell's second husband, Henry Sibthorpe, appears to have played a prominent role in gathering together this collection of original verse and transcribed material, capping the volume with elegies and an epitaph on Southwell's death. Sibthorpe also acted as a kind of editor at a few points in the manuscript. (Jean Klene has noted his comment on an overused rhyme on fol. 49r: 'wyf/ lyfe to ofte'.)[24] This manuscript demonstrates yet another variety of manuscript miscellany: a place for original verse, some of it autograph, and for compiled material, not in Southwell's hand, which raises the question of the degree to which the manuscript should be considered Southwell's venture.

In terms of religious and political sites of production, Constance Fowler was at the centre of a Catholic circle of poets and readers in Staffordshire during the 1630s, and Sarah Cowper compiled a collection of satirical political and libertine verse. Fowler's miscellany demonstrates Catholic literary activity at a time when persecution continued to force it underground. Libertine verse also had to circulate clandestinely. Cowper compiled ten manuscripts which have been classed as commonplace books, but a number of these would be considered miscellanies.[25] One of these, 'The Medley' (Hertfordshire County Record Office, Penshanger MS D/EP F37), is an enormous collection of alphabetically arranged extracts and additional verse, dated 1673. Harold Love has discovered that most of its contents appeared in another manuscript, the miscellany of George Villiers,

2nd Duke of Buckingham. Cowper seems to have obtained this material from her friend Martin Clifford, Buckingham's secretary, to whom she has attributed the first item of each section of epigrams, maxims and similes (with 'M.C.').[26] Cowper was not unusual in transcribing large amounts of material from one source; manuscript items tended to circulate in groups. A second Cowper miscellany, MS D/EP F36, contains a number of scribally circulated lampoons, indicating her interest in state poems and clandestine satires. Cowper's manuscripts indicate one woman's access to political concerns of the day, through its scribally published libertine verse.

Another manuscript which places a woman in a sphere thought typically to exclude women is Folger Shakespeare Library MS x.d.177. Elizabeth Clarke put her own stamp on a collection probably compiled initially at the University of Oxford (given references to Brasenose College and to Carfax) in about 1595. The first compiler has written jests, poems and extracts, which include satirical accounts of priests, law courts and the court, pastoral love poetry and obscene stories. Clarke has signed the first page four times, and has reversed the manuscript so that the final page forms a new first page, signing her name in the top right corner of this page (fol. 8v reversed). She has also transcribed some verse: stanzas three and two of a three-stanza poem first printed in Thomas Stanley's *Poems* of 1651. This poem was later published in many songbooks and miscellanies, including Henry Lawes's *The treasury of musick*.[27] The poem also enjoyed a circulation in manuscript (see Crum W339 and Folger Shakespeare Library MS v.a.169, Part II, p. 29). None of the variants in the extant versions of the poem I have seen follow the alterations made by Clarke, which include changing the lines 'Ide rather marry a Disease, / Than court the thing I cannot please' to 'then Court a Lady I cannot plese'. The substitution of 'Lady' for 'thing' suggests the kind of compiler intervention exhibited in so many miscellanies, indicating perhaps in this case a desire to reinstate the humanity of the disgruntled male speaker's object of desire.

Miscellanies compiled by women do not survive in the same numbers as those compiled by men, nor are they as easily identifiable with known sites of manuscript production and circulation of verse, such as the universities, Inns of Court and coffee houses. Nevertheless, women's verse and prose miscellanies with varied contents, originating in and moving to varied sites of production, enable us to gain a more accurate picture of women's writing practice during the early modern period. These documents reveal evidence of reading, compiling, adapting, appropriating, writing and engagement with literate culture in a way that few other sources of the period can.

NOTES

1. Mary Hobbs, *Early Seventeenth-Century Verse Miscellany Manuscripts* (Aldershot: Scolar, 1992); Arthur F. Marotti, *Manuscript, Print, and the English Renaissance Lyric* (Ithaca, NY: Cornell University Press, 1995); Harold Love, *Scribal Publication in Seventeenth-Century England* (Oxford: Clarendon Press, 1993); H. R. Woudhuysen, *Sir Philip Sidney and the Circulation of Manuscripts 1558–1640* (Oxford: Clarendon Press, 1996); Peter Beal (comp.), *Index of English Literary Manuscripts*, vol. I: 1450–1625, 2 parts (London: Mansell, 1980), vol. II: 1625–1700, 2 parts (1987–93).

2. See the essays in George L. Justice and Nathan Tinker (eds.), *Women's Writing and the Circulation of Ideas: Manuscript Publication in England, 1550–1800* (Cambridge: Cambridge University Press, 2002) and Victoria E. Burke and Jonathan Gibson (eds.), *Early Modern Women's Manuscript Writing: Selected Papers from the Trinity/Trent Colloquium* (Aldershot: Ashgate, 2004).

3. See, for example, Mary Hobbs, 'Early Seventeenth-Century Verse Miscellanies and Their Value for Textual Editors', *English Manuscript Studies 1100–1700* 1 (1989), 182–210.

4. Michel de Certeau, *The Practice of Everyday Life*, trans. Steven Rendall (Berkeley: University of California Press, 1984); Roger Chartier, 'Texts, Printing, Readings', in Lynn Hunt (ed.), *The New Cultural History* (Berkeley: University of California Press, 1989), pp. 154–75.

5. Wendy Wall, 'Authorship and the Material Conditions of Writing', in Arthur F. Kinney (ed.), *The Cambridge Companion to English Literature 1500–1600* (Cambridge: Cambridge University Press, 2000), pp. 64–89 (64–5).

6. Claudia A. Limbert and John H. O'Neill, 'Composite Authorship: Katherine Philips and an Antimarital Satire', *Papers of the Bibliographical Society of America* 87 (1993), 487–502 (492); Margaret J. M. Ezell, *Social Authorship and the Advent of Print* (Baltimore: Johns Hopkins University Press, 1999).

7. For an edition of Fowler's manuscript see Deborah Aldrich-Watson (ed.), *The Verse Miscellany of Constance Aston Fowler: A Diplomatic Edition* (Tempe, AZ: Arizona Center for Medieval and Renaissance Studies in conjunction with Renaissance English Text Society, 2000).

8. For an edition see Jean Klene (ed.), *The Southwell–Sibthorpe Commonplace Book: Folger MS v.b.198* (Tempe, AZ: Medieval and Renaissance Texts and Studies, 1997).

9. Marcy L. North, *The Anonymous Renaissance: Cultures of Discretion in Tudor–Stuart England* (Chicago: University of Chicago Press, 2003), pp. 29–30.

10. Evelyn S. Newlyn, 'A Methodology for Reading Against the Culture: Anonymous, Women Poets, and the Maitland Quarto Manuscript (c.1586)', in Sarah M. Dunnigan, C. Marie Harker and Evelyn S. Newlyn (eds.), *Women and the Feminine in Medieval and Early Modern Scottish Writing* (Basingstoke: Palgrave Macmillan, 2004), pp. 89–103 (92–8).

11. For an edition see W. A. Craigie (ed.), *The Maitland Quarto Manuscript*, Scottish Text Society (Edinburgh: Blackwood, 1920).

12. An electronic edition of the manuscript is being prepared by Raymond G. Siemens at the University of Victoria.

13. Elizabeth Heale, 'Women and the Courtly Love Lyric: The Devonshire MS (BL Additional 17492)', *Modern Language Review* 90 (1995), 296–313 (303).
14. These were first discovered by Ethel Seaton, '"The Devonshire Manuscript" and its Medieval Fragments', *Review of English Studies* n.s. 7 (1956), 55–6.
15. Heale, 'Women and the Courtly Love Lyric', pp. 306–7; Paul G. Remley, 'Mary Shelton and her Tudor Literary Milieu', in Peter C. Herman (ed.), *Rethinking the Henrician Era: Essays on Early Tudor Texts and Contexts* (Urbana: University of Illinois Press, 1994), pp. 40–77 (55–8).
16. David Norbrook, '"This blushinge tribute of a borrowed muse": Robert Overton and his Overturning of the Poetic Canon', *English Manuscript Studies 1100–1700* 4 (1993), 220–66 (221).
17. Josephine A. Roberts, 'Introduction', *The Poems of Lady Mary Wroth*, ed. Roberts (Baton Rouge: Louisiana State University Press, 1983), pp. 32–5. She notes three contemporaneous manuscripts that contain the exchange.
18. Jason Scott-Warren, 'Reconstructing Manuscript Networks: the Textual Transactions of Sir Stephen Powle', in Alexandra Shepard and Phil Withington (eds.), *Communities in Early Modern England: Networks, Place, Rhetoric* (Manchester: Manchester University Press, 2000), pp. 18–37.
19. Love, *Scribal Publication*, p. 80. Scott-Warren, 'Reconstructing', uses the terms, p. 20.
20. Raymond Southall, *The Courtly Maker: An Essay on the Poetry of Wyatt and his Contemporaries* (New York: Barnes and Noble, 1964), pp. 15–25 and 172–3; Southall, 'The Devonshire Manuscript Collection of Early Tudor Poetry, 1532–41', *Review of English Studies* n.s. 15 (1964), 142–50; Helen Baron, 'Mary (Howard) Fitzroy's Hand in the Devonshire Manuscript', *Review of English Studies*, n.s. 45 (1994), 318–35 ('Table 1: Analysis of Hands in the Devonshire MS', pp. 329–33).
21. Remley, 'Mary Shelton', p. 47; Baron, 'Mary (Howard) Fitzroy's Hand', pp. 325–6.
22. Margaret Crum (ed.), *First-Line Index of English Poetry 1500–1800 in Manuscripts of the Bodleian Library Oxford*, 2 vols. (Oxford: Clarendon Press, 1969), T1217, S387, S1076.
23. I am grateful to Gillian Wright for this information.
24. Jean Klene, ' "Monument of an Endless affection": Folger MS v.b.198 and Lady Anne Southwell', *English Manuscript Studies 1100–1700* 9 (2000), 165–86 (177).
25. For a list see Anne Kugler, *Errant Plagiary: The Life and Writing of Lady Sarah Cowper 1644–1720* (Stanford, CA: Stanford University Press, 2002), p. 219, n. 55.
26. Harold Love, *English Clandestine Satire 1660–1702* (Oxford: Oxford University Press, 2004), pp. 282–3 and 'How Personal is a Personal Miscellany? Sarah Cowper, Martin Clifford and the "Buckingham Commonplace Book"', in R.C. Alston (ed.), *Order and Connexion: Studies in Bibliography and Book History* (Cambridge: D. S. Brewer, 1997), pp. 111–26.
27. Henry Lawes, *The treasury of musick* (London, 1669), Book 1, p. 27. See Galbraith Miller Crump (ed.), *The Poems and Translations of Thomas Stanley* (Oxford: Clarendon Press, 1962), pp. 387–8, for a list of additional sources in which the song was printed.

READING LIST

Bawcutt, Priscilla. 'Scottish Manuscript Miscellanies from the Fifteenth to the Seventeenth Century'. *English Manuscript Studies 1100–1700* 12 (2005), 46–73.

Burke, Victoria E. and Jonathan Gibson (eds.). *Early Modern Women's Manuscript Writing: Selected Papers from the Trinity/Trent Colloquium.* Aldershot: Ashgate, 2004.

Clarke, Elizabeth (director). The Perdita Project. http://www.warwick.ac.uk/english/perdita/html/. An online catalogue of early modern women's manuscript compilations.

Clarke, Elizabeth and Lynn Robson (eds.). *Still Kissing the Rod?* Special issue of *Women's Writing* 14.2 (2007).

Hardman, Philippa (ed.). *Medieval and Early Modern Miscellanies and Anthologies.* Special issue of *The Yearbook of English Studies* 33 (2003).

Hobbs, Mary. *Early Seventeenth-Century Verse Miscellany Manuscripts.* Aldershot: Scolar, 1992.

Justice, George L. and Nathan Tinker (eds.). *Women's Writing and the Circulation of Ideas: Manuscript Publication in England, 1550–1800.* Cambridge: Cambridge University Press, 2002.

Love, Harold. *Scribal Publication in Seventeenth-Century England.* Oxford: Clarendon Press, 1993.

Marotti, Arthur F. *Manuscript, Print, and the English Renaissance Lyric.* Ithaca, NY: Cornell University Press, 1995.

North, Marcy L. *The Anonymous Renaissance: Cultures of Discretion in Tudor–Stuart England.* Chicago: University of Chicago Press, 2003.

Woudhuysen, H. R. *Sir Philip Sidney and the Circulation of Manuscripts 1558–1640.* Oxford: Clarendon Press, 1996.

4

MARCY L. NORTH

Women, the material book and early printing

Despite the discouragements women writers faced in early modern England, female authors and translators were surprisingly visible in the early print market.[1] In most years from 1545 on, a buyer at a London bookseller's stall would have found one or more publications attributed to a woman.[2] If first-edition, singly authored, literary publications proved scarce, as they sometimes did, the bookseller could have pointed the buyer to popular reprints of women's devotional and didactic works or to the many smaller contributions of women: Queen Elizabeth's prayers tucked into any of two dozen editions of Thomas Sorocold's *Supplications of Saints*, Margaret Ascham's prefatory epistle to her late husband's *Scholemaster*, or one of several poems in verse miscellanies attributed to anonymous women. The numbers of women authors in print do not come close to those of male authors, but women were conspicuous enough in early print to make female authorship a relatively familiar, even conventional, phenomenon.

Works by and including women authors looked much like the other items for sale at the bookseller's stall, if not like the folios of the most ambitious and prolific men, then at least like the publications of the majority of male authors. Women's publications were reprinted only slightly less often than those by minor male authors. Shorter compositions by both men and women were often used by printers to supplement more substantial primary texts. Women were frequently identified with initials or class titles, and this practice was common for male authors, too. There are conventions that women's publishers favoured – posthumous publications and smaller formats, for instance – but few that are associated exclusively with women. The path leading to publication may have been more difficult for women, but, once in print, the appearance and fate of men's and women's texts were comparable.

Clearly, one cannot measure the visibility of early women in print by counting only those who acted intentionally to publish substantial bodies of original work. This authorship model describes a few later seventeenth-century women such as Margaret Cavendish and Aphra Behn, but it excludes the vast majority of women authors. It also excludes many male authors who did not have the talent, daring and connections of Edmund Spenser and Ben Jonson or who saw publication not as a profession but as a way to advertise their civic skills. Publishers did not need an author's permission to print a text they had acquired, and many publications before the eighteenth century were not initiated by the authors at all. Works were commonly ushered into print by friends or published posthumously by devotees. Manuscripts could be stolen for the printer, too, though authors exaggerated this problem to justify their publications. Like the male authors of the period, women reached print in a variety of ways that do not fit modern notions of literary career and authorial autonomy.

Measuring the visibility of women in print by looking solely at literary publications also obscures women's influence. Early readers did not see at the bookseller's stall what we see today in a textbook of Renaissance literature. Works touching on religion were the single most marketable kind of publication in early print culture, and they appealed to both male and female authors. Didactic and practical instruction literature, humanist translations and polemics appeared in vast numbers, too. Volumes of English poetry were much less common. Isabella Whitney's 1567 *Copy of a Letter to her Unconstant Lover*, for instance, is one of only three volumes of original English verse printed that year. By the 1630s, the balance of genres had shifted somewhat with the popularity of printed play texts, but literature (even understood very broadly) still accounted for less than 20 per cent of the book market. Against this backdrop, women's preferences for publishing devotional and didactic works indicate that they were very much in tune with the book industry and were choosing genres not just because they were considered appropriate for women but because they promised to attract readers.[3]

In this chapter on women and the material book, I analyse how publications by women authors fit with the normative conventions of the print industry. My evidence is in the physical characteristics of books and pamphlets, the numbers of editions and the framing of authorship within specific publications. I divide my investigation into discussions of book size, reprints, small contributions to larger volumes, and, finally, attribution and anonymity. I take a twofold approach, establishing what was conventional for both men and women and focusing on a few authors and texts that achieved exceptional prominence. If we want an accurate picture of the influence of early women authors in print, then we need to let go of modern ideals of literary authorship and compare women's publications to the full range of formats, genres, and authors that readers might have found between 1445 and 1645 at a London bookseller's stall.

Formats

The page size, or 'format', of a publication varied considerably in early print culture. Some books were so large they could only be read on a lectern and some were small enough to hang from a belt or hide in a pocket. A book's format was determined by the number of times a single large sheet of paper (about 19 x 25 inches) was folded to make individual leaves. Sheets folded once formed the large and expensive folio. Two folds created the most common and versatile size, the quarto. Three folds yielded an octavo, a convenient format that was easy to transport. Formats smaller than the octavo were compact enough to carry in a pocket or purse.[4]

The large folio came to have cultural significance in the early book market. Folios were expensive and awkward to carry, so they tended to find homes in aristocratic libraries, large churches, or institutions with the space to exhibit a large volume. The folio was the format of choice for display Bibles and volumes of religious prominence. Publications by nobility, collected works by prominent authors, song books and certain classics were printed in folio. Works of history and lengthy collections of legal and governmental records, substantial instruction manuals, dictionaries and other reference books also came out in folio. Folios signalled not only the aspirations of the author, but also the ambition of the printer, who counted on élite buyers and abiding interest to make his or her investment worthwhile.

In the sixteenth century, women authors only appeared in folios as minor contributors to larger works. Mary Tudor's translation of Erasmus is included in the folio *Paraphrase of Erasmus upon the Newe Testamente* (1548). Anne Askew's examination testimony is one of several accounts of Protestant martyrs that John Foxe compiled in *Actes and Monuments* (1563). Foxe's folios were available for public perusal in large churches. Sir John Harington included a poem by Anne Killigrew in the notes to Book 37 of his folio translation of *Orlando Furioso* (1591). The folio, one should note, was not a common format for any author in the period, male or female, so women's reliance on smaller formats does not necessarily mean they were denied some customary authorial privilege. In 1591, only a few publications appeared in folio besides *Orlando Furioso* – a geometry volume, two sets of statutes, a Tacitus edition and a Bible. The other 300 publications were much more modest in size.

With the seventeenth century, it grew fashionable for living English poets to publish collected works in folio when they felt they had earned classic or laureate status. Samuel Daniel's 1601 *Works* set the precedent, though Daniel's immediate model was Philip Sidney's posthumous *Arcadia* and poems, the second edition of which had been a folio (1593). Although today our traditional canon of Renaissance literature draws heavily from authors whose works eventually reached folio, the majority of seventeenth-century authors never achieved folio publication.

In 1621, Mary Sidney Wroth also made the decision to imitate Sidney, her paternal uncle, by publishing her *Urania* and sonnet sequence together in an ostentatious, first-edition folio. In many ways, Wroth's *Urania* merited a large, expensive format. Wroth's high social status, her Sidney family legacy, the length of the work (close to 600 pages) and the collected genres of romance and poetry all argued for folio publication. Wroth's romance nevertheless met with criticism from her peers, and it was not reprinted. Nine years later, Elizabeth Cary's translation, *The Reply of the Most Illustrious Cardinall of Perron* (1630), appeared in folio. Although Cary remained anonymous, her dedication to Queen Henrietta Maria made it clear that she was, like the Queen, a Catholic woman. This publication was suppressed, most obviously because of the book's Catholicism. Still, it can hardly be coincidence that the first two folio publications initiated by women were ill received. Even towards the middle of the seventeenth century, when Margaret Cavendish's folio editions of her own poetry contributed to her reputation for eccentricity and extravagance, folios remained exceptional. They called attention to themselves at the bookseller's stall and claimed for their authors and translators a certain bravado. Folio publication made Wroth's, Cary's and Cavendish's literary ventures seem all the more transgressive to their detractors, not just because women were using print, but because they were choosing a grandiose (even provocative) format.

Like the majority of male authors, early modern women appeared most often in quarto and octavo. Many first editions of literature were printed in quarto. Whitney's *Copy of a Letter* (1567) and *Sweet Nosgay* (1573), Aemilia Lanyer's *Salve Deus Rex Judaeorum* (1611), Elizabeth Cary's *Tragedie of Mariam* (1613), Diana Primrose's *Chaine of Pearle* (1630) and Mary Fage's *Fames Roule* (1637) all appeared in quarto. Elizabeth Colville, Lady Culros's *Godlie Dreame* (1603) came out in quarto initially, although subsequent editions were in smaller formats. Second editions often appeared in smaller formats, as printers took aim at new audiences.

One finds a number of women's devotional texts and prayers in extremely small formats. Several editions of Catherine Parr's *Prayers or Meditacions* appeared in 16mo (one-sixteenth of a full sheet), and Elizabeth Tyrwhit's *Morning and Evening Prayer* (1574) was printed as a 32mo, a book about four inches tall. Alice Sutcliffe's *Meditations of Man's Mortalitie* (1634) appeared in a duodecimo, a popular seventeenth-century format with twelve leaves per folded sheet. These devotional publications were marketed to readers who wanted to carry the books with them during the day and consult them in quiet moments. It was the devotional genre and the way it was used, not the gender of the author, that encouraged the small formats; prayers by men also appeared in small volumes. These tiny books could nevertheless be said to characterize women's publication in the earlier years, if only because several women wrote devotional works that became exceptionally popular.

The influence of reprints

Before the second half of the seventeenth century, women authors rarely published more than one or two works in a literary career. Some women no doubt wrote prolifically, but not all of their works reached print. As such, the prominence of women authors in print depended more on the reprinting of their works than on the number of works they wrote.[5] In the sixteenth century, noblewomen who undertook translations or devotional projects found an eager print audience. The two reigning Queens rendered the idea of female authorship more familiar to print audiences in their official letters and proclamations, but their academic and creative exercises, especially Elizabeth's, were also influential. Elizabeth's translation of Marguerite de Navarre's *Godly Meditations* went through four sixteenth-century editions, all of them crediting Elizabeth on the title page, and Elizabeth's prayers had an extremely long life as an acknowledged part of Sorocold's *Supplications of Saints* (1612).

The most influential sixteenth-century noblewoman may have been Henry VIII's last Queen, the Protestant Catherine Parr, whose *Prayers or Meditacions* went through almost twenty editions before 1600. They were printed primarily in small octavo and sextodecimo formats. Like most profitable texts, Parr's prayers were also included within other works, *Psalms or Prayers* (1568), for instance, and Thomas Bentley's 1582 *Monument of Matrones*. Parr's visibility in print should not be underestimated. Print was still a relatively new technology in England when Parr's works appeared in 1545. Only about 130 titles were printed that year, three of which were editions of Parr's prayers. With her name and status on the title page, she was as prominent as any other author published that year. Certainly, it helped to be Queen, but the prayers remained popular long after Parr's death. Several editions even came out during the Catholic reign of Mary Tudor with false dates to protect the Protestant printers and readers.

Also achieving prominence in print were several women whose trials and executions made them exemplary figures in Protestant historiography. Lady Jane Grey, whose father-in-law tried to have her crowned Queen in 1553, and Anne Askew, who defied Henry VIII's bishops in defending her reformed theology, both produced small bodies of work that were reprinted again and again in the sixteenth century. Askew's *First Examinacion* was initially compiled by John Bale in 1546, and *An Epistle of the Lady Jane* first appeared in 1554. There is something apocryphal about these women in that their stories are bigger than their contributions as authors, but martyrs, like queens, kept women's names and voices in circulation, reminding readers that, since women could and did write in times of trial, they also had the capacity to write in less trying times.

From 1560 to 1640, the number of titles printed annually doubled, tripled and then quadrupled in a remarkable expansion of print production. The print audience also broadened to include a greater diversity of readers, and professional authorship became a real possibility for ambitious writers. It is against this backdrop that one genre, mother's advice literature, gained momentum and sustained its popularity through reprints. The phenomenon of mother's advice grew out of two print industry successes: *A Crystall Glasse, for Christian Women* (1591), which recorded the last words of Katherine Stubbes, and the humanist genre of father's advice literature.

Philip Stubbes's account of his young wife's virtue and early death was printed in 1592 as a short pamphlet in black letter, the typeface used for ballads and other works aimed at less educated audiences. Stubbes employed very plain rhetoric in an obvious effort to reach a broad audience. The technique worked, and the pamphlet became one of the most reprinted publications of the early seventeenth century. Katherine was praised in the pamphlet not for her silence but for reading and speaking out in the name of her reformed religion. When a puerperal infection struck after her son's birth, a fate she had earlier predicted, her husband and friends recorded her learned but accessible 'confession of faith' as she lay on her deathbed.

The Stubbes pamphlet contained many components of mother's advice literature – broad appeal, a mother's devotion to family, foretold death, posthumous publication and a heroine so virtuous she cannot be held to earthly standards of female modesty. Yet Katherine's advice did not speak to earthly concerns in the way that mother's advice literature would, and Katherine's words were so obviously mediated by her husband that today they are rarely included in the canon of women's literature. The more immediate voice and practical quality found in mother's advice literature came instead from a humanist-inspired fashion for advising sons. Cicero's *De Officiis* (published in 1606), James I's *Basilikon Doron* (1599) and its adaptation, *The Fathers Blessing* (1616), Lord Burghley's *Certaine Preceptes* (1611) and *Sir Walter Raleigh's Instructions to his Sonne* (1632) together accounted for fifty editions and reprints in the early seventeenth century. The genre of parental advice is hardly new, as the classical example suggests, but this particular wave of publication made women's contributions seem timely rather than anomalous.

There were several popular mother's advice publications. Elizabeth Grymeston's *Miscelanea* (1604) went through four editions and Elizabeth Jocelin's *Mothers Legacie to her Unborne Childe* (1624) saw five. None, however, was reprinted quite as often as Dorothy Leigh's *Mothers Blessing* (1616). This unusually long work of nearly 300 duodecimo pages was reprinted almost two dozen times. Leigh sought publication before her death so that her sons would not need to share the manuscript copy of her advice:

> But when I had written these things unto you, and had (as I thought) something fulfilled your Fathers request, yet I could not see to what purpose it should tend, unlesse it were sent abroad to you: for should it be left with the eldest, it is likely the youngest should have but little part in it. Wherefore setting aside all fear, I have adventured to shew my imperfections to the view of the world. (sigs. B8r–v).

In the *Crystall Glasse*, the husband's mediation had allowed Katherine Stubbes to neglect worldly concerns and focus on the heavenly. Leigh, by contrast, seems to have made a practical, earthly decision with a keen understanding of print's advantages. Only the title page tells us that the work was published posthumously. The editorial mediation in Grymeston's and Jocelin's publications also focused attention back on the woman author. Grymeston's publication had almost no mediation, other than a dedicatory poem. The anonymous introduction to Jocelin's *Legacie* (figure 13) took the form of an 'Approbation' and framed the *Legacie* as an inheritance that the executor was legally obliged to publish.[6] Although the executor's duty was to 'approve' the last will and testament, this was the first step to fulfilling the author's wishes.

Other examples of mother's advice followed, most of them exploiting the success of these three reprinted publications. M. R.'s *Mothers Counsell* (1630) was more didactic and less personal than the *Legacie,* but it also framed its contents as a last will and testament. In *The Countesse of Lincolnes Nurserie* (1622), Elizabeth Clinton used mother's advice as a premise to encourage women to breastfeed their infants. This brief work saw only one edition, perhaps because the subject was considered topical. Ez. W.'s *Answer of a Mother unto hir Seduced Sonnes Letter* (1627) offered a rhetorically skilful argument against the son's Catholicism. What these later publications demonstrate is how the role of mother–author, especially after the success of Leigh's work, was adapted and exploited in the print market.

Devotional and advice literature by women found early success in the reprint market, but women's more literary works were rarely reprinted

Figure 13. Early eighteenth-century edition of Elizabeth Jocelin, *Mothers Legacy*, in 24°
(13 × 7 cm) with signature of a female owner on the paste-down.

before the second half of the seventeenth century. Isabella Whitney's two volumes were the most ambitious collections of original verse published by a woman in the sixteenth century, and they saw only one edition each. Aemilia Lanyer's poetry was not reprinted, and neither was the work of Elizabeth Cary, Diana Primrose, or Mary Fage. It is difficult to measure the success or failure of these single editions. The audience for poetry was smaller than the audience for devotional literature, and one edition may have satisfied that audience. Whitney's *Letter* could not have failed entirely, for printer Richard Jones was willing to publish Whitney's second, longer work in 1573. In Whitney's generation, minor print poets such as Llodowick Lloyd and Thomas Watson produced original works that did not reach second editions, and several 1590s sonnet sequences, by Barnabe Barnes, Giles Fletcher, William Percy and Bartholomew Griffin, were never reprinted. Even very prolific print authors such as Nicholas Breton and Thomas Nashe did not see every publication reprinted.

Although second editions came to signal the success of a male poet's work in the seventeenth century, this trend does not mean that a one-edition work was a failure. Even in the 1630s, when the disparity between men's and women's reprint numbers was greatest, men's original poetry remained less marketable than other genres. Many of the male counterparts of Lanyer, Cary, Primrose and Fage also produced single-edition works. Richard Brathwait's conduct manual, *The English Gentleman*, did quite well, but at least two of his poetry volumes, *The Golden Fleece* (1611) and *Poets Willow* (1614), were not reprinted. Fulke Greville's posthumous *Workes* (1633), Lawrence Leonard's *Arnalte and Lucenda* (1639) and Mildmay Fane's *Otia Sacra Optima Fides* (1648) were not reprinted in the early modern period. Any bibliography of minor poets will yield even more examples. Publications of women's poetry, confined to single editions as they were, may not have resonated across several generations in the way that Catherine Parr's prayers did, but they compared favourably to other minor poetry publications of their generations and may have been read and applauded by a limited audience.

The visibility of minor authors

It was not until the late seventeenth century that women authors produced substantial oeuvres and could compete with the more productive male authors. Women's smaller contributions nevertheless made an impression in print; their poems, letters and prefaces were numerous, and some of them were placed very prominently within their publications. Two modern bibliographical resources, the *Biographical Dictionary of English Women Writers, 1580–1720* and *Early Modern Women Poets: An Anthology*, reveal that dozens of women contributed one or two poems to early publications and published little else.[7] Poems attributed to anonymous women in miscellanies and other compilations easily double this figure. In the ten years between 1610 and 1620, for instance, one finds a poem attributed to the 'Maid of Honor' in *The Crown Garland of Golden Roses* (London, 1612, sig. B3r–v), a poem in *Sir Thomas Overburie his Wife* (London, 1616) thought to be by Cecilia Bulstrode (sig. ¶4–v), and a dedicatory poem by Marie Lily in her father's *Two Sermons* (London, 1619, sig. A4v). In these same ten years, anonymous women's answer poems and a poem by Mary Sidney Herbert appeared in Francis Davison's *Poeticall Rhapsodie* (London, 1611, pp. 85, 185–6, 156–8). Scholars are hesitant to include in the canon of women's literature every poem in a woman's voice, especially since male poets often wrote from the feminine perspective. For an early reader, however, dedications and answer poems in larger works may have seemed to be credible women's compositions. Considered together, these published poems show that women poets were not exceptionally rare, though they tended to publish in a manner reminiscent of manuscript culture, privileging occasion, social dialogue and amateur status over literary career.

Supplementary or complementary texts were extremely common, and they came from the pens of both men and women. Although title pages do not always advertise this fact, many early publications contained more than one author. Samuel Daniel's sonnets were first published at the back of Sidney's *Astrophel and Stella* (1591), and sonnets believed to be by Anne Locke were appended to her translation of the *Sermons of John Calvin* (1560). Printers and primary authors found letters and prose pieces attractive complements as well. A letter from Penelope Rich was included in her brother's *Apologie of the Earle of Essex* (1600), and a letter from Jane Glencorse appeared in *Newes from Ireland* (1642). Ursula Quarles's memorial biography of her husband, Francis Quarles (figure 14), was the first item in *Solomons Recantation* (1645). The popularity of dedicatory poems and reprints that had been 'augmented' made the practice of including secondary authors an effective marketing tool. Sometimes, the position of a secondary piece in a volume and the volume's popularity gave a woman author considerable exposure. This was the case with Quarles's biography. Margaret Ascham's preface to the *Scholemaster*, too, introduced a broad audience to her editorship of Roger Ascham's classic pedagogical treatise. Although modern scholars may object to the way secondary women authors depended on more important male authors to occasion their contributions, the mediation performed by these women was not unlike that of Philip Stubbes, who receives primary credit for narrating his wife's life and death.

Attribution and anonymity

The title page evolved in the sixteenth century to advertise the contents of a printed work – it was posted in public places much like a flyer. The title page could also promote an author or mark the absence of one. In the sixteenth century, many authors and translators were identified on the title page by initials or simple ascriptions, perhaps because the author's status was not yet marketable or perhaps because brief ascriptions were sufficient in the smaller print market. Isabella Whitney, Anne Dowriche, Anne Locke and Margaret Tyler were all identified with initials. In the seventeenth century, a growing number of women of middling status reached print, and title pages show a new interest in articulating precisely class distinctions, familial connections and credibility. Aemilia Lanyer is 'wife to Captain Alfonso Lanyer servant to

A
SHORT RELATION OF THE
Life and Death of M^r. *Francis Quarles*,
by *Vrſula Quarles*, his ſorrowfull
Widow.

Hough it be inconſiſtent with the duty of a
wife, to be injurious in any reſpect to her
husband ; yet in this my bold undertaking
I fear I ſhall be ſo to mine : which I doubt
not but he would have forgiven, if he had
been living, as proceeding from love; and I hope his friends
will pardon (now he is dead) as being the laſt duty I can
perform to a loving husband. Thoſe that ſee with what
pen his Works are written, will ſay his life deſerved a more
skilfull Artiſt to ſet it forth : which office though many
might have been procured to undertake ; and to which I
doubt not, but ſome would voluntarily have offered them-
ſelves, if they had known that ſuch a thing had been intended : yet have I (with much zeal, though ſmall diſcretion)
adventured upon it my ſelf, as being fully aſſured that none
can be more ſenſible of the loſſe of him, then I, though
thouſands might have expreſt that loſſe to the world with
more Art and better judgement.

He was a Gentleman both by birth and deſert : deſcen-
ded of an ancient Family, and yet (which is rare in theſe
laſt and worſt times) he was an ornament to his Anceſtors.
His Father was *James Quarles* of Rumford Eſquire ; Clerk
of the Green-cloth and Purveyor of the Navie to Queen
Elizabeth, and yonger brother to Sir *Robert Quarles*. His
education was ſuitable to his birth ; firſt, at ſchoole in the
A 2   Countrey,

Figure 14. Ursula Quarles, 'The Life and Death of Mr. Francis Quarles', sig. A2,
preface to Francis Quarles's *Solomons Recantation* (1645).

the Kings Majesty'. *Antidote against Purgatory* (1634) was 'written by that virtuous and rightworthy gentle-woman (the honour of her sex for learning in England) M^s. Jane Owen, late of God-stow, in Oxfordshire, deceased', and *Fames Roule* (1637) is 'by Mistress Mary Fage, wife of Robert Fage the younger, Gentleman'.

With this new attention to identity, it is surprising to learn that women's use of anonymity and pseudonymity increased in the first half of the seventeenth century – at least we think so. Initials and simple ascriptions remained conventional for both men and women, but two other models of ascription, the satirical pseudonym and the Catholic religious name, were also adapted by women authors for the print market. The best-known examples of pseudonymous publication are found in the controversy over the worth of women. Although we cannot be certain that Esther Sowernam (*Esther Hath Hang'd Haman*) and Constantia Munda (*The Worming of a Madde Dogge*) are female, their learned and witty 1617 retorts to Joseph Swetnam's *Araignment of Lewd, Idle, Froward, and Unconstant Women* (1615) showed print readers that women authors could play satirically with names. The pseudonyms also gave these women the freedom to use invective and *ad hominem* attacks. Sowernam and Munda did not necessarily seek the protection of pseudonyms because they were women – they might have been protecting their social standing instead.

The Catholic exiles whose translations were smuggled into England took new religious names as sisters living in Continental convents. They may have also sought protection through their new names, perhaps for their families still in England. It is nearly impossible today to determine the birth name for the translator of François de Sales's *Delicious Entertainments of the Soule* (1632). The *Short Title Catalogue* simply refers to her as Prudentiana Deacon. *The History of the Angelicall Virgin Glorious S. Clare* by Luke Wadding (1635) claims Magdalen Augustine as its translator, though scholars differ on whether Magdalen is Catherine Bentley or Elizabeth Evelinge. However inconvenient early modern anonymity is for modern editors, we need to see it not as something that disqualifies a potential woman author from inclusion in the canon, but as an example of women making use of print's potential as they undertook more daring publications.

The easing of print restrictions in the 1640s and the resulting pamphlet culture encouraged many authors and publishers to play with the attribution conventions of the previous generation. Of particular interest in this period are publications of questionable female authorship. In the 1640s, petitions from large groups of women began to appear in print with some frequency.[8] We know that some of them were indeed initiated by women, but pamphleteers also published satirical petitions around the same time, such as *The Virgins Complaint for the Losse of their Sweet-Hearts, by these present Wars, and their owne long solitude and keeping their virginities against their wills* (1642). In their mockery of the petition genre, satirists depicted female political action and authorship as a travesty, but their parodies also signalled that female petitioners were conventional enough to be mocked effectively. A few very interesting women's petitions seem to hang in the balance between serious grievance and mockery. *The Midwives' Just Petition* (1643), for instance, argues against war on the grounds that, if no children are conceived while husbands are fighting, midwives will be out of business. Unlike in the case of the *Virgins Complaint*, modern scholars have taken this petition somewhat seriously.[9] As the fashion for petitions and their parodies spread in the 1640s, women authors did not necessarily retreat. It is possible they were responsible for some of the ambiguous petitions and had appropriated the mockery of female authorship for their own causes.

The flurry of 1640s pamphleteering seems to have encouraged parodists and serious authors alike to hide behind female authorship and women's conventional genres. A work claiming to be an early Tudor prophecy by 'Mother Shipton', for instance, was reprinted over two dozen times, often with other 'older' prophecies that had long since come true. The *Short Title Catalogue*, however, lists no copy of *The Prophesie of Mother Shipton* before 1641. Yet another print genre that women authors embraced, the defence of women, was imitated in *The Womens Sharpe Revenge* (1640) by 'Mary Tattle-well and Joan Hit-him-home, spinsters'. Like *The Midwives' Just Petition*, this work is sometimes read as a serious defence.

Eleanor Douglas, an eccentric prophet and noblewoman and one of the most prolific women writers of the mid seventeenth century, also took advantage of lax print regulation to experiment with authorial attribution. Between 1640 and 1643, she personally directed the printing of half a dozen prophetic tracts, most of them the length of popular pamphlets. In them, she used anagrams of her own name to establish her connection with the biblical Daniel, displayed proper names with different typefaces and tested the usefulness of traditional print practices. Douglas's 'Preface' to her *Appeale to the High Court of Parliament* (London, 1641) is a mocking, obscure text that begins: 'The roade way not to baulke, a preface omitted neither to the reader: complement, although layd aside, soft lineing of that sort, these therwith prefaced not; rather preferred for all weather serviceable, a peece of plain Leather' (sig. A3). Much like the pamphleteers imitating and mocking women's authorship, Eleanor Douglas turns upside down a convention in which authors address the public, and she does so to condemn the artificial relationship between authors and readers that print encouraged. Serious and parodic manipulations of attribution conventions date back to the beginning of print, but the parody of so many different genres associated with female authorship in the early 1640s suggests that women's publication practices were becoming somewhat more distinct and definable.

In early modern England, women achieved visibility in print comparable to that of minor male authors, not because they were prolific or because they achieved laureate status, but because early printing practices favoured inclusion of minor authors, political and social dialogue, reprinting of popular favourites, and imitations and parodies of what had become conventional. Although female authors continued to have their detractors, the print industry, in its everyday practices, was just as likely to grab the work of a woman as that of a man. When the first women begin to establish prolific literary careers in the 1650s and 1660s, the concept of the female print author was already well established.

NOTES

1. On factors that discouraged women from printing, see Wendy Wall, *The Imprint of Gender: Authorship and Publication in the English Renaissance* (Ithaca, NY: Cornell University Press, 1993) and Elaine Beilen, *Redeeming Eve: Women Writers of the English Renaissance* (Princeton, NJ: Princeton University Press, 1987).
2. Much of my evidence comes from the online *English Short Title Catalogue*, available through The British Library, London. I offer broad findings more often than specific numbers because information about early editions is still incomplete.
3. For information about women and print genres, see Helen Wilcox (ed.), *Women and Literature in Britain: 1500–1700* (Cambridge: Cambridge University Press, 1996).
4. For more information on book production, see Bradin Cormack and Carla Mazzio, *Book Use, Book Theory: 1500–1700* (Chicago: University of Chicago Library, 2005); John Barnard, D. F. McKenzie and Maureen Bell (eds.), *Cambridge History of the Book in Britain*, vol. IV, 1557–1695 (Cambridge: Cambridge University Press, 2002); Lucien Febvre and Henri-Jean Martin, *The Coming of the Book: The Impact of Printing, 1450–1800* (London and New York: Verso, 1997); and H. S. Bennett, *English Books and Readers: 1475–1640*, 3 vols. (Cambridge: Cambridge University Press, 1952–70).
5. Kimberly Ann Coles discusses the importance of women's reprints in *Religion, Reform, and Women's Writing in Early Modern England* (Cambridge: Cambridge University Press, 2008).
6. After the first edition, the 'Approbation' is signed by 'Tho. Goad'.
7. Maureen Bell, *A Biographical Dictionary of English Women Writers: 1580–1720* (Boston, MA: G. K. Hall, 1990); Jane Stevenson and Peter Davidson (eds.), *Early Modern Women Poets: An Anthology* (Oxford: Oxford University Press, 2001).
8. See Mihoko Suzuki's chapter on seventeenth-century petitioners in *Subordinate Subjects: Gender, the Political Nation, and Literary Form in England, 1588–1688* (Aldershot: Ashgate, 2003).

9. The petition is included in Suzanne Trill, Kate Chedgzo, and Melanie Osborne (eds.), *Lay By Your Needles Ladies, Take the Pen: Writing Women in England, 1500–1700* (Oxford: Oxford University Press, 1997).

READING LIST

Barnard, John, D. F. McKenzie and Maureen Bell (eds.). *Cambridge History of the Book in Britain*. Vol. IV, 1557–1695. Cambridge: Cambridge University Press, 2002.

Bell, Maureen. *A Biographical Dictionary of English Women Writers: 1500–1720*. Boston, MA: G. K. Hall, 1990.

Burke, Mary, Jane Donawerth, Linda Dove and Karen Nelson (eds.). *Women, Writing, and the Reproduction of Culture in Tudor and Stuart Britain*. Syracuse, NY: Syracuse University Press, 2000.

Clarke, Danielle and Elizabeth Clarke (eds.). *'This Double Voice': Gendered Writing in Early Modern England*. Basingstoke: Palgrave Macmillan, 2000.

Coles, Kimberly Ann. *Religion, Reform, and Women's Writing in Early Modern England*. Cambridge: Cambridge University Press, 2008.

Cormack, Bradin and Carla Mazzio. *Book Use, Book Theory: 1500–1700*. Chicago: University of Chicago Library, 2005.

Demers, Patricia A. *Women's Writing in English: Early Modern England*. Toronto: University of Toronto Press, 2005.

Ezell, Margaret. *Social Authorship and the Advent of Print*. Baltimore: Johns Hopkins University Press, 1999.

Febvre, Lucien and Henri-Jean Martin. *The Coming of the Book: The Impact of Printing, 1450–1800*. Trans. David Gerard. London: Verso, 1997.

Longfellow, Erica. *Women and Religious Writing in Early Modern England*. Cambridge: Cambridge University Press, 2004.

Salzman, Paul. *Reading Early Modern Women's Writing*. Oxford: Oxford University Press, 2007.

Stevenson, Jane, and Peter Davidson (eds.). *Early Modern Women Poets: An Anthology*. Oxford: Oxford University Press, 2001.

Wall, Wendy. *The Imprint of Gender: Authorship and Publication in the English Renaissance*. Ithaca, NY: Cornell University Press, 1993.

Wheale, Nigel. *Writing and Society: Literacy, Print and Politics in Britain, 1590–1660*. London: Routledge, 1999.

Wilcox, Helen (ed.). *Women and Literature in Britain: 1500–1700*. Cambridge: Cambridge University Press, 1996.

PART TWO

Sites of production

5

CAROLINE BOWDEN

Women in educational spaces

'Bought of Mrs Mary Woodrofe February the 8, 2 shades. Receved of Mrs Atkinson the som of fortey shelling for them. I say receved by me, Kattarn Roberts.'[1]

This receipt for the purchase of two lace scarves ('shades') written in her own hand by Kattarn (possibly Katharine) Roberts, working as a sales-woman in 1672, allows us both to question our understanding of women's literacy and to consider the means by which Roberts and other women of her social class learned to write receipts acceptable to book-keepers in substantial households. Even for well-educated women whose families left copious documents relating to their estates and households, there are few records regarding girls' education. Important questions about the education of girls and women remain to be answered. For instance: where did women such as Katharine Roberts, about whom we know little or who left only fragmentary evidence of their ability to write in receipts, short inscriptions in books, or initialled witness statements, learn to write? This chapter will consider educational spaces, whether publicly accessible or private, large or small, immaculately maintained or rough, which sheltered a variety of activities that can be defined broadly as educational.

This present volume demonstrates very clearly the growth of women's writing over the sixteenth and seventeenth centuries in England. However, explaining how and where girls were educated remains challenging, because as a number of historians and literary scholars have shown, opinions varied over what girls should be taught, and schools for girls were lacking.[2] We know that the curriculum for those girls of the landed classes who were educated in this period might encompass reading, writing, music, cookery and medicine. For poorer girls, teaching was much more restricted, including at best basic reading, writing and occasionally numeracy. Yet as more research is carried out and more evidence uncovered, we need to explain how women from social classes ranging from the daughters of aristocrats to the daughters of tradesmen and shopkeepers were able to write so competently with so little formal schooling.[3]

Women and writing literacies

The term 'writing' applied to early modern women covers a very wide range of levels of competence from inscribing initials on a document to writing entire letters in Greek or creating original works of literature. This is hardly surprising given the variations in parental opinion on how or indeed how much girls should be educated, even in families where parents were able to pay for teaching for their daughters or to provide it themselves. Historians and literary scholars have approached early modern girls' education from two main directions: firstly by finding evidence of reading and writing skills; secondly by looking for evidence of schools, teachers, tutors and governesses. Such research has expanded our knowledge of individuals from the gentry and upper classes: those parts of society able to keep records and maintain an archive. However, it adds little to our understanding of how (and when) poorer women, who may have left nothing more than a signature, learned to write, nor how girls with little formal education were able to write long original works.

It is worth approaching women's writing from a different direction and broadening our understanding of the process of becoming literate. In our own time, as scholars mostly living in countries with universal state education, we have become used to thinking that learning to read and write takes up several years of teaching and learning in primary schools. However, there are alternative models from parts of the world where there is little formal state education, particularly for girls, and where different educational spaces are found. Research on the effectiveness of literacy schemes recently undertaken in areas with little provision of formal schooling for girls, can, I believe, help us understand the situation in early modern England with its lack of schooling available to girls.[4]

The concept of 'functional literacy' adopted in critiques of modern literacy schemes focuses on the learning of skills that can immediately be used for a purpose identified as important by the learner. It is one that would be recognized in the seventeenth century by Katharine Roberts, our receipt-writer, as well as women in twenty-first century Uganda and India who learn to read and write because, for instance, they want to be able to set up micro-businesses and sign for loans. One literacy scheme in Kerala, southern India, provided 300 hours of teaching to women participants spread over one year to accommodate peak periods of labour such as harvest in order to achieve functional literacy.[5] It needs constant practice to maintain even the basic writing skills achieved at the end of such a short course. Becoming literate this way requires high motivation from the learner and commitment to continuing practice. Research has shown that teachers on literacy schemes do not have to be formally qualified to be effective: success has been achieved using instructors who are given minimal training. Instructors must be sympathetic to the participants, use materials closely related to the interests of the learners and build on the individual enthusiasm and motivation of the female learners.

This modern research points up the significance of a number of factors which are also relevant to early modern England: in particular the importance of individual motivation as an impetus to learning; the need to continue practising skills in order to avoid losing them; the existence of appropriate teaching (by untrained teachers) in spaces where the learners feel comfortable and learning materials relevant to the life of the learner. In developing countries women from poorer families have a very limited amount of time to devote to learning because of domestic and family responsibilities, but many see the value that the ability to write could add to their circumstances. For the better off, motivation to continue learning is driven by other factors such as bringing up children, piety, managing the household or the family business. There are many similarities in the circumstances of women in early modern England. By understanding the impact of the literacy schemes with their focus on individual effort, motivation and continuing practice, we will be in a better position to understand how women in early modern England who received some, albeit limited, formal teaching in schoolrooms were able to improve their skills largely by their own efforts.[6]

The receipt quoted at the head of this paper comes from a collection of documents generated by tradespeople supplying goods and services to Sir Robert and Lady Shirley living in London between 1672 and 1675. It is one of a number written by women working in small businesses who were able to write well enough to summarize the transactions in their own hand. Among the other women writing their own bills and receipts was Mary Black for 'an hermine muffe with tails and spekt ... 21 yeards and a halfe of hermine ... and a border for gloves' costing £4.11.0 which she noted had been paid by Mrs Atkinson (probably a housekeeper). In September 1675 Mary Griffiths wrote out a receipt for £1.06.0 for gloves and damask powder.[7] Mary Griffiths's hand is rounded, even, fluent and easy to read, indicating years of practice. Other receipts generated by women are found among the financial papers relating to the Countess of Huntingdon's household from the 1630s onwards. Most of the writers had acquired more than basic literacy skills and were able to write whole sentences with a degree of fluency which suggests regular practice. A few receipts from women have only names or initials: the rest is in another hand.

There is other evidence of women of the 'middling sort' being able to write. For instance, in the early seventeenth century, Ann Bowyer, the daughter of a Coventry craftsman, put together a commonplace book.[8] Ann Bowyer has been identified as the mother of Elias Ashmole, with the result that we have some contextual background for her, although no detail regarding her education. Her level of competence is far above that of most of the receipt writers although they may have come from a similar social background.

As we have already seen in the studies of modern-day literacy campaigns, training in both reading and writing is seen as providing only the initial impetus for the student. A second crucial element to women's literacy is continuing practice. After the first courses, literacy is still fragile; the learner has skills that can be developed or lost depending on how often and how well they are used. This is also true of the seventeenth century. I would argue that the women supplying seeds, shades or lace to Sir Robert and Lady Shirley fall into this category. The uncertainty of the writing hand in several of these receipts, coupled with poor spelling, suggests very limited access to teaching. Yet, however uncertain their writing, the women in this sample of documents were sufficiently competent to collect money owed and to write receipts acceptable to the book-keepers at the big houses they supplied. Necessity was a powerful factor driving these women to become and remain literate. Where did they learn to write?

Schooling for girls

Formal schooling was available to some early modern girls from poorer families: even in the sixteenth century there were petty or elementary schools (mostly in urban areas) able to take in girls. In theory, school teachers were licensed by the ecclesiastical authorities. However, in practice domestic schools holding fewer than six pupils did not have to be licensed, and Jay Anglin argues that there must have been many more than the forty-seven schoolmistresses identified by the authorities teaching in twenty-eight different parishes in the Elizabethan diocese of London.[9] It was in these kinds of schools that our receipt writers may have gained their basic skills. A few poor girls were admitted to Christ's Hospital, London from its foundation in 1552, where they were able to learn to read and (from 1658) to write. Little is known about the quality of licensed teachers, and Anglin has evidence that some of the women who taught in these schools were unable to write. At the other end of the spectrum, there were writing teachers such as Mrs Elizabeth Beane, active in London in the 1680s, whose pupils demonstrated considerable artistic prowess along with arithmetical and cal-ligraphic skills in their copy-books.[10]

The number of schools open to girls did increase over the seventeenth century with the foundation of schools specifically for daughters of parents able to pay for their education. In the early years of the seventeenth century, a number of formal schools, mainly for daughters of merchants and gentle-men, sprung up in areas such as Deptford, Hackney and Putney just outside London, and Red Maids school opened in Bristol in 1634. The standard of education provided in these schools and the length of time spent there by the pupils varied considerably, but they would have provided sufficient ground-ing that pupils could later develop on their own. The fees payable at these schools would probably have placed them beyond the reach of parents of women like Katharine Roberts, our receipt-writer.

For devout Catholic parents able to pay fees and willing to lose contact with their daughters for the duration of their education, there were convent schools on the Continent. From 1600, more than fourteen schools for girls were created by the new English religious foundations for women established in exile in Flanders and France. Some of these schools were small and short-lived; others focused mainly on providing a place where girls could remain until they were old enough to join the convent as novices. The larger schools were set up by nuns whose religious purpose was to educate girls until they were able to choose whether to join a convent or return to the world to become wives and mothers. Susan Hawley, founder of the English Sepulchrines in Liège, established a school which taught writing, reading, needlework, French and music. The Augustinian Canonesses in Paris had a popular school with a curriculum that included reading, writing and casting accounts: while at school the girls read and spoke French. The pupils lived within the convent walls and were expected to follow a code of behaviour only slightly less strict than that of the postulants who were planning to join the convent, with-out taking holidays and visiting their parents. Over time convent schools educated a substantial number of mostly upper-class English girls.[11]

The European schools established by the Mary Ward Sisters – followers of Mary Ward (1585–1645), a visionary Englishwoman from Yorkshire – survived the suppression of Ward's institute in 1631. Since the Sisters were never enclosed and in the schools were treated as laywomen wearing respectable rather than monastic dress, the schools were very different from those established in the enclosed convents. The quality of the education they offered drew pupils in large numbers, and from 1669 the first school was opened in England in Hammersmith. The Bar Convent in York from its opening in 1686 took in girl pupils; however, its main educational activity dates from the eighteenth century.

Informal educational spaces

The daughters of landed families whose parents decided to educate them were likely to have been taught over several years by tutors and governesses or by their parents at home, although we know little about the contents of the curriculum or the exercises they performed. The provision of education in families was gendered, with girls receiving less tuition than boys, and in some cases it is clear that girls gained only very basic skills. We have evidence in family accounts of payments for teaching in a number of families. As early as the mid sixteenth century, evidence in household accounts shows that Margaret Willoughby was being educated at Wollaton near Nottingham with her brother Francis. In the Fane family three generations of women were educated at home. Firstly, Grace Sharington (later Lady Mildmay) was educated by a governess. Then her only daughter, Mary, who became Countess of Westmoreland, and Rachael, her granddaughter, were both brought up and taught at Apethorpe, Northamptonshire. Rachael Fane's notebooks give rare evidence of the contents of a young girl's lessons in the first half of the seventeenth century and include a delightful masque that she created one Christmas to be performed by the children of the house.[12] Many Catholic girls were also educated at home: Mary Ward spent several years being educated in the household of Sir Ralph and Lady Grace Babthorpe at Osgodby near York in the 1590s. A hundred years later, as the eldest of eleven children, Anne Gerard took her dead mother's place: 'She taught them all her self to read writ work &c. so that their father never spent one penny on their education', before she joined the Carmelite convent in Antwerp in 1725, aged forty-six.[13]

Since the decisions regarding a daughter's education were made on an individual basis by parents, the educational activities in households varied considerably. On the one hand, it is possible to find Latin scholars such as the four surviving daughters of Sir Anthony Cooke (Mildred, Anne, Elizabeth and Katherine), and the four daughters of Sir John Wiseman (Jane, Bridget, Anne and Barbara), who were taught Latin by their fathers at home. Both these families, coincidentally, lived in Essex: the first Protestant, the second Catholic. However it should be noted that a classical education for girls was sufficiently rare to be commented on at the time. In contrast, there are many other women from a similar social background whose uncertain hands and spelling suggest rather limited education and practice. Although parents provided teaching for their daughters to leave them with skills they considered appropriate to their status and marriage prospects, this was not necessarily the final level of their educational achievements revealed in the writings they left. Many women continued learning, creating their own opportunities and making their own educational spaces in their households.

Continuing education

Motivation for learning was driven by a number of factors: for many women from landed families it was their family and estate responsibilities, religious convictions, intellectual interests or music that led them to take the initiative either to continue reading and writing in solitude or to forge informal networks. At all educational levels, a combination of personal initiative and social and economic circumstances explains how most women moved from the standard of writing competence they reached at the end of the period of their schooling to the level they practised as adults. There must have been some women at the beginners' level who, because they lacked opportunities to practise, lost the skills they had learned in their lessons. This pattern has been found across a number of contemporary literacy schemes, including that in Kerala in Southern India.

The country houses built by the landed classes in early modern England provided women with educational spaces for themselves, their families and their servants. For instance, at the end of the sixteenth century, Mary Sidney Herbert, Countess of Pembroke, was at the centre of literary and scientific activities involving both women and men who gathered round her at Wilton House, near Salisbury. She was herself a strong influence on her niece Mary Wroth (1587–c.1653), who spent time at Wilton. While she initially enjoyed court life and performed in masques by Inigo Jones and Ben Jonson from 1604, Wroth's life changed on the death of her husband in 1616. It is thought that she may have started writing for publication in order to pay off some of the considerable debts he left on his death. Margaret Cavendish, Duchess of Newcastle, living with her husband in exile in the Rubens House in Antwerp between 1648 and 1660, engaged with visiting scholars and used the time to write prolifically. Then and later on her return to England, Cavendish was part of an intellectual circle which embraced scientific as well as literary studies. Lady Ranelagh's house in Pall Mall in the 1640s has been described as the nearest equivalent in England to a Parisian aristocratic ladies' intellectual salon. Lady Ranelagh was not formally educated but was close to her brother (Robert Boyle) who was, and she is described in the *Oxford Dictionary of National Biography* as a leading woman intellectual of her day. Lady Ranelagh was part of the Hartlib circle and a proponent of girls' education. As well as carrying out experiments herself, her house was a centre for new science and her brother built a laboratory there in 1676. In rather different circumstances, women from a less exalted social background played a central role in the intellectual pursuits of the religious community founded by Nicholas Ferrar at Little Gidding that was active 1625–57, contributing to the concordances and the records of the meetings that were held. In the situations outlined here, we have women who can be described as autodidacts: they clearly advanced their own education beyond that which was provided by their parents, seizing and even creating opportunities to follow their intellectual interests.

An interest in learning could also be a more solitary preoccupation for women with closets or private chambers serving as spaces for study or work, particularly in houses built from the latter part of the sixteenth century. Evidence for this comes from a number of sources: for example, the painting of Mary Neville, Lady Dacre, seated at her desk with quill pen in hand, is one of a handful of images of women engaged in the act of writing. The professional scribe Esther Inglis (as discussed in the Introduction to this volume) depicts herself in the act of writing in a number of her works. A full-length painting by an unknown artist shows Lady Grace Mildmay with her hand on her open manuscripts on a table, with a quill ready for use in an ink pot. Some inventories give clues as to the presence of women's closets, although books are rarely listed as part of the contents. One of the most spectacular of these rooms must be the painted closet of Lady Anne Drury at Hawstead Place in Suffolk. The panels, illustrating a series of inspirational emblems and mottos, were possibly painted by Lady Anne herself before 1610. However, any room in the house could be a learning space. According to her daughter's biography, Elizabeth Cary, Lady Falkland, was a true autodidact, having taught herself a number of languages, including Latin, when she was a child. As a young bride, she was sent to live with her mother-in-law, who seems to have disapproved of her and confined her to an upstairs room without any books. Cary turned it into an educational space by using the opportunity to write poetry.[14]

Still-rooms (rooms in which stills were kept for the distillation of perfumes and cordials) and kitchens were also transformed into educational spaces. Here women practised and developed skills learned earlier and trained others to prepare the herbs and distillations for medicines used in the household and the local area. Numerous recipe collections testify to the existence of female networks of knowledge exchange. Besides the well-known practices of Lady Grace Mildmay and Lady Margaret Hoby are many others, including those carried out in the household of Mary, Countess of Shrewsbury. Two of the Countess's daughters, Aletheia Talbot and Elizabeth Grey, were responsible for the publication of important books of household science in the mid seventeenth century: *Natura Exenterata* (1655) and *A Choice Manual of Rare and Select Secrets* (1653) respectively.

Explanations of motives for learning are given in many funeral sermons. Although these cannot be considered unbiased sources, such sermons illustrate some of the factors driving women to continue learning. Women of the landed classes with servants had time, and for some, book learning was part of their responsibilities in the household, either teaching children or encouraging the servants to learn. Both Lady Margaret Hoby and Lady Anne Clifford refer to reading with their servants and annotating the books; Elizabeth Isham, who remained unmarried, taught her brother's daughters. Some women inscribed their books with family details, comments on receipts, reflections on particular passages or simply their names.[15] In these volumes, we have evidence of the interaction between individual and text and of continuing reinforcement of writing skills. Other women drew on the family book collections to compile miscellanies and commonplace books. Support for women's writing activities was provided by a range of manuals available to individuals in increasing numbers in the seventeenth century, including Clement's *Petie Schole* (first published 1576), Coote's *English School-master* (1596) and Billingsley's *The Pen's Excellencie* (1618). None of these manuals was suitable for beginners, but they could serve to underpin lessons initially learned from tutors or parents; once girls could read, they had access to these books for themselves.[16]

As I have already suggested, religious piety provided a powerful motivation for many women to continue their practice of writing. Piety led some women to translate texts of considerable length or write commentaries on biblical and other religious texts. According to John Mush her biographer, Margaret Clitherow, a Catholic convert who was executed in York for failing to plead her case, viewed her time in prison as a school. Clitherow learned to read English and developed a written hand during her three periods of imprisonment in York Castle between 1577 and her execution in 1586. Writing skills are evident in the copious sermon notes made by Protestant women, including Lucy Hastings, Countess of Huntingdon. Hester Biddle and Sarah Cheevers were among many Quaker women writing pamphlets, preaching sermons in public and travelling on behalf of the movement. Mary Percy was the first of many English nuns who translated or compiled works for the libraries of the newly founded convents; her translation of the *Abridgment of Christian Perfection* was printed in 1612. Other women, such as Elizabeth Grymeston, were driven by a sense of maternal responsibility to write moral instructions for their children in case of their own death. The 'educational' spaces occupied by these women thus range from a prison cell, a church during Sunday worship and Quaker meeting houses to an enclosed Benedictine convent in Brussels. This diversity emphasizes the importance of considering individual motivation for women who wrote in spite of repeated advice that they should be if not silent at least circumspect and modest.

The English convents were educational spaces for Catholic women: here the educational skills of potential members were developed, new members were initiated into the religious practices of the convent, extensive libraries were built up and records were kept. Detailed records were very important in creating a sense of identity and community: the copying of lengthy biographies of founders, exemplary lives, conventual annals and rules placed writing at the centre of daily life, alongside reading and the performance of the office. Although these institutions created in exile served a minority religious group, they are important when considering female intellectual culture in early modern England. More than 2,500 English women became members of enclosed convents between 1600 and 1700, and, in addition, there were many who joined the Mary Ward Sisters and lived unenclosed. As well as serving their members, convents also affected the lives of the girls who attended their schools, the laywomen who retired to live in their buildings, the locals and English visitors who attended their services and provided patronage. Published books generated by the convents spread their influence further afield.

Conclusion

This chapter has argued that much, possibly most, of girls' education in early modern England took place outside formal educational spaces with the result that many women were largely self-taught. Basing our approach on the research methodology built up over a number of years by educationists and sociologists evaluating current literacy schemes in developing countries, we can better understand the way that individual determination drove many women, after initial teaching, to continue to improve their writing skills on their own. We must look over a wide canvas for educational spaces. This chapter has only been able to scratch the surface of the argument, but I hope that it provides guidance to enable readers to look out for themselves and find many more early modern English women in educational spaces.

NOTES

1. Huntington Library, San Marino, CA, Hastings Papers, HAF Box 20 Folder 32. I am grateful to the Huntington Library for granting the Fellowship which led to the finding of these documents, thus originating the arguments discussed here.

2. Surveys of current research can be found in Kenneth Charlton, 'Women and Education', in Anita Pacheco (ed.), *Companion to Early Modern Women's Writing* (Oxford: Blackwell, 2002); Kenneth Charlton and Margaret Spufford, 'Literacy, Society and Education', in David Loewenstein and Janel Mueller (eds.), *The Cambridge History of Early Modern English Literature* (Cambridge: Cambridge University Press, 2002), pp. 15–54.

3. For a study of the importance of informal education see Thomas Laqueur, 'The Cultural Origins of Popular Literacy in England 1500–1850', *Oxford Review of Education* 2.3 (1976), 255–75. On women's handwriting, see Heather Wolfe's chapter in this volume.

4. See, for example, *Report of Evaluation of the Functional Adult Literacy Programme in Uganda* (Kampala: Ministry of Gender, Labour and Social Development, 1999); Krystyna Chlebowska, *Knowing and Doing: Literacy for Women* (Paris: UNESCO, 1992); Polly Driven, 'Women and Nonformal Education in West Africa: Policy and Practice', in Marianne Bloch *et al.* (eds.), *Women and Education in Sub-Saharan Africa* (Boulder, CO: Lynne Rienner Publishers, 1998), pp. 83–95. For an English account of a contemporary self-taught woman (Rose Stripp Williams), see Yvonne Roberts, 'The Plot Thickens', *The Guardian,* 15 February 1999.

5. G. Sambasiva Rao (ed.), *Problems of Women's Literacy* (Mysore: Central Institute of Indian Languages, 1979), p. 143.

6. This approach to understanding women's education in early modern England builds on the work of other historians who have already studied countries where widespread literacy was gained outside formal schooling. For instance, the Swedish historian of education Egil Johansson, who studied the literacy campaign in Sweden from the end of the seventeenth century, argued that the majority of the population learned to read scriptures almost entirely without the use of schools. See Johansson, 'Literacy Campaigns in Sweden', in Robert F. Arnove and Harvey J. Graff (eds.), *National Literacy Campaigns: Historical and Comparative Perspectives* (New York and London: Plenum Press, 1987), pp. 65–98. Similarly, Egil Eklof has argued that in pre-1917 Russia most peasants learned to read and write outside the formal school system. Eklof quoted in editors' Introduction to *ibid.*, p. 13.

7. Huntington Library, Hastings MSS, Box 21, Folder 2 and Box 22, Folder 25.

8. Victoria Burke, 'Ann Bowyer's Commonplace Book (Bodleian Library Ashmole MS 51): Reading and Writing Among the "Middling Sort"', *Early Modern Literary Studies* 6.3 (January 2001), 1–28.

9. Jay Anglin, *The Third University: A Survey of Schools and Schoolmasters in the Elizabethan Diocese of London* (Norwood, PA: Norwood Editions, 1985).

10. Emily Bowles Smith, ' "Let them Compleately Learn": Manuscript Clues About Early Modern Women's Educational Practices', www.folger.edu/html/folger_institute/mm/EssaysES.html accessed 7 January 2008.

11. See Caroline Bowden, 'Community Space and Cultural Transmission: Formation and Schooling in English Enclosed Convents in the Seventeenth Century', *History of Education* 34.4 (July 2005), 365–86.

12. Caroline Bowden, 'Education for Authorship?' in Victoria Burke (ed.), *Early Modern Women's Manuscript Writing* (Aldershot: Ashgate, 2004), pp. 157–80.

13. Nicky Hallett, *Lives of Spirit: English Carmelite Self-Writing of the Early Modern Period* (Aldershot: Ashgate, 2007), p. 13.

14. Heather Wolfe (ed.), *Elizabeth Cary, Lady Falkland: Life and Letters* (Cambridge, MA: RTM Publications, 2001), p. 109.

15. See Heidi Brayman Hackel, *Reading Material in Early Modern England: Print, Gender, and Literacy* (Cambridge: Cambridge University Press, 2005) and Edith Snook, *Women, Reading, and the Cultural Politics of Early Modern England* (Aldershot: Ashgate, 2005). See also Snook's chapter in this volume.

16. On writing manuals, see also Heather Wolfe's chapter in this volume.

READING LIST

Charlton, Kenneth. *Women, Religion and Education in Early Modern England.* London: Routledge, 1999.

Daybell, James. 'Interpreting Letters and Reading Script: Evidence for Female Education and Literacy in Tudor England'. *History of Education* 34.6 (November 2005), 695–715.

Gray, W. S. *The Teaching of Reading and Writing.* Paris: UNESCO, 2nd edn, 1969.

Hunter, Lynette and Sarah Hutton (eds.). *Women, Science and Medicine 1500–1700.* Stroud: Sutton Publishing, 1997.

Lindmark, Daniel (ed.). *Alphabeta Varia: Orality, Reading and Writing in the History of Literacy.* Umea, Sweden: Umea University, 1998.

Walker, Claire. *Gender and Politics in Early Modern Europe: English Convents in France and the Low Countries.* Basingstoke: Palgrave, 2003.

6

WENDY WALL

Women in the household

Opening a seventeenth-century manuscript recipe collection, I discover a book given to Anne Dewes by her mother Mary Granville upon the occasion of Anne's marriage to John Dewes. Scrawled in different hands are typically miscellaneous recipes: 'To make one sleep', 'For a sore breast', 'To boil a haunch of venison', 'To make Bread', 'To Make an Admirable good water against Melancholy', 'The Manner of distilling a water of honey', 'To preserve walnuts', 'To boile a capon larded with lemons', 'To make a syrip of Gillflowres', 'To cleane teeth well', 'To Make a cake Mrs Margaret Melbourns Way'. Nestled among these culinary, household and medical recipes (or 'receipts', as they were called) is one that surprises me: 'To Make Inke, Verie good'.[1] As housewives preserved fruits, concocted curatives and created cakes, they apparently also made ink from rainwater, vinegar gum, copperas (the proto-sulphate of iron) and oakgalls (an excrescence produced by insects on trees, used as a dye). Granville's text includes, in fact, three different ink recipes. Lest we think her tastes idiosyncratic, we might consider that published recipe books also included different ways of making ink, including invisible ink.[2] The materials of writing could be, it seems, conceptualized as part of early modern household production.

In one of her popular manuals, *The Gentlewomans Companion* (1673), Hannah Woolley, in fact, imagines writing as a household art. Directing governesses how to teach girls, Woolley classifies needlework as a 'practice' of the 'pen' and groups writing alongside preserving and distilling:

> Having qualified them for reading, you should so practice them in their pen, as not to be ignorant in a *Point de Venice*, and all the Productions of the Needle, with all the curious devices of *Wax-work*, *Rock-work*, *Moss-work*, *Cabinet Work*, *Bengle-work*, &c. and in due time let them know how to Preserve, Conserve, Distill; with all those laudible Sciences which adorn a compleat Gentlewoman.[3]

Practising with a pen enables girls to undertake decorative crafts such as 'rock-work', which was a sewing stitch, but also a collage made out of pebbles. For Woolley, writing is a manual skill fundamental to the 'laudible Sciences' of housewifery (*Gentlewomans Companion*, p. 9). Instructions on how to form good letters thus are positioned alongside advice on roasting carps, candying flowers, curing eye sores and distilling wine.

Even housewives who did not make ink or write undertook tasks that can be seen as intellectual production, work that might shed light on contradictions in early modern ideologies of gender. In *Othello*, Iago quips that women are 'Players in [their] huswifery and huswives in [their] beds'.[4] Playing on the double meaning of 'housewife,' Iago misogynistically suggests that every industrious housewife masks an inner hussy. The problem signified lexically by the word 'housewife' touched on a general problem: although the early modern household was ideally meant to solidify social and gender norms, it was also a space of considerable authority, anxiety and fantasy for its residents. By considering practices in the home as well as 'writing' in and around the household, this chapter seeks to make sense of the dual nature of housewifery. Focusing particularly on carving and confectionary, I ask questions designed to remind students of the historically distinctive and textured contours of pre-industrial European domesticity: how could rituals of the *domus* express – but also scrutinize – idealized social relations? How did home practices and representations allow the negotiation of identity and authority? How were the circulation of manuscripts and printed guides implicated in domestic life?

Can you carve for yourself?

In Shakespeare's *Merry Wives of Windsor*, the mischievous Falstaff contemplates seducing Mistress Ford in order to replenish his depleted coffers. He is drawn to her in part because he sees her glances and speeches as indicating her availability: 'She discourses, she carves, she gives the leer of invitation' (1.3.45–6). It is somewhat unexpected to a modern reader to hear that Mistress Ford's ability to 'carve' is seen as sexy. What does Falstaff mean?

As they gloss 'carve' in this passage to mean a general sociality, editors signal their uncertainty as to its exact definition. The Riverside editors wonder if 'carve' means 'shows courtesy (?) or speaks affectedly (?)'; the *Norton Shakespeare*'s gloss is also hesitant: 'is courteous?' The Arden editor speculates that carving might be seen as an aphrodisiac because it could involve a curious wiggling of the finger at the table, a 'digitary ogle'.[5] Carving certainly denoted the simple task of cutting and serving meat at the table. But it seems to have become a synonym for being hospitable, a meaning susceptible to sexual innuendo in part because the gracious hostess was to apportion meat generously, showing attentiveness to her guests' needs and their status.

Yet to Falstaff's mind, carving involves an expressive agency much like discoursing. While we might imagine this to be Falstaff's peculiar view, it is also evident in Laertes's description of Hamlet to Ophelia: 'He may not, as unvalued persons do, / Carve for himself' (*Hamlet*, 1.3.19–20). Carving indicates freedom of choice. As Woolley indicates in *The Gentlewomans Companion*, it is a social action that tests the manners of both agent and recipient: 'If you be carved with any thing ... which you do not like, conceal ... your repugnancies', she warns (p. 70). Mistress Ford's right to allocate food and to discriminate amongst guests bespeaks an authority extending out of the literal task of cutting. While medieval manuscripts routinely assign carving to male servants in noble households, printed English household manuals *c.* 1600 locate this affect-laden act as part of the middling-class housewife's repertoire.

Early modern English domestic guides suggest that carving should be orderly. 'A *Pig* must be chined down the Back, the Head being cut off fair, the Ears laid upon the Shoulders, and the Jaws by the front; the Ears by Ladies being accounted best', one text advises.[6] Carving is an 'Anatomical Art', which, according to *The Genteel House-keepers Pastime*, 'teaches its Practitioners to know the Dissection of Parts, the scituation of Joynts and Ligaments, and the true position of the ... eminent Muscles. Nor does it shut out the most excellent Sciences of Arithmetick and Geometry: for the skillful Carver knows how to ... dispose the best of Delicacies to the most eminent Persons.'[7] Classified as a learned 'pastime', carving, whether for the servant or mistress, straddles the line between physical craft and social knowledge. In its demand for precise manoeuvring and a fine-tuned sense of decorum, carving is part of the history of manners.

Yet the figure of the woman with a knife in her hand is treated with some anxiety in the period, for housewives were not only to carve decorously at the table but also to hack animals as part of butchery. The language of household guides is graphic: '[Y]ou shall crush and breake the bones well, from Pigges and Rabbets you shall cut off the feete before you spit them, and the heads when you serve them to table', directs Gervase Markham in *The English Housewife*.[8] One book of secrets offers this recipe: 'Take a great fatt Capon that is well fleshed, and pull it while it is alive, and take forthe onely the guttes and the bellie, and when he is dead, stampt it in a Morter grostly.'[9] The violence of kitchen work is shown as well in the daintily written manuscript book of Anne Bankes (Lady Borlase), which includes a recipe requiring that the reader bludgeon young moles without killing them. She advises: 'Cutt the throats of them whilst alive & Let them bleed on a puter Dish or Plate as much as you can make them, then rip up the Bellies & take out the Lungs gutts Young anes & all the Inards Blood & all', finally grinding the baked organs into a powder.[10] The crushing of animals' bodies as part of medical and cookery recipes reveals the flipside of decorous carving.

Because curatives were interlaced with culinary recipes in the period, the figure of the human body often hovers near the scene of kitchen carnage. Many cures require the housewife to act on human flesh, scarifying wounds and piercing sites of infection. In this sense, the housewife's anatomical knowledge extended from butchery to physic. Elsewhere in this volume, Mary Fissell discusses the work of female medical practitioners; for my purposes, it is sufficient to note that household guides sometimes call upon the imagery of 'flesh' in a way that links carving to healing. This linkage is evident in literary texts that present characters who are frightened about being chopped and cooked into homely stews, jellies and broths.[11]

Carving also surfaces as potentially powerful in its capacity to serve as a lexicon for the housewife to master. The 'proper terms for carving', as they came be known, were outlined in early texts written for servants such as the 1508 *Boke of Carving*, and then assigned to the housewife when reprinted in guides such as Thomas Dawson's 1597 *The Second Part of the Good Huswives Jewell* and John Murrell's 1638 *Two Books of Cookery and Carving*.[12] In *The Accomplisht Ladys Delight*, Woolley acknowledges how common this vocabulary has become: 'Because many Books of this Nature have the Terms of Carving added to them, as being necessary for the more proper Nominating of things; I have thought good also to add them.'[13] 'Proper Nominating' was fairly extensive, Woolley explains: 'In cutting up all small Birds it is proper to say thigh them, as thigh that Woodcock, thigh that Pigeon':

> But as to others say, mince that Plover, wing that Quail ... Allay that Pheasant, untack that Curlew, unjoynt that Bittern, disfigure that Peacock, display that Crane, dismember that Hern, unbrace that Mallard ... spoyl that Hen, sawce that Capon, lift that Swan, reer that Goose ... unlace that Coney, break that Deer, leach that Brawn ... splat that Pike ... tame that Crab, barb that Lobster, &c.[14]

Terms such as 'thigh', 'mince' and 'unjoynt' join with less specifically culinary words, such as 'disfigure', 'dismember', 'break' and 'spoyl', before wandering into exotic injunctions to 'reer', 'splat', 'splay', 'tusk' and 'barb' animals. The sheer copiousness of Woolley's language practice stands out on the page, in over thirty-five vivid verbs. The decorum supposedly established by proper manners takes on an almost maniacal fervour, as the carver enacts a stylized verbal performance of different ways to dismember and display flesh. This tutorial locates an autoptic vision of early modern culture – the epistemological drive to dissect and master the body – specifically within the confines of daily work.[15] It is no wonder that Falstaff associates carving with emotionally charged discoursing.

Readers might have made connections between carving and a ruled flirtation, as does a lover in a poem by Richard Brome, who declares his dissatisfaction with the niceties of courtship:

> I neither know, nor love to play
> And fool my time away:
> Nor talk in *Dialects* to please your *fancy*:
> Nor *carve* the *Capon* or the *Quaile*
> But *hew* it through from *head* to *tail*.[16]

While frivolous lovers delicately carve, this speaker reveals true passion by ripping apart poultry without respect for coy rituals. Brome's text is in keeping with the *Art of Courtship*, whose title page boasts that it includes 'Amorous dialogues, Complemental Expressions, Poems Letters, Discourses upon sundry occasions ... directions for courtship and behavior; And rules for carving of Flesh, Fish, Fowls and cutting up Pastry'. Carving, classified with the 'amorous dialogues' of flirtation, hints at appetites that are almost ordered – but not quite. It materializes a social being who has the power to display the unruliness that manners were meant to harness.

Falstaff's suggestion that Mistress Ford has stepped across the line separating hospitality from lewdness is echoed in ubiquitous puns in the period on carving as castration or flirtation. Her 'digitary ogling' smacks of something threateningly alluring, a trait extending out of her role as a merry housewife. At issue, in the text and in practice, were cultural fantasies about gender, particularly the way that the expression of proper decorum invited their imagined violation. The housewife was always potentially a huswife because, in part, she wielded the knife as part of her duty to serve.

Edible art

In Ben Jonson's *The Staple of News*, Lickfinger pronounces that cooking and serving depend on an expansive knowledge of astronomy, military strategy, chemistry, engineering, philosophy, architecture and poetry. 'A Boyler,

Range, and Dresser were the *Fountaines* / Of all the knowledge in the *universe*', he declares, as he waxes rhapsodic about the cook's role as creator:

> A *Master-Cooke*! Why, he's the *man* o' men,
> For a *Professor*! he designes, he drawes,
> He paints, he carves, he builds, he fortifies,
> Makes *Citadels* of curious fowle and fish.
> Some he *dri-dishes*, some *motes* round with *broths*.
> Mounts *marrowbones*, cuts *fifty angled custards*.[17]

Lickfinger's praise for the chef as a maker of worlds reminds us that proximate to the meaning of 'carving' as cutting is that of creating an artistic or graphic design. 'Cutwork' was, in fact, a term used to describe openwork embroidery designs or appliqué pattern work.[18] Housewives as well as professional chefs used 'carved moulds' to create designed edibles, much like the artistic 'fowle and fish' that Lickfinger admires. Confections such as Lady Borlase's 'To make paste for a lace tart or to make Little Cakes cut in works' (*Receiptes Booke*, p. 65) were among the most popular subjects found in early modern recipe books. Working with sugar plate and almond-based marzipan, housewives were invited to cut and to print novel 'conceits'.

John Partridge's 1573 *Treasurie of Commodious Conceites*, debuting as the first printed cookbook in England written for women, sought a class-conscious readership interested in imitating less costly forms of the banqueting dishes (as desserts were termed) presented at court or in great households. Marzipan could supply the material for making witty simulacra of the world, seen, for instance, when Partridge directs:

> Take and cut your leafe of golde, as it lieth upon the booke, into square peeces like Dice, & with a Conies tailes end moysted a little, take the golde up by the one corner, lay it on the place being first made moyste, and with another tayle of a Conie dry presse the golde down close. And if ye will have the forme of an Harte, or the name of Jesus, or any other thing whatsoever: cut the same through a peece of paper, and lay the Paper upon your Marchpane, or Tart: then make the voide place of the Paper … moyste with Rosewater, laye on your golde, presse it downe, take off your Paper, and there remaineth behinde in golde the Print cut in the saide paper.[19]

Mixing sugar paste and cutting gold leaf, the housewife could create a tart shaped as an animal or marked with the 'name of Jesus', recipes which require that the reader have a book and paper to stencil words and designs. As in other guidebooks, the reader is encouraged to copy or write poems in and on food, and to 'cut' and 'print' sugar images or words in the kitchen.[20]

Hugh Plat's *Delights for Ladies* trades specifically on the estranging inventiveness of confectionery. In one recipe, 'A most delicate and stiffe sugar past whereof to cast Rabbets, Pigeons, or any other little birde or beast, either from the life or carved molds', Plat teaches readers to shape isinglass (material from fish) into a glutinous jelly paste and then pour it into carved moulds.[21] In order to make the animal look like a savoury dish rather than a live creature or dessert, the housewife can dredge it with a bread crust mixture so that 'a banquet may be presented in the forme of a supper' (B4[r]). Dessert thus can mark a return of the chicken already consumed. The act of eating similarly becomes performance art when guests are served marzipan plates, saucers, dishes and bowls (B7[r]). After eating a tart, a person might consume the surface on which food was served. In mimicking earlier courses, such conceits might make diners self-conscious about the social rituals and materials of eating. Similarly, other items in Plat's *Delights*, such as marzipan letters, knots, castles, arms and escutcheons, were popular subjects in kitchen art (B9[v]). Creating tasty alphabets to be arranged as monograms, or presenting an edible family coat of arms (the escutcheon), women fashioned and parodied markers of gentility.

Plat goes so far as to write a mock epic prefatory poem to *Delights for Ladies*, where he champions the housewife's ingenuity in using 'compoundes of arte' to rival the natural world:

> I teach both fruits and flowers to preserve,
> And candie them, so Nutmegs, cloves, and mace:
> To make both marchpaine, paste, and sugred plate,
> And cast the same in formes of sweetest grace.
> Each bird and foule, so moulded from the life,
> And after cast in sweet compounds of arte,
> As if the flesh and forme which Nature gave,
> Did still remaine in every lim and part.   (A2[v]–A3[r])

In Plat's language, marzipan chickens bear natural complexions that 'remaine' in every limb, as if the housewife reincarnates live animals when she makes desserts. The *trompe l'oeil* dimension of cooking and confectionery showed that it could parody the very categories and acts deemed essential to social life.

In a manuscript recipe book (*c.* 1610), Sarah Longe includes among her entries for possets, ales, tarts, preserves, boiled meats, puddings and cures a typical but inventive recipe for 'jumballs'. Longe's recipe calls for flour, sugar, eggs, cream, coriander and fennel seed. 'Worke all together well, then roll it into small rolls, and cast it into Knots', she writes.[22] Just as Longe cast biscuit dough into ornamental knots, Granville shaped marzipan into flowers dyed an array of colours.[23] In creating decorative chickens, edible letters, faux flowers or divinely marked cakes, early modern housewives demonstrated that domestic work could serve as something more than a form of female subjection. Rather than placing a premium on productive labour and naturalized hierarchies, these books grant practitioners the freedom to use their imaginations. Listen to one typical directive in a cookbook: 'Make thereof Pies, Birds, Fruits, Flowers, or any pretty things printed with Moulds, and ... use them at your pleasure'.[24] As she 'printed' and manipulated 'pretty' letters in her kitchen craft shop, the housewife was invited to re-imagine an idealized domestic space and its protocols.

As desserts imitating family crests reveal, confections could also mark social distinctions. Promising to deliver marmalades and tarts fit to beautify a nobleman's table, recipe books routinely advertised the cultural capital vested in domestic practices.[25] Some recipe books appeared with the trappings of literary texts, with prefatory poems and frontispieces. Others included celebrity recipes to appeal to readers eager to appear a lady or gentle person (for example, how 'To make a Conserve or Jellie of Quinces, after my Lady Gray Clements sort'[26]). Even aristocratic women signalled their knowledge of other ladies' household tips: Lady Borlase acquaints us with how Lady Fanshaw preserves pippins and how Lady Curson conserves oranges (*Receiptes Booke*, pp. 107, 108). These dishes marked one's inclusion in the world of countesses, queens and ladies.

Rather than emphasizing status, Gervase Markham's *English Housewife* locates housewifery as part of a national ethic uniting classes and regions. In an encyclopedic manual covering spinning, wool-making, brewing, wine-making and dairying, Markham fantasizes in *The English Housewife* that the English home can be insulated from professionalization and the market. He writes of the housewife's diet: 'Let it proceed more from the provision of her owne yarde, then the furniture of the markets; and let it be rather esteemed for the familiar acquaintance she hath with it, then for the strangenesse and raritie it bringeth from other Countries' (p. 4). Ignoring the possibility that native goods could be purchased at local fairs, Markham equates shopping with foreignness. By accentuating the wife's nationality (rather than her virtue), Markham hints of domestic labour's role in transmitting indigenous culture. He implies that all English people, regardless of class or region, share a set of domestic practices built on country frugality and thrift.

Yet Markham's text is riddled with contradictions. Some tasks that he assigns the housewife had already been taken over by professionals long before his book appeared in print. Kim Hall has also underscored the sleight of hand in works such as Markham's, which celebrate national insularity while relying on expensive imported ingredients. Hall argues that the housewife functioned figuratively to 'nationalize' goods by laundering foreign products into home-born forms.[27] Eschewing 'strange' foodstuffs, Markham's housewife expresses a particular fantasy of class and nation. But even Markham can't resist the occasional ornamental recipe designed purely for show. Domesticity might hold out the promise of ensuring morality, class status or Englishness, but it also enabled practitioners to mock the principles underwriting these categories.

Household 'writing'

As Juliet Fleming reminds us in her theorization of wall art, tattooing and engraved jewellery, early modern writing had an 'ostentatious materiality ... born of and bound in matter'.[28] In shaping almond paste into letters and in signalling status by carving meat, early modern women engaged in highly representational material acts. In this way, domestic practice constituted a form of writing (and here it might be instructive to remember that the Old English word 'carve' was held to be cognate with the Greek 'graf-ein', meaning 'to write'). Tasks such as carving and cookery were bound up with a fantasy life and with the manipulation of letters, much like the textile 'writing' that aristocratic women routinely undertook when they stitched alphabetic samplers and embroidered stories in household objects.[29]

For Woolley, the forming of letters was a logical extension of other domestic arts. She thus gives in *Compleat Servant Maid* detailed advice to girls on how to cut a quill with a penknife:

> Having a Penknife with a smooth, thin, sharp edge, take the first or second quill of a Goose wing and scrape it, then hold it in your left hand with the feather end from you, beginning even in the back, cut a small piece off sloping, then to make a slit enter the knife in the midst of the first cut, put in a quill and force it up, so far as you desire the slit should be in length ... and fashion the nib by cutting off both the sides equally down, then place the nib on the nail of your left hand thumb, and to end it draw the edge into it slanting and being half thorow turn the edge almost downright and cut it off. (p. 23)

Having carved a quill with these precise slices, the reader is taught the bodily control and attention to proportion that allow the girl to write, or 'cut' letters. Yet the pen-knife, as we have seen, came in handy for 'cutworks' of all kinds. In her recipe for making fruit cakes, Lady Borlase says of fruit tarts, 'turn them forth with a pen-knife uppon glass sheetes, & cut them into what fashion you please' (*Receiptes Booke*, p. 158). The tools used to enable writing (the goose quill made from the goose cooked for dinner, perhaps) double as the tools of domestic artistry.[30]

In addition to their work in housewifery, women such as Sarah Longe, Mary Baumfylde, Katherine Brown, Mary Granville, Elinor Fettiplace, Anne Bankes (Lady Borlase), Elizabeth Fowler, Susanna Pack and Jane Buckhurst collected recipes in books that were altered and transcribed by others as they circulated within the lively manuscript culture in and outside the home.[31] While painting a vivid picture of the pesticides, narcotics, hygiene products, foods and medicines common in domestic life, these texts also offer a peek at how household writing functioned. Mary Baumfylde's collection, which includes 'A secret quintessence' calling for opium and directions on how to decapitate a pig, accrued different signatures as it circulated to men and women, including 'Abraham Sommers' and 'Katherine Thatcher'. Sarah Longe's book, which offers instructions for preserving gooseberries, healing sore nipples and making 'Queen Elizabeth's fine cake', furnished the site on which she could display her autograph in ornamental penmanship. Longe's book ends with a beautifully penned index that classifies recipes according to type. Whoever wrote the index to another anonymous recipe book took it as an occasion to practise their letters while organizing the text. In forming sectional headers, he or she repeated each letter of the alphabet four times, with increasing elaboration. And Lady Margaret Hoby mentions that she listened to books read aloud as part of the 'Huswiffrie' that kept her busy.[32]

Other recipe collections emphasize the social networks informing domestic work. Jane Buckhurst records Lady Abergavenny's way of making a sack pudding, noting as well that her 'receipt for the yellow jaundice' is 'approved by Mrs. Rogers'. Concerned about her property in a world where texts circulate, Buckhurst writes on the flyleaf that if anyone finds her book, they should return it to her. Elinor Fettiplace left her recipe collection, written in different hands, to her niece and goddaughter, Ann Poole. And Lady Borlase, who apparently liked exotic almond 'flummeries' cut 'in the shape of Dice' (*Receiptes Booke*, p. 98), dutifully recorded: 'These receipts following are my mother's' (p. 86). As this list suggests, recipe books were bearers of memory, indicators of artful practices, occasions for signalling ways of reading and writing, and signs marking family and community networks. They were an intricate part of women's manuscript participation in the culture of early modern writing.[33]

Considering the full array of tasks done in the household as well as manuscript recipe collections widens the range of what counts as domestic writing. In carving pens from goose quills, shaping letters, scribbling poems in walnuts, concocting ink, reading cookery books and circulating handwritten recipes, women did deal domestically with the materials of writing.

They also expressed themselves through other non-written signifying practices sometimes imagined within the vocabulary of 'writing': carving, cutting, printing, impressing. In their roles as household managers and workers, women and servants were given licence to test various ideologies. As such, the home could become the site where the hussy as well as the housewife materialized simultaneously.

NOTES

1. Anne Dewes (née Granville), manuscript book at the Folger Library (v.a.30), p. 42.

2. John Partridge, *The Widdows Treasure* (London, 1595), B5v; *A Queens Delight, Or the Art of Preserving, Conserving and Candying*, appended to W. M., *The Queens Closet Opened* (London, 1655), pp. 270–1.

3. Hannah Woolley, *The Gentlewomans Companion* (London, 1673), p. 9. The authorship of this text is in dispute.

4. William Shakespeare, *Othello*, in *The Riverside Shakespeare*, ed. G. Blakemore Evans (Boston: Houghton Mifflin, 1974), 2.1.112. Unless specified otherwise, citations to Shakespearean texts will be to this edition.

5. *The Riverside Shakespeare*, ed. Evans, 1.3.45, note 45, p. 294. *The Norton Shakespeare*, ed. Stephen Greenblatt *et al.* (New York and London: Norton, 1997), 1.3.38, note p. 1241. Arden editor Harold Oliver raises the idea of the 'digitary ogle', a provocative display of the hand while carving at the table, only to dismiss it. See *The Merry Wives of Windsor*, ed. Harold J. Oliver (New York: Routledge, 1973), 1.3.42, note p. 23.

6. Anon., *The Art of Courtship* (London, 1686), B1v.

7. Anon., *The Genteel House-keepers Pastime: Or, the Mode of Carving at the Table* (London, 1693), pp. 4–5.

8. Gervase Markham, *The English Housewife* (London, 1623), part of 'Country Contentments', p. 85.

9. *A Compendium of the rationall Secretes of the worthie Knight and moste excellent Doctour of Physicke and Chirurgerie, Leonardo Phioravante Bolognese* (London, 1582), 3rd book, p. 59.

10. *Ladie Borlase's Receiptes Booke*, ed. David E. Schoonover (Iowa City: University of Iowa Press, 1998), p. 132. On the domestic torture of animals, see Patricia Fumerton, 'Introduction: A New New Historicism', in *Renaissance Culture and the Everyday* (Philadelphia: University of Pennsylvania Press, 1999), pp. 1–4.

11. For one example, see Francis Beaumont and John Fletcher, *The Nice Valour*, in *The Works of Mr. Francis Beaumont and Mr. John Fletcher*, 10 vols. (London: J. and R. Tonson and S. Draper, 1750), x: 326.

12. Thomas Dawson's *The Second Part of the Good Huswives Jewell* (London, 1597), irregular pagination, B2r–B3v; John Murrell's *Two Books of Cookery and Carving* (London, 1638), pp. 151–2.

13. Hannah Woolley, *The Accomplisht Ladys Delight* (London, 1675), p. 369.

14. Hannah Woolley, *The Compleat Servant Maid* (London, 1683), p. 35.

15. See Jonathan Sawday, *The Body Emblazoned* (New York: Routledge, 1995), pp. 1–15.

16. Richard Brome, 'Reasons of Love', in *Songs and Other Poems* (London, 1661), p. 23.

17. Ben Jonson, *The Staple of News* (London, 1625), 4.2.19–22, p. 52.

18. *OED* II. 5a, 6a, 6b, 7.

19. John Partridge, *Treasurie of Commodious Conceites, and hidden Secrets* (London, 1573; 1584), A7r.

20. See, for example, anon, *A Closet for Ladies and Gentlewomen* (London, 1608), pp. 30–8.

21. Hugh Plat, *Delights for Ladies* (London, 1602), B3v.

22. 'Mrs Sarah Longe her receipt book' (*c.* 1610). The Folger Library (v.a.425), p. 45.

23. Anne Dewes, recipe book, p. 50.

24. M. B. (or Lord Ruthven), *The Ladies Cabinet Enlarged* (London, 1655), p. 30.

25. See the title page to John Murrell, *A New Booke of Cookerie* in *Two Books of Cookery and Carving* (London, 1638).

26. John Partridge, *Treasurie* (London, 1627), B4v.

27. Kim Hall, 'Culinary Spaces, Colonial Spaces: The Gendering of Sugar in the Seventeenth Century', in Valerie Traub, M. Lindsey Kaplan and Dympna Callaghan (eds.), *Feminist Readings of Early Modern Culture: Emerging Subjects* (Cambridge: Cambridge University Press, 1996), pp. 168–90. See also the now classic work by Sidney W. Mintz, *Sweetness and Power: The Place of Sugar in Modern History* (New York: Viking, 1985).

28. Juliet Fleming, *Graffiti and the Writing Arts of Early Modern England* (Philadelphia: University of Pennsylvania Press, 2001), p. 13.

29. See Ann Rosalind Jones and Peter Stallybrass, *Renaissance Clothing and the Materials of Memory* (Cambridge: Cambridge University Press, 2000), pp. 134–71; Susan Frye, 'Sewing Connections: Elizabeth Tudor, Mary Stuart, Elizabeth Talbot, and Seventeenth-Century Anonymous Needleworkers', in Susan Frye and Karen Robertson (eds.), *Maids and Mistresses, Cousins and Queens: Women's Alliances in Early Modern England* (New York: Oxford University Press, 1999), pp. 165–82.

30. On the materials of writing, see also the chapter by Heather Wolfe in this volume.

31. See recipe books by Mary Baumfyld (v.a.456), Sarah Longe (v.a.425), Jane Burkhurst (v.a7), Katherine Brown (v.a397) and the anonymous v.a.19 in The Folger Library. See also *Elinor Fettiplace's Receipt Book*, ed. Hilary Spurling (London: Viking, 1986).

32. *Diary of Lady Margaret Hoby, 1599–1605*, ed. Dorothy M. Meads (Boston and New York: Houghton Mifflin Co., 1930), p. 109.

33. Margaret Ezell, *The Patriarch's Wife: Literary Evidence and the History of the Family* (Chapel Hill and London: University of North Carolina Press, 1987), pp. 36–61; Ezell, *Social Authorship and the Advent of Print* (Baltimore, MD, and London: Johns Hopkins Press, 1999), esp. pp. 210–44. Before Hannah Woolley's late seventeenth-century recipe books, the only female-authored publications that might be classified as domestic were mother's advice books. See Sylvia

Brown (ed.), *Women's Writing in Stuart England: The Mothers' Legacies of Dorothy Leigh, Elizabeth Josceline and Elizabeth Richardson* (Thrupp, Stroud, Gloucestershire: Sutton Publishing, 1999).

READING LIST

Hall, Kim. 'Culinary Spaces, Colonial Spaces: The Gendering of Sugar in the Seventeenth Century'. In Valerie Traub, M. Lindsey Kaplan and Dympna Callaghan (eds.), *Feminist Readings of Early Modern Culture: Emerging Subjects*. Cambridge: Cambridge University Press, 1996, pp. 168–90.

Hobby, Elaine, 'A Woman's Best Setting Out is Silence: The Writings of Hannah Wolley'. In Gerald Maclean (ed.), *Culture and Society in the Stuart Restoration: Literature, Drama, History*. Cambridge: Cambridge University Press, 1995, pp. 179–200.

Lehmann, Gilly. *The British Housewife: Cookery Books, Cooking and Society in Eighteenth-Century Britain*. Blackawton, Devon: Prospect Books, 2003.

Pennell, Sara. '"Perfecting Practice": Women, Manuscript Recipes and Knowledge in Early Modern England'. In Victoria Burke and Jonathan Gibson (eds.), *Early Modern Women's Manuscript Writing: Selected Papers from the Trinity/Trent Colloquium*. Aldershot: Ashgate, 2004, pp. 237–58.

Wall, Wendy. *Staging Domesticity: Household Work and English Identity in Early Modern Drama*. Cambridge: Cambridge University Press, 2002.

7

ELIZABETH CLARKE

Women in church and in devotional spaces

The interaction between sacred space and sacred writing is a multifaceted one, especially in the seventeenth century when the nature of sacred space and the nature of sacred writing, particularly women's writing, are subject to so much change. The meaning of 'church' in the period under consideration is fought over in words and, occasionally, in battles. Sometimes, for women and for men, words take the place of physical buildings, and become a kind of sacred space in themselves – this can be true of books, particularly the Bible. However, throughout the early modern period there are examples of women writing prayers and devotions of the kind that could be used in the Church of England, from Elizabeth Tyrwhit's 1574 *Morning and Evening Prayer, with divers Psalmes, Himnes and Meditations*, included in Thomas Bentley's *The Monument of Matrones* (1582), to Elizabeth Percy's *Meditations and prayers to be used before, at, and after the receiving of the holy sacrament of the Lord's Supper* a century later. Such writing, anchored in the physical space of the Church of England, had a rather different significance in the late sixteenth century than it was to have in the late seventeenth century.

Elizabeth Tyrwhit's 1574 volume exists in a single, tiny, gilt girdle-book in the British Library, which may once have belonged to Elizabeth herself, and which is reminiscent of the way that Catholic Books of Hours, so popular with women until the Reformation, were seen as dress accessories.[1] This volume is at once intimate jewellery and political theology, from a woman closely associated with Catherine Parr: its contents are an individualistic adaptation of the Church of England liturgy. Thomas Bentley's compilation of female devotions features Elizabeth Tyrwhit alongside other women, such as Frances Abergavenny and Dorcas Martin, whose writing was not readily available in 1582. *The Second Lampe of Virginitie Containing Divers godlie Meditations, and Christian Praiers made by sundrie vertuous Queenes, and other devout and godlie women in our time* is one of seven 'Lampes' in the series that makes up *The Monument of Matrones*, and Patricia Brace claims that the individual voice of Elizabeth Tyrwhit is absorbed into the Order of Service of the Church of England thanks to the structural changes Bentley made to her work.[2] The fact that liturgical and individual prayer can so easily be merged perhaps indicates that at this date, church liturgy could speak for the individual woman.[3] Bentley's massive publication is conscious of its status as a document of state religion in Reformation England, particularly as it relates to women, and Queen Elizabeth has high prominence in the volumes of *The Monument of Matrones*, which are dedicated to her. The work is often careful to distinguish itself from Catholicism, and it celebrates martyrdom in the tradition of Foxe's *Actes and Monuments*, of which it is perhaps seen to be a women's version, nearly twenty years after Foxe's volume, so important to the church in England, appeared. Lest this should in any way be perceived as a legalistic and formal use of sacred space, whether in church or out of it, Bentley precedes all the prayers in the fourth 'Lampe' with a warning. These prayers are not intended 'nicelie, curiouslie or strictlie to you to observe hours, daies, feasts, times or seasons, bind you unlawfullie to an impossibilitie, as of necessitie to use all or everie of these praiers and meditations, in place, maner, and forme as they are set downe' (*Monument of Matrones*, sig. B3r). The implied enemy here is Catholicism, with the perceived formality that ties sacred words to time and place. As we shall see, this Reformed concern about the 'place, maner and forme' of sacred discourse, and its link with sacred spaces, was a cause of conflict over the next century.

Mary Sidney's poetic Psalm paraphrases are an important and strategic devotional work, which with the forty-three Psalms paraphrased by Philip Sidney before his death, constitute the famous manuscript, extant in eighteen copies, of the Sidney Psalter.[4] This is an élite production, one copy of which was presented to Queen Elizabeth, probably not designed for use in public worship. The interpretation of these Psalms is clearly in the Reformed tradition, based on the Geneva Bible and the Book of Common Prayer, and possibly many other Reformed sources which have been suggested for them.[5] The annotations to Psalm 84 in the Geneva Bible, which expresses a longing for the physical space of the House of God, identify the Old Testament 'Tabernacle of the Lord' with the distinctly New Testament, and Reformed, 'assembly of the Saintes'.[6] They point out that in the Old Testament only the priests were allowed into the Holy of Holies: not only is there no particularly holy place in the pre-Laudian Church of England forbidden to ordinary Christians, but there is also no distinction in Reformed theology between ministers and lay people. As Mary Sidney paraphrases it, Psalm 84 expresses a longing for the presence of God, imaged as God's house, as in the first stanza:

> How Lovely is Thy dwelling
> Great God in whom all greatness is belonging
> To view thy Courts, farr, farr from any telling
> My Soul doth long and pine with longing.[7]

In Sidney's choice of words and images there is a concrete sense of a real building: for example, her choice of metaphor in stanza 3 for the person who frequents the House of God, 'household man', is the sixteenth-century description of a servant in a Tudor house. A similar sense of devotion to the actual fabric of the temple is shown in Psalm 122:

> O what lively delight, O what a jollity
> This newes unto me brought newly delivered
> That Gods house ruined should be reedifyd
> And that shortly we should evry man enter it.   (Psalms, p. 163)

It is as necessary for the Reformed reader to interpret the Old Testament temple as the New Testament church as for the woman reader to include herself in the masculine noun here, but both manoeuvres were common-place. For Mary Sidney, although she is the last living spokesperson of the Dudley–Sidney alliance, which lobbied for decades for English support for Continental Protestantism against Catholic domination, there is as yet no fracture between the physical building of the church and the spiritual community of the saints.[8]

Publishing in a very limited way her sacred poem *Salve Deus Rex Judaeorum* in praise of an aristocratic group of women in 1611, Aemilia Lanyer appended a radical new verse form that combined a vivid description of physical space with a sense of the sacred. 'The Description of Cooke-ham' has been described as possibly the first country-house poem in English: like Jonson's *To Penshurst* it is a panegyric to the head of the house, the Countess of Cumberland, imagining the dependence of the estate on the physical presence of its aristocratic resident. However, this poem does not offer details of the house, but of the grounds, which are sacralized by the devotional activity going on there to the extent that Christ and his disciples are imagined as present with Margaret Clifford in a physical interaction of place and word:

> In these sweet woods how often did you walke,
> With Christ and his Apostles there to talke;
> Placing his holy Writ in some faire tree,
> To meditate what you did therein see.[9]

Meditation on the Holy Bible – and perhaps Aemilia Lanyer's poetry itself – is the mental space within which it is possible to give sacred experience a physical location: Jesus himself dwells with the Clifford women in this garden, and sacred buildings are not needed.

The *Monument of Matrones* had envisaged a physical movement from closet, that archetypal site for a woman's private devotion, to church and back again, with the spiritual activity of prayer linking the two sacred spaces, one for communal worship, and one for individual communion with God.[10] From the 1620s, a different attitude to holiness, prioritizing physical space, began to dominate the Church of England with the rise of William Laud (who became Archbishop of Canterbury in 1633). There were profound consequences for women's writing. A combination of reverence for sacred spaces, concern for set language and obedience to spiritual authority was typical of Laudianism in the 1630s, much to the discontent of traditional Puritans.[11] One woman whose autobiographical writing seems to chart a move from Puritan dislike of set prayers and church ceremonies to something more like a Laudian understanding of sacred space is Elizabeth Isham (1609–54), who was brought up in Puritan Northamptonshire, whose mother articulated Puritan theological attitudes and whose house was frequented by John Dod, the early Nonconformist and inveterate anti-Laudian whom Isham cannot help admiring. Writing in 1638 in a more polarized religious climate, Isham recalls childhood Christmases in nearby ancient Lamport church with some nostalgia, equating the materiality of celebrations in church, so beloved of Laudians, with the Puritan, spiritualized conception of building the church:

> I call to mind the knowledge that I had in these times, of our Lord and Saviour Jesus Christ, which I well remember by the celebration of his Feasts, and especially the feast of his Nativitie ... surely it is a good thing to rejoyce in these Feasts; and in the holydays which are keept in memory of the Apostles which are the foundation of the Church. Jesus Christ himselfe being the chiefe corner stone. in whom wee being members thereof groweth unto an holy Temple.[12]

For Isham, there is no conflict between the metaphorical and physical conceptions of sacred space, although she clearly is aware of the politico-religious struggle over such ideas that is just beginning. She asks to be forgiven for taking part in church ceremonies with music and vestments without fervently believing in their validity: however, Elizabeth Isham's willingness to question Puritan orthodoxies about sacred space is consonant with her embracing of Royalism during the civil war.

Devotion to physical space and poetic word is often explicitly political in the seventeenth century. Henrietta Maria, Charles I's Queen, opened a lavish new Catholic chapel designed by Inigo Jones in Somerset House in 1635, and encouraged the production of literature (admittedly not female-authored) at her court: Henry Hawkins's emblem book in praise of the Virgin Mary, *Partheneia Sacra* (1633), is an illuminating instance of the courtly combination of sacred word and physical space in book form. Elizabeth Richardson, Baroness of Cramond, was 'persuaded' to publish a collection of prayers in 1645 that is clearly meant to represent a reconstruction of Church of England practice in the face of a Westminster Assembly that had just abolished it.[13] Her set prayers are in direct opposition to the volume that was intended to replace the Prayer Book, *A directory for the publique worship of God* (1645), which was careful not to prescribe actual words of prayer even during the church service: *A directory* suggests subjects for prayer, but the minister 'is left to his liberty as God shall direct and inable him'.[14] Elizabeth Richardson is certainly not in favour of such extemporary prayer: 'When thou enterest into the house of God, take heed thou offerest not unto him the sacrifice of fooles, but before thou prayest, prepare thyself, thy heart and tongue.'[15] In her volume, the prescription of prayers to be said on 'first awaking' every morning and at various points during the day until last thing at night seems to be an attempt to control secular experience rather than the joyous permeation of Reformed devotion to all places and times of the Christian's life envisaged earlier in the early modern period.[16]

During the civil war period another Royalist woman, Lady Hester Pulter, wrote about being excluded from the church building. Pulter's period of spiritual isolation, perhaps from her local church in Cottered, Hertfordshire, which had a side chapel full of memorial engravings to her ancestors, coincides with a sense in her poetry that she is cooped up in her country house, Broadfield Hall. There are echoes of Psalm 84 in this poem, especially in the reference to the sparrow:

> Must I thus ever interdicted bee
> My Gracious God to thee and onely thee
> I will complain pardon and pitty mee
> Have I thy sacred Pledges took in vain
> Or heard thy Blessed word applaus to gain
> That thou dost thus thine Ordinances restrain
> If it bee soe thy mercy I implore
> To lay my sins upon my saviours score
> And mee unto thy Church again restore
> The wanton sparrow and the Chaster Dove
> Within thy sacred temple Freely move
> But I ay mee am kept from what I Love.

The sense of imprisonment and restraint is typical of much of Pulter's poetry, although here it is specifically lack of access to the 'sacred temple' that she laments. Pulter looks forward, in a manner characteristic of her poems, to free access to Heaven, that everlasting and secure sacred space. This sense of exclusion may be because the vicar of Cottered celebrated Communion in an unfamiliar and more Puritan manner, as his survival in post throughout the Interregnum indicates. Clearly, the church building is a sacred space that matters to Pulter: like the Laudians, she calls it a 'sacred temple'. Much of her poetry, for which she habitually uses epithets of liberation and enlargement, postdates the era when Pulter could find church attendance congenial, and she describes instead a mental space which seems to substitute for a place of Christian worship: Pulter finds God in the natural world, whether she is looking out at the stars, or examining the flowers in her garden. Confined to her bed with her fifteenth child at the age of forty-three she goes on a kind of astrological pilgrimage:

> Sad, sick and Lame as in my bed I Lay
> Least Pain and Passion should bear all the sway
> My thoughts beeing free I bid them take their flight.[17]

Pulter imagines the planets in a Copernican sequence – very advanced for 1648 – and rehearses their mythological significances, but it is all conceived within a Christian framework, and she is writing what she sees as Christian poetry. Pulter shows great powers of observation wherever she goes on her country estate, in her garden, examining her flowers, looking at the river, and uses the only freedom that she has – that of thought – to muse on the significance of everything she comes across in a Christian context. In this way she produces a blend of science and nature with the truths of the Christian religion that is unusual in this period: the denial of traditional sacred space leads Pulter to carve out a poetic realm that to some extent serves as a place for her to exercise devotion.

In the Interregnum, with Presbyterians controlling many Church of England buildings, including prestigious establishment cathedrals (although a wall was built in Exeter Cathedral to allow room for the Independent congregation to meet as well), it was clear that physical space was no longer presumed to be the primary site of spirituality. In the early years of the civil war, before their army acquired good discipline, Parliamentarian soldiers carried out unofficial acts of defilement in church buildings such as drinking, smoking and urinating as 'a defiant and dramatic illustration of the rejection of the idea that holiness could abide in any particular place'.[18] Hester Pulter of course was outraged at such behaviour, railing at those who turned the church into 'a stable and a stews'.[19] By the 1650s prestigious places of worship were available for use by more radical Protestants, as Independent Anne Venn, daughter of a famous Parliamentarian soldier, testifies; she attended Westminster Abbey in the 1650s. Venn's 1658 auto-biographical publication, *A wise virgins lamp burning*, is full of references to places, often coupled with the ministers she heard there. Place is fore-grounded in Venn's early struggle over whether to go to church or to carry out her devotions at home: the subtitle of her book, *Gods sweet incomes of love to a gracious soul waiting for him Being the experiences of Mrs. Anne Venn*, reveals the emphasis of radical sects on personal experience rather than public worship. The specificity of this document in terms of place and time (one particularly intense experience of God happened at Isaac Knight's house in Fulham, a week before the battle of Worcester) is not to do with a sense of sacred space, or the liturgical calendar: it is about providing a his-torical context in which the spiritual blessing took place, to give it a stronger sense of validity. Also important in this document is the power of the written word to lessen the impact of the sense of place, as when the nine-year-old Anne Venn uses the published sermons of John Dod to escape the ungodly atmosphere of the house in which she is living.

The proliferation of sects who worshipped outside of traditional church spaces further helped to delocalize the perception of the divine for a large part of the Christian community in mid to late seventeenth-century England. No longer was the physical church or the recited liturgy the anchor for orthodox spiritual experience, and during the Interregnum, particularly for women, the centre of the spiritual life was located elsewhere. A new literary form gave this new sense of religious life a textual, if not a physical, location. The spiritual journal, in which Reformed Christians, particularly women, recorded their devotional lives, was increasingly recommended to the faith-ful in the Interregnum.[20] Isaac Ambrose's popular epic of the Christian life, *Prima, Media, Ultima*, placed important emphasis on recording spiritual experience, offering excerpts from his own journal as educative illustration.[21] The 'Evidences' of salvation in such a spirituality are not in the sacraments taking place in the church building, but in experiences of God which could happen in any place and at any time: Ambrose replaces the ejaculations to be said on holy days and in holy spaces with meditations that can take place at any time in the everyday lives of a soldier, a tradesman, a farmer. According to Ambrose, even the minister performs his most important duties not in his church, but in his closet (*Prima, Media, Ultima*, p. 196). The recommended space for meditation is somewhere solitary, and preferably in the open air (p. 194). Mary Rich, Countess of Warwick, preferred the 'wilderness' in her garden as a place for communion with God, despite regularly frequent-ing both the local Episcopal church and the Nonconformist chapel. Rich's favourite biblical quotation is from Canticles 7:12, 'there will I give thee my loves'.[22] 'There' in the Song of Songs is the vineyard: for Mary Rich her special place is in her garden, her 'wilderness', where she spends many hours in communion with Christ. Rich's spiritual journal is a record of what happened there, and in any other place God spoke to her. The years after the Argyll rebellion, when Henrietta Lindsay's husband was fleeing from justice in Holland, and before his triumphant return with William of Orange, were clearly full of incident: Lindsay obliquely alludes to events in Windsor, London, Amsterdam and Rotterdam. However, the drama of her narrative is in her perception of Christ's absences and presences, a drama no doubt underlined for contemporary readers by their understanding of how spiritual favours interacted with temporal favours to make circumstances of place and time irrelevant. Lindsay's detailed journal charts every appearance of Christ to her, wherever it takes place. Here is her description of 'a hid enjoyment' that she experienced while visiting the court at The Hague in 1687: 'one half-hours access to the Son of God, who in the remotest corners of this earth and in the hardest circumstances than most of the world would think possible to bear up under, yet O quhat lot can he not sweeten and make delightsome, quhen his blessed countenance ... is felt and found in it'.[23]

In the Restoration, after the 1662 St Bartholomew's Day ejection of many Nonconformist ministers from their former church buildings, the Cavalier Parliament employed legislation to reinforce new definitions of sacred space. The Conventicle Act of 1664 forbade religious assemblies of more than five people outside Church of England buildings: the Five Mile Act in the following year banned clergymen from residing within five miles of churches from which they had been ejected. It is not surprising that an increasing number of Nonconformist sects developed an entirely different definition of sacred space. Margaret Fell Fox, in *A testimonie of the touch-stone*, expounds an elaborate spatial metaphor for the true church that is entirely spiritual:

> What ground have ye to build upon, when you know nothing of him, but what ye have from a profession without you? Oh consider seriously! and turn your minds to the light, which will let you see your foundation to be rotten and sandy: which ye foolish builders are building in your imaginations, Babel in the Air ... where is your foundation? where is your ground? where is your root, who denies the corner stone, the light Jesus Christ, the light and Rock of ages, which all the Prophets, and Apostles, and holy men of God is founded and built upon?[24]

Elsewhere Fell accuses the gathered churches of inventing sacred space: 'this sort ... *creeps into houses*, and calls them Churches, (when as the Apostle saith, the Church is in God)'.[25] In 1663–4, Fell is on trial in Lancaster and asked not to hold meetings in her house. In a time when the Church of England and its buildings are once again dominant, Fell makes her position clear:

> What dost thou call a Church the house or the people, the house ye all know is Wood and Stone, but if thou call the people a Church, to that I shall answer; as for the Church of *England* that now is, I was gathered unto the Lords truth, unto which I now stand a witness before this Church was a Church.[26]

In fact, for some women exclusion from church buildings marked their entry into authorship, as they justified themselves against accusations by male church leaders. Thus Susanna Parr, excommunicated from the tiny Independent church meeting at Exeter by Mr Stucley because of her attendance at the Presbyterian meeting, wrote *Susanna's apologie against the elders* in 1659. Twenty years later, Anne Wentworth was excommunicated by Hanserd Knollys from his Baptist church. Anne, who had prophetic leanings, produced several pamphlets in self-justification, including *A true account of Anne Wentworths being cruelly, unjustly, and unchristianly dealt with by some of those people called Anabaptists* (1676). For Fell, Parr and Wentworth, designated places for worship became suspect because of the way that male authority took charge of space, controlling who might enter there and who should speak there. Margaret Fell Fox's 1666 volume *Womens speaking justified, proved and allowed of by the Scriptures all such as speak by the spirit and power of the Lord Jesus* discredits all external authority and allows only the power of the Spirit and the verbal authority of the Bible, which may be conferred on women as well as men.

High Calvinist Lucy Hutchinson is one of the major religious authors of the period. Calvinism is not concerned with sacred buildings; Hutchinson's theological writing shows an interest in the location of the Holy Spirit in the human body, and how the human being can sense His presence with them, whatever their physical place. The climax of Hutchinson's writing, and the only part of it to be printed in the seventeenth century, is a poetic paraphrase of Genesis entitled *Order and Disorder*, five cantos of which were published anonymously in 1679.[27] The poem makes a fascinating comparison with another poetic version of Genesis, 'The Sacred Historie', composed in the 1660s in manuscript by a woman, probably the Catholic Mary Roper.[28] Both writers were very much out of favour with the church establishment of their time: the relationship to sacred space in the real world is not comfortable for either of them, and for both of them the Bible offers sanctuary for their hopes and beliefs. In the method of reading the sacred text deeply familiar to early modern women, both writers locate their aspirations and fears for seventeenth-century England in the experience of the Biblical characters. Mary Roper is clearly using one of them – Joseph – as a type of Charles II. She breaks off her version of Genesis to deal with contemporary events in a section called 'May 29 1669', the ninth anniversary of Charles' entry into London, and she makes the comparison of Charles II with Joseph explicit.

> God who Joseph Did in Prison Save
> Deliverance unto our Soveraigne Gave
> Our King, Like Joseph, was in Great Distresses
> But God Brought Him from troubles Wildernesses
> *(Early Modern Women's Manuscript Poetry*, p. 157)

The rest of Roper's poem celebrates God's providential care in providing for Charles, illustrated by a picture of Boscabel Oak, in which Charles hid after his defeat at Worcester in 1651. Lucy Hutchinson's version of Genesis is also relevant to contemporary politics, although she does not break into her narrative with political poems, as Roper does. In the fifteen cantos of *Order and Disorder* which remained in manuscript, Hutchinson uses digression and changes of tense to signal that she is locating seventeenth-century evils within her interpretation of the biblical text. Cain is identified specifically as a seventeenth-century high churchman, a 'formal hypocrite' who worships in the physical church building although he is not one of the elect (*Order and Disorder*, p. 98). The reason that Cain's sacrifice is not accepted is that there is no sincerity in his heart. Like the Laudians whom the Restoration Anglican church explicitly celebrated, he merely enjoys the holy ceremonies: they are 'performances' (p. 90).

By 1682, the closeness of Church of England worship to the Catholic liturgy, and the devotion to the edifices of the physical church, are the cause of political controversy. A 1691 volume written for 'a devout lady', *The ladies preparation to the monthly sacrament*, is typical.[29] This volume includes prayers and ejaculations for every stage of the Communion service. A vivid impression of the space of the church is created by the physical anchoring of the prayers at certain locations. There are prayers to be said 'when you enter the Church' (*The ladies preparation*, p. 108), 'when you cast your eye on the *Font* and the *Pulpet*' (p. 109) and 'when you Kneel before the Altar' (p. 111). There is a strong sense of decorum to be observed in church: the lady should get there early (p. 108), meditate while the elements are prepared (p. 113) and rehearse appropriate prayers while others are communicating (p. 123). *The ladies preparation* aspires to control thought and action in a variety of contexts in a deeply conservative manner, reminding the modern reader that in the late seventeenth century, in an age when 'obedience' was an important theological concept, the Church of England lady was likely to be Tory in politics. On the walls of Bath Abbey is an example of poetry by a woman, but it is a very conservative one. It is a poem by Elizabeth Peirce, who died in 1671, aged nineteen. Lovingly recorded is the fact that this poem was not published, but found, in Peirce's closet, after her death: it serves as her epitaph.[30] It thus fits into that seventeenth-century attitude to women's writing commented on by Wendy Wall: the only space in which a woman is allowed to become an author is the limited one that opens up immediately after her death.[31] Physically, the poem is Peirce's memorial stone: textually, it is comparable to the publication entitled 'A Female Legacy', of which those by Elizabeth Jocelin and Dorothy Leigh became bestsellers in the seventeenth century.

Religious buildings in the early modern period were imbued with the politics of state and of gender: many women preferred the devotional spaces of their own mind to any physical place, and constructed for themselves in their own writing imaginative locations where they could be confident in their relationships with God. Thus An Collins writing in 1652 locates her sacred space, where she writes her godly poetry, within her own head:

> As a garden is my mind enclosed fast
> Being to safety so confind from storm and blast
> Apt to produce a fruit most rare
> That is not common with every woman
> That fruitfull are.[32]

In the Interregnum, prophetesses such as Anna Trapnel and Sarah Wight were able to disseminate their God-given prophecy from sickbeds in houses and hostelries in London and Cornwall, where they appeared to be in trances, or unable to eat, or dying.[33] Although their words had to be mediated by male scribes and male authority, such women escaped the restrictions of sacred space, with its connotations of conventional religion and its emphasis on male speech and writing, by reducing the importance of the external world to the extent of the apparent degeneration of their own physical bodies.[34] In doing so they automatically boosted the significance of their own imaginative constructions of the spiritual, which Nigel Smith has recently characterized as giving access to 'a completely surreal plane of reality, one that was paradisal in shape, or that was a sacred realm in which the dreamer or visionary lived'.[35] Excluded from churches for one reason or another, women often used their writing to create mental devotional spaces of their own.

NOTES

1. Patricia Brace, 'Tyrwhit, Elizabeth, Lady Tyrwhit (*d.* 1578)', *Oxford Dictionary of National Biography*; Eamon Duffy, *Marking the Hours: English People and their Prayers 1240–1570* (New Haven, CT: Yale University Press, 2006), p. 56.

2. Elizabeth Tyrwhit, *Morning and Evening Prayer, with divers Psalmes, Himnes and Meditations,* 1574, selected and introduced by Patricia Brace, in *The Early Modern Englishwoman: A Facsimile Edition of Essential Works*, ed. Betty S. Travitsky and Anne Lake Prescott, Series 1, Part 3, vol. 1 (Aldershot: Ashgate, 2003), p. xii.

3. There is a discussion of Catholic Books of Hours, and whether they are individualistic or intended to extend the domain of the church, in Duffy, *Marking the Hours*, pp. 97–102.

4. For a bibliographical account of the state of the manuscripts, see Gavin Alexander, 'A New Manuscript of the Sidney Psalms', *Sidney Journal* 18.1 (2000), 43–56. The manuscript described by Alexander has now been catalogued as British Library Egerton MS 3789.

5. Danielle Clarke (ed.), *Isabella Whitney, Mary Sidney, and Aemelia Lanyer: Renaissance Women Poets* (Harmondsworth: Penguin, 2000), p. xxv.

6. *The Bible translated according to the Ebrew and Greeke, and conferred with the best translations in divers languages; with most profitable annotations upon all the hard places, and other things of great importance, as may appeare in the epistle to the reader* (London, 1599), p. 229.

7. Sidney, Psalms, in Clarke, ed. *Renaissance Women Poets*, p.108.

8. Clarke, ed., *Renaissance Women Poets*, p. xvi.

9. *The Poems of Aemilia Lanyer*, ed. Susanne Woods (New York: Oxford University Press, 1993), p. 133.

10. Lena Cowen Orlin, *Elizabethan Households: An Anthology* (Washington: Folger Shakespeare Library, 1995), pp. 70–8. In her latest book, Lena Orlin questions the view that closets were primarily for devotion, arguing that they were sites for the display of valuable goods: *Locating Privacy in Tudor London* (Oxford: Oxford University Press, 2007), p. 299.

11. See Andrew Spicer, '"What kinde of house a kirk is": Conventicles, Consecrations and the Concept of Sacred Space in Post-Reformation Scotland', in Will Coster and Andrew Spicer (eds.), *Sacred Space in Early Modern Europe* (Cambridge: Cambridge University Press, 2005), pp. 81–103.

12. Princeton University Library, Robert H. Taylor Collection RTC01 no. 62, fol. 8r, transcribed by Alice Eardley. For the Isham Project, which is putting Elizabeth Isham's manuscript writing online, see www2.warwick.ac.uk/fac/arts/ren/projects/isham/.

13. See Victoria E. Burke, 'Richardson, Elizabeth, *suo jure* Baroness of Cramond (1576/7–1651)', *Oxford Dictionary of National Biography*.

14. *A directory for the publique worship of God, throughout the three kingdoms of England, Scotland, and Ireland* (London, 1645), pp. 2, 38.

15. Elizabeth Richardson, *A Ladies Legacie to her Daughters* (London, 1645), p. 10.

16. For more on this controversy, see Christopher Durston, 'By the Book or with the Spirit: the Debate over Liturgical Prayer in the English Revolution', *Historical Research* 79 (2006), 50–73.

17. Leeds University Library, Brotherton Collection MS Lt q-32, fol. 76b, fol. 71b, transcribed by Alice Eardley.

18. Julie Spraggon, *Puritan Iconoclasm during the English Civil War* (Woodbridge: Boydell and Brewer, 2003), p. 203.

19. Leeds University Library, Brotherton Collection MS Lt q-32, fol. 114b.

20. For a list of surviving manuscript journals by women, see Elizabeth Clarke, 'The Use of Women's Manuscripts in a Widening Political Arena', in James Daybell (ed.), *Women and Politics in Early Modern England, 1450–1700* (Basingstoke: Palgrave Macmillan, 2004), p. 226.

21. Isaac Ambrose, *Prima, Media, Ultima* (London, 1650), p. 164.

22. British Library MS Add. 27,358, fol. 17v.

23. David George Mullan (ed.), *Women's Life Writing in Early Modern Scotland: Writing the Evangelical Self, c. 1670–1730* (Aldershot: Ashgate, 2003), p. 321.

24. Margaret Fell Fox, *A testimonie of the touch-stone, for all professions, and all forms, and gathered churches (as they call them)* (London, 1656), p. 1.

25. Margaret Fell Fox, *False prophets, antichrists, deceivers which are in the world, which John prophesied of, which hath long been hid and covered, but now is unmasked in these last dayes with the eternal light which is risen* (London, 1655), p. 4.

26. *The examination and tryall of Margaret Fell and George Fox (at the severall assizes held at Lancaster the 14th and 16th days of the first moneth, 1663, and the 29th of the 6th moneth, 1664)* (London, 1664), p. 13.

27. Lucy Hutchinson, *Order and Disorder*, ed. David Norbrook (Oxford: Blackwell, 2001), is a modern-spelling edition of all twenty cantos, from the printed version and from manuscript.

28. Leeds University Library, Brotherton Collection MS Lt q-2. Extracts from the manuscript are printed in Jill Seal Millman and Gillian Wright (eds.), *Early Modern Women's Manuscript Poetry* (Manchester: Manchester University Press, 2005), pp. 153–68.

29. *The Ladies preparation to the monthly Sacrament. Consisting of prayers, meditations, and ejaculations, before, at, and after receiving the Lords supper* (London, 1691).

30. I am indebted to Siobhan Keenan, who also found this poem in the manuscript commonplace book of Katherine Thomas, National Library of Wales MS 4340A, where it had been copied in 1694.

31. Wendy Wall, *The Imprint of Gender: Authority and Publication in the English Renaissance* (Ithaca, NY: Cornell University Press, 1993), p. 286.

32. An Collins, *Divine Songs and Meditacions*, ed. Sidney Gottlieb (Tempe, AZ: Medieval and Reniassance Texts and Studies, 1996), pp. 55–6.

33. H. Jessey, *The exceeding riches of grace advanced by the spirit of grace, in an empty nothing creature, viz. Mris Sarah Wight*, 2nd rev. edn (London, 1647); Anna Trapnel, *The cry of a stone, or, A relation of something spoken in Whitehall* (London, 1654).

34. See Hilary Hinds, *God's Englishwomen: Seventeenth-Century Radical Sectarian Writing and Feminist Criticism* (Manchester: Manchester University Press, 1996), pp. 87–96; Diane Purkiss, 'Producing the Voice, Consuming the Body: Women Prophets of the Seventeenth Century', in Isobel Grundy and Susan Wiseman (eds.), *Women, Writing, History 1640–1740* (London: B. T. Batsford, 1992); and

Susan Wiseman, 'Unsilent Instruments and the Devil's Cushions: Authority in Seventeenth-Century Women's Prophetic Discourse', in Isobel Armstrong (ed.), *New Feminist Discourses: Critical Essays on Theories and Texts* (New York: Routledge, 1992), for different approaches to this phenomenon.

35. Nigel Smith, 'The Rod and the Canon', *Women's Writing* 14 special issue: *Still Kissing the Rod? Early Modern Women's Writing in 2005* (2007), ed. Elizabeth Clarke and Lynn Robson, p. 234.

READING LIST

Beilin, Elaine. *Redeeming Eve: Women Writers of the English Renaissance*. Princeton, NJ: Princeton University Press, 1987.

Clarke, Danielle. *The Politics of Early Modern Women's Writing*. Harlow, Essex: Longman, 2001.

Eales, Jacqueline. *Women in Early Modern England 1500–1700*. London: UCL Press, 1998.

Hannay, Margaret P. (ed.). *Silent but for the Word: Tudor Women as Patrons, Translators, and Writers of Religious Works*. Kent, OH: Kent State University Press, 1985.

Longfellow, Erica. *Women and Religious Writing in Early Modern England*. Cambridge: Cambridge University Press, 2004.

Orlin, Lena Cowen. *Locating Privacy in Tudor London*. Oxford: Oxford University Press, 2007.

Veevers, Erica. *Images of Love and Religion: Queen Henrietta Maria and Court Entertainment*. Cambridge: Cambridge University Press, 1989.

8

KAREN BRITLAND

Women in the royal courts

Of the three Queens I will consider here (from 1550 to 1700), only one, Elizabeth, was a reigning monarch: Anna of Denmark and Henrietta Maria of France were Queens Consort, the wives of James I and Charles I respectively. As the anointed Queen of England, Elizabeth was the centre of the country's political life: the courts of Anna and Henrietta Maria, established alongside those of their husbands, often provided places from which reservations about the monarch's policies could be articulated. It is interesting to see, in these very different courts, how struggles for inclusion in the Queen's inner circle broke out among courtiers, particularly at the start of each reign. Rather than being ephemeral to the political process, the court of a Queen Consort was, at the very least, a significant locus of power-broking, as well as of literary patronage and literary production.

Early studies of Anna and Henrietta Maria presented these Queens as politically naive and culturally frivolous in a way rarely applied to Elizabeth I. Alfred Harbage, for example, described Henrietta Maria as a 'charming lady' who dignified 'a love of festive toys and tinsel' which in Anna of Denmark 'had seemed childish frivolity'. This backhanded compliment infantilizes both Queens and leads, unsurprisingly, to the value judgement that 'Henrietta had not a jot of literary taste.'[1] In contrast, Elizabeth I is often presented as a woman of impeccable sense, whose education and knowledge impressed foreign ambassadors. This nationalistic construction elevates the English Elizabeth at the expense of her foreign counterparts, yet, if the study of these royal courts reveals anything, it is that the women associated with them were deeply involved in the continental exchange of texts, goods and personnel. Anne Boleyn, Elizabeth's mother, visited the French court in the wedding train of Mary Tudor, Henry VIII's sister. Anna and Henrietta Maria, both of whom married across national borders, maintained connections with their natal families, with Henrietta Maria, particularly, having siblings in the ruling families of France, Spain and Savoy. It is impossible to consider the cultural patronage of these women and those who attended them in a purely national context: the books they read, the letters they wrote and the religions they espoused were all profoundly influenced by developments abroad.

In this context, the education received by such women takes on an interesting hue. While Diane Purkiss, for example, has suggested that noblewomen's education was intrinsically ornamental, surmising of Jane, Lady Lumley's facility in Greek and Latin that, 'the very fact that a girl could not use an elaborate humanist education enhanced its value as conspicuously useless', in a court society where preferment was largely dependent on patronage ties, where foreign ambassadors abounded and where continental fashions were often imitated, this kind of education was invaluable.[2] Although women could not take up public roles as orators, the art of conversation as a means of social promotion increased in importance throughout the sixteenth and seventeenth centuries until, in 1646, the Frenchman François du Soucy could observe: 'For those who are in the courts, the wise counsel of their wives, their shrewdness, their cabals, are a thousand times more effective for the fortune of the houses than the efforts of men before Princes and Kings. It is at their homes that people assemble, it is there that all is decided.'[3] This chapter will trace the international connections maintained by Elizabeth, Anna and Henrietta Maria at the same time as it discusses the nature of their courts and the writing undertaken by women who profited by, or were excluded from, them.

Elizabeth I

Catherine Parr, Henry VIII's sixth wife, has been credited with emphasizing the importance of education for royal and noble children. John N. King describes how Parr's circle (which included the Duchesses of Suffolk, Richmond and Somerset) encouraged the translation of Protestant religious works and patronized religious and educational 'reformers' such as Roger Ascham, John Aylmer, John Foxe and Thomas Wilson.[4] During Elizabeth's adolescence, with an older brother and sister still living, it seemed highly unlikely that she would inherit the English throne. Instead, her future was likely to mirror that of her aunt, Mary, married at the age of eighteen to the King of France. Indeed, when Elizabeth was only thirteen months old, negotiations began for her betrothal to the Duke of Angoulême, third son of François I. In this context, a facility with languages would be beneficial, permitting Elizabeth to operate in a European court without the potentially disruptive intermediary of an interpreter.

Women of the previous generation, including the French King's sister, Marguerite de Navarre, whose *Miroir de l'âme pécheresse* Elizabeth was soon to translate, had proved themselves useful members of the royal courts. Anne Lake Prescott has noted that the Duke of Norfolk, Elizabeth's great-uncle, believed Marguerite was 'the most frank and wise woman he ever spake with', a comment that elevates both Marguerite and the court of which she was a part.[5] In a Europe that saw constant intermarriage between its ruling houses, women played important patronage roles: King, for example, has noted that Lady Jane Grey's 'contemporary correspondence with Bullinger in Latin, Greek, and Hebrew shows that the learning of noble English women was well known in Continental circles' (King, 'Patronage and Piety', p. 52). In other words, the English nobility did not exist in isolation, but were in constant contact with the leading artists, thinkers and rulers of Europe. International royalty patronized and shared foreign tutors: Elizabeth I was trained in Italian by Baldassare Castiglione; Queen Anna patronized the Anglo-Italian John Florio; Prince Charles in England and Henrietta Maria in France shared the same French dancing master. Noblewomen's education and their cultural and religious awareness, far from being ornamental, were important social and political networking tools.

In this international, dynastic context, Elizabeth's translation of Marguerite de Navarre's *Miroir*, given to Catherine Parr as a New Year's gift in 1544, is particularly interesting. Why Marguerite's work was chosen for the young woman to translate is unknown, although Prescott suggests that the book would have reinforced the 'Erasmian and Reformist tone' of Catherine's circle (Prescott, 'Pearl of the Valois', pp. 64–5). The French text might also have been owned by Anne Boleyn, who had known Marguerite, and might, therefore, have had familial significance.[6] It certainly connected Elizabeth to a famously erudite Princess and, for a Protestant, was free of controversial Catholic elements such as purgatory and saints.[7] Elizabeth's childhood exercise in translation was a multivalent one that served to link her to her stepmother's reformist circle, to her mother, to Marguerite and to a tradition of female devotional writing.

From the start, then, Elizabeth was encouraged to value writing and the bonds it established within and between courts. Not only did she present her translation of the *Miroir* to Catherine Parr, she also translated Catherine's own *Prayers or Meditacions* into Latin, French and Italian, presenting these to Henry VIII in 1545. She likewise prepared at least four manuscript books as New Year's gifts for Henry and Catherine, together with a translation of Bernardino Ochino's *De Christo Sermo* for her brother Edward.[8] Throughout her own reign, Elizabeth was also presented with books as New Year gifts and was actively involved in the manuscript circulation of verses, responding, for example, to a poem by Sir Walter Ralegh – which expressed concern about the rise of a new court favourite – with lines that began familiarly, 'Ah, silly Pug, wert thou so sore afraid? / Mourn not, my Wat, nor be thou so dismayed.'[9] In a broader literary sense, she also participated in the propagation of court iconography and cannot even be said to have been the passive observer of entertainments put on for her pleasure. Most notably, in 1575, at Kenilworth, country home of Robert Dudley, Earl of Leicester, Elizabeth declined to view an entertainment, ostensibly because of the weather, but more probably, in King's words, because of her 'distaste for its advocacy that she choose a husband and marry'.[10]

As Queen of England, Elizabeth was part of an international community of monarchs. When her last suitor, the Duke of Alençon, died in 1584, she wrote in French to his mother, Catherine de Médicis, expressing her sorrow for the latter's loss. In 1593, hearing news of Henri IV's conversion to Catholicism, she wrote him a passionate letter of dismay, again in French; and she also received poetic missives from poets favoured by other courts. For example, Pierre de Ronsard, the Valois court's most celebrated poet, sent her a French sonnet in which he begged for clemency for Mary, Queen of Scots.[11] Royal women's writing and cultural patronage in this period operated in the service of an international politics as much as a domestic one: it was also constantly inflected by religion.

A religious context certainly informs the literary activities of Mary Sidney Herbert, Countess of Pembroke, in Elizabethan England. Margaret Hannay has described how 'she used her *Psalmes* for political commentary in the spirit of the Geneva Protestants who were so closely allied with her family', noting also that her translation of Philippe de Mornay's *Discours de la Vie et de la Mort* was undertaken in support of Mornay and his Huguenot cause.[12] Even her translation of Robert Garnier's history play, *Marc Antoine*, had a potentially political colouring, helping, in Hannay's words, 'to naturalize Continental historical tragedy in England, using Roman history to comment on English politics in a way that anticipated Shakespeare' (Hannay, '"Your Vertuous and Learned Aunt"', p. 17). Here, then, a French source was adapted into English and appropriated, in part, for a specific political cause.

Despite her own literary output, the Countess of Pembroke is most popularly known as the dedicatee of her brother Philip's *The Countess of Pembroke's Arcadia*, which she saw through the press in 1593. In many ways, she was responsible for her brother's posthumous reputation as a soldier, patron and writer: a reputation that informed much English Protestant writing after his death in 1586. The *Arcadia*, together with Edmund Spenser's 'May Eclogue', which, in Leah Marcus's words, associated May-day customs with the 'corruptions' of Catholicism, became emblematic of Protestant pastoral discourse in England.[13] Evoking Virgil's *Eclogues*, these works helped construct an English literary tradition based on classical precedents that rivalled similar developments in Europe. Pastoral writing was a truly European phenomenon, flourishing in Italy, Spain and France, and giving rise to influential publications such as Guarini's *Il pastor fido*, Montemayor's *Diana* and Racan's *Les Bergeries*. Although these tales usually unfold in a featureless pastoral environment, they often include international journeys and characters from various lands. As such, they reflect the noble society of which they are a part. Couched as romantic fantasies, pastorals could articulate a political or religious position, comment on the vagaries of noble service and demonstrate how good breeding might lead to a virtuous life. Intrinsically European in their influences and locations, Spenser's and Sidney's pastoral writings nevertheless helped to define a strongly Protestant national literature in service to Elizabethan England.

Anna

Helen Hackett has suggested that romance writing in England increased in popularity from the Elizabethan period on to the Stuart courts of James and his consort Anna, while Marcus notes that pastoral, under the Stuarts, became more closely associated 'with the monarch's own policy initiatives' as James and his son tried to encourage people to leave London for the provinces (Marcus, 'Politics and Pastoral', pp. 139–40). Notably, in 1621, Prince Charles danced before his father in Ben Jonson's masque, *Pan's Anniversary*, in a manner that evoked Spenser's 'April Eclogue' and Elizabethan progress entertainments, as well as using the image of the pastoral god, Pan, to praise King James as a vigorous and peaceful ruler.[14] In other words, the Stuart regime appropriated pastoral as a cultural tool through which it both looked back to an Elizabethan golden age and located James as the father and head of the nation.

Lady Mary Wroth's romance, published in 1621, should be placed in this context. Helen Hackett has noted that it 'displayed detailed knowledge of the *Arcadia*, *The Faerie Queene* and other romances', and was one of two romances in the period authored by a woman (the other was Margaret Tyler's 1578 *Mirrour of Princely Deedes and Knighthood*).[15] Wroth was Sidney's niece, and the title page of her work echoes *The Countess of Pembroke's Arcadia* when it terms itself *The Countesse of Mountgomeries Urania*. Taking its models from male-authored works and appearing when the Stuart regime was reappropriating pastoral for the state, Wroth's text foregrounds the travails of female characters and is ostensibly concerned with love. From its first publication, the *Urania* was also understood to be a *roman-à-clef*, shadowing courtly figures in its noble characters: its heroine,

Pamphilia, is typically taken as a representation of Wroth, while Pamphilia's faithless lover, Amphilanthus, is supposed to shadow William Herbert, Wroth's cousin and the supposed father of her two children.

Critical attention has traditionally focused on these elements of Wroth's text. However, it can also be read as a continuation of the Elizabethan discourse that couched political negotiations in the language of love. For example, in Book 3 of the *Urania*, Pamphilia is reminded that the truer her subjects are to her, the firmer her own loyalties will be (p. 411). Similarly, a woebegone woman describes how a nobleman did not reward her generous love, but behaved 'like a King that takes a Present and likes it, but thinks it his Subjects due to present it, and so meanes not to reward the bringer, scarce the giver'.[16] The society in the *Urania* is built on reciprocal relationships where interfamilial alliances underpin international treaties, friends avenge the honour of wronged relations and good deeds promote social health. Concomitantly, the society it depicts is intrinsically unstable precisely because loyalties may change, contracts can be broken and kings and lovers can prove ungrateful.

Gary Waller has noted that the men in the *Urania* 'are in continual movement' while the women 'are either expected to wait at home, however restless or trapped they appear, or else are continually at risk for their boldness'.[17] 'Judging from Wroth's writings', he says, 'a recurring fantasy for women in the period is that they might emulate the autonomy and mobility of the courtly-chivalric heroes' ('Mary Wroth', p. 39). Wroth's text certainly presents an international stage on which a Prince might travel from campaigns in 'Germany', through 'Dalmatia', to 'Morea' and thence to 'Mattinea'. However, it does not incarcerate women at home, nor does it necessarily represent their travel as 'bold'. Although solitary travel is sometimes problematic for women in this text, they also undertake it without incident (Musalina, for example, uneventfully travels home to Romania: *Urania*, p. 422). In sum, in the *Urania*, just as in Europe as a whole, women are an important force for social cohesion both nationally and internationally. The text does, perhaps, offer a fantasy of women's involvement in literary and social affairs, but critical discussions should acknowledge the integral role noblewomen played in factional politics at home and abroad.

The most comprehensive body of critical work on women in politics focuses on Anna of Denmark, whose education, like Elizabeth's, was managed by European tutors. Anna's mother, Sophie of Mecklenburg, patron of the alchemist Tycho Brahe, had significant intellectual abilities, and Anna was probably educated with the same attention as her brother, the future King Christian IV of Denmark.[18] For thirteen years before arriving in England, Anna, as James VI's consort, had been deeply involved in Scottish politics and she continued to assert a political presence in London. The first English Queen Consort since Catherine Parr, she too gathered about her a group of ladies with literary and cultural interests, and her court, always separate from that of her husband, was potentially a locus of opposition to his policies.

Recent work on Jacobean cultural patronage, and particularly on court masques, has focused on the roles of Anna, Prince Henry and the Duke of Buckingham, arguing that their cultural activity was a means of advising (as well as complimenting) the monarch. Clare McManus, for example, has suggested that Anna's first surviving masque (Samuel Daniel's *Vision of the Twelve Goddesses*) 'gazed back at Elizabeth's female community and forward to Anna's court', pointing out that, in the first decade of the reign, 'the court's masquing stage was occupied almost entirely by women'.[19] Similarly, Kathryn Schwarz sees the spectacle of Anna and her ladies in the *Masque of Queens* (1609) as harking back to Elizabeth's reign and virtually upstaging King James.[20] In other words, early in the reign, Anna wielded a forceful cultural and political presence.

Such performances were not, though, always looked on with equanimity. Anna's *Masque of Blackness* (1605) caused a particular stir because the Queen and her ladies performed in costumes that Dudley Carleton, a court observer, deemed 'too light and curtizan-like for such great ones'.[21] Interestingly, Carleton also noted the struggle for precedence between foreign ambassadors at this entertainment: court masques served a political purpose, not only in their subject-matter, but also in who was invited to watch and perform in them. The French ambassador, Guy Le Fevre de la Boderie, was often convinced he had been slighted, and complained bitterly that Anna favoured his Spanish counterpart.[22] Royal masques, far from being trivial, could illuminate inter-courtly allegiances and indicate the direction of political policy.

As well as signalling a court's international agenda, masques also indicated domestic favour. The change of reign in 1603 meant that new personnel could make a mark alongside the new Queen, and, on James's accession, several English noblewomen journeyed to Scotland to congratulate his wife. This paid off, particularly for Lucy Russell, later Countess of Bedford, who became one of Anna's most favoured ladies. Unsupplanted despite the efforts of families who had enjoyed favour close to Elizabeth, Russell danced in all the Queen's major masques, including *Blackness*, *Beauty* and *The Masque of Queens*, and had her portrait painted in the costume she wore for *Hymenaei*. Born in 1581, she was the kinswoman of Sir Philip Sidney and the Countess of Pembroke through her grandmother, Lucy Sidney. Barbara Lewalski has described her as 'easily the most important patroness of the

Jacobean court, except for Queen Anne herself', noting that she 'influenced the queen's patronage directly and had the ear of the king's ministers and favourites'.[23] Proficient in several languages, she was one of the dedicatees of John Florio's translation of Montaigne's *Essays* in 1603, and was also a particular patron of John Donne (Lewalski, 'Lucy, Countess of Bedford', p. 74).

Russell was also a patron of drama: Shakespeare's *Titus Andronicus* received its only recorded performance in her house, and, in 1617, she organized an entertainment for Anna entitled *Cupid's Banishment*, performed by young women from the Ladies Hall at Deptford.[24] This included a speech by one 'Mistress Watkins' who acted Fortune, which, as McManus has noted, prefigured Alice Egerton's performance in Milton's *Masque at Ludlow* by seventeen years and might be a 'unique instance of female speech in a Jacobean court masque' (*Women on the Renaissance Stage*, p. 180). The entertainment was performed at the Queen's house in Greenwich and can be interpreted, as McManus notes, either as 'a statement of Anna's marginalisation' or 'as evidence of the shift in the locus of courtly power away from its Whitehall centre at a time when performance at court had been appropriated by James's male favourites' (p. 180). In other words, this entertainment bears witness to the existence of not one royal court, but two. Performed by girls and organized by one of Anna's chief women, it served to praise the Queen Consort, making evident her independent cultural position, even as it potentially demonstrated her slide from influence.

This marginalization had implications for the Queen's dependants. Courts were not exclusively made up of royal and noble families, but also of musicians, poets, secretaries, cooks and scullery maids. For some, they offered great opportunities: for others, they were dangerous and exploitative environments. Aemilia Lanyer, celebrated mistress of Elizabethan courtier Henry, Lord Hunsden, experienced both aspects of this life at court. During her early years, she belonged to the Countess Dowager of Kent's household, and later joined the circle of Margaret, Countess of Cumberland, and her daughter, Anne Clifford. Lanyer's poem, 'The Description of Cooke-ham', celebrates her time at the Countess of Cumberland's country residence, and is included in her only published volume, *Salve Deus Rex Judaeorum* (1611).

The title page of this curious volume identifies its author as 'Wife to Captaine *Alfonso Lanyer* Servant to the Kings Majestie', securing Lanyer's identity through her relationship to two men (her husband and the King). However, as Susanne Woods discusses in 'Narrative poetry' in this volume, Lanyer's work sets out to exculpate women, asserting that Eve should not be entirely blamed for mankind's fall, and noting that men alone were responsible for Christ's crucifixion. Invoking the example of Herod, the poem links tyranny in kings with tyranny in husbands, and, by surrounding Christ with sympathetic female figures such as his mother and the weeping '*daughters of Jerusalem*', divorces kingship and divinity, showing women to be more naturally attuned to Christ through their mutual capacities for humility and compassion.[25] It therefore radically breaks down the hierarchy that places husbands as gods over their wives, at the same time as it calls into question the notion that kings such as Herod wield divinely sanctioned authority.

This privileged connection between women and the suffering Christ is subsequently extended to Lanyer's patron, '*my Lady of Cumberland*', in a manner that gives Cumberland strong religious authority and positions her as chief in a list of famously devout women, including Deborah, Judith and Hester (*Salve Deus*, F4v). At this point in the poem, the imagery of Queen Anna's circle seems to be obliquely invoked. In 1609, Anna had danced in Jonson's *Masque of Queens*, accompanied, notably, by Anne Clifford. The masque presented eleven heroic women led by the Queen as Bel-Anna. Lanyer's poem, placing Cumberland amongst devout women, spiritualizes the idea of Anna's masque, and brings together, through its multiple dedications, a similar group of noblewomen. Indeed, if one includes Lanyer's addresses to 'all vertuous Ladies', 'The Vertuous Reader' and 'the doubtfull Reader' (a3r–f3v), the number of dedicatory addresses in her edition, like the number of Queens in Anna's masque, is twelve. Female community, here and in the printed quarto of the masque, occurs textually, operating through literary allusion and historical precedent to create a sense of group identity.

Despite this sense of textual community, the later part of Lanyer's life was troubled. As a widow, she briefly ran a school in St Giles-in-the-Fields, but never achieved under Anna the same kind of court successes she had enjoyed under Elizabeth. Nevertheless, her writing at once expressed her gratitude for patronage and asserted her intellectual and spiritual independence. Indeed, as Woods has noted, *Salve Deus Rex Judaeorum* makes no apologies for its creation of 'a community of good women for whom another woman is the spokesperson and commemorator'.[26] Like Wroth's *Urania*, it posits women's virtue as a cornerstone of society, and is both a homage to, and the product of, a supportive, female community.

Henrietta Maria

After Anna's death in 1619, England remained without a Queen's court until 1625, when Charles I married the fifteen-year-old Henrietta Maria. Once again, competition for places around the Queen Consort was rife, and it is interesting that Lucy Hay, wife of the Earl of Carlisle, seems to have modelled herself on the Countess of Bedford. Bedford had been instrumental in arranging Lucy's marriage and acted as hostess at entertainments given by Carlisle.[27] In 1618, following Bedford's example, Lucy attempted to mount an entertainment before the ailing Anna, yet this was cancelled, probably by the Queen.[28] Nevertheless, it demonstrated Lucy's ambitions and showed that, just as Wroth modelled herself on the Countess of Pembroke, she intended to imitate Bedford.

Lucy's initial overtures to Henrietta Maria seemed successful as, like Bedford, she supplanted arguably more eligible candidates for queenly favour, such as the wife and sister of the Duke of Buckingham. In 1627, for example, she accompanied Henrietta Maria to suppers with the Countesses of Exeter, Oxford and Berkshire which did not include either of the Buckingham women.[29] Like Bedford, she was committed to her family's concerns, remaining largely loyal to the group assembled for the cancelled masque. However, unlike Bedford, she did not remain the Queen's favourite for long. In 1629, she was discredited by a rival faction led by the French ambassador. Although she continued to work for her own and her family's advancement, she never again enjoyed Henrietta Maria's confidence. Her career, though, shows clearly how courtly women were integral to factional politics, both nationally and internationally.

Henrietta Maria is most famously known for her promotion of French culture and a Catholicized neo-Platonism. Within this discourse, physical beauty becomes the external manifestation of a virtuous soul, and a beautiful woman's chief purpose is to inspire her admirers towards pure chastity. Henrietta Maria appeared in court masques in the guise of figures such as Divine Beauty, her personal symbolism combining her husband's iconography with French and allusively Catholic images.

She was also the first English Queen to take a speaking role in a play when, in 1626, she appeared with her French ladies in *Artenice*, a pastoral previously popular at the French court. This performance caused disquiet among English commentators, one writing after the event that he heard 'not much honour of the Queen's mask, for if they were not all, some were in men's apparell'. The most interesting aspect of Henrietta Maria's performances, however, is not cultural, but political. In 1633, she again acted in a play, this time performed in English and commissioned from Walter Montagu, a courtier who often travelled between the European courts. His play, *The Shepherds' Paradise*, which saw Henrietta Maria perform as Bellessa, a rural queen, gestured to the wars ravaging Europe, suggesting that Bellessa/Henrietta Maria might act as a peacemaking force. Charles, like his father, advocated a policy of non-intervention in Europe: Henrietta Maria, and the group of Protestant families with whom she was loosely allied, advocated a more interventionist role, hoping ultimately to restore Charles's dispossessed sister and nephews to the Palatinate throne.

This pastoral illustrates how Henrietta Maria's Catholicized, French imagery was strangely compatible with an English, Protestant tradition of pastoral. It also demonstrates a political continuity across several generations at the English court. In the early 1630s, Henrietta Maria allied herself with families who had affinities with the earlier Sidney grouping, favouring Henry, Earl of Holland, son of Penelope Rich (immortalized by Sidney in *Astrophil and Stella*), and his cousin, Henry Percy. This shows the continued influence of important courtly families whose womenfolk were indispensable as marriage-brokers, cultural and religious patrons, and factional negotiators.

Despite her affiliations with this group of Protestants, which became less close as the 1630s progressed, Henrietta Maria also interested herself in the fortunes of the recusant writer Elizabeth Cary, to whom she was probably introduced by Buckingham's wife, Katherine. Indeed, Cary's relationship with the Caroline court is fascinating for what it tells us about female courtly patronage. The wife of Henry Cary, Lord Deputy of Ireland, she converted to Catholicism in 1626 and, cast off by her husband, established herself in London. Henry was adamantly against a reconciliation and Charles I was equally severe in the affair, but was petitioned repeatedly by the Duchess of Buckingham, who also pressed her husband to intercede on Elizabeth Cary's behalf. Charles remained firm, but Cary refused to recant and stayed in London, receiving at least one fifty-pound loan from the Duke of Buckingham's mother. Eventually the King arranged for her to receive a pension of £300 a year, drawn from her husband's salary, but, in 1630, she was still pleading poverty and took a chamber, for a while, at the French ambassador's house, an arrangement that might well have been facilitated by Henrietta Maria.

Two of Cary's literary works from this period show how a noblewoman's religious and political sympathies cannot always easily be separated from her literary output. One, a translation of Cardinal du Perron's *Reply*, was published in Cary's lifetime and was an unashamed declaration of her Catholic allegiances. The other, a history of Edward II, probably written earlier than the translation, remained in manuscript long after her death. It was finally published in two versions in 1680: one, a handsome folio, was said to have been written by 'E. F. in the year 1627', the other, a smaller octavo, was asserted to have been 'Writ by the Right Honourable HENRY Viscount FAULKLAND' (Cary's husband, Henry, had been created Viscount Falkland in 1620). Recent scholarship confirms that the folio volume was written by Cary (the initials 'E. F.' standing for 'Elizabeth Falkland'); a suggestion borne out by evidence within the text.

The years 1627–8 saw a resurgence of tales about malign court favourites as Buckingham's political influence made him increasingly unpopular: in 1627, Michael Drayton published a new edition of *Barons' Wars*; Francis Hubert's Elizabethan verses on Edward II were republished in an unauthorized edition; and Ben Jonson's *Mortimer His Fall* might also date from this period. Most significantly, perhaps, François Garnier, 'procurer general' to Henrietta Maria, was asked by the Queen to translate John Stow's account of Edward II into French, indicating that her circle was interested in this unfortunate monarch and his French wife (see Leeds Brotherton Library, MS 97).

If Elizabeth Cary's *Edward II* was written in 1627, then it should be included in this collection of stories that evince distrust of favourites. Although she was supported by Buckingham's female relatives, and although her husband had profited from his early patronage, the 1680 text is equivocal about such a man's power, seeming, particularly in the character of Spencer, to allude to the highly influential Duke. Edward's Queen, Isabel, is distrustful of him, and we are told that, 'To win a nearer place in her opinion, he gains his Kindred places next her person; and those that were her own, he bribes to back him.'[30] This had certainly been Buckingham's strategy towards Henrietta Maria and her French attendants in 1626. The text also observes that, if 'any one held him at too smart a distance, prizing his integrity and honour before so base a traffique, he was an ill Member of State, and either silenc'd, or sent to an *Irish* or *Welsh* Employment' (*History … of Edward II*, pp. 52–3). Although it is problematic to extrapolate biographical details from Cary's text, there is perhaps an oblique reference here to her husband's posting to Ireland. At once a critique of favouritism, the text might be read as a bid to win back her husband's good will and to insinuate herself into the favours of the Queen.

Cary's translation of Cardinal du Perron's *Reply*, dedicated to Henrietta Maria in 1630, is a much less equivocal bid for patronage. Du Perron's original text was contentious, and part of a theological argument with James I.[31] Cary's translation addressed Henrietta Maria as a woman who was 'fittest to protect a woman's work', and a Catholic 'fittest to receive the dedication of a Catholicke-worke'. The tone of the dedication is reverential but direct, and the writer's confidence in her work reinforced by an address 'To the Reader' which asserts:

> *I will not make use of that worne-out forme of saying, I printed it against my will, mooved by the importunitie of Friends: I was mooved to it by my beleef,*

*that it might make those English that understand not French, whereof there
are manie, even in our universities, reade* Perron; *And when that is done, I
have my End.*[32]

This is a strikingly shameless assertion of a deliberate decision to go into
print. It also asserts Cary's linguistic abilities and, in its deeply theological subject-matter, asserts her intellectual strength and her commitment
to Catholicism. Most importantly, in its choice of subject-matter and its
dedication to Henrietta Maria, it places Cary alongside the English Queen
Consort within a decidedly European religious context.

From the young woman who would become Elizabeth I to the recusant
Elizabeth Cary, women's education fitted them for life at the English courts.
Until we recognize the roles played in factional politics by women such as
the Countess of Bedford and Lucy Hay, we will not properly appreciate
their importance to these systems, nor the figurations of female characters
in courtly texts. Women's writing at court was bound up with their family
positions and social networks. Indeed, to be a member or a client of the
famous Sidney–Pembroke family was to partake of an intensely privileged
literary status. The loss of courtly privilege, for both men and women, frequently led to reduced opportunities for promotion, financial reward and
recognition. Lady Mary Wroth, Aemilia Lanyer, Lucy Hay and Elizabeth
Cary all, in different ways, suffered the disapproval of the royal courts,
but were adept enough to negotiate for patronage and survival. In sum,
despite injunctions for their silence and obedience, women were integral to
courtly politics and cultural patronage in England and throughout Europe.
If one were to seek for an emblem to describe their international significance, one might be tempted to find it in Wroth's picaresque romance
where women, as well as men, undertake journeys across borders, where
they are involved in the brokerage of international deals and where they
are constantly involved in a negotiation between their social positions and
their private desires.

NOTES

1. Alfred Harbage, *Cavalier Drama* (London: Oxford University Press, 1936),
   pp. 10–11.
2. Diane Purkiss (ed.), *Three Tragedies by Renaissance Women* (London: Penguin
   Books, 1998), p. xv.
3. François du Soucy, *Le Triomphe des Dames* (Paris, 1646), pp. 145–6; quoted in
   Nancy Klein Maguire, 'The Duchess of Portsmouth: English Royal Consort and
   French Politician, 1670–1685', in R. Malcolm Smuts (ed.), *The Stuart Court and
   Europe* (Cambridge: Cambridge University Press, 1996), pp. 247–73 (258).

4. John N. King, 'Patronage and Piety: the Influence of Catherine Parr', in Margaret P. Hannay (ed.), *Silent but for the Word: Women as Patrons, Translators, and Writers of Religious Works* (Kent, OH: Kent State University Press, 1985), pp. 43–60.

5. Anne Lake Prescott, 'The Pearl of the Valois and Elizabeth I: Marguerite de Navarre's *Miroir* and Tudor England', in Hannay (ed.), *Silent but for the Word*, pp. 61–76 (65).

6. See *The Mirror of The Sinful Soul*, ed. Percy W. Ames (London: Asher and Co., 1897), p. 31. See also Susan Snyder, 'Guilty Sisters: Marguerite de Navarre, Elizabeth of England, and the *Miroir de l'âme pécheresse*', *Renaissance Quarterly* 50.2 (1997), 443–58 (453, note 24).

7. Marguerite's religious affiliations have been strongly debated, but she was probably a reforming Catholic, rather than a closet Protestant: see Renja Salminen's analysis in Marguerite de Navarre, *Le Miroir de l'Ame Pécheresse*, ed. Renja Salminen (Helsinki: Suomalainen Tiedeakatemia, 1979), especially pp. 71–82.

8. Jane A. Lawson, 'This Remembrance of the New Year: Books Given to Queen Elizabeth as New Year's Gifts', in Peter Beal and Grace Ioppolo (eds.), *Elizabeth I and the Culture of Writing* (London: British Library, 2007), pp. 133–71 (138–9).

9. *Elizabeth I: Collected Works*, ed. Leah Marcus, Janel Mueller and Mary Beth Rose (Chicago: University of Chicago Press, 2000), p. 308.

10. John N. King, 'Queen Elizabeth I: Representations of the Virgin Queen', *Renaissance Quarterly* 43.1 (1990), 30–74 (46).

11. See John Nichols (ed.), *The Progresses and Public Processions of Queen Elizabeth*, 3 vols. (London: Society of Antiquaries, 1823), II: 425.

12. Margaret P. Hannay, '"Your Vertuous and Learned Aunt": The Countess of Pembroke as a Mentor to Mary Wroth', in Naomi J. Miller and Gary Waller (eds.), *Reading Mary Wroth* (Knoxville: University of Tennessee Press, 1991), pp. 15–34 (17).

13. Leah S. Marcus, 'Politics and Pastoral: Writing the Court on the Countryside', in Kevin Sharpe and Peter Lake (eds.), *Culture and Politics in Early Stuart England* (Basingstoke: Macmillan, 1994), pp. 139–59 (152).

14. See Martin Butler, 'Ben Jonson's *Pan's Anniversary* and the Politics of Early Stuart Pastoral', *English Literary Renaissance* 22.3 (1992), 369–404 (376).

15. Helen Hackett, '"Yet Tell Me Some Such Fiction": Lady Mary Wroth's *Urania* and the "Femininity" of Romance', in Clare Brant and Diane Purkiss (eds.), *Women, Texts & Histories 1575–1760* (London: Routledge, 1992), pp. 39–68 (46); Helen Hackett, *Women and Romance Fiction in the English Renaissance* (Cambridge: Cambridge University Press, 2000), p. 7. See also Lori Humphrey Newcomb's discussion of Wroth under 'Prose fiction' in this volume.

16. Mary Wroth, *The Countesse of Montgomeries Urania* (London, 1621).

17. Gary Waller, 'Mary Wroth and the Sidney Family Romance: Gender Construction in Early Modern England', in Miller and Waller (eds.), *Reading Mary Wroth*, pp. 35–63 (39).

18. See Mara R. Wade, 'The Queen's Courts: Anna of Denmark and her Royal Sisters', in Clare McManus (ed.), *Women and Culture at the Courts of the Stuart Queens* (Basingstoke: Macmillan, 2003), pp. 49–80 (54).

19. Clare McManus, *Women on the Renaissance Stage* (Manchester: Manchester University Press, 2002), pp. 106, 98–9.

20. Kathryn Schwarz, 'Amazon Reflections in the Jacobean Queen's Masque', *Studies in English Literature, 1500–1900* 35.2 (1995), 293–319.

21. Quoted in *Ben Jonson*, ed. C. H. Herford and P. and E. Simpson, 11 vols. (Oxford: Clarendon Press, 1941), x: 448.

22. See La Boderie, *Ambassades de Monsieur de la Boderie en Angleterre*, 5 vols. (Paris, 1750), III:13–24.

23. Barbara K. Lewalski, 'Lucy, Countess of Bedford: Images of a Jacobean Courtier and Patroness', in Kevin Sharpe and Steven N. Zwicker (eds.), *Politics of Discourse: The Literature and History of Seventeenth-Century England* (Berkeley: University of California Press, 1987), pp. 52–77 (52).

24. See Gustav Ungerer, 'An Unrecorded Performance of Shakespeare's *Titus Andronicus*', *Shakespeare Survey* 14 (1970), 102–9.

25. Aemelia Lanyer, *Salve Deus Rex Judaeorum* (London, 1611), D4r–v.

26. Susanne Woods (ed.), *The Poems of Aemilia Lanyer* (Oxford: Oxford University Press, 1993), p. xxxi.

27. See John Chamberlain, *The Letters of John Chamberlain*, ed. N. E. McClure, 2 vols. (Philadelphia: The American Philosophical Society, 1939), II: 55.

28. See Nathaniel Brent to Dudley Carleton, 2 January 1618: The National Archives, London, SP 14/95/3, fol. 6.

29. See Archives du Ministère des Affaires Etrangères, Paris: Fonds de la Correspondence Politique – Angleterre (origines–1871), vol. 42, fol. 61v.

30. E[lizabeth] F[alkland], *The History ... of Edward II* (London: J. C. for Charles Harper, Samuel Crouch and Thomas Fox, 1680), p. 52.

31. See William Brown Patterson, *King James VI and I and the Reunion of Christendom* (Cambridge: Cambridge University Press, 1997), pp. 182–9.

32. [Elizabeth Cary], *The Reply of the ... Cardinall of Perron* (Douay: Martin Bogart, 1630), ã2v.

READING LIST

Barroll, Leeds. *Anna of Denmark, Queen of England*. Philadelphia: University of Pennsylvania Press, 2001.

Bennett, Lyn. *Women Writing of Divinest Things: Rhetoric and the Poetry of Pembroke, Wroth and Lanyer*. Pittsburgh, PA: Dusquesne University Press, 2004.

Brant, Clare and Diane Purkiss (eds.). *Women, Texts & Histories 1575–1760*. London: Routledge, 1992.

Hackett, Helen. *Virgin Mother, Maiden Queen: Elizabeth I and the Cult of the Virgin Mary*. Basingstoke: Macmillan, 1995.

Hannay, Margaret Patterson (ed.). *Silent but for the Word: Women as Patrons, Translators, and Writers of Religious Works*. Kent, OH: Kent State University Press, 1985.

King, John N. 'Queen Elizabeth I: Representations of the Virgin Queen'. *Renaissance Quarterly* 43.1 (1990), 30–74.

Lewalski, Barbara K. 'Lucy, Countess of Bedford: Images of a Jacobean Courtier and Patroness'. In Kevin Sharpe and Steven N. Zwicker (eds.), *Politics of Discourse:*

The Literature and History of Seventeenth-Century England. Berkeley: University of California Press, 1987, pp. 52–77.

Lytle, Guy Fitch, and Stephen Orgel (eds.). *Patronage in the Renaissance*. Princeton, NJ: Princeton University Press, 1981.

Marcus, Leah S., Janel Mueller and Mary Beth Rose (eds.). *Elizabeth I: Collected Works*. Chicago: University of Chicago Press, 2000.

McManus, Clare. *Women on the Renaissance Stage*. Manchester: Manchester University Press, 2002.

McManus, Clare (ed.). *Women and Culture at the Courts of the Stuart Queens*. Basingstoke: Macmillan, 2003.

Miller, Naomi J. and Gary Waller (eds.). *Reading Mary Wroth: Representing Alternatives in Early Modern England*. Knoxville: University of Tennessee Press, 1991.

Peck, Linda Levy (ed.). *The Mental World of the Jacobean Court*. Cambridge: Cambridge University Press, 1991.

Veevers, Erica. *Images of Love and Religion: Queen Henrietta Maria and Court Entertainments*. Cambridge: Cambridge University Press, 1989.

Woods, Susanne. *Lanyer: A Renaissance Woman Poet*. Oxford: Oxford University Press, 1999.

9

FRANCES E. DOLAN

Women in the law courts

Any reader of early modern drama is familiar with the scene of a woman on trial.[1] Formally charged and tried, these notorious women get the chance to defend themselves, yet they face charges rather than bringing them. Women, as individuals and as a group, were also constantly 'arraigned' in print by such writers as the notorious Joseph Swetnam in his diatribe *The Araignment of Lewd, Idle, Froward, and Unconstant Women* (1615). As a consequence, defenders of women writing under female pseudonyms defended themselves and their sex by putting their attackers on trial in print, as in Esther Sowernam's pamphlet response to Swetnam, *Esther Hath Hang'd Haman*, in which 'she' proposes to arraign 'lewd, idle, froward, and unconstant men, and Husbands',[2] or in the play *Swetnam the Woman-hater, Arraigned by Women* (1620). In addition, individual women turned to print to defend their own virtue against formal and informal charges. While the adversarial trial provided a useful structure for depicting and conducting the battle of the sexes, it offers a skewed if vivid image of women's relationship to law courts.

My goal in this chapter is to sketch the range of women's engagements with the law in sixteenth- and seventeenth-century England, and the various relationships between women's legal engagements and their writing. Women did not enter courtrooms only under duress as defendants. They regularly entered courtrooms of their own volition as plaintiffs or witnesses. Just as women attended the theatre, they also attended notorious trials as spectators. Insiders in some ways, they were included on different terms than men were. In law courts, women were constrained yet strategic; in some ways subordinated and in other ways (perhaps even simultaneously) privileged and powerful. Women's entry into and experience with law courts was shaped not only by gender but also by their social, economic, marital and moral status, their ethnicity, their religion and by the highly variable circumstances that drove them to law in the first place.

The law was at the centre of early modern English culture, as a venue or occasion for conflict exploration and resolution, as a repository and generator of tropes and plots and as a vocabulary for the assertion and defence of entitlements and the imposition of obligations. Legal knowledge was broadly diffused through the culture; the law constrained, offered resources to and conferred authority on many different kinds of people in widely varying circumstances. The law was not one institution but many; it was not one body of knowledge but many overlapping, sometimes contradictory, knowledges. Rather than a monolithic or homogeneous set of standards imposed from above on hapless victims, the law was a haphazard, interactive mechanism with which increasing numbers of people interacted. Rates of litigation rose briskly 'with many courts inside and outside London more than doubling their business between 1550 and 1600'.[3] Women were active participants in this elaborate machine, participants who were, if anything, especially motivated to learn how to use the law to their advantage.

What law courts women were 'in' and why

Women could not serve as judges, attorneys, legal clerks or jury members. They could, however, serve on 'juries of matrons', the often randomly gathered groups of women who searched other women's bodies for proofs of virginity or recent childbirth, or for the marks taken as proofs of witchcraft.[4] On such occasions, women were able to trade on their presumed knowledge of the female body and to assert it as the basis of authoritative testimony, albeit often at the expense of the women they searched. Women also served as witnesses in a wide variety of causes; other women were more likely than men to ask women to testify on their behalf, but women also testified against other women.[5]

It is difficult to summarize women's legal status succinctly since different bodies of law offered different restrictions and opportunities. Under the common law, an unmarried woman (or 'feme sole') had approximately the same legal rights and responsibilities as a man; she could own and sell property, bequeath her property by will, make contracts, sue and be sued. Upon marriage, however, the husband assumed his wife's legal rights and responsibilities, subsuming her separate legal stature into his own by a process called 'coverture', under which the wife (a 'feme covert') was absorbed into or covered by the couple's 'unity of person'. The idea that husband and wife were one person under the common law was a legal fiction and was always acknowledged and contested as such. Yet this idea was also far-reaching in its impact and tenacious in its survival. As a consequence, women, particularly married women, appeared infrequently in common law courts such as the Court of Common Pleas or the Courts of the King's Bench or Queen's Bench (depending on who was on the throne), which was the most important common law court and had extensive criminal jurisdiction. Timothy Stretton, for example, finds women litigants in 10 to 13 per cent of the cases he samples in the 1560s from Common Pleas and Queen's Bench.[6]

Women appeared in criminal courts, sometimes by choice, but often not. These courts would include assize or circuit courts, the Queen's or King's Bench, and the Star Chamber Court, a London prerogative court that dealt with any matter deemed particularly threatening to the state. It is in the assize courts that we most often find the records of particularly 'feminized' – and distinctively early modern – crimes, by which I mean those crimes that were defined in terms of the perpetrators' female gender or for which most of the accused were women. Such crimes include neo-natal infanticide, witchcraft and petty treason (a form of murder defined as especially egregious because a subordinate attacked an authority figure, that is, a wife killed her husband or a servant killed his or her master).[7] Lurid, purportedly true stories of witches and women who killed their husbands and children were popular in pamphlets and ballads, and sometimes on the stage as well. The gendered definitions and representations of these crimes shed light on contemporary anxieties about intimacy, interdependency, domestic life and women's power over the people for whom they cared. Yet witches and petty traitors have diverted us from women's more mundane law-breaking. Using the records of Cheshire County quarter sessions and biannual Palatinate great sessions (equivalent to assizes although not a circuit court), Garthine Walker directs our attention away from supposedly feminized crimes towards the many other reasons that women entered criminal courts as defendants, plaintiffs and witnesses. Walker shows that women were involved in most categories of crime, although they usually constituted a minority of those prosecuted. Criminal women were not marginal figures; they were wives, mothers and mistresses.[8]

We find women most frequently in equity courts and church courts, that is, those in which they were less bound by common law restrictions than they were in common law and criminal courts. Thus the feature of married women's status that supposedly restricted their legal participation might also have motivated some of them to go to law and to seek out those jurisdictions in which they had the best options. With regard to their control over property, married women, to some extent, could get around the restrictions of coverture, or be stripped of its protections, via equity law through the Courts of Chancery and Exchequer (courts of royal prerogative). Records of women's litigation suggest that many married women assumed and asserted a right to maintenance and to some control of the property they brought into their marriages. Women acted as executors for their husband's estates, as guardians for underage children or wards and even as their husband's attorneys. Sometimes they defended their own rights *against* their husbands. They brought suit alone or with others.[9]

Women were plaintiffs or defendants in a third of the cases Timothy Stretton has studied in the Court of Requests, 'the poor man's Chancery', a national equity court in Westminster (in London). The majority of these women were married. For instance, wives often brought suits or were sued with their husbands. Instigated or supported by their husbands, many wives also brought in business that they had chosen not to litigate as single women or widows. Some even sued their husbands. Single women came to court to claim bequests or allowances or unpaid wages; widows came as executrixes of their husbands' wills, to collect debts, to prove their ownership of contested assets, to retain control of the marital home and to protect their assets in preparation for another marriage. However, women 'were less free than men to indulge in business dealings, to press bond penalties or openly to seek gain for themselves'. Women were especially liable to be seen as 'clamorous' – making too many or too aggressive demands, pursuing frivolous nuisance suits – if they did not have a male representative or partner as most, but not all, did.[10]

Women also figured importantly as litigants in church courts, which worked to regulate social conduct and sought to reform more than punish (and, indeed, might sentence an offender to public penance or excommunication but not to imprisonment or corporal punishment). Here, too, married women might sue without their husbands or attempt to settle their marital disputes. It has been argued that the London church courts became a 'women's court' in part because, as Susan Amussen puts it, 'reputation was a gendered concept in early modern England'.[11] Women thus turned to the courts to defend their sexual honour as the very fragile basis of their reputations – charging others with defaming them, suing for breaches of contract (or promise) that rendered their marital status unclear, standing charged of or bringing charges of sexual offences (such as incest, adultery and fornication), or petitioning for a marital separation or annulment. According to Laura Gowing, canon law was 'more open to women's legal agency than common law' because of its preoccupation with areas in which women were especially invested or assumed to be especially authoritative (not that this meant they were always respected as reliable witnesses).[12] As a consequence, women, mostly from the ranks of London's trades and crafts, brought 80 per cent of sex and marriage cases in London church courts by the early seventeenth century. This feminization of litigation happened outside London as well, although later and less extensively.[13] Women also grew to be the majority of those taking care of routine business in ecclesiastical probate courts, in which nearly three quarters of those 'appearing in court to prove wills, exhibit inventories and file accounts' were women.[14]

Although equity and church courts provided important venues for early modern women, these courts were interrupted during the English civil war and never quite recovered their momentum or stability thereafter.[15] Ultimately, common law outlasted both equity and ecclesiastical law, coming to dominate in England and its colonies. Yet equity courts, for instance, had meanings or influence extending beyond their actual jurisdiction. Walker suggests that in addition to or through the actual work of these courts, 'equity had evolved as a legal category to provide remedies in situations in which precedent or statutory law might not apply or be equitable' and so 'provided a resource upon which people drew in other jurisdictions and for other purposes'.[16] Luke Wilson and Lorna Hutson have argued that developments in equity law shaped representations of interiority and intention in Renaissance poetry and drama. Thus equity might have impinged even on women writers who never entered its courts.[17]

'Writing' and women's legal engagements

Before women appeared in court, as defendants, plaintiffs or witnesses, they usually had to give statements, called depositions or examinations. They gave these to male clerks, who shaped them according to the needs of legal procedure and convention, and the specific requirements of the court. Some women might have felt that having their words carefully recorded by a scribe and incorporated into a legal proceeding gave their speech and experience new authority. On the other hand, 'when women came into the court, they were made aware from the start that their testimony was understood differently from that of men' because they were assumed to be unreliable witnesses. They could give sworn testimony, although doubt was sometimes expressed as to whether women understood the oaths and their implications.[18]

Witness statements or depositions survive from many jurisdictions. Often the most fully developed stories appear in church court depositions; their wealth of narrative detail is one of the reasons social historians have found them invaluable. The question is whether we can read the surviving documents as records of women's 'voices' or as in any way women's 'writings'. As Stretton cautions, for example, 'given the obscuring filters created by male counsel, male scribes and male judges, it is unlikely that much survives in the records that could be labelled authentic female "voices"'.[19] Yet even such cautious scholars also seek in court records some trace of the kinds of voice we simply do not find in other kinds of sources; approaches vary from claiming that legal clerks transcribed depositions pretty much as they heard them to claiming that depositions contain some hint of voices or stories prior to or in excess of scribal shaping. The more we question what constitutes 'authentic' women's writings, the less distinctive the mediation of legal records may come to seem. According to Diane Purkiss, for instance, '*any text* produced by an early modern woman was prone to male intervention, in the process of composition as well as at the point of transcription or printing'.[20] As Lynne Magnusson says of letters in which women requested various kinds of redress or assistance: 'Our conceptions of authorship may not easily accommodate verbal practices that are social not only in that they repeat set forms but also in that secretaries or family members were often collaborators in the composing process.'[21] Although Magnusson works on letters rather than depositions, she invites us to think in terms of collaboration rather than mediation. Scholarship on the drama, most notably that of Jeffrey Masten, has revealed that playwriting was collaborative. This knowledge seems hard for many critics to assimilate; the author as possessive individual is far from dead in discussions of early modern literature. But collaboration might be a productive way of describing what was required of women going to law, who often depended on men to represent their words and their interests.[22]

The scene of the woman alone at the bar prevents us from thinking about these cross-sex, cross-class, intergenerational collaborations. Yet these collaborations might be similar to those that have been crucial to the history of women's writing, from Margery Kempe, dictating her autobiography to priests, to John Bale's redaction of the examinations of Anne Askew or Henry Jessey's transcription and publication of Sarah Wight's prophecies. In preparation for entering law courts and in the courts themselves, women were often able to press their claims because men helped them. When they wrote letters of appeal, they usually addressed men, whom they asked to represent their interests to yet other men. Queen Elizabeth herself instructs those who carry and present her letters on what to say to their recipients.[23]

Thinking about women's collaborations with men, we must also focus on how often women were themselves not 'in' court but rather pleading and planning from a distance. It might be argued that the women who work at a distance maintain the most control over the words on which they depend, and so are the easiest for us to recognize as writers. When Elizabeth Cary is barred from court, she conducts her business by letter. As she writes to Lord Conway, 'I cannot follow you, otherwise than by letter, both for want of a coach, and besides, because I am forbidden the court' and so asks him to 'be my solicitor'. In her long-running and ultimately fruitless attempt to get financial support from her husband, from whom she is separated largely because of her conversion to Catholicism, Cary seems to prefer documents to presence. Her petition to the Privy Council depicts her in the third person: 'for her personal appearance at the Councel table, she desires it may be spared because she is unwilling to appear in any place to oppose her lord, and as unwilling to appoint anybody to that purpose, thinking it unmeet to confront him'; if her husband objects 'anything against her humble desire (which she thinks he cannot) she then desires that an Answer in paper may be accepted from her'.[24] Cary was examined before the King's Bench and the Star Chamber in 1636 regarding the smuggling of her two young sons out of the country; she also sent constant letters of appeal to the court. Cary was so well connected that the most important people in the kingdom were informed of and involved in her marital, financial and parental struggles. She did not need to go to the Court of Requests; writing directly to the King and the Secretary of State, she secured their attempts to help her although even they could not get her husband to pay. Writing constitutes her participation in litigation and litigation is thus one of the provocations that make her a writer.

Cary presented her legal knowledge as a kind of patrimony – what 'she, being a Lawyer's daughter, was not wholly ignorant of' – and as a means of protecting her entitlements as a viscountess, wife and mother.[25] Other aristocratic women also turned to the law to defend their privileges. Like Cary, they achieved mixed results. A barrister, John Hawarde, describes an incident in 1606 in which a titled widow, Lady Rachel Russell, asserts her right to appeal to the Star Chamber Court and to state her case in her own terms but in which the male personnel of the court object to her self-assertion. Elizabeth I had granted both plaintiff and defendant claims to the property in question; Russell had 'custody' or use of the castle, park and manor of Dunnington; the Earl of Nottingham, who was Lord Admiral, had 'fee simple of them all', or what we might now call 'ownership'. The Earl and his men had arrived at the castle when Lady Rachel was absent; denied entrance, they had broken in, taken up residence and then barred Lady Rachel when she returned. At the time of the court hearing, Russell had not yet regained admission to the castle; she charged the Earl and his men with 'riot'. King James refused to intervene. At the hearing, the Privy Council suggests that 'the Lord's own servants entering but into his own house could not be rioters'. Lady Rachel expresses outrage that her claim is disputed and that she is not granted the status of 'Lady Dowager'. What interests me about this episode is that she appears in court on her own behalf and insists on speaking. Just as the judges are about to wrap up the proceedings without giving Lady Rachel satisfaction, 'the Lady, interrupting them, desired to be heard, & after many denials by the Court, violently & with great audacity began a large discourse, & would not by any means be stayed nor interrupted, but went on for the space of half an hour or more'. The lords of the Privy Council 'much distasted these fond speeches' and tried to stop her,

> but she still went on, & all the Court & presence murmuring & making great noise, giving no ear to anything she said, her own Counsel going from the bar also; yet she went on without any change, or any way abashed at all, in a very bold & stout manner, without any show of any distemperature, or any loud speaking, but showing a very great spirit & an undaunted courage, or rather will, more than womanlike, whose revenge by her tongue seemed to be the sum of her desire.[26]

Lady Rachel does not get satisfaction in that her claims are not supported and her speech is ignored and condemned. Even her attorney abandons her at the bar. The Lord Chancellor laments that 'we have suffered you to wrong yourself, this court, and our Majesty his service' and the judges 'all wished it had been ended, & never brought to this'. Yet Hawarde admits to some admiration for her. He also imagines that she demands of the occasion a form of satisfaction that is wholly under her own control: her 'revenge by her tongue seemed to be the sum of her desire'. Hawarde's detailed account of Russell's speech, its motive and its effects, materializes it into a text and grants it an afterlife.

Women also recorded or documented their legal engagements. Anne Clifford is a particularly famous and well-studied litigant, largely because she documented her decades-long legal battles in a series of diaries. Her father died in 1606, leaving his estate to his brother and then to his brother's son; the estate was to return to his daughter Anne only if the male line failed. Anne and her mother argued that his will was illegal because, since the estate was first conferred by a royal grant, it had been passed down to direct descendants, who could be either male or female. Anne's first husband, Richard Sackville, Earl of Dorset, was willing to negotiate with her uncle and cousin; she and her mother were not. She and her mother filed suits; she filed suit alone; she and her second husband, Philip Herbert, Earl of Pembroke and Montgomery, filed suits together in 1632 and 1637. But she got control of the property only in 1643 – when the male line did, indeed, fail. In the end, Clifford won because first, she never gave in or gave up and second, she outlived her rivals. The diaries make clear that Anne monitored these legal battles both intimately, through her subtle domestic struggles with her family members and whispered consultations at court, and at a distance, via letters and assisted by male secretaries, attorneys and advisers.

Arguably, it was litigation, and the documentation it required, that made Clifford a 'literary figure'.[27] Cary, Russell and Clifford developed considerable legal knowledge and were extremely persistent. Their self-assertions were in defence of élite privileges (financial maintenance from a husband, royal grants and inheritances) and of prerogatives often understood as traditionally feminine – control over their children, for instance. They used the law not to demand change but rather to defend their stake in the continuity of lands, titles and the 'old faith'.

But less privileged women were also compelled to write by their appearances in court. Let me give two vivid examples from 1680. Standing on a scaffold awaiting hanging for arson, Margaret Clark interrupted the proceedings to explain to spectators that she had 'left an account in a writing' of her very limited complicity – and the guilt of the man who had been acquitted. Although Clark refers to herself as the writer, she seems to have depended on the kind of collaboration that produced depositions, albeit after rather than before her trial: 'her words being taken from her Mouth in short hand, and when written out, read unto her, who then likewise affirmed the same to be True' and signed 'the same with her own hand'. Through the interventions of the High Sheriff, a minister and others present, this text was printed; thus Margaret Clark was able to participate in the depiction and interpretation of her crime and its punishment.[28] Elizabeth Cellier took the remarkable step of writing and printing an account of her own imprisonment and trial for treason, *Malice Defeated: or a Brief Relation of the Accusation and Deliverance of Elizabeth Cellier* (1680), in which she recounts how she successfully defended herself before the King's Bench and achieved acquittal. She was then tried and convicted in the Old Bailey for publishing this text, which was deemed a scandalous libel of individuals, the government and the laws of the nation. Cellier's unwilling appearance as a defendant thus prompted her into print, which in turn led to her criminal accountability for her text.[29]

Litigation motivated women to write in still another way. Some women writers created a parallel legal universe in which they needed little or no assistance, asserted control over their own affairs and self-representation, flaunted their knowledge and emerged successful. I think of this as a parallel rather than an alternative universe because even as women writers imagine it, they also structure it in terms of existing legal venues and vocabularies. For example, as scholars have shown, many women, even married ones, left wills, thus asserting some control over their property and its transmission. But women had to have something in order to leave it. Writers such as Isabella Whitney invented forms that enabled them to leave immaterial legacies, as in Whitney's 'Last Will and Testament', or texts purporting to be maternal legacies to unborn children. Margaret Cavendish restages her unsuccessful attempt to petition Parliament for a share of her husband's sequestered estate in a range of scenes of efficacious petitioning in her plays and in her prose fiction *The Description of a New World, Called the Blazing World* (1666).[30] In conclusion, some women built on the knowledge they had of litigation, often from their own suits of one kind and another, but used their powers as writers to imagine courts in which they were not only successful plaintiffs but judges, clerks and attorneys as well.

NOTES

1. Subha Mukherji, *Law and Representation in Early Modern Drama* (Cambridge: Cambridge University Press, 2006), pp. 206–32; Linda Woodbridge, *Women and the English Renaissance* (Urbana: University of Illinois Press, 1984), pp. 244–71, 96–7, 300–22.
2. Esther Sowernam, *Esther Hath Hang'd Haman* (London, 1617), title page.
3. Timothy Stretton, *Women Waging Law in Elizabethan England* (Cambridge: Cambridge University Press, 1998), p. 41. See also Cynthia Herrup, *The Common Peace: Participation and the Criminal Law in Seventeenth-Century England* (Cambridge: Cambridge University Press, 1987); J. A. Sharpe, 'The People and the Law', in Barry Reay (ed.), *Popular Culture in Seventeenth-Century England* (New York: St Martin's, 1985), pp. 249–56.
4. James C. Oldham, 'On Pleading the Belly: A History of the Jury of Matrons', *Criminal Justice History* 6 (1985), 1–64; Rachel Weil, 'The Politics of Legitimacy: Women and the Warming-Pan Scandal', in Lois G. Schwoerer (ed.), *The Revolution of 1688–1689: Changing Perspectives* (Cambridge: Cambridge University Press, 1992), pp. 65–82.
5. Laura Gowing, *Domestic Dangers: Women, Words, and Sex in Early Modern London* (Oxford: Clarendon Press, 1996), p. 49; Clive Holmes, 'Women: Witnesses and Witches', *Past and Present* 140 (August 1993), 45–78.
6. Stretton, *Women Waging Law*, p. 40.
7. Frances E. Dolan, *Dangerous Familiars: Representations of Domestic Crime in England, 1550–1700* (Ithaca, NY: Cornell University Press, 1994); Joy Wiltenburg, *Disorderly Women and Female Power in the Street Literature of Early Modern England and Germany* (Charlottesville: University of Virginia Press, 1992).
8. Garthine Walker, *Crime, Gender and Social Order in Early Modern England* (Cambridge: Cambridge University Press, 2003), p. 76.
9. Amy Louise Erickson, *Women and Property in Early Modern England* (London and New York: Routledge, 1993), pp. 114–15. See also Geoffrey L. Hudson, 'Negotiating for Blood Money: War Widows and the Courts in Seventeenth-Century England', in Jenny Kermode and Garthine Walker (eds.), *Women, Crime and the Courts in Early Modern England* (Chapel Hill and London: University of North Carolina Press, 1994), pp. 146–69; Natasha Korda, *Shakespeare's Domestic Economies: Gender and Property in Early Modern England* (Philadelphia: University of Pennsylvania Press, 2002), pp. 11–12, 39–47; Craig Muldrew, '"A Mutual Assent of Her Mind"? Women, Debt, Litigation and Contract in Early Modern England', *History Workshop Journal* 55 (2003), 47–71.

10. Stretton, *Women Waging Law*, pp. 7, 71, 95, 218, 145, 107, 110, 53, 233.

11. Richard M. Wunderli, *London Church Courts and Society on the Eve of the Reformation* (Cambridge, MA: Medieval Academy of America, 1981), p. 76; Susan Amussen, *An Ordered Society: Gender and Class in Early Modern England* (New York: Basil Blackwell, 1988), p. 104.

12. Gowing, *Domestic Dangers*, p. 38.

13. *Ibid.*, pp. 32, 36, 48.

14. Erickson, *Women and Property*, p. 32.

15. Stretton, *Women Waging Law*, p. 233.

16. Walker, *Crime, Gender, and Social Order*, p. 230.

17. Lorna Hutson, 'The "Double Voice" of Renaissance Equity and the Literary Voices of Women', in Danielle Clarke and Elizabeth Clarke (eds.), '*This Double Voice': Gendered Writing in Early Modern England* (New York: St Martins Press, 2000), pp. 142–63; Luke Wilson, *Theaters of Intention: Drama and the Law in Early Modern England* (Stanford, CA: Stanford University Press, 2000).

18. Gowing, *Domestic Dangers*, pp. 50–1, 53, 234, 251.

19. Stretton, *Women Waging Law*, p. 13.

20. Diane Purkiss, *The Witch in History: Early Modern and Twentieth-Century Representations* (London and New York: Routledge, 1996), p. 93; Lena Cowen Orlin, 'A Case for Anecdotalism in Women's History: The Witness Who Spoke When the Cock Crowed', *English Literary Renaissance* 31.1 (Winter 2001), 52–77, esp. 77.

21. Lynne Magnusson, 'A Rhetoric of Requests: Genre and Linguistic Scripts in Elizabethan Women's Suitors' Letters', in James Daybell (ed.), *Women and Politics in Early Modern England, 1450–1700* (Aldershot: Ashgate, 2004), pp. 50–66, esp. p. 52. See also Carolyn Sale, 'The "Roman Hand": Women, Writing and the Law in the *Att.-Gen. v. Chatterton* and the Letters of Lady Arbella Stuart', *English Literary History* 70 (2003), 929–61; Alison Thorne, 'Women's Petitionary Letters and Early Seventeenth-Century Treason Trials', *Women's Writing* 13.1 (March 2006), 23–43.

22. Jeffrey Masten, *Textual Intercourse: Collaboration, Authorship, and Sexualities in Renaissance Drama* (Cambridge: Cambridge University Press, 1997) and 'Material Cavendish: Paper, Performance, "Sociable Virginity"', *Modern Language Quarterly* 65.1 (March 2004), 49–68; Catharine Gray, *Women Writers and Public Debate in Seventeenth-Century Britain* (Basingstoke: Palgrave, 2007), pp. 29–31; Maureen Quilligan, *Incest and Agency in Elizabeth's England* (Philadelphia: University of Pennsylvania Press, 2005); Stretton, *Women Waging Law*, p. 123.

23. *Elizabeth I: Collected Works*, ed. Leah Marcus, Janel Mueller and Mary Beth Rose (Chicago: University of Chicago Press, 2000), p. 212; *Elizabeth Cary, Lady Falkland: Life and Letters*, ed. Heather Wolfe (Tempe: Arizona Center for Medieval and Renaissance Studies, 2001), p. 281. I have modernized and standardized spelling and punctuation here and in other quotations.

24. Cary, *Life and Letters*, p. 256 (5 April 1626), p. 300 (27–31 August 1627), p. 357 ([April] 1630).

25. *Ibid.*, 201.

26. *Les Reportes del Cases in Camera Stellata (1593–1609), from the original ms. of John Hawarde*, ed. William Paley Baildon (privately printed, London, 1894), pp. 271–8, esp. pp. 276–7.

27. Mary Chan and Nancy E. Wright, 'Marriage, Identity, and the Pursuit of Property in Seventeenth-Century England: The Cases of Anne Clifford and Elizabeth Wiseman', in Nancy E. Wright, Margaret W. Ferguson and A. R. Buck (eds.), *Women, Property, and the Letters of the Law in Early Modern England* (Toronto: University of Toronto Press, 2004), pp. 162–82, esp. p. 177; *The Diaries of Lady Anne Clifford*, ed. D. J. H. Clifford (Phoenix Mill: Alan Sutton, 1990); Julie Crawford, 'The Case of Lady Anne Clifford; or, Did Women Have a Mixed Monarchy?' *PMLA* 121.5 (2006), 1682–9.

28. *A Warning for Servants: and a Caution to Protestants* (London, 1680), C4v; *True Confession of Margret Clark* (London, 1680); Frances E. Dolan, ' "Gentlemen, I have one thing more to say": Women on Scaffolds in England, 1563–1680', *Modern Philology* 92.2 (1994), 157–78, esp. 171–7.

29. Rachel Weil, ' "If I did say so, I lyed": Elizabeth Cellier and the Construction of Credibility in the Popish Plot Crisis', in Susan D. Amussen and Mark A. Kishlansky (eds.), *Political Culture and Cultural Politics in Early Modern England: Essays Presented to David Underdown* (Manchester: Manchester University Press, 1995), pp. 189–209; Frances E. Dolan, *Whores of Babylon: Catholicism, Gender, and Seventeenth-Century Print Culture* (Ithaca, NY: Cornell University Press, 1999; Notre Dame, IN: University of Notre Dame Press, 2005), pp. 157–210; and Jody Greene, *The Trouble with Ownership: Literary Property and Authorial Liability in England, 1660–1730* (Philadelphia: University of Pennsylvania Press, 2005), pp. 88–103. A record of Cellier's trial for 'seditious libel' is available through the Proceedings of the Old Bailey online (t16800910–12).

30. Wendy Wall, *The Imprint of Gender: Authorship and Publication in the English Renaissance* (Ithaca, NY: Cornell University Press, 1993), pp. 279–340; Julie Crawford, ' "Pleaders, Atturneys, Petitioners, and the like": Margaret Cavendish and the Dramatic Petition', in Pamela Allen Brown and Peter Parolin (eds.), *Women Players in England, 1500–1660: Beyond the All-Male Stage* (Aldershot: Ashgate, 2005), pp. 241–60.

READING LIST

Amussen, Susan. *An Ordered Society: Gender and Class in Early Modern England*. New York: Basil Blackwell, 1988.

Erickson, Amy Louise. *Women and Property in Early Modern England*. London and New York: Routledge, 1993.

Gowing, Laura. *Domestic Dangers: Women, Words, and Sex in Early Modern London*. Oxford: Clarendon Press, 1996.

Hunt, Margaret R. 'Wives and Marital "Rights" in the Court of Exchequer in the Early Eighteenth Century'. In Paul Griffiths and Mark S. R. Jenner (eds.), *Londinopolis: Essays in the Cultural and Social History of Early Modern London*. Manchester: Manchester University Press, 2000, pp. 107–29.

Prest, Wilfred. 'Law and Women's Rights in Early Modern England'. *The Seventeenth Century* 6.2 (1991), 169–87.

Stretton, Timothy. *Women Waging Law in Elizabethan England*. Cambridge: Cambridge University Press, 1998.

Walker, Garthine. *Crime, Gender and Social Order in Early Modern England*. Cambridge: Cambridge University Press, 2003.

10

MARY E. FISSELL

Women in healing spaces

Women wrote about health, healing and the body in a variety of spaces in early modern England. When we look from the top down, that is from the perspective of a physician, we see few women healers, and even fewer women writers. However, if we start at the bedside, we see women involved in a wide range of healing activities, many of which they preserved in one form of writing or another. In order to understand the kinds of women's writings that have survived, we need to frame those texts in two larger contexts, that of medical work, and that of women's speech.

Historians used to think that medical work in early modern England was organized the way that physicians imagined that it should be: with themselves at the top, overseeing their inferiors. We now recognize that vision for the fantasy that it was. There were many kinds of health care providers in early modern England. The basic four clearly identified occupational groups were midwives, apothecaries, surgeons and physicians. Of these, women were eligible for entry only into the ranks of midwives. They were barred from universities and thus from becoming physicians, and they were not apprenticed to surgeons or apothecaries.

However, these groups represented only a portion of England's female healers. Many, many others practised in part-time or occasional fashion. Equally if not more important, many women were responsible for the health of their household, diagnosing, prescribing and preparing medicines at home. We will never know the full extent of women's health care practice, but women were a substantial portion of practitioners.

These formal structures of medical work help explain why there was not a substantial quantity of published medical works written by women. Such occupational structures did not reward publication by women. However, when we broaden the remit, and ask about women's writings about health, healing and the body, we discover a range of works by women. Women wrote letters in which they described their health and that of their families; they preserved recipes in manuscript notebooks; they advertised their services; and a few exceptional women wrote books on medical topics. Nevertheless, most of women's knowledge about the human body remained in the oral realm in this period, so we need to situate written texts within a much larger world of knowledge about the body that was transmitted in speech. We can eavesdrop, for example, at a late seventeenth-century doorway when a poor woman begging alms gave a woman a recipe to cure excessive menstruation.[1] Rare indeed are moments such as these that have been fixed in texts. However, they serve to remind us that writing down medical knowledge was an unusual practice for many women, so that the shape of extant texts reflects only a small portion of women's knowledge of health and healing.

All early modern women and men were accustomed to narrating their own ill health to others, even if only an infinitesimal proportion wrote down such descriptions. The nature of the patient–practitioner relationship and the diagnostic habits common to every sort of healer were grounded in stories of sickness told by patients. Physical examination as we know it was not practised, and so it was the story as much as or more than the body that required interpretation. Consequently, women's narratives of illness are often buried in practitioners' casebooks, in some instances in what appear to be their own words.[2]

Women's writing about health, healing and the body centred on three spaces: the still-room, the sickroom and the birthing room, each of which generated characteristic forms of writing. The closet, cabinet or still-room – a place where women might collect papers and store medicines – was strongly associated with the recipe book. The sickroom produced a substantial amount of writing about experiences of illness both told from the perspective of the sufferer and embedded within narratives written by caretakers. Finally, the birthing room generated a printed midwifery text written by a woman. Women also talked about experiences of childbirth in letters and diaries, although detailed descriptions are rare.

The still-room

Recipe or receipt books are one of the most significant forms of early modern women's writing about health and healing; substantial numbers of them survive in manuscripts well as a few printed texts.[3] We cannot always know the author or authors of such works – some provide a detailed genealogy of composition, with inscriptions of compilers on a fly-leaf, while others remain mute about their origins, leaving us to speculate about sequences of various handwritings. Both men and women wrote recipe books, and in some cases, a particular book was compiled by both sexes over a couple of generations.

A number of recent dissertations provide the first substantial scholarship on recipe books, and they suggest that these sources have much to tell us about women and healing.[4] Recipe books are highly formulaic. They are composed of a string of recipes, sometimes put into categories by their compilers, but more often in seemingly random order. Some writers numbered their recipes, and/or added tables of contents or indices to help them find their way through the recipes they had amassed. This seemingly random order derives, of course, from the mode of composition: people added to recipe books over time, as they accumulated more recipes. Some books clearly had a jump start – as Elaine Leong has documented, they seem to have been assembled by copying another remedy book as a kind of starter-kit, and then added to over time, and even over generations.[5]

Recipes themselves followed a formulaic pattern: a heading, usually indicating what ailment the recipe treated, but sometimes indicating provenance, as in 'my Lady Ann's cordial'; directions for making the remedy; and sometimes directions for use, such as, take two drops in a glass of wine in the evening. Many manuscript and printed books include recipes for cooking as well as healing. Often writers annotated their recipes with indications of efficacy, using the medieval formulation *probatum est* or its English equivalent, 'proven'. Most recipes seem to have been for commonplace and chronic ailments rather than dramatic life-threatening ones – coughs, skin ailments, sore eyes and the like more than, say, plague or acute fevers.

Although these entries are quite spare, in the sense of lacking a narrative frame or a lot of paratextual apparatus, careful readings have begun to open up recipe books, revealing details about their composition and use. These books offer a window into the social worlds of healers who compiled and used them. First, many of these books included recipes which appear to be of practical use – that is, they are composed of ingredients that early modern readers would have been able to assemble from a kitchen garden, a trip to a market and/or an apothecary's shop. Compared to books intended for physicians, domestic recipe books do not emphasize polypharmacy (that is, medicines with many many ingredients), nor very expensive, exotic ingredients. The material worlds these texts permit us to imagine seem to fit with what we know of the domestic circumstances of the middling sorts and their betters.

These texts also show us the social worlds of their compilers through the attributions of recipes. Some recipes were acquired for specific ailments – for example, 'Cousin Hannah Browne for my daughter Katherine when weak January 16th 1709' (Leong, 'Medical Recipe Collections', p. 143) – but most were collected when the social occasion arose for exchange. For example, in *Natura Exenterata*, a 1655 printed collection of 1702 recipes ascribed to Aletheia Talbot, there is a catalogue of all the 101 people from whom the recipes were collected, ordered by rank, with male aristocrats like Sir Walter Raleigh at the top, followed by doctors, men, most of whom are 'Mr', then aristocratic women, then ordinary women.[6] Not all names indicated personal exchange – 'Paracelsus', for example, tells us that Talbot had read his works. In the text itself, sequences of recipes hint at actual meetings. On pages 6 and 7, for example, there is a sequence of six recipes given by Mrs Downing, including a salve for a 'rankled' sore, a powder to stanch bleeding wounds and another that can be used for nosebleeds, conjuring up an image of the two women meeting face to face, or perhaps exchanging letters.

We are also beginning to appreciate the technical sophistication of some women's recipe books. For example, a manuscript recipe book associated with Lady Margaret Clifford (1560–1616) testifies to a high level of alchemical knowledge, with many recipes and allusions to a broad range of alchemical works. The manuscript is in two hands, neither of which appears to be Lady Margaret's, leading one historian to suggest that the book was prepared by scribes for Lady Margaret's use from her readings in a variety of libraries.[7] Distilling and making chemical remedies was not limited to a few in Elizabethan England; women took up distilling as a household practice, and some female healers adopted Paracelsian remedies quickly and eagerly.

In some cases, women made their own copies of existing recipe collections, while others were copied by scribes or servants, such as that 'written by Andrewe Plowden servante to mistris Honor Henslow, 1601'.[8] Manuscript recipe books were thus in dialectic relationships with each other, the nature of their composition highly recursive and interlinked with the production and reproduction of other manuscripts. Similarly, printed and manuscript texts were in a reciprocal relationship – a manuscript recipe book might contain individual recipes from printed sources, but then itself become the copy-text for a printed text – recipes from which would then be recycled back into other manuscripts!

Both manuscript and printed recipe books point to the circumstances of their composition in an unusual way: they echo the material facts of domestic medicine in form and title. The series of individual recipes, assembled both for specific circumstances ('for my daughter Katherine when weak') and as a kind of all-purpose household first-aid kit, mimics the closet or still-room or cabinet in which women kept their remedies. The evidence we have from such healers as Lady Grace Mildmay or Elizabeth Freke shows that these women made some multi-purpose remedies in fairly large batches and then stored them for years. Printed texts go a step further and title themselves after the spaces within which medicines were made and/or stored: for example, *The Queens Closet Opened*, allegedly the personal recipes of Queen Henrietta Maria, and *The Ladies Cabinet Opened*. Others associate recipes with small treasures or jewels, valuables kept in cabinets or closets. While we no longer consider the contents of bathroom cabinets 'treasures' or 'jewels', the preparation of early modern remedies might involve large quantities of expensive materials. When Elizabeth Freke's maidservant ran away, after a period of illness, Freke was furious and snarled about the costs of the medicines she had administered to the ungrateful servant: 'forty shillings would nott pay for her cordialls shee had outt of my closett'.[9] Freke did in fact keep her home-made cordials in a closet, as well as in a cabinet in her bedroom, literally echoing recipe-book titles. Many recipe books by both men and women refer to their contents as 'secrets', a multivalent word in this period. 'Secret' referred to any material process whose workings were not wholly explicable. But 'secrets' also referred to female genitals, potentially eroticizing hidden knowledge.

Although recipe books go back to the Middle Ages as a genre, and were among the first types of medical book to be printed, they became immensely popular during the 1650s, for reasons not yet clear. Certainly many forms of print boomed during the Interregnum, in part due to the lapse of the government's system of censorship. Some of the surge in receipt books, however, is likely to be due to copycat printing – once one such book sold many copies, printers rushed other recipe books into print. The book that led the boom seems to have been Elizabeth Grey, Countess of Kent's 1653 *A Choice Manual of Rare and Select Secrets in Physick and Chyrurgery*, although Lord Ruthven's *The Ladies Cabinet Opened* of 1639 may also have kickstarted the rise in popularity of the genre. Over the seventeenth century, recipe books were about 20 per cent of the total vernacular medical books published each decade, but in the 1650s, recipe books were almost a third of such titles.

Recipe books can be considered a form of technical writing, much like the artillery manuals or mining guides that gradually shifted from manuscript to print circulation. Unlike these, however, recipe books were written by both women and men. Because women had long been associated with domestic medicine, women continued to compile recipe books and to circulate individual recipes between manuscript and print. The recipe as a form remained fairly constant over the early modern period, continuing to require a reader to bring a good bit of tacit knowledge to the text (how to 'seethe' a liquid; where to find a herb and how to properly identify it) in order to use the text effectively.

The sickroom

The recipes so painstakingly prepared were used to heal a wide variety of complaints. From our vantage point, early modern illness was interminable. People were bedridden for what seem to us incredible lengths of time – months or even years. The fundamentals of medical care provided by doctors and domestic healers alike continued to be based upon the four humours. Sick bodies were helped to recover by promoting the body's own healing processes – thus, if an illness provoked vomiting, perhaps a medicine that also caused vomiting would help the body rid itself of whatever noxious substance was causing harm. Such evacuative therapy must have generated a huge amount of work, largely performed by women, changing linens and doing laundry, but most of it was never discussed in writing.

Women's writing about the sickroom either describes an individual's own suffering or details a woman's own healing practices, both usually in letters or diaries. When women wrote about their own ill health, they often employed one or more of three languages: those of spiritual accounting, grievance (or 'social accounting'), or the body as instrument.

Women were the front line of domestic healing. In October 1660, Abigail Harley described in a letter to her widower brother-in-law the care that she was giving to his infant daughter while he was away. The baby was very ill; she had fits, made some choking or rattling sounds in her throat, and slept poorly. Abigail made a drink of maidenhair, violet leaves and hyssop in a sugar syrup for her and sat up all night with the baby. The next day, Abigail continued to administer remedies of her choosing, sent for a doctor, and got two other women to watch and pray with her. Abigail explained, 'we are waiting to see what the Lord will do with her'.[10] Many collections of family papers contain detailed accounts of a family member's illness, written to someone far away. Such letters document the details of care (showing distant family members that everything possible was being done), brace the reader for the possibility of worse news and join writer and reader together in trying to accept God's will for the sick person.

Some women functioned as informal healers for their locale, offering health care as a form of charity or good works. Often they write about such activities in frustratingly brief ways – at least for historians seeking details of healing practices. Such women recorded their work more as a form of spiritual accounting than as a medical aide-memoire. For example, Lady Margaret Hoby (1571–1633), who lived in Hackness, Yorkshire, kept a diary from 1599 to 1605. Hoby seems to have had a substantial healing practice, especially in surgery. When a serving-man cut his foot with a hatchet, she dressed his wound that day, and for at least another ten days. Her practice resembled those of contemporary surgeons, who changed dressings and applied a large variety of ointments on a daily basis. Hoby put her healing work in the frame of spiritual accounting, 'After I had prayed I dressed the sores that came to me', she wrote on 2 February 1600.[11] Hoby had been educated in the Puritan household of Catherine, Countess of Huntingdon, and her diary echoes that of other godly writers who sought God's plans for them in the minute details of everyday life. For some other healers, such texts were literal accounting, that is, notes to help them collect fees. For example, Cumbria County Council has published the diary of a nameless Kendal midwife who practised from 1669 to 1675. The text is not a diary in the sense of life-writing; instead it is more of an account book, listing the newborn child, the father and the house or area where the family lived.[12] However, very few of these documents describing the work of female healers survive, since many of them worked in an informal economy or as charity.

Lady Margaret Hoby also shows us the sickroom from the patient's perspective. Her experiences of illness are noted in the same terse way as her activities as a healer. Illness was often just a stumbling block to spiritual exercises: 'I passed the afternoon with little reading because of my sickness', she notes on 13 January 1600 (*Diary*, p. 100), having dragged herself to church in the morning and afternoon. Many writers used religious language to describe illness. God was pleased to hear a sick person's petition, or preserved an injured person from an even worse wound, or spared someone's life – illness was often an intimate and sustained connection with the divine. When early modern women understood illness in such religious ways, they were, knowingly or unknowingly, following the advice of scores of devotional works, such as Thomas Becon's *The Sick Man's Salve* (1561), published in at least thirty editions.

Another language of ill health was that of grievance, or perhaps what we might call 'social accounting'. Elizabeth Freke (1642–1714), a deeply dissatisfied gentry woman living in rural Norfolk, noted down episodes of illness along with her unhappiness with her husband and son, and her many run-ins with servants who stole from her, were rude, or otherwise did not perform their duties as she wished. Her diary seems to have functioned as a testament to her continued ill-use, a space for grumbling and a record for her own ailing memory. Freke served the medical needs of her household, making large quantities of medicines and keeping an extensive recipe book. Compared to the spiritual accountants like Hoby, we learn more about Freke's own ailments, including dreams that foretold catastrophic falls. One of the themes that emerges most clearly from Freke's tale of woes is the very long time frame of early modern convalescence. She was in bed for months and even years from some ailments. Her diary is also one of the few accounts charting a slow descent into frailty associated with old age.

Finally, writings from the sickroom might use the body as an instrument through which God could communicate. As in the Middle Ages, the female body was a potent source of metaphor and meaning, and some women's bodies testified to a range of beliefs and ideologies. Often, as in the case of patient narratives, we must unpack a woman's authoring of her bodily practices from a text written by a man. Perhaps we can best understand these texts as joint productions, co-authored by male healer and female patient. Sarah Wight and Henry Jessey are a good example of this kind of cultural co-production.[13] In 1647, Wight, a fifteen-year-old girl, took to her bed, refusing to eat, remaining blind, deaf and bedridden for two months. Her distraught widowed mother brought in a range of ministers, including Henry Jessey, to heal her daughter. Sarah was struck by the conviction that she was damned while Jessey sought to persuade her of God's goodness and pull her back from the brink. Only after Wight apparently resigned herself to death did she experience a turn-around. Her bed became a sort of pulpit, with Wight quoting passages from Scripture and then explicating them. Wight also functioned as a kind of prophet, with women and girls seeking her counsel. Wight, then, can be understood in a variety of ways – as a female prophet similar to other radical women in the tumultuous 1640s and 1650s; as an adolescent girl struggling with her relationship with her mother; as a Nonconformist sunk in spiritual despair – but in any case, these are stories in some way authored by Wight. She uses the curious double move common to female prophets, of claiming to be able to say nothing, yet serving as God's instrument, and thus speaking God's words. When Sarah recovered, her mother took her to the country, and Henry Jessey published his account of the affair as *The Exceeding Riches of Grace Advanced* (1647). The book went into eight editions by 1700, by far his most successful work.

The sickroom was thus the site for a range of women's writing about health, healing and the body. As with many other texts of the period, women's sickroom writing drew upon Scripture and upon a huge quantity of devotional literature. In our time, so-called 'pathographies' or autobiographies of encounters with sickness are a genre unto themselves, but such was not the case in the early modern period. Often writing about the body was secondary to writing about the soul.

The birthing room

The third space that structured women's writing about health and healing was the birthing room, a special case of the sickroom. When a woman went into labour, she sent for her 'gossips', those female friends, neighbours and kin whom she had invited to support her through the long hours of labour. The word 'gossips', deriving from 'god-siblings', points to one of the most important frames for women's writing about childbirth – that of religion. Men were not usually admitted to the room unless a surgeon was called in for an emergency. After the birth, women 'lay in', in theory spending a month in bed before being 'churched', that is, going to church for the first time and participating in a special service of thanksgiving.

Although experiences of the birthing room – both giving birth and attending upon other women – must have been central to many women's adult lives, such experiences were rarely described in writing. Knowledge about reproduction was strongly gendered female and was almost always transmitted orally.[14] While we might wish to eavesdrop on those gossips, sources only rarely permit us any insight into their conversations. Nonetheless, three forms of women's writing about childbirth survive: prayers, life-writings and a guidebook.

First, women wrote prayers to be said during labour and delivery. As with many other forms of women's writing in this period, such prayers are often part of larger male-authored texts, mediated in various ways. In 1582 Thomas Bentley published his *Monument of Matrones*, a huge compendium of prayers for women.[15] The fifth section of the book is devoted to childbirth, including prayers to be said by the midwife, for the midwife, by the labouring woman and by and for her attendants. Some of these prayers include powerful descriptions of the pain of childbirth. Bentley collected prayers rather than writing them all himself, but we are not certain how many of these were actually written by women. Bentley's work was followed by a flood of smaller publications meant specifically for childbearing women, such as John Oliver's *A Present for Teeming Women*, first published in 1663. In manuscript sources, such as the papers of Elizabeth, Countess of Bridgewater (1626–63), we occasionally find a woman's own prayers about childbearing.

Much richer are those few women's writings that describe childbirth in letters or diaries. Best known of these is the writing of Alice Thornton (1626–1707), a godly Yorkshire woman who wrote three volumes of memoirs, subsequently published in the nineteenth century as a single volume of autobiography.[16] As Sharon Howard has noted, Thornton's descriptions of the pangs of childbirth draw upon religious tropes. In particular, Thornton uses the language of torture, describing childbirth as being on the rack. These images draw upon Foxe's Book of Martyrs, and can be understood as developing a model of identity formation through profound physical testing associated with the Marian Protestant martyrs celebrated by

Foxe. Individual suffering in childbirth could thus be redemptive and even a source of strength.

The other primary way that Thornton wrote about childbirth was in terms of God's providence, a theme common to many women's life-writings. Indeed, Thornton's memoir begins with a description of being saved from death at the age of three through God's providence. The opening phrases of the prayer said at the churching of women put childbirth into this same structure of thought – it was God himself who had given a woman her safe deliverance. Almost any misfortune or trying event – falling off a horse (or narrowly avoiding falling off a horse!), catching a chill, Thornton's evading capture by soldiers – all could be, and often were, interpreted as the workings of God's providence. Ill health or the pangs of labour could be suffused with meaning instead of merely endured when understood in this way.

Perhaps the best-known early modern women's writing about childbirth is *The Midwives Book* (1671), a midwifery guide written by Jane Sharp (*fl.* 1641–71). On the title page, Sharp proclaims herself to be 'Practitioner in the Art of Midwifry above 30 years'. Although, scholars have not been able to find biographical details about Sharp, some of her turns of phrase and her dedication to Lady Elleanour Talbutt suggest a West Country background.

Whatever Sharp's life experiences, her book is at once deeply conventional and fully flavoured with an individual personality. Like almost every other midwifery guide in the period, the text is not original. Sharp drew upon texts such as Nicholas Culpeper's *Directory for Midwives*, his translation of Daniel Sennert's *Practical Physick*, Peter Chamberlen's *Dr Chamberlain's Midwifes Practice* and others. As Elaine Hobby has demonstrated in the introduction to her superb edition of Sharp, Sharp borrowed extensively from other texts, but she tweaked them, altering the gender politics implict in the medical advice.[17] For example, Culpeper tells a story about a woman who would not be content until she gave birth to a boy, despite having had many healthy daughters. Finally she had a son, but he proved a 'fool', and Culpeper has the husband say 'Wife, thou wast never contented till thou hadst a Boy, and now thou hast gotten one that will be a Boy al the daies of his Life.' Sharp removes the preachy husband, merely noting that 'Some' (perhaps men as well as women?) are not content unless they have a son, and she makes the birth of a fool possible but not certain: 'God sometimes hears their prayers, and sends them a Boy, it may be a Fool, that will be a boy as long as he lives' (Hobby, Introduction to Sharp, *The Midwives Book*, p. xxv). Sharp's language permits the possibility that the pressures of primogeniture, or just sexism, weighed upon both parents, and makes Culpeper's punitive consequence merely a possibility rather than certainty. Sharp's book is remarkable because she seems to see so clearly into some of the gender politics implicit in male-authored texts whilst building her own book from them.

In conclusion, women's writing about health, healing and the body in the early modern period extended across many genres and was produced in a number of key sites. When we look at the still-room, the sickroom and the birthing room, two larger themes emerge. First, it is clear that women's writing, like that of men, could be a patchwork process of appropriation and re-use. Our own notions of authorial invention and autonomy are not relevant to much of the writing considered here. Instead, we must pay close attention to how material was circulated, borrowed and altered to fit an individual text. Second, difficult as it is for our own body-obsessed era to believe, early modern women were rarely driven to write about their own experiences of their bodies as such. Instead, religious belief drew them to their writing desks, shaped their prose and probably structured even their experiences of their own bodies. We need to continue to recover the ways in which the Bible and devotional literature formed a lens through which women saw health and illness.

NOTES

1. Collection of medical recipes, Royal College of Physicians, MS 504, p. 28, reproduced in Patricia Crawford and Laura Gowing (eds.), *Women's Worlds in Seventeenth-Century England* (London: Routledge, 2000), p. 30.
2. Mary E. Fissell, 'The Disappearance of the Patient's Narrative and the Invention of Hospital Medicine', in Roger French and Andrew Wear (eds.), *British Medicine in an Age of Reform* (London: Routledge, 1991), pp. 92–109.
3. On recipe books, cookery and household writing, see also Wendy Wall's chapter in this volume.
4. Jennifer K. Stine, 'Opening Closets: The Discovery of Household Medicine in Early Modern England' (Ph.D. thesis, Stanford University, 1996); Alisha Rankin, 'Medicine for the Uncommon Woman: Experience, Experiment, and Exchange in Early Modern Germany' (Ph.D. thesis, Harvard University, 2005); Lisa K. Meloncon, 'Rhetoric, Remedies, Regimens: Popular Science in Early Modern England' (Ph.D. thesis, University of South Carolina, 2005).
5. Elaine Leong, 'Medical Recipe Collections', in 'Seventeenth-Century England: Knowledge, Text and Gender' (Ph.D. thesis, Oxford University, 2005), p. 143.
6. Philiatros, *Natura Exenterata* (London, 1655).
7. Penny Bayer, 'Lady Margaret Clifford's Alchemical Receipt Book and the John Dee Circle', *Ambix* 52.3 (2005), 271–84.
8. Leong, 'Medical Recipe Collections', p. 138.
9. Elizabeth Freke, *The Remembrances of Elizabeth Freke, 1671–1714*, ed. Raymond A. Anselment (Cambridge: Cambridge University Press, 2001), p. 285. Anselment's edition wholly supersedes the 1913 Carbery edition, which silently combines two different texts. The Freke manuscripts are in the British Library, Add. MSS 45718 and 45719.

10. Abigail Harley to Sir Edward Harley, 9 October 1660. British Library, Add. MS 70115; reprinted in Crawford and Gowing, *Women's Worlds*, p. 202.
11. Margaret Hoby, *The Diary of Lady Margaret Hoby*, ed. Dorothy M. Meads (Boston: Houghton Mifflin, 1930), p. 100.
12. *The Diary of a Kendal Midwife* (Kendal: Cumbria County Council, 2002).
13. Henry Jessey, *The Exceeding Riches of Grace Advanced* (London, 1647). On women prophets, see Hilary Hinds's chapter in this volume.
14. Patricia Crawford, 'Sexual Knowledge in England, 1500–1750', in Roy Porter and Mikulas Teich (eds.), *Sexual Knowledge, Sexual Science: The History of Attitudes to Sexuality* (Cambridge: Cambridge University Press, 1994), pp. 82–106; Mary E. Fissell, 'Making a Masterpiece: The *Aristotle* Texts in Vernacular Medical Culture', in Charles E. Rosenberg (ed.), *Right Living: An Anglo-American Tradition of Self-Help Medicine* (Baltimore, MD: Johns Hopkins University Press, 2003), pp. 59–87.
15. Thomas Bentley, *The Monument of Matrones* (London: Printed by H. Denham, 1582), B1r.
16. Alice Thornton, *The Autobiography of Mrs Alice Thornton of East Newton, Co. York*, ed. C. Jackson (Edinburgh: Surtees Society, 1875). East Riding of Yorkshire Archives Service, Beverley, DDHV/75/1. Copy in the British Library, RP 2346. Sharon Howard, 'Imagining the Pain and Peril of Seventeenth-Century Childbirth: Travail and Deliverance in the Making of an Early Modern World', *Social History of Medicine* 16 (2003), 367–82.
17. Jane Sharp, *The Midwives Book. Or the Whole Art of Midwifry Discovered*, ed. Elaine Hobby (Oxford: Oxford University Press, 1999).

READING LIST

Bar-On, Yaarah. 'Neighbours and Gossip in Early Modern Gynaecology', in Willem de Blécourt and Cornelie Usborne (eds.), *Cultural Approaches to the History of Medicine*. London: Palgrave, 2004, pp. 36–55.
Fissell, Mary E. *Vernacular Bodies: The Politics of Reproduction in Early Modern England*. Oxford: Oxford University Press, 2004.
Gowing, Laura. *Common Bodies: Women, Touch, and Power in Seventeenth-Century England*. New Haven, CT: Yale University Press, 2003.
King, Helen. *Midwifery, Obstetrics and the Rise of Gynaecology: The Uses of a Sixteenth-Century Compendium*. Aldershot: Ashgate, 2007.
Knoppers, Laura Lunger. 'Opening the Queen's Closet: Henrietta Maria, Elizabeth Cromwell, and the Politics of Cookery'. *Renaissance Quarterly* 60 (2007), 464–99.
Marland, Hilary (ed.). *The Art of Midwifery*. London: Routledge, 1993.
Pelling, Margaret. *Medical Conflicts in Early Modern London: Patronage, Physicians, and Irregular Practitioners, 1550–1640*. Oxford: Clarendon Press, 2003.

PART THREE

Genres and modes

11

DANIELLE CLARKE

Translation

'from translation all Science had its of-spring'[1]

Writing to William Temple in September 1653, Dorothy Osborne complains bitterly about the quality of English translations of French romance: 'they were still soe much french in words and Phrases that twas impossible for one that understood not french to make any thing of them'.[2] Osborne's attitude reveals a set of expectations about what a translation should be like; namely, that it should not betray its status as a translation at all, and that to do so is to put in place a significant barrier if not to comprehension, then to reading pleasure. It is a complaint more usually found in relation to texts assumed to have higher cultural status than romance – classical literature and scripture, for example – but it signals the crucial balance that the translator seeks to strike between fidelity or accuracy and comprehensibility. Osborne's complaint epitomizes the fact that sixteenth- and seventeenth-century England was what translation theorists designate a 'target culture'. Technically, this means that translation activity into English was focused on the perceived needs of English culture, rather than on respecting the cultural or historical integrity of the 'source culture'.[3] This statement, whilst broadly true, conceals as much as it reveals. Translation activity in early modern England is variegated, multiple and serves a host of different functions; it is both literary (broadly defined) and pragmatic (practical manuals of instruction, as well as legal and trading documents). Translation is viewed as high status literary activity, and as unsung pedestrian drudgery, as William de L'Isle suggests when he claims that 'I, that am not worthy ... to hould a Trencher to the Muses, have (with bouldness inough) thrust my hand into the dish amongst them.'[4] The evidence of translations reveals an interest in the appropriation of textual content alongside a not always articulated concern with bolstering lexical range and authority, and with aligning English with Latinate stylistic authority. Translated texts constitute a significant proportion of both printed and manuscript texts until (and beyond) the

Restoration, but it is only post-Restoration that we find significant critical reflection on the translation process.

Translation practice in the Renaissance is in no sense linear; it is not a movement with rules and objectives, but it is omnipresent. Rather, translation is one very powerful means by which the early moderns mediate and measure their relationship with their contested heritage. Translation and translated texts continually confront questions related to power and status: which texts are 'worthy' of translation? Which classes of people should be able to read which texts? How does the existence of a vernacular translation affect the élite who previously had exclusive access to that text? The great Elizabethan translations are often lauded more for their influence on later writers, notably Shakespeare, than for any inherent qualities of their own, although many of the most 'popular' works of the Tudor and early Stuart periods were in fact translations, or had their origins in translated work. Romance, in particular, was often translated, or heavily indebted to translated sources – here, the fact of translation often goes unremarked, a symptom of the fact that these texts largely fell outside of the humanist system of value.[5] Alongside these manifold paradoxes lies another – that while translation is central to programmatic humanist pedagogy, and forms the epistemological category that structures much of early modern thinking about language, style and meaning, it is disproportionately present in the remaining record of women's literary production. This paradox – that a culturally authoritative form of literary production was seemingly an accepted activity for women – will form the focus of this essay.[6]

Translation in context

'Translation' is arguably neither a mode nor a genre (although it can be said to be both); neither does the term refer to a single type of textual activity. Translation as a category is at least binary in its conceptual core, and translation practice entails divergent practices, theories and attitudes to language and textuality. As such, it can be seen both as a philosophical, conceptual category, and as a powerfully material *praxis*; in general, the English Renaissance inclines rather more to the latter view than the former. The historical, literary or political significance of a translation may be articulated on numerous textual axes: a passage (or more) that has been excised or expanded; the choice of translation style (literal, paraphrase, imitation); the choice of source text; the dedicatee; the timing of publication; the selection of genre; the importation of new genres; specific vocabulary choices; the creation of interpretive communities or political/ideological alliances. Alongside these potentially lofty contributions to textual culture it is important to recall translation's status as a form of active reading, an intensified encounter with the linguistic contours of the source text and a type of productive *copia* in relation to the target text. Female as well as male translators were frequent coiners of words, as well as attempting to reproduce the rhetorical tropes and figures of their sources in their work. There is often a disjunction between the alleged purpose of translation, and the text's final effect; notions of authorial intention can only help us so much in analysis, as translation is the ultimate manifestation of the dispersal of textual authority. Biographical explications are liable to be particularly misleading. A translation that starts life as a diversion, or as an exercise, may well subsequently have an unexpected impact; equally, the act of translation itself may be a highly coded political or ideological intervention where the guise of another's words can help to evade the authorities.[7] For women translators, all of these functions of translation are potentially available, precisely because of the decentring of authorial responsibility or authority that the act of translation necessarily entails. All translations may occupy multiple positions on the continuum between submission to and mastery of the source text; it is this flexible ambiguity that makes translation such a ready outlet for women writers in the period. Where the boundaries between legitimate engagement with the written word via a restrictive concept of translation as submission and other types of textual productive are porous, conscious attempts at containment will be limited at best.

It is tempting to draw a parallel between the historical invisibility of the translator as a generator of textual meaning, and the relative invisibility of the early modern woman writer, both in her own culture, and in later literary history. To do so, however, would be to underplay the centrality of translation, and translators, in early modern culture; by the same token, many women writers and translators in the period were known, acknowledged and lauded for their translation activity, not all of which was circulated in a domestic setting.[8] To suggest that translation was, in any sense, a marginal activity in the Renaissance would be to mistake the character of literary production in the period. Sixteenth-century England, in particular, was what we might term a 'culture of reception', rapidly and rather unevenly assimilating a literary and scholarly heritage into an unstable and evolving vernacular, to the end of creating an élite culture not only to rival imperial Rome, but commensurate with England's burgeoning imperial and commercial supremacy. In line with this imperially inflected project, an expanding Renaissance readership encountered many foundational texts in translation: Golding's *Metamorphoses* (1565–7); North's version of Plutarch's *Lives* (1579); Harington's *Orlando Furioso* (1591); Florio's Montaigne (1603); Chapman's Homer (1611); and Shelton's *Don Quixote* (1612), to name just a few key texts. Not infrequently, translations were presented as forms of linguistic conquest, as Samuel Daniel's dedicatory poem to Sylvester's translation of Du Bartas's *Divine Weekes* implies:

> Thus to adventure forth, and re-convay
> The best of treasures, from a Forraine Coast,
> And take that wealth wherin they gloried most,
> And make it Ours by such a gallant pray ...[9]

Equally, if not more important, is the impact of biblical translation, and the commitment to making Scripture available in the vernacular. The translation of the Bible and the very particular difficulties that it posed facilitated a debate about key aspects of translation – what is lost? What is fidelity? Why does accuracy matter? The accessibility of the Bible in English in turn created a demand for the translation and circulation of other kinds of texts – commentaries and sermons (Calvin, for example), theological works, prayer books and meditations, all of which found an eager and ready readership in the emergent class of literate women.

The readership of a translation is immediately bifurcated into those reading with knowledge of the source texts and languages, and those who are not – in each case, the reading experience will be very different, and entails a quite different set of intertextual relationships. Where the translated text is only known to the reader through the target language, translation has the effect of appropriation and assimilation, making the text seem familiar, native – which is one reason why translations are such happy hunting grounds for lexicographers and historians of the English language. A reader familiar with the source language and text will bring a different set of textual relationships to bear, and the intertextual dynamics will tend to be diachronic, rather than synchronic, as is the case when the translated text is read primarily in relation to other vernacular texts. To put this slightly differently, whilst translation is obviously a distinct type of literary production, it does not necessarily fall into a singular category for the reader, who will, in most cases, encounter it as a text with the same status as other texts. This relative marginality or slipperiness of ownership can be exploited as a form of agency to figures who otherwise lack it (women), and as a form of evasion for those who might wish to place some distance between author and text (this category might also include women). Translations then are not necessarily primarily oriented towards the source, and this might be argued to be a distinctive feature of much of women's translation activity, namely that it is positioned in relation to other English writings, looks to the contemporaneous rather than the ancient, and is less constrained by the functional learning habits of the grammar school.

As well as being the means by which texts, stories, ideas and technologies were moved from one locus to another, translation activity formed the backbone of early modern grammar school pedagogy. One primary practical means by which a pupil's knowledge of grammar was tested was through the practice of translation, to and from Latin, and in the case of Roger Ascham's systematization of this practice, through so-called 'double translation'. In this instance, a text was translated from Latin into English, and the student then translated the English sentence back into Latin – the objective being to come as close to the original as possible. Such exercises were undertaken both individually and collectively and involved a minute concentration on the grammatical elements of language, with other structures of meaning being relegated to secondary importance, at least in the early stages.[10] For an academically minded boy, such encounters must have engendered an intimate sense of linguistic difference, indeed of the very impossibility of attaining the end to which the exercise was ultimately geared. The texts encountered in this way would gradually have increased in difficulty and complexity as the pupil progressed, and the apt student's developing skill would have led him towards the looser (and equally influential) counterpart of translation, imitation. And this is where distinctions and definitions start to get a little murky. Conventionally, a translation will be defined on the basis of its apparent proximity to or distance from the original text; here 'fidelity' is the overwhelming criterion, yet 'literalism' is frequently seen as a fault.[11] Of course, as post-structuralist interpretations of translation have been at pains to point out, the notion of a stable textuality awaiting reproduction is at best misleading, but these kinds of assumptions have a significant bearing on the kinds of expectations that structure women's intervention as translators, namely that they will 'serve' the source text, faithfully reproducing it without appropriating any of its cultural capital for their own purposes.[12]

The metaphorical language used in translation discourse is often strongly gendered, with the terms shifting according to where the power is deemed to reside in the (usually) hierarchical relationship between translation and original. What is striking about Renaissance discourses is the shift between an early language of submission to foreign language texts (usually in Latin or Greek), to a language of mastery, where the original is presented as feminized, as passive, and to be subordinated to the masculine power of English. These positions are often expressed metaphorically by means of designating the original text as a female body, which needs to be reclothed in a different 'dress' (language), a reworking of classical metaphors for the relationship between form and content. Honoré D'Urfé's heroine, Astrea, for example is now encouraged to crosse the seas, and to try what welcome she shall meete with here in ENGLAND. And though it cannot be, but her riding-suite will take much away from her originall beauty (it being the fortune of few Bookes to be bettered by the translation) yet she is so confident of her owne Worth, that she expects acceptance onely for herselfe, and not for her ornaments.[13]

The connection between notions of value and gender is strongly suggested in John Florio's suggestion that 'all translations are reputed femalls, delivered at second hand' (*Essayes*, A2r); other critics assert that creativity is seen as 'original and "masculine"', whilst translation is often viewed as 'derivative and "feminine"'.[14] One might argue that this feminization of the concept of translation as a form of submission arises in order to differentiate such activity from the apparently more productive textual encounters with antecedent texts valorized through imitation and *copia*, but it perhaps also suggests some notion of suitability based on homology, where the cultural function of both translation and women is to reproduce and transmit cultural and economic capital. Translation thus is one of a number of rather porous concepts that attempt to determine or measure intertextuality, and the degree of difference between original/source and translation/version/ imitation. Arguably, translation can also be pressed into service to describe other kinds of textual transformations, *translatio* being the Latin term for metaphor; some women writers clearly use intermediary texts when they translate, working sometimes from other English versions, or from translations from Latin texts in other modern languages.[15]

Women, texts and translation

For many literate women from upper-class English families, translation formed part of a series of educational activities that collectively emphasized and reinforced virtue and woman's role within the household. The non-institutional site of the home was generally the place where, sometimes with the aid of a tutor, girls learned foreign languages. Translation activity rarely formed part of a programmatic education, and it usually focused on the learning of French or Italian, as a form of female accomplishment, or 'ornament'. There were exceptions to this, of course; some girls were taught Latin and, occasionally, Greek, and their contribution to female translation output is disproportionately significant.[16] Girls who might be called upon to take on a role in the public sphere, as a ruler, for instance, were educated in much the same way as their male peers, which demonstrates that arguments relating to female education in the period are not so much concerned with ability, as with suitability. In theory, at least, attempts to circumscribe female literary production by advocating translation on the grounds that it involves attention to small matters of detail, and submission to the source text, were justified, like other restrictions placed on female education, by the notion that women's contribution was to be made in the private sphere, where virtue mattered above all. Many extant translations by women might well be classified as classroom exercises; Elizabeth Cary's translation of Ortelius clearly falls into this category, although her precocity rightly suggested that this foundation would be built upon.[17] Early works by Elizabeth I, Catherine Parr and Lady Lumley fall into this category too. It is perhaps significant that many of these women continued their writing activity, thus informally and non-institutionally following some kind of pattern or model in their acquisition of literary skill and training. Some writers use translation judiciously but not exclusively; Cary, for example, generally eschews translation later in her writing life, but deploys it at a particular moment of personal and ideological crisis. Her translation of Jacques Davy Du Perron's *Reply* (1630) clearly arises out of her conversion to Catholicism, and is a not so oblique way of announcing that; it also attempts to cement ties with the female Catholic circles focused on the Villiers family; finally, it attempts to encourage the proselytizing tendencies of Henrietta Maria. These contextual effects are arguably at least as important as the actual content of the text, which whilst dense with authoritative allusions and precedents, ultimately advances few new arguments on the topic of papal supremacy.

Women's literary activity was fundamentally shaped by what happened in the household; most writing women from the Renaissance period would have learned to read at home, rather than in the haphazard and informal environment of the petty schools. Some would have acquired literacy in later life, or been taught by peers, or have been taught more formally in the setting of a convent or school. Initial encounters with translated texts usually focused on the most important translated text of all, the Bible. Whilst it is not the purpose of this chapter to focus on women as readers and consumers of translated texts, the Bible is an exceptional case, primarily because its translated status, together with its authority and position as legitimate reading for women, spawned a wide range of translation activities on the part of women. In the first instance, its use demonstrates one dominant notion of translation in relation to women, that of virtuous occupation. This relies on a very limited concept of translation, one that envisages little expansion beyond a word-for-word engagement with the text; in this, it is more closely allied to copying than to the kinds of transformative operations that we routinely expect from Renaissance translators. In turn, such activity is imagined as a form of occupation, keeping the impressionable mind from straying beyond prescribed limits; it presupposes the translator as a *tabula rasa* who will receive the ideas of the source intact. In this scenario, the female translator is an almost invisible ligature between source text and translation, which is assumed to be a process of simple replication. However, there is a big difference between prescription and practice, and the authorized encounter with a text as varied and complex as the Scriptures provided a springboard for a legitimized form of textual engagement and production, not only with the rhetorical richness of the Bible itself, but also with its forms and genres (witness poetry derived through imitation and meditation from the biblical model – Anne Lok, Mary Sidney, Anne Southwell, *Eliza's Babes*, Diana Primrose, Aemilia Lanyer).

Beyond the strict confines of the Bible itself, women were sometimes actively encouraged to consult commentaries and theological explanations, and beyond that to participate in (and often to direct) household prayers, discussions and readings. For many women, these kinds of informal networks seem to have provided a context (a putative readership, perhaps) for the translation of key works of theology. Like other kinds of printed texts, many translations (whether undertaken by men or by women) come with conventional disclaimers, or humility *topoi*; nevertheless, women translators show a marked preference for the kinds of texts that might be seen to be their own justification, even when those texts are ultimately radical or controversial. Even when the text itself may fall outside of such prescribed limits, the terms in which it is presented are often defined against the notion of the ideal: 'it is a womans work, though in a story prophane, and a matter more manlike then becommeth my sexe'.[18] There is no doubt, whatever the nature of the text translated (drama, poetry, theology, romance), that for most women, the household and the family are the crucible within which this kind of activity is forged and encouraged. While translation, as suggested above, was a key element of Renaissance classroom pedagogy, it was also practised less formally within the educational regimes of highly placed households. Many of the women who translate, for example, Lady Lumley, or the Cooke sisters, come from noble households where there is a deep commitment to humanist learning.[19] Father figures are often crucial here, as their enthusiasms are passed on to apt daughters in the absence of willing or able sons. Equally, such interests would have prompted the idea of a connection between education and virtue, which may well have improved a young woman's eligibility in the marriage market. In other cases, particularly where families and kinship networks exhibit commitments to particular theological and/or political positions, a woman's translation activity will often turn out to cohere with wider cultural practice within a given kinship network; Mary Sidney, Countess of Pembroke is a high-profile example of this phenomenon, but there are many other examples.

Translated texts – whether a narrow or a broad definition is used – constitute a significant proportion of the output of early modern women, and it is perhaps revealing that it is during this period that the term 'translatresse' is coined to denote female translation activity. Interestingly, the term is used both pejoratively and positively; William Chillingworth uses it to refer to Elizabeth Cary's translation of Du Perron's *Reply*, but Dame Agnes More refers to herself as a 'translatresse' in her translation of St François de Sales's *Delicious Entertainments of the Soul*.[20] Translations by early modern women can be found in virtually all genres and modes – poetry, prose, drama; romance, history, theology – and are fairly evenly spread over the period, rising proportionally in line with the overall increase in women's printed output. Works of religious controversy are well represented, both Catholic and Protestant.[21] Particular texts recur in women's translations, hinting at the possibility that certain materials were considered to be of particular interest to women, but also that most women – even literate ones – had limited access to printed books. In addition, the re-translation of the same text is of a piece with translation activity more generally in the period, namely that it is time-bound and context-driven; the Sternhold-Hopkins Psalter was not the Psalm translation for the Protestant aesthetic espoused by the Sidney circle in the 1580s and 1590s; Golding's fourteeners did not articulate the Ovid required by the early Stuarts.

An example of such a text is Petrarch's sequence of linked poems, *I Trionfi*, which adapts the model of the Roman triumph to a series of moral tableaux – it is written in *terza rima*, which is notoriously difficult to render into passable English verse. Nevertheless, the text has been interpreted as 'an invitation to female poetics', presumably because of the depiction of Laura as a speaker.[22] There are three extant translations of the text by women: Elizabeth I's partial translation of the *Triumph of Eternity*, usually considered to be a schoolroom exercise; Mary Sidney, Countess of Pembroke's version in *terza rima* of the *Triumph of Death*; and Anna Hume's translation of the first three triumphs (Love, Chastity and Death), published in Edinburgh in 1644.[23] Both Elizabeth I's and Mary Sidney's translations are manuscript texts, although certainly Mary Sidney's translation was known to her contemporaries – it is included with a letter of December 1600 from Sir John Harington to Lucy, Countess of Bedford; in addition, Thomas Moffett pleads with her to 'Let *Petrarke* sleep, give rest to *Sacred Witte*' in his *The Silkewormes, and their Flies*.[24] That three women translated this text is testament to the fact that our understanding of women's engagement with literary culture in the Renaissance requires constant revision.[25] The iconography arising from Petrarch's poem was widely assimilated and re-used in performances, portraits and spectacles, and Petrarchan discourse – more usually derived from the *Canzoniere* – was pervasive in the poetry of the period, but is more usually assumed to entail a problematic objectification of the feminine, and its ultimate subordination to masculine sexual and rhetorical supremacy.[26] Yet the evidence of these translations suggests that Petrarch's writings held a good degree of interest for women as texts to engage with, and that they also perceived the political potential in what appeared to be 'suitable' texts for women.[27] The *Triumph of Death* in particular was a text with political resonance, with its emphasis on the ultimate capitulation of beauty and chastity to death; a highly topical issue in the waning years of Elizabeth's reign, and one that raised serious succession and political issues. Mary Sidney's version, whilst not in any sense a 'free' translation, uses stylistic and lexical choices to hint at the possible political application of the depiction of the death of Laura, and her transformation into a resonant figure – death triumphs over beauty, and eternity ultimately triumphs over death. One of the more conspicuous examples of this is the refraction of the Countess's phrasing through another text that she was working with – probably contemporaneously with the *Triumph of Death* – the Psalms. In the second part of the poem, Laura describes her own death:

> I not denye (quoth she) but that the crosse
> Preceeding death, extreemlie martireth,
> And more the feare of that eternall losse.
> But when the panting soule in God takes breath;
> And wearie heart affecteth heavenlie rest,
> An unrepented syghe, not els, is death.[28]

Careful stylistic choices serve to ally this moment more closely with the Christian tradition; 'crosse', 'martireth' give a distinctively Protestant cast to Petrarch's *dolgia forte*. The influence of the Psalms is rather more obvious in the Countess's rendering of 'ma pur che l'alma in Dio si riconforte', as she allies the soul's desire for God with more secular discourses which pun on the heart/hart homophone, as well as evoking Psalm 42: 'As the hart braieth for the rivers of water, so panteth my soule after thee, O God.'[29]

Translated texts by women – and by men – are not only significant for their content or their style, but they frequently innovate formally and generically as well. The case of the *Triumphs* is an unusual one, because the poetic tradition seems to have melded with the more dramatic, performance tradition, but in other cases, generic innovation can be traced directly to translated texts. Although in many ways an exception, the translated output of the Countess of Pembroke is highly significant, not least because of her self-conscious selection of texts that fell within decorous bounds, and her subtle exploitation of their potential for agency and intervention in the public sphere. She was also deeply interested in questions of form and genre, and reveals the way in which rhetorical and stylistic invention could operate from the margins of humanist pedagogy. A good example of this is her 1592 *Antonius: A Tragedie* (reprinted in 1595 as *The Tragedie of Antonie*), a translation of Robert Garnier's Senecan drama, *Marc Antoine*. The play is the first English drama to represent the figure of Cleopatra – with some degree of sympathy – and effectively introduced the form of the closet drama to England, where it was enthusiastically taken up by members of the Pembroke circle, and was strongly associated with veiled political commentary and criticism. The selection of a play to translate that was concerned with a transitional point in Roman history was certainly political in the context of the 1590s, as concerns about Elizabeth's succession – and the excesses of her court and the extravagance of her iconography – came into sharp focus. The play is directly interested in the relationship between public action and private morality, and with the need to moderate and control sexual passion; interestingly, it is the figure of Cleopatra who embodies repentant virtue, and chooses death over capitulation to Rome. The translation sticks closely to Garnier's original, not so much because of 'how hesitant she was to appear assertive', but because of the potential political application of the text.[30] Such disciplined adherence to the form and meaning of the text also leads the Countess of Pembroke to innovate in other ways, as she introduces word-play and distinctive coinages – the repeated use of the word 'measure', for example, and her use of figures such as chiasmus and anaphora. A representative example of this kind of rhetorical and stylistic patterning can be found in Charmian's attempt to dissuade Cleopatra from suicide:

> CH. Live for your sonnes. CL. Nay for their father die.
> CH. Hardharted mother! CL. Wife, kindhearted, I.
> CH. Then will you them deprive of royall right?
> CL. Do I deprive them? No, it's dest'nies might.[31]

Women's translation activity in the Renaissance has yet to be fully explored and adequately documented, partly because translated texts present such challenges to our notions of what texts and authorship consist of.[32] This has perhaps led to the marginalization of materials – however significant – translated by women in the period, and this is largely due to our inability, as modern readers, to locate and interrogate gender in these kinds of texts. Yet translation provides a rich seam of evidence of women's active participation, not only in the literary culture of the Renaissance, but in all aspects of culture.

NOTES

1. John Florio, trans. Montaigne, *Essayes*, A5r. For modern views that echo Florio's, see George Steiner, *After Babel: Aspects of Language and Translation* (Oxford: Oxford University Press, 1975).
2. *The Letters of Dorothy Osborne to William Temple*, ed. G. C. Moore-Smith (Oxford: Clarendon Press, 1928), p. 91.
3. A reliable guide to terminology and basic translation theory is Susan Bassnett, *Translation Studies* (London: Methuen, 1980); see also Lawrence Venuti, *The Translator's Invisibility: A History of Translation* (London: Routledge, 1995).
4. *Virgils Eclogues Translated into English* (London, 1628), 3v.
5. See, for example, *Argenis, Amadis de Gaule, The History of Astrea, Ariana, Eromena*.
6. The forthcoming *Oxford History of Literary Translation in English*, vol. II, ed. Robert Cummings, will give detailed background on the key topics; useful secondary material can be found in Robert Cummings, 'Recent Studies in English Translation *c.* 1520–*c.* 1590', *English Literary Renaissance* 37 (2007), 274–316.
7. For a well-known example, see *The Annales of Cornelius Tacitus*, trans. Henry Savile (n.p.: 1598), and David Womersley, 'Sir Henry Savile's Translation of Tacitus and the Political Interpretation of Elizabethan Texts', *Review of English Studies* 42 (1991), 313–42.
8. No systematic statistical analysis has been done, and the list of works attributed to women grows all the time; but see Patricia Crawford, 'Women's Published Writings 1600–1700', in Mary Prior (ed.), *Women in English Society 1500–1800* (London: Methuen, 1985), pp. 211–64.
9. Samuel Daniel, *The Complete Works in Verse and Prose*, ed. A. B. Grosart, 5 vols. (London: Hazell, Watson and Viney, 1885–96), I: 281.
10. See William E. Miller, 'Double Translation in English Humanistic Education', *Studies in Translation* 10 (1963), 163–74, and for a development of Ascham's model, John Brinsley, *Ludus Literarius: or, The grammar schoole* (London, 1612).
11. See Jonathan Goldberg, 'The Countess of Pembroke's Literal Translation', in Margreta de Grazia *et al.* (eds.), *Subject and Object in Renaissance Culture* (Cambridge: Cambridge University Press, 1996), pp. 321–36.
12. See Walter Benjamin, 'The Task of the Translator', in *Illuminations*, ed. Hannah Arendt, trans. Harry Zolen (New York: Harcourt, Brace and World, 1968), pp. 69–82; Jacques Derrida's reading of Benjamin's essay is 'Des Tours de Babel', in *Difference in Translation*, ed. Joseph F. Graham (Ithaca, NY: Cornell University Press, 1985), pp. 165–207.
13. *The History of Astrea. The First Part*, trans. John Pyper (London, 1620), A3r–v.
14. Lori Chamberlain, 'Gender and the Metaphorics of Translation', in Lawrence Venuti (ed.), *Rethinking Translation: Discourse, Subjectivity, Ideology* (London: Routledge, 1992), pp. 57–74 (57).
15. See Eugene Vance, who argues that the 'generic term for figures of thought was … *translatio*', *Mervelous Signals: Poetics and Sign Theory in the Middle Ages* (Lincoln: University of Nebraska Press, 1986), p. 315. For a contrary view, see Rita Copeland, *Rhetoric, Hermeneutics and Translation in the Middle Ages:*

Academic Traditions and Vernacular Texts (Cambridge: Cambridge University Press, 1991), p. 235, n. 74.

16. See Jane Stevenson, *Women Latin Poets: Language, Gender, and Authority from Antiquity to the Eighteenth Century* (Oxford: Oxford University Press, 2005).

17. See Michael Drayton's dedicatory poem to Elizabeth Tanfield, in *Works*, ed. J. W. Hebel, 5 vols. (Oxford: Blackwell, 1959), v: 123–4. The translation is of 'The Mirror of the Worlde' and is now in the Bodleian Library, MS Dep.d.817.

18. Diego Ortúñez de Calahorra, *The Mirrour of Princely Deedes and Knighthood*, trans. Margaret Tyler (London, 1578), A3r.

19. See Mary Ellen Lamb, 'The Cooke Sisters: Attitudes toward Learned Women in the Renaissance', in Margaret P. Hannay (ed.), *Silent but for the Word: Tudor Women as Patrons, Translators, and Writers of Religious Works* (Kent, OH: Kent State University Press, 1985), pp. 107–25, and Alan Stewart, 'The Voices of Anne Cooke, Lady Anne and Lady Bacon', in Danielle Clarke and Elizabeth Clarke (eds.), *'This Double Voice': Gendered Writing in Early Modern England* (Houndmills: Macmillan, 2000), pp. 88–102.

20. See *OED* entry; *Delicious Entertainments of the Soul* (Douai, 1632), sig. a2r. The possibility of a connection between the two women, given Cary's connections with continental Catholics, is intriguing but unproven.

21. See, for example, Catherine Bentley, trans. Luke Wadding, *The history of the angelicall virgin glorious S. Clare* (Douai, 1635); Anne Prowse, trans. Jean Taffin, *Of the markes of the children of God* (London, 1609); Lady Elizabeth Russell, trans. John Poynet, *A way of reconciliation of a good and learned man* (London, 1605).

22. Nona Fienberg, 'Mary Wroth and the Invention of Female Poetic Subjectivity', in Naomi Miller and Gary Waller (eds.), *Reading Mary Wroth: Representing Alternatives in Early Modern England* (Knoxville: University of Tennessee Press, 1991), pp. 175–90, 184.

23. See Leicester Bradner (ed.), *The Poems of Queen Elizabeth I* (Providence, RI: Brown University Press, 1964), pp. 13–16; p. xiv.

24. London, 1599, A3r.

25. Another woman (E[lizabeth] D[ouglas]) contributed dedicatory sonnets to William Fowler's translation of the *Triumphs*. See *The Works of William Fowler*, ed. Henry W. Meikle, 2 vols. (Edinburgh: Scottish Text Society, 1914–40), I: 19.

26. See D. G. Rees, 'Petrarch's "Trionfo Della Morte" in English', *Italian Studies* 7 (1952), 82–96, and for details on Renaissance uses of *I Trionfi*, see Danielle Clarke, '"Lover's Songs Shall Turne to Holy Psalmes": Mary Sidney and the Transformation of Petrarch', *The Modern Language Review* 92 (1997), 282–94.

27. See, for example, Katherine Duncan-Jones, 'Bess Carey's Petrarch: Newly Discovered Elizabethan Sonnets', *Review of English Studies* 50 (1999), 304–19.

28. Text in *Isabella Whitney, Mary Sidney and Aemilia Lanyer: Renaissance Women Poets*, ed. Danielle Clarke (Harmondsworth: Penguin, 2000), II: 46–51.

29. *Geneva Bible* (1560), fol. 243v.

30. Tina Krontiris, *Oppositional Voices: Women as Writers and Translators of Literature in the English Renaissance* (London: Routledge, 1992), p. 68.

31. *Narrative and Dramatic Sources of Shakespeare*, ed. Geoffrey Bullough, 5 vols. (London, 1957–75), vol.v, lines 555–8.
32. Brenda Hosington's forthcoming book should remedy this.

READING LIST

Cummings, Robert. 'Recent Studies in English Translation c. 1520–c. 1590'. *English Literary Renaissance* 37 (2007): 274–316.

Ferguson, Margaret. *Dido's Daughters: Literacy, Gender, and Empire in Early Modern England and France*. Chicago: University of Chicago Press, 2003.

Goldberg, Jonathan. 'The Countess of Pembroke's Literal Translation'. In Margreta de Grazia *et al.* (eds.), *Subject and Object in Renaissance Culture*. Cambridge: Cambridge University Press, 1996, pp.321–36.

Hannay, Margaret P. *Philip's Phoenix: Mary Sidney, Countess of Pembroke*. New York: Oxford University Press, 1990.

Hannay, Margaret P. (ed.). *Silent but for the Word: Tudor Women as Patrons, Translators, and Writers of Religious Works*. Kent, OH: Kent State University Press, 1985.

Hermans, Theo (ed.). *The Manipulation of Literature: Studies in Literary Translation*. London: Croom Helm, 1985.

Krontiris, Tina. *Oppositional Voices: Women as Writers and Translators of Literature in the English Renaissance*. London: Routledge, 1992.

Robinson, Douglas. 'Theorizing Translation in a Woman's Voice: Subverting the Rhetoric of Patronage, Courtly Love and Morality'. *Translator* 1 (1995): 153–75.

12

JAMES DAYBELL

Letters

Letters are undoubtedly the most ubiquitous written form surviving from the pens of early modern women. Letter-writing was a quotidian activity connected to the rhythms of women's everyday lives. Perhaps more than any other type of text, letters – given their apparent immediacy and auto-biographical flavour – lend themselves to intersecting methods of inquiry: historical, literary, palaeographical, linguistic and gender-based. They shed important new light on female education and literacy and on the nature of early modern women's writing; reflect family, gender and other social relations; map the social and political activities of networks of female let-ter-writers; and permit the reconstruction of sixteenth- and seventeenth-century *mentalités*. Recent work has challenged traditional perceptions of women's letters as largely 'private', non-political forms and of letter-writing as a solely male activity.[1] Furthermore, new approaches to Renaissance let-ters have encouraged scholars to rethink the ways in which we read, inter-pret and understand women's letters.[2] Letters are not simply depositories of 'historical fact', windows into women's souls or indeed vehicles capable of echoing unproblematized women's voices down the centuries. Increasingly, correspondence is viewed as a highly complex genre that requires layers of careful unpacking, an awareness of the multi-dimensional nature of episto-larity (literally, the 'letterness' of letters) and sensitivity to social and cultural meaning inscribed textually and materially for full understanding.

Early modern women's letters survive in three main types of repository: in state papers, in legal and institutional archives and among family collec-tions. While a small proportion of letters can be read in modern printed (and increasingly online) editions, the majority need to be consulted in manu-script.[3] Correspondence in archives can be located using standard printed calendars, as well as through finding other bibliographical resources and the catalogues of research libraries and local record offices, though count-less missives doubtless lie decaying in private muniments rooms. Numbers of surviving letters increase over the course of the period with rising female literacy levels: more than 3,500 Elizabethan letters written by over 750 individual women are extant, and in excess of 10,000 women's letters survive for the period to 1642 – a fraction of the letters written at the time. These figures, however, pale in comparison with men's correspondence, which survives in far greater numbers. This partly reflects higher levels of male literacy and familiarity with letter-writing, the greater range of opportunities that male writers had to employ letters in official or business capacities, and male archival policies which discriminated against women's letters. John Knox's 'godly and comfortable letters', for example, were preserved for posterity, but the replies of his female correspondents are lost.[4]

The ways in which archives were formed have an important bearing on the nature of correspondence that exists today. Letters in state and legal repositories tend to be highly practical, connected with judicial, patronage and business matters. Although family collections contain letters of a more 'personal' nature, the surviving material may be unrepresentative of the range of letters written during the period. The paucity of missives of a sexual nature, for example, may reflect wilful destruction or may suggest that they were regarded as too ephemeral for preservation. Serendipitous finds occasionally permit the reconstruction of epistolary exchanges, but usually only one side of the correspondence remains. Letters of particular individuals also commonly survive unequally for different periods of their lifetime; years of marriage or widowhood are usually more fully represented than childhood or adolescence; runs of correspondence covering the entire life cycle of particular women are rare. More broadly, letters capture a mere snapshot in time, generating a view of women's lives as static rather than evolving and of the relationships they document as constant rather than fluctuating. Correspondence was also occasioned by practical concerns, crises and events; it reflects certain emotional states or conditions, such as grief, love, need. These characteristics are at the heart of the epistolary genre.

Analysis of the social status of women letter-writers indicates that letter-writing represents a larger area of early modern female activity than many hitherto have assumed, one that was socially and geographically diversified. Letter-writing skills extended below the ranks of the aristocracy, court élites and the wives and daughters of courtiers and humanists to encompass 'middling' groups.[5] The majority of women of landed and mercantile status had regular dealings with pen, ink and paper during the period, which further contributes to reconsiderations of levels of female literacy.[6] Indirect evidence, including scriveners' diaries and accounts, court depositions and popular literature, indicates that women lower down the social scale were involved in epistolary cultures, a useful corrective to conceptions of letter-writing as an élite preserve. Although most scholarly attention has focused on England, female letter-writing during the sixteenth and seventeenth centuries extended well beyond its borders, into Scotland, Wales and Ireland, throughout Europe and across the Atlantic to New England. Furthermore, a handful of women were involved in the traditionally male, Latin world of the European-wide Republic of Letters: Margaret Roper corresponded with the Dutch humanist Erasmus; and, in the seventeenth century, Dorothy Moore and her niece Katherine, Lady Ranelagh were intimately associated with the epistolary networks of the Royal Society and Samuel Hartlib, whose scriptorium disseminated intellectual and religious ideas in Britain and Europe.[7] An examination of networks of correspondents helps to map the ambit of women's social worlds. While chiefly centred upon the family and household, contacts were not confined to the 'domestic' sphere as traditionally defined: Elizabeth, Countess of Shrewsbury sat at the centre of a pan-European news and intelligence network; Mary Phelippes, wife of cryptographer Thomas Phelippes, took over her husband's correspondence with a web of European spies after his imprisonment in the wake of the Gunpowder Plot; and the seventeenth-century gentlewoman Anne Newdigate cultivated useful court contacts by post.[8]

Attention to the mechanics of composition – who wrote letters, how and under what conditions – exposes various archetypal epistolary practices that in combination work to erode, but not completely erase, notions of early modern letter-writing as private, personal and singular. While many women wrote themselves, a significant proportion of letters were penned by amanuenses (distancing female signatories from personal writing technologies) or exhibit signs of collaboration. Letters were dictated to scribes; written from notes by secretaries; constructed from templates or models by clerks; passed to family members and friends for comment; they were drafted and reworked by legal counsel and government officials. For some women, use of a scrivener or secretary was enforced by illiteracy; for others (as with fully literate men) it was a matter of choice influenced by circumstance and convention. Ill health and infirmity might lead women to sit with a scribe; the messy mundanity of writing itself did not sit easily with early sixteenth-century ideas of nobility. Throughout the period, formal business correspondence was conventionally penned by secretaries, while by the start of James I's reign it was increasingly expected that women would indite intimate and family letters with their own hands.[9] The scribal and textual peculiarities of letters refigure them as potentially communal and collective, rather than merely individual and exclusive, providing a more complex understanding of issues of authorship and early modern subjectivities. Definitions of what constitutes a 'woman writer' therefore must incorporate cultural writing practices that are collaborative as well as those that are individual.

The customs of delivery and reading shed further light on the generic sophistication of early modern women's letters. Prior to the evolution of the post office, letters were delivered in a makeshift manner, entrusted to bearers (servants, merchants, carriers and even passing travellers) who represented corporeal extensions of the letter; meaning was therefore generated orally as well as textually.[10] The exigencies of dispatch, the sudden arrival and departure of a bearer, could encourage an urgent immediacy among letter-writers, different from the studied rhetorical manoeuvrings evident in formal business missives. Letters were frequently sent unsealed, passed among family members and read aloud to assembled company; letters were circulated scribally and sometimes published in print. Elizabeth I's condolence letter to Margaret Norris on the death of her son, the military commander Sir John Norris, circulated widely in manuscript throughout the seventeenth century. A godly letter from Lady Jane Grey to her sister Katherine was included by Miles Coverdale in his 1564 edition of martyrs' letters, presumably by virtue of her royal status.[11] The insecurity of the epistolary medium, however, promoted a degree of self-censorship among writers distrustful of letters going astray and falling into the wrong hands. Alongside these communal practices, therefore, developed an emerging concept of privacy; correspondence was increasingly regarded as singular, the property of the recipient. The opening of another person's missive (even by a spouse) became socially taboo, thought worthy of apology. As female literacy rose over the period, women's letters became increasingly private spaces, detached from secretarial gaze. Husbands and wives traded intimacies and secrets in correspondence; young girls were encouraged to practise their epistolary skills in order to allow them greater control over their own affairs in later life; clandestine or highly sensitive information was transmitted by women using ciphers, informal codes and secret devices.[12] The learned Anne Bacon (1528–1610) used a kind of cipher in letters to her son Anthony by transliterating into Greek characters critical comments about Archbishop Whitgift in order to conceal them from the prying eyes of servants. Anne, Countess of Northumberland used a series of coded symbols to represent names of different people in her correspondence with the recusant exile William Cotton concerning Spain and the Netherlands.[13] Increased personalization of letter-writing led to letters being utilized for an expanding range of purposes by the end of the period.

Read for their contents, women's letters demonstrate the breadth of female activities, which extended from the household economy and estate management, domestic and religious patronage, medicine and education, to involvement in local, national and European politics. The majority of letters touch on business concerns defined in the broadest sense; women wrote for pragmatic reasons, garnering advice and information in their dealings. While practicalities might provide the initial impetus to correspond, a plethora of topics are mentioned in passing; letters thus act as useful records for reconstructing the everyday lives and experiences of early modern women. They reveal much about contemporary social practices, and activities often 'hidden from history' that spanned the female life cycle, including pregnancy, childbirth, breast-feeding and the selection of godparents; attitudes to the education and upbringing of children and wardship; customs of courtship and marriage arrangement, death and bereavement. Religion, however, is strikingly absent from most sixteenth-century women's everyday correspondence (with important exceptions like the redoubtable Puritan widow Anne Bacon); the degree of religiosity involved in the formation of outward epistolary selves was muted during a period of continual flux created by religious and political upheavals. By the mid seventeenth and early eighteenth centuries, though, epistolary and religious conditions were increasingly secure, and the letter developed more fully as a forum of female piety and sociability, intellectual discussion and spiritual counsel.[14] Broad similarities exist between the content of men's and women's letters, although female letter-writers, as Anne Laurence and Rosemary O'Day have argued, bring an alternative viewpoint to those of men on social affairs. Indeed, Barbara Harris, using early Tudor women's correspondence, argues for a distinctly 'female point of view' about pregnancy and childbirth.[15] Moreover, letters offer a unique perspective on early modern women, different from male-voiced prescriptive texts; essentially secular, they differ from diaries, which generally conform to strict religious interpretive models.

The word 'letter' is in many ways a catch-all term that belies the rich variety of epistolary forms, both 'real' and 'fictional'. When scholars refer to women's correspondence, however, they ordinarily mean vernacular prose letters, which can be divided formally by function and sub-genre (love letter, letter of condolence, petitionary and 'familiar' letters) and are distinct from other types of epistolary writing, such as the verse epistle, dedicatory epistle and epistolary novel. 'Domestic' or 'familiar' epistles encompassed a wide range of subjects and purposes. Indeed, William Fulwood argued that such correspondence was 'more in use than any other for so much as their nature they are very necessary, to let our frendes understande of our estate, and of our businesse be it of helth, prosperitie, sicknesse, adversitie, or any other domesticall and familiar thyngs'.[16] The permeability of generic boundaries blurs strict divisions between 'familiar', 'domestic' or 'familial' correspondence, and 'business', 'state' or 'political' letters. In practice, early modern women's correspondence was rarely limited to single issues, but covered diverse topics, a characteristic feature that precludes individual epistles from any simplistic or reductive mode of classification. In a letter to her father, Richard Bagot, Anne Broughton provided details of two murder trials, sent foodstuffs and clothing, thanked him for his gift of venison and imparted assorted news of family and friends. Writing during the civil war to her sister-in-law Anne More, the Parliamentarian Lady Elizabeth More interspersed news of her own health and teething updates of her young son Will with details of troop movements at Bedford and in Hertfordshire.[17]

Letters were, however, not without conventions and protocols. Printed Renaissance letter-writing manuals and manuscript formularies offered model letters for women writing in different social situations. An early example is Christine de Pisan's *The Treasure of the City of Ladies*, last published in 1536 in French, which includes 'an example of the sort of letter the wise lady may send to her mistress'.[18] Elizabethan epistolographies also catered for a female audience. William Fulwood's *The Enemie of Idlenesse* (1568) presents letters from a wife, a sister, a mother and a daughter, and an epistle from a lady to her lover. The 1595 edition of Angel Day's *The English Secretary* contains 'a letter remuneratory from a gentlewoman of good sort to a nobleman her kinsman', and 'a letter gratulatorie from a wife to her husband'.[19] The mid seventeenth century witnessed the development of English manuals specifically directed at women, including Jacques Du Bosque's *The Secretary of Ladies* (1638), Henry Care's *The Female Secretary* (1671) and Hannah Wolley's *The Gentlewoman's Companion* (1672). The degree to which manuals scripted women's epistolary interactions is uneven. Beyond standard formulae, salutations, modes of address and closural forms, women's informal correspondence was a relatively elastic, protean genre, unconstrained by slavish convention. Formal letters, however, are a different matter, where deviation from prescribed norms provoked social anxiety. Letters of petition making requests to government officials and monarchs most closely adhere to standard forms, often following the kinds of classical rhetorical devices outlined by Erasmus and Day. Women's letters of petition, recommendation and intercession also reveal familiarity with rhetorical and epistolary forms in terms of structure, language, strategies and manuscript layout. While there is evidence that women owned letter-writing manuals and that young girls received tuition in letter-writing, it is more likely that this conversance with epistolary conventions was gained through contact with the form.[20]

Modes of address, language and tone shed light on the nature of women's social interactions; letters thus act as useful indicators of women's status and role within society. Above all what emerges from analysis of a range of women's correspondence – with social subordinates, superiors and equals, and with men as well as women – is the variety of their social relationships, which differed in emotional intensity depending on the personalities, character and backgrounds of individual writers. Letter-writing could reinforce social distinctions through polite conventions of address or through deferential language and tropes such as apologies for 'scribbled lines'; yet positions of social and familial seniority also conferred status and authority on women. Gender codes were porous, creating overlapping areas of female responsibility; marked differences existed between restrictive authoritarian precepts and actual practice.[21] In writing to servants women acquired a voice of command; as mothers they wrote with a mixture of counsel and censure; as wives they wrote with trust and affection. Operating within the confines of male authority, women achieved significant social influence as power was negotiated on an individual basis.

Furthermore, letter-writing in sixteenth- and seventeenth-century England was a political activity. Women were well aware of the politically freighted nature of language; codes of deference and social courtesy were intricately utilized in communications with family and officials; negative gender assumptions of female incapacity were manipulated for strategic effect. Moreover, the letter was the chief written form through which women exerted power and influence. 'Networking' letters give evidence of women's cultivation and maintenance of kinship and patronage networks. The passing on of news (as a form of gift) in letters cemented social contacts, and kept female correspondents abreast of current events and public opinion. Margaret Hill wrote regularly from London to her cousin Richard Carnsew in the West Country, keeping him informed of events in the capital; in one of her letters she enclosed a newsbook and a copy of the Earl of Essex's funeral sermon.[22] During the early seventeenth century the staunchly Puritan widow, Lady Joan Barrington, regularly received copies of corantos or newsbooks with letters from family and friends. Postal connections were also vital as channels of information, and in the 1650s the Ghent Benedictine nuns put their postal services at the disposal of Charles II for delivering Royalist mail. Letters of intercession on behalf of family and clients reveal the extent of female involvement in areas of patronage normally perceived as male, including the appointment to secular and ecclesiastical office. Read with attention to language, women's letters of intercession display a rich vocabulary of favour and 'political friendship'. Female letter-writers employed a Senecan language of mutual benefits, promising repayment of favours in kind and assuring the friendship of themselves and husbands. Frances Bridges, Lady Chandos, assured Sir Julius Caesar, Master of the Court of Requests, that she would 'be ever ready to requite' him 'in a greater matter when occasion shalbe offered'.[23] The easy familiarity with which women utilized a language of favour and reciprocity suggests the high degree of confidence and authority with which many women intervened in political arenas as an ordinary part of their social duties as family members, mistresses of households, landowners and patrons in their own right.[24]

The early modern period as a whole witnessed the emergence of more personal epistolary forms and the increasing range of flexible uses for which letters were employed, a development from the pragmatic medieval form bound by the *ars dictaminis* which impeded emotional content and personality. Letters have traditionally been interpreted as 'autobiographical' documents, uniquely self-reflective, expressive of 'women's voices' and capable of shedding light on women's self-perception. As texts, letters are indeed characterized by strongly autobiographical elements, and often convey a rich flavour of a writer's 'personality'. Written in the first person, with a firm sense of authorial identity, they describe the dealings, events and experiences of writers' everyday lives; they establish relationships between writers and the recipients of their letters; as the conveyors of sentiments and feelings they express various emotional states; and they display women's opinions, attitudes and judgements on a range of matters. Letters are, therefore, viewed as outward exhibitions of self-expression, representations of the outer self; letter-writers possess the language to describe personal thoughts and feelings: 'I', 'my', 'mine' and 'my self'. How far women's letters of the period can be considered 'autobiographical', however, is an important question, especially in light of recent theoretical and critical approaches to the 'self' and 'selfhood', which challenge received notions of the 'self' or 'selves' as linguistic, cultural or social constructs subject to historical relativity.[25] In one sense, letters represent a 'technology of the self', a vehicle through which female letter-writers composed a self or selves through writing. The very process of writing a letter prompted women to view themselves in relation to others, for example, a daughter writing to a parent, a wife corresponding with a husband, a female suitor petitioning a government official.[26] Female letter-writers were further prompted to categorize themselves by social status, gender, nationality and religion, as well as by more identifiable traits such as character, temperament, health, age, appearance and education. Letters occasioned by dispute or conflict convey among the most vivid expressions of self in terms of individual rights; female letter-writers deftly marshalled a language of equity in their epistolary confrontations. In addition to this presentation of an outer self, letters are also arguably reflective of interiority, a woman's 'inner self' (or more precisely how this was represented). During the early modern period, letter-writing performed an increasing range of functions that led to a degree of inwardness. In some ways, letter-writing appears to have provided a form of cathartic or psychological release, through which women formulated and worked out issues and concerns. Letters written to confessors or preachers on matters of spiritual development encouraged confessional self-examination, a practice that continued well into the seventeenth century, especially within Puritan circles. The experience of illness or dying prompted similar inward contemplation: symptoms and diseases were self-diagnosed, pain and 'affliction' described. This was a time when to be ill or sick – as with states of madness, passion and overt sorrow or grief – was not to be one's 'proper' self.[27]

By the second half of the seventeenth century the letter-writing genre emerged as a forum for literary and creative writing and fictionalized social commentary, which contrasts with the everyday practicality of medieval women's letters, such as those of the female correspondents of the Paston, Cely, Plumpton and Stonor families and women like Alice de Bryene. Two centuries later, the letters of Dorothy Osborne (1627–95), for example, mark a significant stylistic and generic shift in letter-writing, as the letter form was appropriated by women for an expanding variety of purposes. Written during the period of her clandestine courtship with Sir William Temple (1652–4), Dorothy Osborne's letters – despite Virginia Woolf's dictum that 'letters did not count' as 'literature'[28] – are often praised for their *literariness*; Osborne is lauded as a 'prose stylist', her letters as attaining a 'fictional' quality, replete with narrative tensions and literary *topoi* and discernible echoes of the French romance tradition.[29] Osborne's letters emerge as artfully studied texts, conscious of rhetorical conventions and epistolary protocols, and exhibit her prodigious talents as a letter-writer. In one letter to her future husband, she wrote, 'You will never read half this letter, tis soe scribled, but noe matter, tis much worth it', a typical balance of epistolary decorum, modesty and assured self-confidence.[30]

In the decade after Osborne wrote, the *Sociable Letters* of Margaret Cavendish, Duchess of Newcastle, printed in her lifetime (1664), offered witty semi-fictional letters conversing on topics ranging from war and peace, literature, science and medicine, to marriage, divorce, infidelity and single life for women. By publishing this collection of letters, Cavendish was writing in a genre that had long been established as an intellectual, public forum acceptable for women in Renaissance Italy.[31] Moreover, in her *Philosophical Letters: or, Modest Reflections upon some Opinions in Natural Philosophy* (also printed in 1664), Cavendish drew connections with continental philosophers and the Royal Society. Katherine Philips's letters to Sir Charles Cotterell were published posthumously in two editions as *Letters From Orinda to Poliarchus* (1705); examples of her letters were published earlier as 'Letters by the late Celebrated Mrs Katherine Philips' in *Familiar Letters Written by the Right Honourable John late Earl of Rochester, And*

Several Other Persons of Honour and Quality (1697).[32] The preface of this collection declares its purpose to be 'entertainment'. These printed letters were examples of a highly literary form – 'they are so able to make their own Panegyrick' – intended for emulation, since they avoid 'uncorrect Looseness in her stile or starch'd Affectation'.

Another famous woman of letters for whom letter-writing was a highly conscious art is Mary Wortley Montagu. Writing at the turn of the eighteenth century, Lady Montagu utilized correspondence as a vehicle for lengthy description and narrative, her letters representing a form of epistolary travel-writing. Letter-writing in this case provided a creative outlet for a woman impelled to write and 'entertain' an audience. The Turkish Embassy letters were reworked from originals, organized into albums and published posthumously a year after Montagu's death, a record of her achievements as a serious writer. Finally, given the generic similarities between the letter and the epistolary novel during this period, literary scholars have often approached female letter-writing as a precursor of novels written by women.[33]

Early modern women's letters were highly complex and developing forms that defy easy categorization; they straddled the divide between 'private' and 'public' texts, they circulated in manuscript and print, and could be 'real' and 'fictional'. This generic flexibility lent them an organic quality; the epistolary mode was appropriated for an increasing range of functions and acted as an umbrella for different writing styles; letters often accompanied other texts, such as poems, recipes, accounts and printed books. The sophistication of the epistolary medium extended further to how letters were read. Letters attained meaning not only as 'documents' and 'texts', but also as material objects situated within specific reading contexts; paper, handwriting, ink, seals and manuscript layout were all culturally coded. Over the early modern period, epistolary skills were diffused among broader sections of the female population; letter-writing changed from an occasional activity associated with secretaries and scribes to an everyday task connected with personal writing technologies. Thus, letters represent the most common extant type of early modern women's writing and are numerically unrivalled as intimate records of their lives and experiences. They highlight the degree to which female letter-writers occupied a liminal space, operating in the spheres of overlap between the 'public' and the 'private', the 'political' and the 'domestic'. Often mistakenly viewed as quintessentially 'domestic', private and penned by leisured and landed social groups, early modern women's letters instead represent a relatively democratic form, and were often collaborative and innately political.

NOTES

1. James Daybell (ed.), *Early Modern Women's Letter Writing, 1450–1700* (Basingstoke: Palgrave, 2001).
2. James Daybell, 'Recent Studies in Sixteenth-Century Letters', *English Literary Renaissance* 35.2 (2005), 331–62, and 'Recent Studies in Seventeenth-Century Letters', *English Literary Renaissance* 36.1 (2006), 135–70.
3. Printed collections include Alison D. Wall (ed.), *Two Elizabethan Women: Correspondence of Joan and Maria Thynne, 1575–1611* (Devizes: Wiltshire Record Society, vol. 38, 1982); Sara Jayne Steen (ed.), *The Letters of Lady Arbella Stuart* (Oxford: Oxford University Press, 1994); Joanna Moody (ed.), *The Private Correspondence of Jane Lady Cornwallis Bacon, 1613–1644* (Madison, NJ: Fairleigh Dickinson University Press, 2003).
4. Patrick Collinson, 'The Role of Women in the English Reformation Illustrated by the Life and Friendships of Anne Locke', *Studies in Church History* 2, ed. G. J. Cuming (London: Nelson and Sons, 1965), 258–72.
5. James Daybell, *Women Letter-Writers in Tudor England* (Oxford: Oxford University Press, 2006), pp. 37–8.
6. Carol L. Winkelmann, 'A Case Study of Women's Literacy in the Early Seventeenth Century: The Oxinden Family Letters', *Women and Language* 19.2 (1996), 14–20.
7. Soeur Marie-Claire Robineau, Sister Gertrude-Joseph Donnelly, E. E. Reynolds and F. Bierlaire, 'Correspondance entre Erasme et Margaret Roper', *Moreana* 12 (1966), 29–46, 121; Lynette Hunter, 'Sisters of the Royal Society: The Circle of Katherine Jones, Lady Ranelagh', in Lynette Hunter and Sarah Hutton (eds.), *Women, Science and Medicine, 1500–1700* (Stroud: Sutton, 1997), pp. 178–97.
8. James Daybell, ' "Suche newes as on the Quenes hye wayes we have mett": The News Networks of Elizabeth Talbot, Countess of Shrewsbury (*c.*1527–1608)', in Daybell (ed.), *Women and Politics in Early Modern England, 1450–1700* (Aldershot: Ashgate, 2004), pp. 114–31; Hatfield House, Hatfield, Hertfordshire, Cecil MS, 123 fol. 132, 119 fol. 65, 197 fol. 41, P. 1144; Vivienne Larminie, 'Fighting for Family in a Patronage Society: The Epistolary Armoury of Anne Newdigate (1574–1618)', in Daybell (ed.), *Early Modern Women's Letter Writing*, pp. 94–108.
9. James Daybell, 'The Social Conventions of Women's Letter Writing in England, 1540–1603', in Daybell (ed.), *Early Modern Women's Letter Writing*, pp. 59–76.
10. Philip Beale, *England's Mail: Two Millennia of Letter-Writing* (Stroud: Tempus, 2005).
11. Steven W. May (ed.), *Queen Elizabeth I: Selected Works* (New York: Washington Square Press, 2004), pp. 225–7; Miles Coverdale, *Godly, Fruitful, and Comfortable Letters* (London, 1564), pp. 662–3.
12. James Daybell, ' "I wold wyshe my doings myght be ... secret": Privacy and the Social Practices of Reading Women's Letters in Sixteenth-Century England', in Jane Couchman and Anu Crabb (eds.), *Women's Letters across Europe, 1400–1700* (Aldershot: Ashgate, 2005), pp. 29–47.
13. *The Letters and Life of Francis Bacon*, ed. James Spedding, 7 vols. (London, Longman *et al.*, 1861–74), I: 112; National Archives, Kew, SP 12/107, 12/108: *c.* June 1576–*c.* February 1577.

14. Mary Morrissey and Gillian Wright, 'Piety and Sociability in Early Modern Women's Letters', *Women's Writing* 13.1 (2006), 44–59.
15. Anne Laurence, '"Begging Pardon for all mistakes and errors in this writing I being a woman and doing it myself": Family Narratives in Some Early Eighteenth-Century Letters', and Rosemary O'Day, 'Tudor and Stuart Women: Their Family Lives Through Their Letters', in Daybell (ed.), *Early Modern Women's Letter Writing*, pp. 194–206, 127–42 (203–4, 128); Barbara J. Harris, 'Property, Power and Personal Relations: Elite Mothers and Sons in Yorkist and Early Tudor England', *Signs* 15.3 (1990), 606–32 (611).
16. William Fulwood, *Enemie of Idlenesse* (London, 1571), 69ᵛ.
17. Folger Shakespeare Library, Washington, DC, Bagot MSS, L.a. 222:24 November 1580; Folger, Loseley MSS, L.b. 701: 2 June (1644).
18. Christine de Pisan, *The Treasure of the City of Ladies* (1405), trans. Sarah Lawson (London: Penguin, 1985), p. 98.
19. Angel Day, *The English Secretorie* (London, 1586; 1595), ii, 64, 67.
20. James Daybell, 'Scripting a Female Voice: Women's Epistolary Rhetoric in Sixteenth-Century Letters of Petition', *Women's Writing* 13.1 (2006), 3–20.
21. Alison D. Wall, 'Deference and Defiance in Women's Letters of the Thynne Family: The Rhetoric of Relationships', in Daybell (ed.), *Early Modern Women's Letter Writing*, pp. 77–93.
22. National Archives, SP 46/71/223, 224, 226, 228: 10/05/1601, 29/03/1602, 23/10/1602, n.d.
23. Arthur Searle (ed.), *Barrington Family Letters, 1628–1632* (Camden Society, 4th Series, 28, London: Royal Historical Society, 1983), pp. 201, 215, 223, 206–7; Claire Walker, '"Doe not supose me a well mortifyed Nun dead to the world": Letter Writing in Early Modern English Convents', in Daybell (ed.), *Early Modern Women's Letter Writing*, pp. 159–76; British Library, London, Add. MS, 12507, fol. 9, 10 March 1604.
24. James Daybell, 'The Rhetoric of Friendship in Sixteenth-Century Women's Letters of Intercession', in Judith Richards and Alison Thorne (eds.), *Rhetoric, Gender, Politics: Representing Early Modern Women's Speech* (London: Routledge, 2006), pp. 172–90.
25. Roy Porter (ed.), *Rewriting the Self: Histories from the Renaissance to the Present* (London: Routledge, 1997).
26. Michel Foucault, 'Technologies of the Self', in L. H. Martin, H. Gutman and W. W. Paden (eds.), *Technologies of the Self: A Seminar with Michel Foucault* (Amherst: University of Massachusetts Press, 1988), pp. 16–49.
27. Roy Porter, '"Expressing Yourself Ill": The Language of Sickness in Georgian England', in Peter Burke and Roy Porter (eds.), *Language, Self, and Society: A Social History* (Cambridge: Cambridge University Press, 1991), pp. 276–99.
28. Virginia Woolf, *A Room of One's Own* (1928; Harmondsworth: Penguin, 1945), p. 63.
29. Sheila Ottway, 'Dorothy Osborne's Love Letters: Novelistic Glimmerings and the Ovidian Self', *Prose Studies* 19 (1996), 149–59.
30. Kenneth Parker (ed.), *Dorothy Osborne: Letters to William Temple 1652–54: Observations on Love, Literature, Politics and Religion* (Aldershot: Ashgate, 2002), p. 100.

31. Maria Luisa Doglio, 'Letter Writing, 1350–1650', in Letizia Panizza and Sharon Wood (eds.), *The Cambridge History of Women's Writing in Italy* (Cambridge: Cambridge University Press, 2000), pp. 13–24.
32. Elizabeth H. Hageman, 'Making a Good Impression: Early Texts of Poems and Letters by Katherine Philips, the "Matchless Orinda"', *South Central Review* 11 (1994), 39–65.
33. Ruth Perry, *Women, Letters and the Novel* (New York: AMS Press, 1980).

READING LIST

Chartier, Roger (ed.). *Correspondence: Models of Letter-Writing from the Middle Ages to the Nineteenth Century.* Cambridge: Polity Press, 1997.

Couchman, Jane and Ann Crabb (eds.). *Women's Letters across Europe, 1400–1700.* Aldershot: Ashgate, 2005.

Daybell, James. 'Interpreting Letters and Reading Script: Evidence for Female Education and Literacy in Tudor England'. *History of Education* 34.6 (2005): 695–715.

'Women's Letters and Letter-Writing in England, 1540–1603: An Introduction to the Issues of Authorship and Construction'. *Shakespeare Studies* 27 (1999), 161–86.

Gibson, Jonathan. 'Letters'. In Michael Hattaway (ed.), *A Companion to English Renaissance Literature and Culture.* Oxford: Blackwell, 2000, pp. 615–19.

Goldsmith, Elizabeth C. (ed.). *Writing the Female Voice: Essays on Epistolary Literature.* London: Pinter, 1989.

Guillén, Claudio. 'Notes Toward the Study of the Renaissance Letter'. In Barbara Kiefer Lewalski (ed.), *Renaissance Genres: Essays on Theory, History and Interpretation.* Cambridge, MA: Harvard University Press, 1986, pp. 70–101.

Jardine, Lisa. *Erasmus, Man of Letters: The Construction of Charisma in Print.* Princeton, NJ: Princeton University Press, 1993.

Magnusson, Lynne. 'A Rhetoric of Requests: Genre and Linguistic Scripts in Elizabethan Women's Suitors'. In James Daybell (ed.), *Women and Politics in Early Modern England, 1450–1700.* Aldershot: Ashgate, 2004, pp. 51–66.

Shakespeare and Social Dialogue: Dramatic Language and Elizabethan Letters. Cambridge: Cambridge University Press, 1999.

Mitchell, Linda C. 'Entertainment and Instruction: Women's Roles in the English Epistolary Tradition'. *Huntington Library Quarterly* 66 (2003), 331–47.

Steen, Sara Jayne. 'Fashioning an Acceptable Self: Arbella Stuart'. *English Literary Renaissance* 18 (1988): 78–95.

13

RAMONA WRAY

Autobiography

Often cited as the most democratic of genres, autobiography in the early modern period crosses the divides of class, religion and political persuasion. At one end of the social spectrum are the autobiographies of Viscountess Elizabeth Mordaunt and Lady Anne Halkett. At the other may be found auto-biographies written by women of the servant and labouring classes, such as Barbara Blaugdone, Barbara Scaife and Anne Herring. In terms of spiritual allegiance, distinctive are Catholic writers such as Lady Lucy Knatchbull and Elizabeth Cellier; arresting too, however, are those Protestant writers who span all possible shades of Nonconformity. Politically, autobiogra-phers frequently appear at several removes from one another, a fact which is graphically illustrated in the instances of Lucy Hutchinson and Margaret Cavendish, who chronicle local or national happenings in addition to their own spiritual and material concerns.

The range of women writing is matched by the spectrum of forms in which they wrote. As the anthology *Her Own Life* (the first point of depar-ture for readers investigating the field) made clear, women in the sixteenth and seventeenth centuries signalled selves across a variety of literary and non-literary genres.[1] The term 'autobiography', then, can be applied to an important body of women's literary and cultural materials which ranges from diary to memoir and from conversion narrative to prophetic statement. This chapter addresses the multiple ways in which early modern women were able to write autobiographically and reflects upon the means whereby the early modern female 'I' might be read with critical currency.

The chapter divides into two parts. Section one discusses the more con-ventional forms of the diary and memoir in which women, mostly from the upper ranks of society, inscribed the minutiae of their daily existences and reviewed life trajectories. It is through an engagement with the representa-tion of largely domestic experiences and through attentiveness to syntactical arrangements, I argue, that the individual woman's relation to contempo-rary ideology can be assessed. In section two, modes of representation such as prose prophecy, the conversion narrative and the legal petition (modes which necessitated personal reflection as part of their overall purpose) are considered. Juxtaposing subjective statement and radical content, these forms reveal the ways in which elements of an autobiographical endeavour are integrated with, and take energy from, more dominant orientations.

Because historical particularity informs the mixed circumstances of autobiographical writing, a nuanced dovetailing of text and context can help us assess the significance of such features as framing device and imported discourse. Moreover, motives for writing can be discerned in a changing and cross-conversing assembly of oral narratives, published autobiographies and manuscript recollections. Throughout, this chapter highlights the importance of different means of communication (whether published or not), while, at the same time, indicating the peculiar reading skills required for unravelling the individual narrative choices of the early modern female autobiographers.

Reading these texts through an autobiographical lens entails recognizing the difficulty of interpreting them in any straightforward fashion. Recent scholars note that, although diaries and memoirs offer a detailed route into the private domestic space, that entry is not unmediated. Crucially, the literary forms examined here cannot offer easy access to a 'true self'. Autobiography, of course, includes facts associated with the speaker; these facts, however, are invariably personally mediated. As Sidonie Smith and Julia Watson argue, as well as 'making "history"', autobiographers also perform 'several rhetorical acts – justifying their own perceptions, upholding their reputations, disputing the accounts of others, settling scores, conveying cultural information, and inventing desirable futures'.[2] The result is not 'truth' in a transparent or unproblematic sense, for the analysis of autobiography necessitates the development of a method attentive to the particular styles of telling, to the individual moments of production and to the overarching intentions and strategies of each author. In the light of this understanding, each section of this chapter also considers some of the practices whereby early modern women's lives and texts might now be critically appreciated.

Reading diaries and memoirs

Diaries and memoirs have significant potential for the study of female lives and histories – they offer an inscription of the private, domestic activities of women while helping us to understand the ways in which domestic roles could extend into, and be restrained by, the larger social and cultural sphere. More generally, this writing provides a sense of how contemporary women imagined themselves and interacted with dominant expectations about gender, class, behaviour and household government. As well as yielding glimpses into quotidian practices, then, diaries and memoirs are vital in establishing the broader contexts that defined the early modern woman's life.

Although they form a minority of extant texts, some diaries, including those of Lady Anne Clifford, Countess of Pembroke, are largely motivated by a secular desire to establish a record of an individual woman's life and achievements. Maintaining a diary on-and-off from 1603 onwards (she died in 1676), Clifford is unusual in that her entries regularly move beyond the domestic and the day-to-day to describe her infringement of the public, and masculine, arena of the law. (Notable in this connection is Clifford's long-running duel with James I over her legal entitlement to her family's Westmorland estates.)[3] However, for most writers of diaries and memoirs, the impetus to write was devotional: writing was generated by the need to record and even enforce a religious routine. Sara Heller Mendelson, while acknowledging 'the real importance of religion in the lives of seventeenth-century women' in her overview of twenty-three Stuart female diaries and occasional memoirs, argues that it 'is probably no accident that three-quarters of the works in the present sample contain considerable devotional content'. 'Feminine piety', she continues, 'always reflected well upon the family, and any tangible display of it might be considered sufficiently edifying to preserve.'[4] Hence, in many extant diaries, emphasis is placed on transcribing prayers, noting attendance at sermons and detailing related religious duties, although most diaries also commemorate a domestic order which encompasses household organization, childbearing and rearing, and work undertaken in the local community (such as nursing and charity provision). An extract from the diary of Lady Margaret Hoby, which was maintained between 1599 and 1605, reveals her investment in regulating domestic and spiritual affairs:

> After private prayers I did eat my breakfast and then went to church: after, I came home and prayed, then I dined and, when I had talked a while with some of my neighbours, I went again to church: and, after the sermon, I went about the house and took order for diverse things which were to be done in my absence, and, at five o'clock, I returned to private prayer and meditation. After I went to supper, then to lector [reading], and so to bed.[5]

The continual documenting of spiritual business, using conventional phrasing and syntax, might suggest a lack of personal reflection or involvement. There is little of what we might expect as a diary's self-analysis, and any introspection is generally in the form of prayer or confession. For example, previous to the extract above, Hoby mentions a Bible reading meeting 'where many sundry distractions withdrew my mind from so profitable hearing as I ought' (*Diary*, p. 93): here, the brief insight into Hoby's psychological state is both enabled by, and contained within, a spiritual frame of reference.

That the close relation in this period between the diary and the devotional tract is both enabling and constrictive invites us to unpack particular patterns of silence, repression and significance. A later seventeenth-century diary maintained by Mary Rich, Countess of Warwick, provides a telling example of the mutually reinforcing lineaments that bind quotidian rehearsal and psychic reflection. For Rich, as for Hoby and Clifford, the writing style is bare and unpolished, its repetitive style in keeping with a diary intended for private use. Commenced on 25 July 1666 and continued until eighteen months before Rich's death in April 1678, the diary seems, on initial inspection, to communicate little more than an everyday sense of Rich's circumscribed conditions. Yet Rich's diary is notable for the ways in which it conveys deep dissatisfaction and repeated disappointments. Phrases such as 'I was very much troubled' and 'I had much sorrow and many tears' reverberate throughout and allow us to identify, in seemingly uncommunicative diary conventions, patterns of personal significance.[6] The numerous instances of marital disharmony which pepper the prose suggest that the source of discontent emanates from Rich's relationship with her husband, Charles: 'When I had supped my lord was out of humour, and disputed with great passion with me ... After I returned home, I fell into a foolish dispute with my lord, in which I was too earnest and too passionate ... I fell into a dispute with him wherein I was very passionately affected and wept much' (*Memoir*, pp. 95, 136, 118). Such statements register a volatile relationship: repeated terms such as 'passion' and 'dispute' point to the pervasiveness of the marital friction. As Rich uses the same terminology to describe her husband's outbursts of rage (another staple of the diary's construction), her narrative takes on some of the properties of a balladic refrain: 'After dinner, without an occasion given, my lord fell into great passion with me ... My lord was passionate with me without any occasion ... He fell violently passionate against me ... My lord, without any occasion given by me, fell into a great passion with me' (pp. 74, 131, 103, 136). Comments such as 'his fierceness made me troubled that I had disputed with him' (p. 95), in conjunction with resolutions not to quarrel with Charles for fear of the consequences, suggest that their disagreements may have gone beyond the verbal and that Rich was the victim of domestic abuse. And, while expressions of despair were a conventional part of spiritual autobiography, Rich's depression clearly worsens after conflicts with her husband. Often the link is explicitly forged by Rich herself. Thus, an observation such as 'After dinner, my lord fell into an exceeding violent passion with me' (p. 153) is invariably followed by a darker tone: 'In the morning I found still upon me a very great melancholy' (p. 154). In the context of crisis and an increased sense of isolation, Rich's mood lightens in the company of her family, again suggesting that her marital relationship is intimately bound up with despair. Attention to linguistic habits, syntactical arrangements and recurring motifs, then, offers heightened awareness of this particular writing subject's domestic conditions. The same may be said for other women writers, including Lady Anne Clifford, whose diary is as remarkable for what it does state as it is for its gaps, silences and understatements. The prose may seem to show a lack of embellishment, yet a localized reading technique can uncover meanings and resonances beyond the surface play of the text.

Mary Jane Moffat and Charlotte Painter argue that the composition of a diary provides women with an outlet for tension through private expression – a means, to cite their phrase, of 'personal accounting' – and seventeenth-century diaries often accord with this process.[7] Certainly, given the repeated marital conflicts recorded, it is possible to contend that writing afforded Rich emotional release and represented, for her, something more akin to modern therapeutic practice, as is suggested in the following extract: 'My mind being still much disturbed, by reason of my lord's passion, I went to prayer, and poured out my complaint before God, and showed him all my trouble; and after ... my heart was much composed' (*Memoir*, p. 131). The language of revelation ('showed him') and release ('poured out') occupies an important place in the diary's narrative strategy. Through God, or rather by means of her diary, Rich discloses the unspeakable in a transaction that brings her comfort and peace of mind. In this connection, it is interesting to note that the entries in Rich's diary after the death of her husband in 1673 are much sparser: indeed, they quickly tail off altogether. The diary for Rich is historically resonant in that it provided a powerful yet legitimate instrument for the representation of her needs and frustrations, desires and aspirations.

Crucially, however, the diary is not the point at which Rich's self-representation concludes. Rich is one of several early modern Englishwomen to write a memoir – a text which moves away from the daily recording procedures of the diary to offer a denser and more retrospective rehearsal of the life story. Rich's memoir, which dates from around 1671 and recounts an entire personal history from birth to old age, is typical of most memoirs produced by women in the period in that it seems not to have been written with publication in mind.[8] Margaret Cavendish's *A True Relation of My Birth, Breeding and Life*, first published in 1656, which claims to have been generated out of ambition and out of a desire 'to live by remembrance in after-ages', is exceptional.[9] More customarily, as with diaries, most extant memoirs can be traced to a devotional imperative. Hence, Alice

Thornton's autobiography of *c.* 1668 is one of many contemporary female 'remembrances' informed by the narrative of God's mercies to the author. Thornton's 'booke', as it is called, announces itself as an account of God's providential dealings, which are revealed in the 'remarkable deliverances' of herself, her husband and children.[10] An incongruous summary, which sits uneasily alongside the gloomy timbre of the autobiography as a whole, is evident here, yet it is still one that clarifies the powerful presence of religion in Thornton's self-authoring enterprise.

While fitting the broad remit of such a religious framework, Rich's memoir is unusual in that it presents a radically different picture from that given in the diary. Like Margaret Cavendish's 'true relation', Rich's memoir (in terms of its plot, characters, language and values) draws heavily on the contemporary literary genre of romance. The result is that, rather than appearing as a violent and abusive tyrant, Charles, as the husband of the memoir, is a gallant, romantic hero. Rich herself is portrayed as a lively, confident and fulfilled mother and wife, and the relationship between husband and wife is depicted as a loving ideal. The disparity between these two versions of Rich's life illuminates the shifting ground between competing constructions of 'truth', between narrative convention and autobiographical insertion, and between generic trajectory and personal life journey. Such is the extent of the reworking of the life, moreover, that any firm relation between 'truth-telling' and the autobiographical act is immediately destabilized.

The discontinuities on display here also point up the fact that, notwithstanding overt religious aims, early modern women's memoirs are often novelistic: they appeal immediately to the modern reader and share strategic similarities with prose fiction. The autobiography of Lady Anne Halkett, dating from 1677 to 1678, is perhaps the most striking of these fiction-suffused productions.[11] Halkett's tales of love and honour, which are set against a backdrop of Royalist defeat in the civil war, are cogently structured and felicitously narrated, employing such novelistic devices as direct address to the reader, episodic development and suspense. Such memoirs tend to be written with an audience in mind, although that audience may be a member of the author's own family. In other memoirs of the period, the impulse to textual transmission is, indeed, explicitly framed in familial or generational terms. Central here is Lucy Hutchinson, who, in *c.* 1665, recorded her earlier desperate flight to London to plead for the life of her Parliamentarian husband (Colonel John Hutchinson had signed the death warrant of Charles I).[12]

If some memoirs employ strategies more commonly associated with the novel, others take on qualities that show a greater affinity with the biography. Lady Ann Fanshawe's manuscript memoirs, composed in 1676 and addressed to her son, comprise 'actions and accidents ... of your father and my life'.[13] The memoir records Fanshawe's life with the statesman, Sir Richard Fanshawe, who worked for the return of Charles II and who briefly held the post of ambassador to Madrid. Once married, women legally became a part of their husbands' property, and therefore it is not surprising that, for many women, the projects of writing their autobiographies and compiling the biographies of their spouses were intimately connected. The work of Theodosia Alleine is pertinent in this respect. Writing the biography of her dissident husband in 1671, Alleine provides ample testimony of the ways in which his experience jeopardizes her own internal and external stability. A prison sentence for him means a prison sentence for her, quite literally, as Alleine makes clear in a passage describing the tension they both felt when preparing for his expected arrest: 'At which time, we sold off all our goods, preparing for a gaol, or banishment, where he was desirous I should attend him.'[14] Taken together, Fanshawe and Alleine's narratives suggest that the biographical project in the period was inextricably intertwined with the autobiographical, and that, for women, the particular and local distinctions between autobiographical and biographical representations are simply not sustainable.

Reading other autobiographical forms

On the whole, only aristocratic women or women from the gentry were permitted the leisure time to write a diary or a memoir, as the names already referred to will have indicated. This is in sharp contrast to women of the middling and even lower sorts, whose participation in radical religious movements shaped their autobiographical writing. The priority for the middling-class woman writer was to commit her life to print as part of a testimony of conversion or as a demonstration of prophetic practice.

For women belonging to these ranks of society, spiritual frames of reference were still important, but here an institutional attachment to a particular church or congregation was often a key consideration as a route to autobiography. A prerequisite for entering one of the gathered churches was the composition of a conversion narrative: aspiring members of the community rendered in public what was essentially a formulaic account. Such accounts are not reducible simply to individual experience. A specific pattern characterized most of the narratives published in the period – usually the author progressed from ignorance and self-deception through spiritual torment to assurance and salvation. Adequately to take stock of the conversion narrative, which makes use of formulae to tell the story of a life, requires a thorough knowledge of the conventions of spiritual writing.

Sarah Davy's *Heaven Realiz'd* (1670), for example, describes her depression before attaining assurance of her salvation: in this sense, the autobiographer follows a convention of the conversion narrative format.[15] But many of the emotions and incidents described in these texts are not simply formulaic: thus Davy gives attention to to childhood, bereavement, illness and patronage (issues that sometimes appear divorced from the conventions of the conversion narrative). Davy also writes in such a way that her own record can have a practical utility: her purpose, she states, is to be 'profitable to some precious soul' (*Heaven Realiz'd*, B7^v). Departures from the standard structure suggest that the conversion narrative provided the author with a framework to make sense of various crises and to assess her feelings and experiences: widely different reminiscences, in short, show that the conversion narrative was not wholly determining or coercive. In contradistinction to the dominant critical view that sees these texts as wholly predictable, it might be argued, then, that situating conversion narratives within contemporary ecclesiastical and congregational practice demonstrates that early modern women were able to find moments of independent expression within otherwise uniform models.

If conversion was one avenue to a registration of the self, the experience of being visited with a prophetic voice was another. Patricia Crawford's checklist of seventeenth-century women's published writings is highly useful in that it demonstrates that the majority of publications by women in the period could be deemed 'prophetic'.[16] Diane Purkiss reminds us that, in early modern terms, 'prophecy was any utterance produced by God through human agency ... includ[ing] hymns, general moral exhortations, scriptural exegeses, prayers, spiritual autobiography and mystical revelations, as well as predictions'.[17] The 'prophetic' was a capacious literary and cultural category that made available a correspondingly rich panoply of autobiographical possibilities.[18]

As one of the most extended sets of autobiographical discourse with a prophetic dimension, the various publications, and one manuscript compilation, of seventeenth-century shipwright's daughter, Anna Trapnel, occupy a singular place. Arguably because of the prevailing characteristics of prophecy, which included corporeal emphases, the need to establish the authenticity of the godly voice, a confrontation with the speaker's status as a conduit and an engagement with political questions (Trapnel was a Fifth Monarchist), the divinely inspired prediction lent itself easily to concomitant reflections on the self. For Trapnel, inscribing the self is indistinguishable from rebutting the manifold charges against her. Trapnel writes not 'to vindicate myself, but the truth' and, in pursuing this aim, the 'truth' of the political movement is legitimated through the telling of the personal history.[19] A number of published autobiographical statements in the period have their genesis in self-vindication or a desire for justice. The public 'truth-telling' of the self in these cases, moreover, forms an alliance with the more formalized entry into the autobiographical sphere exemplified by petitions and depositions. A prevailing imperative for the autobiographer was the routing of false charges. Hence, practising midwife Hester Shaw enters into print in 1653 to refute the malicious slander of her neighbour: 'I was forced to print ... in order to right the world's view', she avers.[20] A parallel case may be found in Susanna Parr's *Susanna's Apologie* (1659). Some three years earlier, Parr had left her Independent congregation, having found that it denied her 'not only the liberty of speaking but of dissenting'.[21] Her actions were generally denounced, and Parr was forced into print to restore the good name which was to her 'worth more than riches and the next in esteem to life itself'.[22] It is from a position of resistant politics, that is itself complicated by contemporary discourses of gender and reputation, that the will to declare the 'I' is generated.

Women's autobiographical writings were sometimes motivated by the desire to clear a public image damaged by troubled family relations. Anne Wentworth's autobiography, published in 1677, justifies the author's decision to leave her husband by relating her eighteen years of suffering at his hands. Most galling for the writer was the possibility that her behaviour would be regarded as immoral: she vigorously denies 'that I keep men company and have rogues come to me, and live a scandalous life in an almshouse' and argues that she is responding to godly injunctions in commemorating the story of her life.[23] Cast in a comparable mould is the request for 'truth and justice' that Mary Blaithwaite, a parliamentary pamphlet-seller, addressed to Oliver Cromwell in 1654 in the wake of the harassment, flogging and physical abuse that she and her family endured at the hands of the local Royalist gentry. This victimization had culminated in her false arrest and incarceration, an action leading to the early demise of her long-suffering husband.[24] In her defensive treatise, Blaithwaite seeks protection from her persecutors and compensation from confiscated Royalist estates and insists that she publishes only out of necessity:

> I am forced after much labour in vain ... to make myself a fool in print, hoping hereby my complaint may come to the ear of that great man, who hath taken upon him the Protection of Commonwealth ... to stir him up to come forth and hear the widows complaint and give relief unto me and my fatherless children.
> (*Complaint*, p. 2)

This prison narrative's construction of a guiltless or persecuted female self, then, is intimately linked to the impetus to set wrongs aright. Yet the 'truth' agitated for in these and associated autobiographical ventures is a problematic category, and we might wish to treat with circumspection Blaithwaite's remarks that 'false and feigned articles' and 'unjust and illegal judgements' (*Complaint*, p. 4) were levelled against her. In cases where a version of 'truth' cannot be easily pinpointed, Julia Kristeva's essay, 'Women Can Never Be Defined', is profitable in underscoring the virtues of negativity. Hence, Blaithwaite's denials – she is not 'one of ... parliament's intelligencers' (p. 3), she does not 'disperse scandalous pamphlets' (p. 5) and she is not part of a group of 'common rogues and thieves' (p. 4) – can function as salient examples of the hypothesis that a 'woman ... cannot "be"'. In 'woman', argues Kristeva, 'I see something that cannot be represented, something above and beyond nomenclatures and ideologies'.[25] Or, to put such a theorized negativity of 'woman' in another way, as do Sidonie Smith and Julia Watson, the subject may herself give utterance to the idea in announcing 'I am not this and I am not this.'[26] Absences, double meanings and a lack of linearity – all of these might illuminate the 'truth' of subjectivity in the same moment that they draw attention to its fluidity, constructedness and transience. In autobiographical practices such as Blaithwaite's, there is no place for the centred subject or autonomous self, as conventional vantage-points, and the discourses through which the self is brought in being, have been dramatically unmoored.

Blaithwaite's 'complaint' shows her locating herself in relation to family; by contrast, other female autobiographers of the middling and lower sorts defined themselves in the context of a broader and non-familial 'we'. It was not unusual, for instance, for women to negotiate a multiple 'we' in the space of a single textual undertaking: typical here are Katharine Evans and Sarah Cheevers, Quaker women who, journeying with female Friends outside England, sent back a jointly authored account of their travels. The Evans and Cheevers 1662 description of imprisonment in Malta is distinctive not only for its elaboration of modalities of political interrogation but also for its integration of the 'I' inside a shared authorial enterprise.[27] More generally in the prison narrative, as elsewhere, women's involvement in religious and political groupings inflects both the initial story and the print manifestation. As the autobiography of internment makes clear, gender is not the only category of identification since collaborative speaking positions – and non-collaborative speaking positions – are structured across other discursive elements, including those relating to sexual choice, nation and class. The utility of the 'we' as an autobiographical feature was that it allowed for a range of identifications to be appropriated, incorporated and emphasized by women embarking upon the establishment of their own sense of community.

In a less explicitly stated dimension of the autobiographical initiative, the 'we' persists in the background of the articulation of the individual subject. Women's voices in a number of literary genres containing autobiographical elements were mediated through a scribe: Anna Trapnel's preacherly pronouncements, for example, were transcribed by a male amanuensis and published by members of her own congregation. As Sidonie Smith notes, 'splittings of all kinds intervene in direct access to the "self" – splittings between author and narrator, between narrator and narrated, between "I" now and "I" then, between "I" and "me", between the ideological "I" and the "I"'.[28] Yet the particularities of Trapnel's texts – *The Cry of a Stone* (1654), *A Legacy for Saints* (1654), *Anna Trapnel's Report* (1654) and *Strange and Wonderful News* (1654) are generically distinct from one another – complicate this system of fractures still further. Immediately evident in Trapnel's work is the unbridgeable nature of the gap between an original point of expression and the existing realization of a speaking subjectivity. Confounding again an easy critical situating of Trapnel is the continual equivocation over the ownership of her voice and life. A familiar feature of Trapnel's writing is the claim that, as author, she neither exists nor matters; rather, a disembodied divinity uses her speech as his own. Such narrative emphases both place at yet another remove the 'I' and raise theoretical difficulties in relation to women's speech and the prevailing characteristics of autobiography. The intransigence of Trapnel's case manifests itself most fully in the representations that mark her summoning of the self, all of which demand careful sifting and extrapolation.

Conclusions

As a subject of study, autobiography both invites us to think about the ways in which the early modern woman inscribed the self and prompts reflection on a body of texts that were key to discussions of difference. It is difficult to think of another genre which crosses so many contemporary categories and constituencies. Autobiography, in this light, offers significant opportunities for reading a range of social and cultural expressions of subjectivity yet, in the same moment, insists that each 'I' be assessed inside discrete framing styles, languages and discourses. One route to a critical assessment of autobiography, this chapter has argued, can be found in recognition of the multiple prompts which initiate self-expression. Similarly, the impact of legal, religious, political and domestic conditions is essential to understanding autobiography's discontinuous discursive registers across the period. Although the dominant impression from autobiography is the subject's mediation of, or interaction with, the wider world, issues of identity and gender construction also operate within the local circumstances of history. The specificity of a gender/genre relationship in such cases, then, derives from the models of identity available to the autobiographer at a particular historical juncture. Perhaps the divergence in forms found in early modern female autobiography is not surprising, since women were experimenting with types of articulation that suited a shifting plurality of selves and circumstances.

This chapter, finally, has explored identity both as a locally constructed paradigm and as a series of often conflicted intersections which illuminated and constrained the female autobiographical subject. To read autobiography in this way is to embark upon a critical journey that necessitates the mixing and matching of method, the scrutiny of silences and stereotypes, sensitivity to the limits and possibilities of the genre and a willingness to find legitimate and illegitimate selves in seemingly invisible traces as well as more obviously stated presences. When defined in this fashion, the theoretical models for understanding women's autobiography take on a correspondingly challenging character as we continue to understand identity in terms of reading the processes and transactions, and representations and interventions, that highlighted the female voice.

NOTES

1. Elspeth Graham, Hilary Hinds, Elaine Hobby and Helen Wilcox (eds.), *Her Own Life: Autobiographical Writings by Seventeenth-Century Englishwomen* (London and New York: Routledge, 1989).
2. Sidonie Smith and Julia Watson, *Reading Autobiography: A Guide for Interpreting Life Narratives* (Minneapolis and London: University of Minnesota Press, 2001), p. 10.
3. See *The Diaries of Lady Anne Clifford*, ed. D. J. H. Clifford (Phoenix Mill: Sutton, 1996), pp. 37, 38, 45, 49, 52, 54, 56, 59, 62, 69, 88, 91, 92, 95, 253, 268.
4. Sara Heller Mendelson, 'Stuart Women's Diaries and Occasional Memoirs', in Mary Prior (ed.), *Women in English Society 1500–1800* (London and New York: Methuen, 1985), p. 185.
5. *Diary of Lady Margaret Hoby, 1599–1605*, ed. Dorothy M. Meads (London: Routledge, 1930), p. 93.
6. Mary Rich, *Memoir of Lady Warwick: Also her Diary* (London: English Monthly Tract Society, 1847), p. 83.
7. Mary Jane Moffat and Charlotte Painter, 'Introduction', in Mary Jane Moffat and Charlotte Painter (eds.), *Revelations: Diaries of Women* (New York: Random House, 1974), p. 5.
8. The memoir was published as Mary Rich, *Autobiography of Mary, Countess of Warwick*, ed. T. Croker (London: Percy Society, 1848).

9. *Paper Bodies: A Margaret Cavendish Reader*, ed. Sylvia Bowerbank and Sara Mendelson (Peterborough: Broadview, 2000), p. 62.

10. Alice Thornton, *The Autobiography of Mrs Alice Thornton of East Newton, Co. York*, ed. Charles Jackson, Surtees Society Series, 62 (Durham: Andrews, 1873), p. 1.

11. *Lady Anne Halkett: Selected Self-Writings*, ed. Suzanne Trill (Aldershot: Ashgate, 2007), pp. 51–143.

12. Lucy Hutchinson, *Memoirs of the Life of Colonel Hutchinson*, ed. James Sutherland (Oxford: Oxford University Press, 1973), pp. 110–14.

13. *The Memoirs of Anne, Lady Halkett and Ann, Lady Fanshawe*, ed. John Loftis (Oxford: Clarendon Press, 1979), p. 101.

14. Theodosia Alleine, *The Life and Death of Mr Joseph Alleine* (London: n.p., 1671), p. 53.

15. Sarah Davy, *Heaven Realiz'd* (London?: n.p., 1670), p. 15.

16. Patricia Crawford, 'Checklist of Women's Published Writings 1600–1700', in Prior (ed.), *Women in English Society*, pp. 211–82.

17. Diane Purkiss, 'Producing the Voice, Consuming the Body: Women Prophets of the Seventeenth Century', in Isobel Grundy and Susan Wiseman (eds.), *Women, Writing, History 1640–1740* (London: Batsford, 1992), p. 139.

18. See also Hilary Hinds's chapter on women's prophecy in this volume.

19. Anna Trapnel, *Anna Trapnel's Report* (London: Thomas Brewster, 1654), A1r–v.

20. Hester Shaw, *Mrs. Shaw's Innocency Restored* (London: T. M. for G. A., 1653), p. 4.

21. Susanna Parr, *Susanna's Apologie against the Elders* (Oxford: Henry Hall for T. Robinson, 1659), p. 21.

22. Thomas Mall, *A True Account* (London: R.W. for Matthew Keinton, 1658), p. 32.

23. Anne Wentworth, *A Vindication* (London: n.p., 1677), p. 4.

24. Mary Blaithwaite, *The Complaint of Mary Blaithwaite* (London: n.p., 1654), p. 5.

25. Julia Kristeva, 'Woman Can Never Be Defined', in Elaine Marks and Isabella de Courtivron (eds.), *New French Feminisms: An Anthology* (New York: Schocken Books, 1981), p. 137.

26. Sidonie Smith and Julia Watson, 'Introduction: Situating Subjectivity in Women's Autobiographical Practices', in Sidonie Smith and Julia Watson (eds.), *Women, Autobiography, Theory: A Reader* (Madison and London: University of Wisconsin Press, 1998), p. 20.

27. See Graham, Hinds, Hobby and Wilcox (eds.), *Her Own Life*, pp. 116–30.

28. Sidonie Smith, 'Construing Truth in Lying Mouths: Truthtelling in Women's Autobiography', *Studies in the Literary Imagination* 23 (1990), p. 150.

READING LIST

Bedford, Ronald, Lloyd Davis and Philippa Kelly (eds.). *Early Modern Autobiography: Theories, Genres, Practices*. Ann Arbor: University of Michigan Press, 2006.

Dowd, Michelle M. and Julie A. Eckerle (eds.). *Genre and Women's Life-Writing in Early Modern England*. Aldershot: Ashgate, 2007.

Graham, Elspeth, Hilary Hinds, Elaine Hobby and Helen Wilcox (eds.). *Her Own Life: Autobiographical Writings by Seventeenth-Century Englishwomen*. London and New York: Routledge, 1989.

Smith, Sidonie and Julia Watson. *Reading Autobiography: A Guide for Interpreting Life Narratives*. Minneapolis and London: University of Minnesota Press, 2001.

14

HELEN WILCOX

Lyric poetry

Near the beginning of the seventeenth century, a gentlewoman married a 'yonge Gent who after forsooke', and in the aftermath of his desertion she 'tooke hir needle in wch she was excelent and wo⸍ked upon hir Sampler thus':

> Come give me needle stitchcloth silke and haire,
> That I may sitt and sigh and sow and singe,
> For perfect collours to discribe the aire
> A subtile persinge changinge constant thinge.
>
> No false stitch will I make my hart is true,
> Plaine stitche my sampler is for to complaine
> Now men have tongues of hony, harts of rue,
> True tongues and harts are one, Men makes them twain.
>
> Give me black silk that sable suites my hart
> And yet som white though white words do deceive
> No greene at all for youth and I must part,
> Purple and blew, fast love and faith to weave.
> Mayden no more sleepeless ile go to bedd
> Take all away, the work works in my hedd.[1]

This early modern lyric poem weaves together many strands (as it were) of the characteristic construction of female experience: the speaker's identity as a 'mayden' or not; her abandonment by a honey-tongued man; the appeal to emotional constancy; her skill in needlework with, symbolically, 'no false stitch'; witty resilience in the face of misfortune; morbid self-absorption; and worldly wisdom even as she appears to abandon the world. If we are to accept the account of the poem offered in the manuscript miscellany in which it appears, the poem was 'written' in the form of a sampler, materially combining the female domestic sphere with formal literary culture – it is, after all, a sonnet, written at the time when that lyric genre was at the height of its popularity in English. The poem's wit lies in its blending of context and metaphor, maintained from the opening request for 'stitchcloth silke and haire' with which to express herself, right through to the pun on women's 'work' in the closing line. A more concise epitome of early modern women's experience embodied in verse would be hard to find.

Of all the genres favoured in early modern English writing, it is the lyric poem which is perhaps most readily associated with women. But do we make this connection too easily and unquestioningly? The genre itself evokes some of the stereotypes of women's culture which may need to be challenged: this form of writing is assumed to be small-scale and private, deploying a personal voice and tending towards the autobiographical.[2] The conversational aesthetic underpinning the lyric, privileging dialogue with a lover or with God, gives rise to some of the finest male writing of the early modern period but might suggest a narrow specificity of scope and subject-matter from the female perspective. The fact that sixteenth- and seventeenth-century women poets flourished as writers of lyric poetry may seem to indicate a prevailing modesty and intimacy in their efforts as literary artists. However, both of these images – of women and of lyric poetry – require exploration and, in some cases, challenge.

With these issues in mind, this chapter will examine (necessarily briefly) the contribution of early modern women writers in English to the lyric tradition. Beginning with the poetic achievement of Mary Sidney's Psalm translations – which are among the greatest technical displays of lyric form in the period – the discussion will then turn to women's use of the sonnet for devotional and amorous subjects, before broadening out to span the enormous range of modes and themes found in early modern women's lyric poetry. These include topographical, scientific and philosophical exploration in verse, social poetic discourse, devotional verse, elegiac lament and lyric self-assertion, as practised by, among others, Anne Lok, Isabella Whitney, Aemilia Lanyer, Martha Moulsworth, Mary Wroth, 'Eliza', Hester Pulter, Margaret Cavendish, Anne Bradstreet, Katherine Philips, Aphra Behn and the aptly named Elizabeth Singer. The ensuing account of the poetry, with implications for our understanding of both gender and genre, is intended as a celebration of this remarkable group of women whose lyric personae exhibit character, wit and imagination on a hitherto unexpected scale.

The primary inspiration and justification of the lyricists' art in the sixteenth and seventeenth centuries was the poetry of the Bible, in particular the Psalms. As Sir Philip Sidney wrote when defending the lyric against its detractors, 'may not I ... say that the holy David's Psalms are a divine poem?'[3] The lyrical mode – poetry as song – was acceptable to God and practised by King David, and thus ought to be good enough for later mortals. Sidney himself set about translating the Psalms into English verse but died before the project was anywhere near completion, and the task of finishing and revising the 150 lyrics was taken on by his sister, Mary. The manuscript was presented to Elizabeth I, herself a lyric poet, in 1599, and sets an immensely high standard with its expressive and innovative variety of stanza form and vocal tone. The creative range of the Sidney Psalms was probably only once surpassed in the early modern period, by Herbert's lyric inventiveness in *The Temple* (1633), a collection surely influenced by Mary Sidney's achievement. The example of Mary Sidney makes us immediately aware of the complexity of the relationship between women poets and the lyric tradition: to translate and versify is to reshape, and to write in the light of the past is not only to inherit examples but also to instigate change. A woman poet was not necessarily an isolated phenomenon standing outside the mainstream of literary history: Mary Sidney intervened in the development of the lyric in English, introducing modes and features that would, in turn, change the way in which men and women wrote their verse. As an admiring John Donne announced, 'We thy Sydnean Psalmes shall celebrate', allowing poet-singers throughout the land to share in the fruits of the Sidneys' 'sweet learned labours'.[4]

Mary Sidney's skill lay not only in her deeply learned approach to the biblical original, but also in the magnificent flexibility of the verse forms in which she wrote her expanded English translation. The dramatic opening stanza of 'De Profundis', her versification of Psalm 130, will quickly demonstrate the expressiveness of lyric form, devised specifically for this individual cry of the Psalmist:

> From depth of grief
>   where droun'd I ly,
> lord for relief
>   to thee I cry:
> my ernest, vehement, crying, prayeng,
> graunt quick, attentive, heering, waighing.[5]

After the jagged brevity of the first four lines, the longer lines of the couplet with their repetitive rhetoric effectively force the voice of complaint upon the attention of the 'heering' and 'waighing' God. These last two words introduce the uncertainty of the divine 'weighing' up: is it for compassion or for judgement? There is a strong investment of a personal presence in the anxious pleading of the speaker/singer here; the original material is greatly extended to give expression to the vehemence of her cries. In several of the Psalms, Mary Sidney's introduction of feminine metaphors appears to render them more specific to her own situation, even re-gendering the biblical text.[6] Throughout the translation we gain a sense of the human tones of the Psalms modified and particularized in the hands of a gifted writer of lyric verse.

The Psalms gave rise to much lyrical writing in the early modern period, whether the sophisticated lute-song stanzas of the Sidney collection or the formally simpler metrical Psalms more amenable to the communal singing favoured by Protestants in the post-Reformation period. Among the other women who contributed to this endeavour, secure in the knowledge that this was a proper and godly literary activity for a female poet, was the late-sixteenth century writer Anne Lok, whose metrical paraphrase of Psalm 51 may usefully be set alongside the verse translation of the same Psalm by Mary Sidney.[7] Lok also gave voice to her devotion in sonnet form, and thus her work encompasses the two predominant lyric forms of the early modern era: expansive Psalm-like song, in which 'we with *David* shall confesse', and the more constrained, intricately constructed sonnet.[8] While the use of the sonnet for spiritual purposes was acceptable in both female and male poets – partly because the gendering of the soul in relation to God tends to place all human speakers in the position of a feminized supplicant – the writing of sonnets of earthly love from the female perspective was rare and often outspoken (as our initial example of the needlework sonnet suggested).

The one leading woman secular sonneteer of the early modern period, Lady Mary Wroth, ran a considerable risk with her writing and found herself censured by a male contemporary, Lord Denny, who complained of her poems and prose romance, insisting that she should 'redeem the time with writing as large a volume of heavenly lays and holy love as you have of lascivious tales and amorous toys; that at the last you may follow the example of your virtuous and learned aunt', Mary Sidney.[9] Fascinatingly, the idea that there might be a new lyric tradition among women poets, stemming from Mary Sidney's example, is here used as a means of attacking Wroth – who did not wilt under fire but responded with a reproof. Wroth's sonnet sequence, *Pamphilia to Amphilanthus*, is an accomplished work which explores the hazards implicit in the female experience of taking the 'thread of love', and makes brilliant use of the interwoven and confining structures of the sonnet to mirror the entrapment of her female speaker:

> In this strang labourinth how shall I turne?
> Wayes are on all sids while the way I miss:
> If to the right hand, ther, in love I burne;
> Lett mee goe forward, therin danger is;
>
> If to the left, suspition hinders bliss,
> Lett mee turne back, shame cries I ought returne
>   Nor fainte though crosses with my fortunes kiss;
>   Stand still is harder, allthough sure to mourne.[10]

As a result of Wroth's daring entry into several 'labourinths' at once – the sonnet form, the expression of female desire, and the manuscript circulation and print publication of secular love poems – there are no grounds for accusing her of 'stand[ing] still'. On the contrary, by means of her adventurous twisting and turning in formal and emotional terms, and her investment of female frustration into the voice of lyric poetry, she undoubtedly moved women's writing 'forward' and stands as a major figure in seventeenth-century poetry.

Although Psalms and sonnets underlie the lyric impulses of much early modern verse, the love of God and the love of men were not the only subjects of women's poetry in the period. Female lyricists explored the significance of their own contexts, too, whether those were classical settings such as Theseus's labyrinth imaginatively reconfigured as the courtly networks inhabited by Wroth, or the very real and immediate environment of Elizabethan London addressed by the sixteenth-century urban poet, Isabella Whitney. In her witty poetic 'Wyll and Testament', conceived as an ironic farewell to the 'famous Citie', Whitney offers a sparkling account of London's topography matched to her experience and mood.[11] The setting of the mid seventeenth-century Hester Pulter's lyric writing, on the other hand, was the house away from London in which she was 'confin'd' – the latter being a loaded choice of vocabulary suggesting the enclosed context of the house and of the birthing chamber where 'confinements' took place. But this location did not prevent Pulter's subject-matter from ranging widely – indeed, the fact that she was 'shut up in A Countrey Grange' seemed to stimulate her imagination and the 'noble freedome of my Mind'. As she contrasts her situation with that of the humblest insects that can roam at liberty, it is clear that she is fascinated by natural history:

> When as each hoarie Moth and Gaudy Fly
> Within their spheirs injoy their Liberty
> The Virgin Bee her luscious Cell forsakes
> And on A Thousand flowers pleasure Takes
> The glistering Beetle casts her stag like Horns
> The next year new her stately Front adorns
> Sheer owls her Unctious Embrio East & West
> To call great Nature who hears her behest
> The silk worm Feeds, then Works, the shee involv's
> Her self, then Breeds, then Flies till shee dissolv's.[12]

This vivid and detailed account was clearly not based on observation alone, but on reading in natural histories and classical accounts, particularly as the mythical 'basilisk' is the next creature in her catalogue. The lyric should thus not be automatically thought of as an outlet for emotion, despite the fact that the unhappy contrast between Pulter's situation and that of the insects gives the poem its initial impetus. Women poets of this period use the lyric to range through their knowledge as well as find satisfaction in their poetic skill. Margaret Cavendish, Duchess of Newcastle, for example, puts forward her philosophical and scientific theories in lyric verse, finding such poetry an apt testing ground for new ideas as well as an opportunity for protest and wit.[13]

If places both real and imaginary, and ideas both inherited and invented, inspired early modern women lyricists, then it is to be expected that the social context, which combines the two, would loom large in their poems. It is indeed typical of the lyric as a genre, and especially of poetry by women in this tradition, that the speaker assumes a specific and often named reader, creating a receptive audience to ensure a favourable response to the poem. In a period when women perceived their own poems to be, in Anne Bradstreet's words, as vulnerable as a child sent 'out of door',[14] it was important that their forays into verse were, as far as possible, embedded in a receptive social environment. Thus an unusually high proportion of women's lyrics are addressed to other women, whether relatives and friends or hoped-for patrons or readers. Aemilia Lanyer, for example (whose longer poems are discussed more fully in Susanne Wood's chapter on narrative poetry), prefaces her *Salve Deus Rex Judaeorum* with a series of shorter poems addressed to women who range from the Queen to 'all vertuous Ladies in generall', asking each of them in their own way to 'grace this little Booke' with their patronage or supportive readership.[15]

This sense of lyric functioning in the social context applies not only to panegyric prefatory and dedicatory verse, but also in many cases to the main texts themselves. Diana Primrose sends her poetic *Chaine of Pearle* (1630) to all noblewomen, urging them to follow the example of the late Queen Elizabeth I, in whose honour it was originally written. The female social context certainly does not imply that the subject-matter is therefore private or domestic, as we might be tempted to assume. Primrose's commended 'pearls' or qualities, each of which is depicted in a separate poem in the sequence or 'chaine', include prudence, justice and 'the Vertues Intellectual',[16] while the purpose of the work as a whole probably reflects a political agenda critical of the status quo in 1630. This serious commitment to writing verse expressing public and moral concerns is reflected in women's lyrics from throughout the early modern era, though it became particularly intense in the mid seventeenth century during the civil war and Commonwealth periods. An Collins, for example, writing devotional and autobiographical lyrics, included among her *Divine Songs and Meditacions*

(1653) a 'Song composed in time of the Civill Warr, when the wicked did much insult over the godly', lamenting the rule of 'Carnall Liberty' and other enemies of truth, which is feminized as 'Lady Verity'.[17] In the 1650s, the radical Anna Trapnel's *Cry of a Stone* interspersed prose with hymns proclaiming her vision of the age and speaking prophetically of the 'rotten wals' to be 'thrown down'.[18] At the end of those turbulent and divisive years, and on the opposite side of the bitter religious and political divide, Katherine Philips wrote lyrics in celebration of the return of Charles II ('Arion on a Dolphin') and delighting in the fact that the rain had stopped in honour of his coronation. Such topical poems, whether angry, visionary or joyful, find their place in the output of the women poets, which belies any sense that their choice of the lyric mode was a badge of retreat or seclusion from the world.

Many lyrics, of course, were written by women on what might be regarded as more conventional subjects, recalling the sampler sonnet with which we began: lyrics of love, or about marriage, or expressing devotion to God. However, it is important to avoid stereotypical assumptions about these poems, too. Katherine Philips celebrated the love between women, most famously in her lyric 'Friendship's Mysterys, to my dearest Lucasia', in which she transformed the inheritance of Donne's secular lyrics into a confident and witty female declaration of the 'religion in our Love'. 'Friendship's Mysterys' was set to music by Henry Lawes, so putting Philips right in the (male) world of lyric as actual song. She also advised young women – before she herself was married – that 'A marryd state affords but little Ease / The best of husbands are so hard to please.'[19] Even though both of these lyrics draw on traditional tropes – passionate same-sex friendship and the praise of the virgin's life – they have the capacity to surprise the modern reader with their apparent outspokenness from a female perspective.

The anonymous author of *Eliza's Babes: Or the Virgins-Offering* (1652) can have a similar effect. She wrote a passionate lyric entitled 'The Lover', for example, but it turns out that the partner in question, her 'lovely Lord', is no earthly husband but Jesus Christ, 'the Prince of Peace'.[20] The boundaries between secular and sacred love are disconcertingly flexible here – in fact, the effect of their overlapping is as dramatic in women's lyrics as in Donne's *Songs and Sonets* or Crashaw's passionate hymns to St Teresa. The range of denominational loyalties in women's devotional verse is also as wide as that spanned by Crashaw at one extreme and Milton at the other: among the female religious lyricists of the early modern period writing in English were the mid sixteenth-century Protestant martyr, Anne Askew, and the early seventeenth-century Catholic nun in exile, Gertrude More. Askew used the ballad form to 'rejoyce in hart' even as death approached; More employed her 'tongue' and 'pen' more privately, but equally to 'extol *Gods* praise' from the depths of her own devotional experience.[21]

To what extent is the lyric an autobiographical mode? Many of the poems referred to in this chapter arose from moments in the personal histories of the poets (one of the recurring characteristics of lyrical verse), and to read women's lyrics is indeed to catch a glimpse of their lives. As the late seventeenth-century religious lyricist Elizabeth Singer wrote, she was about to 'barter for a toy' the gift of 'eternal Joy', when she paused for a moment's reflection on the enormity of what she was doing: 'Oh blest occasion made me *stay to think, / Ere I was hurri'd off the dangerous brink*.'[22] This emphasis on the 'occasion', fundamental to Protestant ideology but also to the link between lyric poetry and particular experience, is nowhere more evident than in the many elegies written by early modern women to record and lament the loss of their children, a reminder of the bitter sufferings of so many women of the period. Yet it would be wrong to treat these poems as though they were merely versified death certificates: they do more than mark mortality. To read a poem like Mary Carey's elegy, 'Written by me at the death of my 4th sonne and 5th Child, Perigrene Payler', is to hear voice and verse, bitter sorrow and sustaining faith, blended together and shaped by the constraints of metre and rhyme:

> I thought my all was given before
> but mercy ordred me one more:
>
> A Perigrene; my God me sent
> him back againe I doe present
>
> as a love token; 'mongst my others,
> One Daughter; and hir 4 deare Brothers.[23]

The significance of her fifth child's name – Perigrene, meaning pilgrim – is not lost on Carey, who firmly believes that his brief sojourn was simply a pilgrimage and his destination was Heaven. The elegy turns into a love poem, and not primarily for the baby but for Christ, to whom Perigrene is given 'as a love token' and about whom Carey goes on to write, 'he is mine; and I am his'. There is a boldness here, even in loss; lament and love, sacrifice and assertion, jostle side by side in Carey's remarkable lyric.

What the first-person voice of lyric poetry offered to early modern women, then, was the chance to create a speaking voice and construct an identity through the patterns of verse. This was often an inherited identity, born of the traditions of the chosen lyric mode such as the stoical voice of elegy, the abandoned lover in sonnet and ballad or the cynical observer in satire and song. In devotional lyric, the voice is that of the Psalmist, and the more familiar the type, the more accessible is the poem:

> I am a stranger, in this world
> The world, seems strang to me
> Lord, hast to take a stranger home
> Who is well known, to thee
>
> This world to me's a borow'd Inne
> I Lodg here, for a night
> And in the morning, I am gone
> Fain I would take my flight.[24]

This lyric, by the Restoration Presbyterian poet Julia Palmer, uses fundamental metaphors of travel – strange places and the need for temporary lodgings – in order to express a profound longing: she would 'Fain' flee the world. The voice is both archetypal and individual, a combination typically afforded by the lyric.

There are some lyrics, however, in which particularity is of greater significance, and a clear early modern example is Martha Moulsworth's 'Memorandum', an autobiographical poem on the borders of lyric and narrative. The poem tells Moulsworth's life story, but her identity and the poetic form are interconnected in a way that suggests a lyric sensibility to the constructed and crafted detail of verse itself. Writing on her fifty-fifth birthday, 'the birth day of my selfe, and of theis lynes', Moulsworth creates a poetic structure to match her age, with a couplet for each year of her life. This is no accident but a deliberate strategy, as her marginal note explains: 'my muse is a tell clocke, & echoeth everie stroke wth a coupled ryme'.[25] The wit of self-assertion can lead to the invention of new and utterly personalized lyric forms.

As the seventeenth century drew to a close, some aspects of lyric came to be severely tested, among them the clarity of gendered voices. If Moulsworth's 'Memorandum' straddles the boundary of narrative and lyric verse, then some of Aphra Behn's lyrics take on the masks of dramatic language (the art through which she earned her living). In her 'Song: Love Arm'd', for instance, she destabilizes the voices of male and female so that it is almost impossible – and perhaps no longer necessary – to work out who is speaking to whom:

> Love in Fantastique Triumph satt,
> Whilst Bleeding Hearts a round him flow'd,
> For whom Fresh paines he did Create,
> And strange Tyranick power he show'd;
> From thy Bright Eyes he took his fire,

> Which round about, in sport he hurl'd;
> But 'twas from mine, he took desire,
> Enough to undo the Amorous World.[26]

While the author is known to be female and Love is clearly male, what are the genders of the desiring speaker and the bright-eyed beloved? In the second half of the poem, the Petrarchan stereotypes of male and female lovers dissolve as victor and victim appear to swap places – revealing the poem to be more of an exploration of lyric voices than a confirmation of gendered roles. The only clarity in the poem's conclusion is that the amorous pair have been the cause of their own downfall, investing Love with the very powers which have destroyed them.

As this final example suggests, it is not appropriate to categorize early modern women's lyric poetry as a site of emotional or even cultural retreat, but rather to witness its potential as a battleground for identity and ideas. It was a form used by women of all social groups – from Trapnel the wheelwright's daughter and Whitney the serving gentlewoman to countesses and queens – and by poets from across the spectrum of religious affiliations. The subject-matter encompassed female experience from childhood to martyrdom and explored issues from public politics to private grief. The lyric mode was often subtle and complex in its structure, yet displayed what Margaret Cavendish called a 'Noble' plainness and conversational ease.[27] Some male contemporaries, not surprisingly, criticized female poets for straying beyond their proper subject (as we have seen in the case of Mary Wroth) and implied that sending their verse outside a limited circle of acquaintances would be improper. Jane Cheyne was praised for keeping her verse within the family, since 'Great Wits (like Princes) best are seen at home',[28] a maxim particularly tuned to the gender politics of the day. However, Cheyne, the 'Great Wit' in question, herself used metaphors which extend the reach of 'home', as in the lyric she wrote as 'An answeare' to her sister, Lady Alice Egerton, who had sent her a 'Songe of I prithy send mee back my Hart'. Joining in the game of poetic exchange between the sisters, but refusing to return her 'hart' or to be limited by this domestic rhetoric, Cheyne adopts the language of the battlefield, seeing her adversary (or sister) as one who would 'challenge' her 'in the feild' and would 'battle sett'. The poem playfully ends with the assertion, 'I then as Maister of the feild / Perhaps may prove your nett.'[29]

Hoping that the early modern female lyric poet does not prove to be our 'nett' – other than in the sense of catching us with her wit and skill – I shall conclude on the implications of Cheyne's penultimate line, 'I then as Maister of the feild'. Lyric was indeed very often the woman poet's field, though it is vital to remember that this could be not just a sheltering or pleasing meadow but also terrain of challenge, mastery and triumph. The poet frequently found herself in skirmishes with science, philosophy and social controversy as well as with the intricacies of love's earthly 'labourinths' and heavenly rewards. The early modern female lyric poet could be a 'Maister' of these varied poetic territories, adapting and appropriating the inherited lyric tradition with technical ingenuity and imaginative flair. Most important, the lyric mode afforded a place for women to make statements beginning 'I then' – whether these were autobiographical assertions or fictional expressions (or, more often than not, a mixture of the two). In their many settings – including the home, the church, the court, the playhouse and the page – these women poets became 'Maister Mistresses' of the lyric art.[30]

NOTES

1. British Library MS Add. 22601, 'Ancient MS Poems, Ballads, Letters, Plays and Sonnets' (c. 1603), fol. 26r. The poem is printed in *Early Modern Women Poets: An Anthology*, ed. Jane Stevenson and Peter Davidson (Oxford: Oxford University Press, 2001), pp. 155–6. This magnificent collection is a vital source of women's lyric poetry from the sixteenth and seventeenth centuries, and as it is widely available (including in paperback), references to it will be supplied whenever a poem cited in this chapter is also included in the anthology.
2. Definitions of 'lyric' vary enormously, but in the context of this volume it is assumed to refer to poetic writing that would not usually be described as either narrative or dramatic. The predominant features of lyric verse in the early modern period include: association with musical performance; technical ingenuity of metrical structures, rhyme and stanza forms; expression of a first-person perspective; and assumption of a social or dialogic context. For a useful account of the genre, see David Lindley, *The Critical Idiom: Lyric* (London: Methuen, 1985).
3. Sir Philip Sidney, *An Apology for Poetry*, ed. Geoffrey Shepherd (Manchester: Manchester University Press, 1973), p. 99.
4. 'Upon the translation of the Psalmes by Sir Philip Sydney, and the Countesse of Pembroke his Sister', John Donne, *The Complete English Poems*, ed. C. A. Patrides (London: Dent, 1985), p. 469.
5. Mary Sidney, from Psalm 130, *Collected Works*, ed. Margaret P. Hannay *et al.*, 2 vols. (Oxford: Clarendon Press, 1998), II: 49.
6. See, for example, the account of the maternal earth in Psalm 104.
7. See Margaret P. Hannay, '"Unlocke my lipps": the Miserere Mei Deus of Anne Vaughan Lok and Mary Sidney Herbert, Countess of Pembroke', in Jean R. Brink (ed.), *Privileging Gender in Early Modern England* (Kirksville, MO: Sixteenth-Century Journal Publishers, 1993), pp. 19–36. Lok was the friend and correspondent of the religious reformer John Knox; she was also the mother of the sonneteer Henry Lok, and later the wife of the Protestant preacher, Edward Dering, whose fervour got him into trouble with the Elizabethan authorities. (In this attempt to place Lok for readers who may not be familiar with her work, we are reminded of how the nature of women's history still leads us to identify and place women socially through their relationships to men.)

8. The quotation is from Lok's 'The necessitie and benefit of AFFLICTION' (line 113), published posthumously in 1615 with her translation of John Taffin's *Of the Markes of the Children of God*; Stevenson and Davidson, *Early Modern Women Poets*, p. 34. Among discussions of Lok's sonnets, see John Ottenhoff, 'Mediating Anne Locke's *Meditation* Sonnets', in Helen Ostovich, Mary V. Silcox and Graham Roebuck (eds.), *Other Voices, Other Views: Expanding the Canon in English Renaissance Studies* (Newark: University of Delaware Press, 1999), pp. 290–310.

9. See *The Poems of Lady Mary Wroth*, ed. Josephine A. Roberts (Baton Rouge: Louisiana State University Press, 1983), p. 34.

10. Lines 1–8 of the opening sonnet in Wroth's 'crowne of Sonetts dedicated to Love', *Poems*, pp. 127–8; Stevenson and Davidson, *Early Modern Women Poets*, pp. 147–8.

11. It is for this reason – the identification of place with personal perspective and emotional self-expression – that it is possible to claim a lyric quality to this poem.

12. Hester Pulter's poetry remained in an undiscovered manuscript in the Brotherton Library, Leeds (MS LT.q.32), until the 1990s. The present quotations are from fol. 79r, p. 153.

13. See, for example, Cavendish's poems on atoms, astronomy and the weather, such as 'Of Cold Winds', *Poems and Phancies* (1664), pp. 38–9; Stevenson and Davidson, *Early Modern Women Poets*, pp. 303–4.

14. Anne Bradstreet, 'The Author to her Book', in *Several Poems compiled with great variety of wit and learning … by a gentlewoman in New England* (Boston, 1678), p. 256; Stevenson and Davidson, *Early Modern Women Poets*, p. 236.

15. *The Poems of Aemilia Lanyer: Salve Deus Rex Judaeorum*, ed. Susanne Woods (New York: Oxford University Press, 1993), pp. 12, 15.

16. Diana Primrose, *A Chaine of Pearle, Or a memorial of the peerles Graces, and Heroick Vertues of Queene Elizabeth of Glorious Memory* (London, 1630), p. 10; Stevenson and Davidson, *Early Modern Women Poets*, p. 227.

17. An Collins, *Divine Songs and Meditacions*, ed. Sidney Gottlieb (Tempe, AZ: Medieval and Renaissance Texts and Studies, 1996), pp. 60, 61; Stevenson and Davidson, *Early Modern Women Poets*, pp. 338–40.

18. Anna Trapnel, *The Cry of a Stone* (1654), ed. Hilary Hinds (Tempe: Arizona Center for Medieval and Renaissance Studies, 2000), p. 34; Stevenson and Davidson, *Early Modern Women Poets*, pp. 296–301. Trapnel was part of the radical sect known as the Fifth Monarchists, who expected the second coming of Christ in the aftermath of the civil war.

19. Katherine Philips, Orielton MSS Box 24, 7/10/2, National Library of Wales. The preceding references to the poems of Katherine Philips were taken from *The Collected Works of Katherine Philips, Volume 1: The Poems*, ed. Patrick Thomas (Stump Cross, Essex: Stump Cross Books, 1990), pp. 71, 73 and 90.

20. *Eliza's Babes: Or the Virgins-Offering* (London, 1652), pp. 24–5; see also the modern critical edition of *Eliza's Babes*, ed. L. E. Semler (London: Associated University Presses, 2001).

21. 'The Balade which Anne Askewe made and sang when she was in Newgate', in *The latter examynacyon of Anne Askewe*, ed. Betty Travitsky and Patrick Cullen (Aldershot: Scolar Press, 1996), fols. 63r–64r (Stevenson and Davidson, *Early*

Modern Women Poets, pp. 16–17); Gertrude More, 'A short oblation of this smal work … to our most sweet and merciful God', *Spiritual Exercises* (Paris, 1658), p. 277 (Stevenson and Davidson, *Early Modern Women Poets*, pp. 225–6). See also Eugene R. Cunnar and Jeffrey Johnson (eds.), *Discovering and (Re)Covering the Seventeenth Century Religious Lyric* (Pittsburgh, PA: Duquesne University Press, 2001).

22. Elizabeth Singer Rowe, *Poems on Several Occasions, Written by Philomela* (London, 1696), p. 43; Stevenson and Davidson, *Early Modern Women Poets*, pp. 515–16.

23. Mary Carey, 'Written by me at the death of my 4th sonne and 5th Child, Perigrene Payler' (1652), in Carey's autograph manuscript in the possession of the Meynell family, p. 150, cited in *Kissing the Rod: An Anthology of Seventeenth Century Women's Verse*, ed. Germaine Greer et al. (London: Virago, 1988), pp. 157–8. See also Bodleian MS Rawlinson D 1308, and Stevenson and Davidson, *Early Modern Women Poets*, p. 310.

24. Julia Palmer, from 'The weary pilgrim', in *The 'Centuries' of Julia Palmer*, ed. Victoria Burke and Elizabeth Clarke (Nottingham: Trent Editions, 2001), p. 29. The edition is one of the fruits of the Perdita Project for the rediscovery and publishing of lost manuscripts by early modern women writers, an initiative to which all scholars of this period are deeply indebted.

25. *'The Birthday of My Self': Martha Moulsworth, Renaissance Poet*, ed. Ann Depas-Orange and Robert C. Evans (Princeton, NJ: Critical Matirix, 1996), p. 20; Stevenson and Davidson, *Early Modern Women Poets*, p. 126.

26. Aphra Behn, *Works*, ed. Janet Todd, 7 vols. (London: Pickering, 1992–6), I: 53.

27. Margaret Cavendish, 'The Claspe', *Poems, and Fancies* (London, 1653), p. 110.

28. From an anonymous 'Elegy' to Jane Cheyne appended to her funeral sermon: Adam Littleton, *A sermon at the funeral of the Right Honourable the Lady Jane …* (London, 1669), H3r.

29. Jane Cheyne, 'An answeare to my Lady Egertons Songe of I prithy send mee back my Hart', Bodleian MS Rawlinson Poet. 16, p. 16; Stevenson and Davidson, *Early Modern Women Poets*, p. 292.

30. With thanks to Shakespeare's Sonnet 20.

READING LIST

Clarke, Danielle and Elizabeth Clarke (eds.). *'This Double Voice': Gendered Writing in Early Modern England*. Basingstoke: Macmillan, 2000.

Cunnar, Eugene R. and Jeffrey Johnson (eds.). *Discovering and (Re)Covering the Seventeenth Century Religious Lyric*. Pittsburgh, PA: Dusquesne University Press, 2001.

Greer, Germaine, et al. (eds.). *Kissing the Rod: An Anthology of Seventeenth Century Women's Verse*. London: Virago, 1988.

Lindley, David. *The Critical Idiom: Lyric*. London: Methuen, 1985.

Ostovich, Helen and Elizabeth Sauer (eds.). *Reading Early Modern Women: An Anthology of Texts and Manuscripts 1550–1700*. New York: Routledge, 2004.

Smith, Barbara and Ursula Appelt (eds.). *Write or be Written: Early Modern Women Poets and Cultural Constraints*. Aldershot: Ashgate, 2001.

Stevenson, Jane and Peter Davidson (eds.). *Early Modern Women Poets: An Anthology*. Oxford: Oxford University Press, 2001.

Summers, Claude J. and Ted-Larry Pebworth (eds.). *Representing Women in Renaissance England*. Columbia: University of Missouri Press, 1997.

Wray, Ramona. *Women Writers of the Seventeenth Century*. Tavistock: Northcote House, 2004.

Wynne-Davies, Marion (ed.). *Women Poets of the Renaissance*. London: Dent, 1998.

15

SUSANNE WOODS

Narrative poetry

Narrative is one of three broad poetic genres in the Western literary tradition. As lyric poetry traces its origins in song and dramatic poetry in religious ritual, so narrative poetry is associated with history and philosophy, particularly the lineage, exploits and ideas of one's own tribe or people. The mnemonic structures of poetic rhythms undoubtedly served an oral tradition as, later, they were seen to serve what Aristotle called the impulse towards harmony.[1] Early modern women poets inherited not only this broad tradition but specific sub-genres and modes of narrative as they evolved through the Middle Ages, notably through courtly romance and stories of the fall of the great, and were re-invented in the sixteenth century on such classical models as Ovidian and historical or epic narratives. In general, educated women had less exposure to Greek and Latin texts than their brothers and found their narrative models in popular English texts.

The most popular verse narratives of the earlier Elizabethan period were the 'tragedies' produced by William Baldwin and others in the *Mirror for Magistrates* (1559–87), a series of poems in the tradition of Boccaccio's *Fall of Princes*. In the later part of Elizabeth's reign erotic Ovidian narratives, including Marlowe's *Hero and Leander* and Shakespeare's *Venus and Adonis*, gained popular attention. Both *Mirror* and Ovidian models fed into other popular narrative genres of the late Elizabeth and early Jacobean period, including the historical and epistolary narratives of Samuel Daniel and Michael Drayton.[2] Literate women were a substantial audience for these works and for pastoral and courtly romances, including Sir Philip Sidney's prose *Arcadia* (1590, 1593), written for his sister, the Countess of Pembroke, and Edmund Spenser's allegorical epic romance in verse, *The Faerie Queene* (1590, 1596), whose first three books he read to Elizabeth's court around the end of 1589. While there is no extant tradition of early modern Englishwomen writing popular courtly romance until Lady Mary Wroth's prose narrative *Urania* (1621), it is possible that some women writers were aware of romances published by women in sixteenth-century

France and Italy.[3] To various degrees women's narrative verse drew from these examples, typically transforming common materials into works of considerable historical and often aesthetic interest.

Biblical narrative also played an important role in the early modern literary imagination, proportionately more for women than for men. While lyric poetry had a long tradition of personal or idiosyncratic expression, narrative poetry was more typically expected to represent and teach the values of a culture. The authority of the speaker was therefore more of an issue in narrative than lyric poetry, making biblical poetics an attractive foundation for the presumably weaker and usually less educated sex. The earliest narratives published by Englishwomen took advantage not only of biblical referents but also of the Protestant doctrine of the unmediated conscience. While women were expected to be household and not public figures, if God were to direct them to speak out, then who could deny it? From early on the *humilitas topos*, the conventional declaration of humility that all poets used in addressing their social superiors, took a form in women's work that might be paraphrased: 'ascribe the faults of this work to my inferior status as a woman and its virtues to God who commanded me to write'. Yet even women's most assertively religious narratives show evidence of wide reading beyond the Bible, and poets seeming to cede to divine and masculine authority find ways of asserting their own.

Three among the earliest of women's poems printed in English show how religion provided a foundation for narratives richer than the term 'religious poem' might imply and also illustrate these women's skill with some of the basic techniques of narrative poetry: Anne Dowriche's *French Historie* (1589), Elizabeth Melvill, Lady Culros's *A Godlie Dreame* (1606) and Aemilia Lanyer's *Salve Deus Rex Judaeorum* (1611). The first makes use of the *Mirror* tradition along with the taste for gory stories fed by the Elizabethan stage. The second is a dream vision, a popular narrative form since the Middle Ages. The third purports to be a retelling of the biblical story of Christ's passion but it is full of references to popular Ovidian and epistolary romances and has its own proto-feminist agenda. As several critics have noted, writing religious poetry, whatever authority the Bible or Protestant theology might allow, was not a 'passive activity' in a time of tremendous religious controversy.[4]

Dowriche's *French Historie* tells the stories of three recent conflicts between the Protestant French Huguenots and their Catholic antagonists. Like the immensely popular prose work first published in 1563, John Foxe's *Actes and Monuments* (commonly known as the Book of Martyrs), Dowriche's book is part of the Protestant reform movement's effort to see God's avenging and redeeming hand in the martyrdom of his saints.

The book is dedicated to her brother, to whom Dowriche offers a token dismissal of her gender: 'if you finde anie thing that fits not to your liking, remember I pray, that it is a womans doing'.[5] And she claims authority from her brother's patronage, from her sources, and especially from her piety of purpose, quoting St Paul at the beginning of her preface 'To the Reader' to insist 'that my onelie purpose in collecting & framing this worke, was to edifie, comfort and stirre up the godlie mindes unto care, watchfulnesse, Zeale, & firventnesse in the cause of Gods truth' (*French Historie*, A3v). Dowriche's preface nonetheless suggests more confidence and ambition than her gestures to male authority might indicate:

> The causes why I have described it in verse are 3. First for mine owne exercise, being a learner in that facultie; Secondlie, to restore againe some credit if I can unto Poetrie, having been defaced of late so many waies by wanton vanities. Thirdlie, for the mere noveltie of the thing, and apt facilitie in disposing the matter framed to the better liking of some mens fantasies, because the same Storie in effect is alreadie translated into English prose. (A4r)

Dowriche presents herself as a serious poet, even if an apprentice in the art.

The verse of *The French Historie* is poulter's measure, rhyming couplets of twelve and fourteen syllables, a popular relative of the ballad and fourteener metres that dominated in mid century but were edging out of style by 1589. Dowriche uses it skilfully, partitioning lines to serve the narrative thrust. The poem begins, for example, with the narrator on a walk in the woods surprised by a cry 'in shrilling voice, and mournful tunes'. The narrator describes his response:

> … casting feare apart, I ranne toward the place,
> To see the wight that did lament, and waile his wofull case.
> Alone, no perill nigh, within a bushie dale,
> A stranger sate: I got aside to heare his dolefull tale. (B1r)

The second of these lines takes advantage of the length to lead the speaker and reader forward. The third line has pauses for emphasis ('Alone' , 'no perill nigh') then runs on to the fourth ('within a bushie dale, / A stranger sate'), which stops abruptly to sit the narrator down and prepare the reader to hear the stranger's lament. The narrator (an '*English-man*') overhears what turns out to be the sorrow of a 'French pilgrime' who discovers his auditor and goes on to tell the stories that have made him so miserable. Each one is a tale of Catholic wickedness visited upon Protestant virtue ultimately followed by God's bloody revenge set in the context of biblical parallels. The second story, for example, is 'the notable, famous, and constant Martirdome of Annas Burgeus, which, being one of the Kings Counsell, was burnt for the Gospel of Jesus Christ' (*French Historie*, D1r) with 'the judgments of the Lord which fell upon King Henrie the second after he had caused Burgaeus to be imprisoned anno 1589. Dilated with examples of Ahab, Amaziah, and Zedechiah, wicked kings, which used like crueltie against the word' (F1r). The French pilgrim concludes his narrative with praise of England and Queen Elizabeth and an admonition against the tragedies that have inflicted France.

The French Historie is a remarkable work, full of blood and bloody revenge all calibrated to biblical pieties and current events. Its publication date, 1589, is only a year after the Spanish Armada and only a few years since Elizabeth worried her more radical Protestant subjects by seeming determined to marry the French Catholic Duc d'Alençon – possibly a circumstance that prompted Dowriche's lengthy warning against the perfidy of French Catholics. Dowriche was capable of writing skilful iambic pentameter, which was rapidly becoming the norm for narrative as well as dramatic verse (she has introductory and concluding material in this metre), but the poulter's measure she chose for her narrative may have condemned this otherwise fascinating work to a smaller audience than it deserves. As far as we know it was not reprinted until modern times.[6]

Both Elizabeth Melvill's *A Godlie Dreame*, first published in 1603 in Scots dialect as *Ane Godlie Dreame*, and Aemilia Lanyer's *Salve Deus Rex Judaeorum* are written in iambic pentameter, and both are in the *ottava rime*, or eight-line stanzas, familiar from French and Italian romance narratives. *A Godlie Dreame* also calls on the popular tradition of dream allegory, while the *Salve Deus* is notably influenced by the *Mirror* tradition and the historical narratives of Spenser, Daniel and Drayton. *A Godlie Dreame* contains accessible language and orthodox Calvinist theology and went through many editions, while the *Salve Deus* is a more literary and idiosyncratic work and was not reprinted until the twentieth century.[7]

Elizabeth Melvill, Lady Colville of Culros, was a member of a prominent Scots Presbyterian family (her father was Sir James Melville of Halhill) and her religious dream allegory focuses on the total depravity and helplessness of the post-lapsarian soul. The poem begins with the speaker mourning the human condition and the weight of her own sins, describing what the modern reader would recognize as psychological depression: 'I loathed my life, I could not eate or drinke'; 'My soule was plunged into most deepe distresse'; 'All merinesse did aggravate my paine, / And earthlie joyes did still increase my woe.'[8] Weeping brings some comfort and the ability to pray but the speaker remains trapped by sin and unable to help herself. Her tears and prayers calm her to sleep but even then she dreams of her wretched condition. The dream also brings 'a sight most sweet' of 'an Angell bright with visage shyning cleare' (*A Godlie Dream*, A3v) that turns out to be Christ, who comforts and leads her across many agonies, 'past the paine', to the threshold of heavenly triumph. The speaker awakes and feels a need to write the dream and present its principal lessons. 'The way to Heaven I see is wondrous hard / ... But let us learne since we are warned so / To cleave to Christ, for he can help us best' (B3r).

The work is written in a skilled Scottish plain style of highly alliterative verse with simple metaphors. Alliteration is an ancient technique for knitting together lines and for emphasis, though sometimes Melvill uses its absence as a form of emphasis, as the technique sets up unfulfilled expectations. At the sight of fiery hell, for example, the simple request for Christ's help that follows two heavily alliterated lines artfully becomes artless expression:

> For feare I faint to see that uglie sight:
> How can I come amongst the bailfull band?
> O helpe me now, I have no force or might.   (B2r)

Also in the tradition of the plain style, Melvill uses metaphors for emphasis but seldom develops them ('The thornie cares of this deceitfull life, / Will rent your hart'; 'In floods of woe when we are like to drowne' (B3v)). Structurally, Melvill's eight-line verses usually serve as verse paragraphs, with important transitions across the verses at just a few key points. When the 'Angell'/Christ first speaks in the dream, the speech begins at the end of the first stanza of sig. A3v and crosses over to the next, taking the speaker and the reader forward into the trial to come. By contrast, at the end of the dream the Christ figure says his last words of the poem and the break between stanzas signals the moment of the speaker's awakening:

> I begouth to fall:
> And cried aloud, and caught him fast againe;
> Lord Jesus come and rid me out of thrall,
> Courage, said he, now thou art past the paine.
>
> With this great feare I started and awoke
> Crying aloud, Lord Jesus come againe: (B3r)

The poem is a vivid example of the Calvinist dilemma and the psychological frustrations it produces. The speaker is miserable and seeks help, but knows she can do nothing to effect her own salvation. Yet the act of prayer suggests that God has reached out to grant her some grace, a sign that she is among the elect. The message of the poem is that we must persevere in holding fast to Christ, yet the theology of the poem continues to assume that we can do nothing to help ourselves. The dream seeks to bridge the gap in logic that inevitably arises. We can and must persevere because Christ will, of his own free grace, give his elect the ability to persevere. And if he chooses to send that message through the weakness of a woman, there is no more to be said about it.

Aemilia Lanyer similarly uses the posture of weakness to affirm her authority to write about God's message to mankind, but however sincere the pose and the piety may be, *Salve Deus Rex Judaeorum* is a serious claim for poetic authority and for a social role for the woman poet. The 1,840-line narrative was preceded by eleven shorter works dedicated to women, including Queen Anna and more directly Lanyer's own patron, Margaret Clifford, Countess of Cumberland, and is followed by the 'Description of Cooke-ham', celebrating an idyllic summer with the Countess and her daughter, Lady Anne Clifford.[9] The long poem itself tells the story of Christ's passion entirely from women's points of view. As she describes it on the book's title page, her long narrative contains '1 The Passion of Christ. 2 Eves Apologie in defence of Women. 3 The Teares of the Daughters of Jerusalem. 4 The Salutation and Sorrow of the Virgine Mary. With divers other things not unfit to be read.' Further, though the title page glances at male authority, describing the author as 'Wife to Captaine Alfonso Lanyer Servant to the Kings Majestie', a concluding envoi 'To the doubtfull Reader' claims nothing short of divine inspiration for the project. The title, which means 'Hail God, King of the Jews', was 'delievered unto me in sleepe many years before I had any intent to write in this manner', and once she had written the poem, she remembered the dream, 'and thinking it a significant token, that I was appointed to perform this Worke, I gave the very same words I received in sleepe as the fittest Title I could devise for this Booke'.[10] Like Melvill, Lanyer uses dream to point to the direct action of God on the Protestant understanding.

The poem is framed by praise of the Countess of Cumberland with a diatribe against false outward beauty which allows the author to point to multiple stories in a variety of narrative traditions. The Countess's inward beauty gives her comfort and praise instead of the tragedy of a Helen or Cleopatra, or, in the English narrative tradition, of a Rosamond (a story made popular by Samuel Daniel) or Matilda (made popular by Michael Drayton).[11] Lanyer's version of beauty very likely owes something to Edmund Spenser's *Foure Hymnes* of earthly and heavenly love and beauty (1596), whose language she occasionally seems to echo (as in lines 185–200, which have verbal or thematic parallels with Spenser's 'Heavenly Beauty', lines 64–101, 183 and 204–10). Lanyer also certainly knew *The Faerie Queene* and may well have heard Spenser reading from it, as she was at court in 1589. Lanyer's version of the passion, with its emphasis on the beauty of Christ both physical and spiritual, is nonetheless very much her own, with hints of a feminized Christ that go back to the Middle Ages.[12]

Lanyer is a sophisticated narrative poet with a good sense of form. Her frame and apparent digressions all tend to support the work's two central premises: that women, even through their weakness, have a stronger claim on Christ's salvation than men, and that the Countess of Cumberland exemplifies that claim by epitomizing the ideal of the church as the 'bride of Christ'. Both of these premises depend in turn on Lanyer's insistence that she has been called by God to write, a point that she declares within the poem itself as well as in the book's envoi. In her concluding praise of the Countess of Cumberland and all that the poem has constructed Lanyer to represent, she asserts her personal authority without apology:

> And know, when first into this world I came,
> This charge was giv'n me by th'eternall powers,
> Th'everlasting Trophie of thy fame,
> To build and decke it with the sweetest flowers
> That virtue yields; Then Madame, doe not blame
> Me, when I shew the World but what is yours,
>   And decke you with the crowne which is your due,
>   That of Heav'ns beauty Earth may take a view.

(lines 1,457–64)

Encomium joins biblical story in what Lanyer claims as her vocation, and indeed her work uses a variety of generic materials, including the religious complaint, meditation and biblical exegesis along with elements drawn from romance and satire.[13] Its best-known section, the defence of Eve in the voice of Pilate's wife, even borrows from the dramatic monologue, as the wife berates her husband and by extension all men for the unforgivable condemnation of Jesus:

> If one weake woman [Eve] simply did offend,
> This sinne of yours, hath no excuse, nor end.

> To which (poore soules) we never gave consent,
> Witnesse thy wife (O *Pilate*) speakes for all.   (lines 831–4)

The *Salve Deus* is a rich poem with considerable appeal to a modern audience, as the proliferation of recent studies has shown.[14] Of all the narrative poems by early modern women writing in English it perhaps best exemplifies the sophisticated plotting that balances the narrative thrust with the pleasures of sections of poetic artistry, what one critic has identified as the 'tension in a poetic fiction between its local schemes of elaboration and recapitulation and the more linear thrust of its discursive structure'.[15] The poem's balance between the central and framing stories (the passion of

Christ, the suffering and virtue of the Countess of Cumberland) combined with set pieces that draw attention to the poetic artistry of the work (such as the description of the beautiful suffering Christ on the cross in lines 1,153–76) makes this narrative satisfying to read for its poetics as well as its story.

Several interesting works that seem to balance between lyric and narrative emerge from the period between Lanyer's *Salve Deus* and the middle of the seventeenth century and are worth mentioning here. Rachel Speght (*fl.* 1617–21), best known as 'the first Englishwoman to identify herself, by name, as a polemicist and critic of contemporary gender ideology' in the prose pamphlet, *A Mouzell for Melastomus*, also published a meditation on death, *Mortalities Memorandum*, preceded in the volume by a dream allegory on the importance of education and knowledge.[16] In 1630 a woman identified on her title page as 'the Noble Lady, Diana Primrose' published *A Chaine of Pearle, or A Memoriall of the peerless Graces and Heroiock Vertues of Queen Elizabeth, of Glorious Memory*. Ten poems or 'pearles' in iambic pentameter couplets praise various aspects of Elizabeth's person and reign, and might have their closest generic cousin in the coronas of sonnets that included Lady Mary Wroth's 'Crowne of Sonetts dedicated to Love'.[17] Unlike the corona, however, Primrose's set of poems does not complete a formal circle and is impelled less by meditation on the late Queen Elizabeth's virtues than the glorious history those virtues presumably secured. The poet shows a reading of the Queen's speeches, sets England's Protestant triumphs, including defiance of the Pope and the Spanish Armada, at the heart of the poem, and concludes with the triumph of English colonialism. Published the same year that Anne Bradstreet and her family emigrated to New England, it provides an interesting reminder of Elizabeth's continuing influence on the imagination of an educated woman, as Bradstreet's more famous poem, 'In honour of that most High and Mighty Princess, Queen Elizabeth, of most happy memory', was to do in 1650. Finally, an autobiographical manuscript poem, 'The Memorandum of Martha Moulsworth, Widdowe', dated 'November the 10th 1632', was discovered at Yale's Beinecke Librarty towards the end of the last century. It recites the story of her three marriages, notes the death of her children and concludes with some wit that she intends to avoid a fourth marriage: 'the Virgins life is gold, as Clarks us tell / the Widowes silvar, I love silvar well'.[18]

Anne Bradstreet's *Tenth Muse Lately Sprung up in America* (1650) marks an important moment for women poets writing in English and for their aspiration to serious narrative genres more particularly. The seventeenth century was in general a more empirical age than its predecessor, culminating in the rise of experimentation in science and the founding of the Royal Society in

1660. Narrative poetry tends away from the allegorical and fantastical and towards the historical and philosophical, finding inspiration in Lucretius's *De Rerum Natura* ('On the Nature of Things') and in the biblical book of Genesis. John Milton's *Paradise Lost* (1667) is the prime example, but there are others. Joshua Sylvester's *The Divine Weeks of the Worlds Birth* (1604), a translation of Guillaume de Salluste Du Bartas's elaboration on Genesis (which Milton knew and admired), became popular and fed an appetite for the origins of things more generally. Bradstreet's book includes a praise of Du Bartas and begins with several long poems that play into the seventeenth-century taste for science and origins: discourses on the four elements, the four human 'constitutions' or humours, the four ages of man and the four seasons of the year. This she follows with historical narratives on the four pre-Christian monarchies, 'The Assyrian, Persian, Grecian, Roman'. The book also contains some poems that are more often read today, including 'A Dialogue between Old England and New, concerning their present troubles' (that is, the English civil wars of the 1640s), praise of Sir Philip Sidney and the poem in honour of Queen Elizabeth with its now oft-quoted lines, 'Let such as say our sex is void of reason, / Know 'tis slander now, but once was treason'.[19] Though Bradstreet's current fame rests largely on those poems that represent her American experience and were mostly published in the posthumous, Boston volume of her poems (1678), the London volume precedes a new wave of Englishwomen poets who may in part have been inspired by her.

Margaret Cavendish, whose *Poems and Fancies* appeared in 1653, may be one of these, as her current biographer speculates.[20] Although it was common enough for both men and women of her class to write poetry, it was not common for them to write on philosophical topics and to publish the results in print. Cavendish's impulses are narrative and dramatic rather than lyric, so that even her short poems (on topics such as atoms, elements and motions) are either discursive or cast as dialogues. One of the most interesting is on poetry itself, 'The Purchase of Poets, or a Dialogue betwixt the Poets, and Fame, and Homers Marriage' (H3v–I1v). In it, Fame lets poets and their friends argue for their wit in an effort to win the right to dwell with her on top of Parnassus. Fame quickly reduces the crowd to three – Ovid, Virgil and Homer. Homer (for whom Ulysses pleads) wins in the end because he is the most original, a trait that Margaret herself highly prized. The narrative concludes with the wedding of Fame and Homer, a jolly party for all the poets and the muses:

> Then did they dance in measure, and in time,
> Each in their turne took out the *Muses* nine.
> In *Numbers* smooth their *Feet* did run,

> Whilst *Musick* plaid, and *Songs* were sung.
> The *Bride* and *Bridegroome* went to bed,
> There Homer got *Fames Maiden-head*.[21]

While allegory itself is old-fashioned, what Cavendish does with it is singular, and, as with her more philosophical poetry and prose, shows the prevailing interest in origins.

The two most prominent women writers of the mid seventeenth century, Katherine Philips and Aphra Behn, were lyric and dramatic poets with little that could be considered narrative and are treated elsewhere in this volume. The most interesting seventeenth-century woman narrative poet after Anne Bradstreet is Lucy Hutchinson (1620–81), who translated Lucretius and wrote a *Memoir* of the life and activities of her husband, the parliamentary Colonel John Hutchinson. Her poem, *Order and Disorder*, exists in a manuscript of twenty cantos elaborating on the book of Genesis, five of which were published anonymously during her lifetime, in 1679.[22] Probably written around the same time or not long after Milton's *Paradise Lost*, it offers interesting comparisons and contrasts with Milton's much more famous work. Hutchinson's political and religious views were similar to Milton's, though not congruent; her Trinitarian God is more orthodox than Milton's more ambiguous father–son relationship in the godhead, for example, and she views liberty as more constrained after the fall than Milton did. Her narrative, too, is different. It proceeds from the beginning of Genesis to near the end and moves in heroic couplets, while Milton's blank verse narrative encompasses the war in Heaven and the fall of Satan and begins the poem in the middle of the story. Hutchinson's linear narrative is common to the tradition of the philosophical poem and shows the influence of Lucretius and Du Bartas. Milton, by contrast, is writing epic, which traditionally begins *in medias res*.

Many interesting comparisons nonetheless remain, with one example the temptation of Eve in *Order and Disorder*, canto 4 and in *Paradise Lost*, book 9. Hutchinson's version is much shorter, but the result of both is remarkably similar. Milton's Eve concludes:

> Here grows the Cure of all, this Fruit Divine,
> Fair to the Eye, inviting to the Taste,
> Of vertue to make wise: what hinders then
> To reach, and feed at once both Bodie and Mind?
> So saying, her rash hand in evil hour
> Forth reaching to the Fruit, she pluck'd, she eat.[23]

Hutchinson's conclusion is discursive rather than dramatic and handled with considerable skill within the bounds of heroic couplets. After the first two lines, which knit together a single idea, the couplet rhymes create emphasis without blocking the forward motion of the story:

> Eve, quickly caught in the foul hunter's [Satan's] net,
> Believed that death was only a vain threat.
> Her unbelief, quenching religious dread,
> Infectious counsel in her bosom bred,
> Dissatisfaction with her present state
> And fond ambition of a God-like height;
> Who now applies herself to this pursuit,
> With longing eyes looks on the lovely fruit,
> First nicely plucks, then eats with full delight,
> And gratifies her murderous appetite.   (4.203–12)

Here 'murderous appetite' is at least as chilling as Milton's comment that Eve 'knew not eating Death' (9.792). As her editor notes, Hutchinson has 'a gift for the sharp satirical maxim' increasingly identified with the balanced couplets of the late seventeenth and eighteenth centuries, as in the narratives of Dryden and Pope.[24] In this her narrative style extends beyond the lingering metaphysical and baroque styles that find echoes in Milton's unique accomplishment.

By the end of the seventeenth century it was no longer unusual for women to publish their poetry. When Mary, Lady Chudleigh (1656–1710), Anne Finch, Countess of Winchelsea (1661–1720) and Sarah Egerton (1670–1723) published books of poems in the first part of the eighteenth century it was not considered remarkable, although publication might still subject women to controversy. The narrative impulse itself moved increasingly towards prose fiction during the century, so that women writers of the later eighteenth and early nineteenth centuries found themselves on the cutting edge of a new genre. Their participation in the narrative modes of the sixteenth and seventeenth centuries, however, remains an enduring accomplishment well worth further study.

NOTES

1. *Aristotle's Poetics*, trans S. H. Butcher, intro. Francis Fergusson (New York: Hill and Wang, 1961), p. 56.
2. E.g., Samuel Daniel, *The Complaint of Rosamond* (London, 1591) and *Poeticall Epistles* (London, 1599); Michael Drayton, *England's Heroical Epistles* (London, 1598).
3. E.g. by Moderata Fonte [Modesta Pozzo], *Tredici canti del Floridoro* (1581), trans. Julia Kisacky and ed. with intro., Valeria Finucci (Chicago: University of Chicago Press, 2006), and Marie-Madeleine Pioche de la Vergne, Comtesse

de Lafayette, *Zayde: A Spanish Romance*, ed. and trans. Nicholas D. Paige (Chicago: University of Chicago Press, 2006).

4. Elizabeth H. Hageman, 'Women's Poetry in Early Modern Britain', in Helen Wilcox (ed.), *Women and Literature in Britain 1500–1700* (Cambridge: Cambridge University Press, 1996), pp. 190–208; Margaret P. Hannay (ed.), *Silent but for the Word: Tudor Women as Patrons, Translators, and Writers of Religious Works* (Kent, OH: Kent State University Press, 1985).

5. Anne Dowriche, *The French Historie: That is: A lamentable Discourse of three of the chiefe and most famous bloodie broiles that have happened in France for the Gospell of Jesus Christ* (London, 1589), A2v.

6. In *The Poets I*, ed. Susanne Woods, Betty Travitsky and Patrick Cullen (Aldershot: Ashgate Publishing, 2002).

7. Both published in facsmile in *ibid.*; see also *The Poems of Aemilia Lanyer: Salve Deus Rex Judaeorum*, ed. Susanne Woods (New York: Oxford University Press, 1993).

8. Elizabeth Melvill, *A Godlie Dream* (Edinburgh, 1606), A2r.

9. See also Karen Britland's discussion in this volume of Lanyer within the context of Queen Anna's court.

10. Lanyer, *Poems*, p. 139.

11. Samuel Daniel, *Complaint of Rosamond* (1592); Michael Drayton, *Matilda* (1594).

12. Janel Mueller, 'The Feminist Poetics of Aemilia Lanyer's "Salve Deus Rex Judaeorum"', in Lynn Keller and Cristianne Miller (eds.), *Feminist Measures: Soundings in Poetry and Theory* (Ann Arbor: University of Michigan Press, 1993), pp. 208–36.

13. See Marshall Grossman (ed.), *Aemilia Lanyer: Gender, Genre, and the Canon* (Lexington: University Press of Kentucky, 1998), notably Barbara K. Lewalski, 'Seizing Discourses and Reinventing Genres', pp. 49–59, and Boyd Berry, '"Pardon … though I have digrest": Digression as Style in "Salve Deus Rex Judaeorum"', pp. 212–33.

14. See the bibliography maintained by Kari Boyd McBride at www.ic.arizona.edu/ic/mcbride/lanyer/lanbib.htm.

15. Clare Regan Kinney, *Strategies of Poetic Narrative* (Cambridge: Cambridge University Press, 1992), pp. 5–6.

16. Barbara Lewalski (ed.), *The Polemics and Poems of Rachel Speght* (New York: Oxford University Press, 1996), p. xi.

17. In *The Poems of Lady Mary Wroth*, ed. Josephine A. Roberts (Baton Rouge: Louisiana State University Press, 1983), pp. 127–34. *A Chaine of Pearle* (London, 1630) is available through the Brown University *Women Writers Online*, www.wwp.brown.edu.

18. *'My Name Was Martha': A Renaissance Woman's Autobiographical Poem*, ed. Robert C. Evans and Barbara Wiedemann (West Cornwall, CT: Locust Hill Press, 1993).

19. Anne Bradstreet, *Tenth Muse Lately Sprung up in America* (London, 1650), O6r.

20. Katie Whitaker, *Mad Madge: The Extraordinary Life of Margaret Cavendish, Duchess of Newcastle* (New York: Basic Books, 2002), p. 139.

21. Margaret Cavendish, *Poems and Fancies* (London, 1653), I1v.

22. Lucy Hutchinson, *Order and Disorder*, ed. David Norbrook (Oxford: Blackwell, 2001).
23. John Milton, *Paradise Lost*, ed. Barbara K. Lewalski (Oxford: Blackwell, 2007), 9.776–81.
24. Norbrook (ed.), *Order and Disorder*, p. xxx.

READING LIST

Beilin, Elaine V. '"Some freely spake their minde": Resistance in Anne Dowriche's *French Historie*'. In Mary Burke *et al.* (eds.), *Women's Writings and the Reproduction of Culture in Tudor and Stuart Britain*. Syracuse, NY: Syracuse University Press, 1998, pp. 119–40.

Dowd, Michelle and Julie Eckerle (eds.). *Genre and Women's Life Writing in Early Modern England: Re-imagining Forms of Selfhood*. Aldershot: Ashgate, 2007.

Gim, Lisa. '"Faire *Eliza's* Chaine": Two Female Writers' Literary Links to Queen Elizabeth I'. In Susan Frye and Karen Robertson (eds.), *Maids and Mistresses, Cousins and Queens: Women's Alliances in Early Modern England*. New York: Oxford University Press, 1999, pp. 183–98.

Grossman, Marshall (ed.). *Aemilia Lanyer: Gender, Genre and the Canon*. Lexington: University Press of Kentucky, 1998.

Hageman, Elizabeth. 'Women's Poetry in Early Modern Britain'. In Helen Wilcox (ed.). *Women and Literature in Britain 1500–1700*. Cambridge: Cambridge University Press, 1996, pp. 190–208.

Kinney, Clare Regan. *Strategies of Poetic Narrative*. Cambridge: Cambridge University Press, 1992.

Lewalski, Barbara. *Writing Women in Jacobean England*. Cambridge, MA: Harvard University Press, 1993.

Price, Bronwen. 'Women's Poetry 1550–1700: "Not Unfit to be Read"'. In Anita Pacheco (ed.), *A Companion to Early Modern Women's Writing*. Oxford: Blackwell, 2002, pp. 282–302.

Smith, Hallett. *Elizabethan Poetry: A Study in Conventions, Meaning and Expression*. Cambridge, MA: Harvard University Press, 1952.

Woods, Susanne. *Lanyer: A Renaissance Woman Poet*. New York: Oxford University Press, 1999.

16

HILARY HINDS

Prophecy and religious polemic

'The time is coming', wrote Mary Cary in 1651, when 'not onely men, but women shall prophesie; not onely aged men, but young men; not onely superiours but inferiours; not only those that have University-learning, but those that have it not; even servants and handmaids.'[1] Cary is prophesying about prophecy itself, her words' sense of urgency suggesting the peculiar pertinence of this discourse to the turbulent mid seventeenth century. Prophecy was a mode of utterance that both testified and contributed to the revolutionary changes of those years. Cary invokes it as a form of address which would sweep away all the usual social strictures regarding who was authorized to speak on matters of public importance: *all* would prophesy, including those habitually excluded from authoritative public discourse – women, young men, inferiors, the uneducated, 'even servants and handmaids'. Cary was a Fifth Monarchist, and so part of a millenarian group actively preparing for the imminent return of King Jesus, but her radical religious politics alone do not account for her enthusiastic anticipation of the revival of prophecy. John Milton had likewise declared that 'now the time seems come, wherein ... all the Lords people are become Prophets'.[2] Milton, close to the heart of revolutionary power, and Cary, a more marginal figure, both understood prophecy to be a timely and vital force in the service of God.

Upon what was this conviction in a far-reaching prophetic imperative based? Cary's and Milton's view of prophecy as open to all was rooted in the Bible: St Paul had told the Corinthians that 'Ye may all prophesy one by one' (1 Cor. 14:31); and he also – despite his prohibition on women's speaking in church – declared prophecy to be open to women as well as men: 'And on my servants and on my handmaidens I will pour out in those days of my Spirit; and they shall prophesy' (Acts 2:18).[3] These biblical texts (among others) were frequently cited by women from radical religious groups as justification for speaking and writing on matters of religious and political significance. These activities proliferated in the 1640s and 1650s, during the civil wars and Protectorate, when women and men of all social ranks engaged in public debate, in the form of prophecy and other kinds of religious polemic, in unprecedented numbers. And yet, despite the Bible's endorsement of prophecy for women as well as men, and despite its acceptance among certain groups, women's participation was the subject of widespread disquiet and vilification. Francis Higginson, an Anglican minister, objected to the Quakers, for example, on the grounds of their openness to both prophetic utterances and women's active participation in their public ministry: 'Sometimes some of them, men, or women, will more like Phrantick people, then modest Teachers of the Gospell … run through, or stand in the streets, or Market-place, or get upon a stone, and cry Repent, Repent, woe, woe.'[4] For Higginson, prophesying in public was tantamount to madness, contrary to a properly 'modest' godly demeanour, and any association of women with 'immodest' acts was sufficient to situate them beyond the bounds of feminine respectability.

It is with the mid seventeenth-century eruption of prophetic and polemical discourse by women that this chapter is concerned. It will explore what characterized prophecy, as well as asking who prophesied and on what kinds of issues. Introducing the idea of prophecy as a 'discourse of desire', it will consider what kinds of investments in an imagined future these texts made. Finally, it will ask how we might account for prophecy as a platform for women's entry into public discourse: how is this mode of speaking and writing gendered, and how did this articulate with prevailing ideas about femininity?

While twenty-first-century meanings of 'prophecy' focus on its prognosticative dimension, seventeenth-century usage inflected it differently, understanding it principally as a form of mediation between the human and the divine, comprehending 'any utterance produced by God through human agency'.[5] This included a broad range of different kinds of divinely informed utterance. The term might refer to 'an activity of biblical exegesis, coupled with personal testimony'; as Mary Cary explained, 'all might prophesy, that is (in the lowest sense) be able to speak to edification, exhortation and comfort'.[6] Used thus, 'prophecy' is akin to preaching, explicating the Bible so as to address the circumstances of its audience. Prophecy also, however, signified a divinely inspired utterance, originating directly from God, the speaker merely a passive conduit for his words. Quakers habitually wrote of being 'moved of the Lord' to speak, and the Fifth Monarchist prophet Anna Trapnel considered herself to be 'made a voice, a sound … even thy voice through her'.[7] Trapnel's phrasing – she is *made* a voice' – frames her capacity to prophesy not as the result of her own spiritual virtues but as something visited upon her. Signs of inspired prophecy might include trances and visions, or the ability to endure extreme physical privation while remaining healthy. Trapnel's prophecies were striking for being accompanied by all these signs: her *Cry of a Stone* (1654) was uttered during an eleven- or twelve-day trance, during which she ate and drank almost nothing, prophesied in extemporary verse and recounted portentous dreams and visions. Ranging from Scriptural interpretation to ecstatic millenarian visions, prophecy was thus a broadly conceived category in the seventeenth century; its many forms were united, however, by a common concern to elucidate an understanding of God's plan for his creation. Its fundamental mode of textual procedure was interpretive, whether of 'the entrails of scripture' (*Cry of a Stone*, p. 17), as Trapnel so evocatively called them, or of contemporary events, natural phenomena, or the body, visions and dreams of the prophet herself. All were understood as elements within God's opaque but providential creation, so all could be scrutinized for signs that would help yield up its meanings.

The prophetic voice, however, was not the only one taken up by women participating in religious debate. In contrast to visionary prophecy, and different too from the careful biblical exegesis of prophets such as Mary Cary, was religious polemic which explicitly engaged with matters of topical religious contention such as church governance, discipline and practice. Whereas prophecies such as Trapnel's are structurally non-linear, stylistically allusive and syntactically loose and accretive, these polemical texts generally conform more closely to the rhetorical patterns and strategies of theological disputation or animadversion, undertaking the 'absorption, reconfiguration and rebuttal' of an opponent's position, or else proceeding through the 'confession' of personal experience in the service of a particular argument.[8] So, for example, Katherine Chidley's *The Justification of the Independant Churches of Christ* (1641) takes on the separatists' arch-critic, Thomas Edwards, and refutes with some rhetorical dexterity his argument against toleration for congregations claiming independence from the national church, while Susanna Parr, in *Susanna's Apology Against the Elders* (1659), defends herself against accusations made by her minister in a long-running dispute about congregational separation from the Church of England.

While these texts differ from prophecies in that they are not directly concerned with mediation between the divine and the human, whether via exegesis or inspiration, they nonetheless have much in common with them. Like prophecies, they habitually support their arguments through biblical citation: Chidley's argument, for example, is buttressed by multiple marginal biblical references. Religious polemic thus shares prophecy's exegetical foundation. Moreover, like prophecies, such polemic is concerned with the elucidation of God's will, and with the demonstration of the author's conformity to it. Indeed, it is the authors' understanding of this – founded in interpretation of the Scriptures, prayer and self-reflection – that motivates and authorizes their polemic. So while Susanna Parr does not claim the status of prophet, she nonetheless interprets the death of her child as a sign from God warning against congregational separatism: 'when I considered the breach that the Lord had made in my family, I beheld how terrible it was to make a breach in his family. Then the work I was engaged in, this sin of separation, appeared nakedly unto me to be no other than a wounding of Christ's body, which is his church.'[9] The origins of prophecy, anchored in the mediation of the divine, might be distinct from those of religious polemic, rooted more in the rational, in rhetoric, and/or in the experiential. Yet the two forms' common interpretive impetus, and their shared providentialist perspective, suggest that they exist on a continuum, undertaking a common work of biblical explication.

If there was indeed a common work of interpretation undertaken in these prophetic and polemical religious writings, how widely was this work taken up? What issues were addressed, and what different forms did these interventions take? Certainly, historians and critics agree that there was a 'dramatic increase' in women's published writing of the 1640s and 1650s, when 'the incidence of female authorship more than doubled'.[10] Most of this increase is accounted for by prophetic and polemical writings, Phyllis Mack calculating that '[o]ver four hundred women prophesied at least once during the second half of the seventeenth century'.[11] The general ferment precipitated by the outbreak of the civil war, together with the breakdown of censorship, fostered an explosion of political and religious debate and a profusion of pamphlet literature, often in the context of the radical religious and political groups that proliferated in these years. The tones and registers of these texts are diverse: they are variously diagnostic and didactic, utopian and dystopian, rapturous and admonitory. Their intended audience is sometimes highly localized, as in Hester Biddle's *Wo to thee City of Oxford* (1655), sometimes sweepingly universalistic, as in Anne Gargill's *A Warning to all the World* (1656). A prophecy might offer an elaborate reading of a single chapter from Daniel, as in Mary Cary's *The Little Horns Doom & Downfall* (1651), rail against current iniquities, as in Trapnel's *The Cry of a Stone*, or soberly map out the character of the forthcoming New Jerusalem, as in Cary's *A New and More Exact Mappe; or, Description of New Jerusalems Glory* (1651). One (Chidley's *The Justification*) mounts a systematic defence of separatist congregations, while another (Anne Wentworth's *A Vindication of Anne Wentworth*) interprets the author's marriage in seamless relation with biblical prophecy and the state of the nation. Some are openly critical of the new political dispensation, such as Mary Howgill's *A Remarkable Letter of Mary Howgill to Oliver Cromwell* (1657), while others, such as Sarah Wight's text, published by Henry Jessey as *The Exceeding Riches of Grace* (1647), resist the deduction of any political dimension to their prophetic trances.[12] The enumeration of specificities and variations could continue indefinitely, for prophecy's address was as wide as its projected audience was diverse, its focus as all-encompassing, its tones as varied, as are to be found in any body of writing.

Beyond these variations, and beside a common foundation in interpretation, is there a common impetus discernible behind this stylistically, thematically and politically disparate corpus? While not always straightforwardly predictive, I would suggest that these texts are united by an explicit and forceful predication on and commitment to an imagined future. In its future-orientation, this writing is palpably driven by a vision of, and a longing for, a different kind of world, and in this we might designate it a *discourse of desire* – whether that desire be for a different kind of social organization, for retribution against unjust oppressors, or for ecstatic union with the returned Christ. It is, I would contend, the energy of this female-authored body of work's desire for more, for better, for different that in no small part makes it so compelling for twenty-first century readers who might be more accustomed to thinking of early modern women as quiescent, deferential and circumscribed by the family. Prophecy and religious polemic scotches the idea that early modern women had no public voice, no stake in delineating and agitating for a particular vision of the future.

It is prophecy's claim on the future, as well as its insistent occupation of public discursive space, which helps account for the hostility that seventeenth-century women prophets encountered from their opponents. Most of these prophecies and polemics were produced in the context of the radical religious sects, such as the Independents, Baptists, Fifth Monarchists and Quakers, who thrived in the 1640s and 1650s, groups whose religious and political agendas existed in seamless relation with each other, and who favoured much more thoroughgoing change than that instigated by Parliament. Prophecy was an important means by which such groups articulated their ambitions and anxieties. As Bertrand Taithe and Tim Thornton suggest, 'Prophecy was not just a wish for change but a call to action', and herein lies prophecy's challenge: rather than being simply an expression of desire, prophecy might also be – and was frequently understood as – 'a call to action', to prepare the way for its own fulfilment.[13] The Fifth Monarchists, in particular, were feared because their words seemed to sanction the use of violence in preparing for Christ's second coming: 'there is a time of the shooting of bullets', suggested Trapnel (*Cry of a Stone*, p. 23); in fact, however, this was largely a rhetorical rather than actual embracing of armed intervention. If the prophetic call to action was not literally a call to arms, opponents were nonetheless correct to discern a thoroughgoing dissatisfaction with the status quo combined with, in some instances, a programme for social, political or legal reform. Prophecy called its readers to invest in, and act in accordance with, its vision of the future by acceding to its interpretation of signs.

How are we to understand this short-lived cultural openness to the politicized public discourse of prophecy, and of women's place within it? Prophecy was most current as a mode of discursive intervention in the mid seventeenth-century years of flux. There was a widespread sense amongst Puritans and sectaries of a nation involved in a divinely sanctioned struggle, whereby 'God is decreeing', as Milton put it in 1644, 'to begin some new and great period in his Church, ev'n to the reforming of Reformation it self: what does he then but reveal Himself ... first to his English-men'.[14] The civil wars, the execution of the King in 1649, the demise of the radical Parliament of 1653, the political uncertainty following the death of Cromwell, and the Restoration of the monarchy in 1660: the meaning of these events was fought over by commentators from the spectrum of religio-political affinities, including prophets, all concerned to further their own understanding of 'the reforming of Reformation'. Prophecy did not entirely cease after the Restoration – some Quakers, despite the movement's greater commitment to quietism, continued to write in a prophetic mode, for example, and the Baptist Anne Wentworth wrote a compelling prophecy in the 1670s – but it no longer spoke within a culture driven by a sense of divine purpose and sympathetic to prophecy's rhetorical modes.

Prophecy, therefore, constituted a short-lived but important element within the revolutionary period's 'structures of feeling' – the phrase coined by Raymond Williams to describe the 'felt sense of the quality of life at a particular place and time'.[15] Significant too within this cultural configuration were contemporary understandings of femininity, and the gendering of prophecy itself: women's own unstable, passive and irrational nature, it was thought, made them peculiarly receptive to prophetic utterance. Women's identity was conceived, at a cultural level, as subject to fundamental transformation: upon marriage, for example, women took on the identities of their husbands, just as when a 'small brooke or little river incorporateth with *Rhodanus*, *Humber* or the *Thames*, the poore Rivolet loseth her name'. This author concludes that a married woman's '*new selfe* is her superior, her companion, her master'.[16] Her 'selfe' is not definitive but contingent, subject to combination with another. The mutability of the selves of female prophets reproduced this essential instability of identity. Moreover, Mack has argued that the efflorescence of prophetic writing depended on it being already marked as a 'feminine' discourse through its association with the non-rational and the passive (visions, dreams and divine inspiration): 'familiar qualities of passivity, irrationality and passion that had formerly justified women's *absence* from the public arena were used to justify their prophetic activities during the Revolution'.[17] Some people respected women prophets precisely for their bodily and spiritual propensity to divine inspiration: as the preface to Trapnel's *Cry of a Stone* put it,

> It is hoped in this day, a day of the power of God, a day of wonders … that anything that pretends [i.e. claims] to be a witness, a voice, or a message from God to this nation, shall not be held unworthy the hearing and consideration of any, because it is administered by a simple and unlikely hand. (p. 2)

For others, however, this susceptibility to the extra-rational provoked anxiety: might not the openness to forces beyond the human make the subject as vulnerable to diabolical intervention as to divine? How were onlookers to determine whether trances were a sign of bewitchment or of godly favour? Trapnel sought to allay such anxieties: when she experienced prophetic trances during her travels in Cornwall, she was suspected of being a witch, but later, following her court hearing for sedition, she reports triumphantly that 'the rude multitude said, "Sure this woman is no witch, for she speaks many good words, which the witches could not"'.[18]

While Trapnel's auditors were ultimately persuaded of her spiritual credentials, later, the cultural tide turned more decisively against such demonstrations of prophetic inspiration. After the Restoration, in particular, radical religion and its perceived excesses were increasingly blamed for the recent troubles. So Joseph Glanvill deplored the 'mischief' which had 'fallen upon religion': 'mysterious, notional preaching hath put many conceited people upon meddling with what they can never well understand, and so hath fill'd them with air, and vanity, and made them proud, phantastical, and troublesome; disobedient to their Governours, and contemptuous to their betters'.[19] 'Mysterious, notional preaching' surely comprehends prophecy as well as more orthodox Puritan discursive practice, and Glanvill's comment places responsibility for the recent disruption of social hierarchies squarely upon radical religion's linguistic excesses. As part of the Church of England's need to discredit enthusiastic sectarian religion, the visionary recourse to the reading of providential

signs was gradually dislodged from a position of widespread cultural acceptance, the femininity of its extra-rational impetus now counting against it.
As a recent scholar concludes: 'By severing the connection between the
female mind and God, and by discrediting its central importance to religious truth and order, those dissenting women who prophesied the downfall of the monarchy or the coming of the Quaker God could be rendered
"Fanaticks", and their attempts to read – let alone produce – the "Signs of
the Times" rejected as mere nonsense.'[20] Women's perceived irrationality
became again an argument against, rather than in favour of, acceptance of
their prophecies, as a commitment to plain speech in religious matters provided one way to discredit religious and political 'enthusiasm'. Tellingly,
Anne Wentworth's detractors in the 1670s claimed that she was mad, and
thus a transgressor against rationality, rather than (as with Trapnel) a
witch, sinning against God.

Accusations of the author's witchcraft, or of her madness, underline the
importance of the speaker/writer herself as a constitutive element of the
composite prophetic 'sign', comprising the figure of the prophet (her earlier
life, her reputation, her community, her bodily state) and the prophetic
words. Those who witnessed the performance of a prophecy were called on
to read the whole multivalent sign as conforming to godly precedent. So
when the Quaker Dorothy Waugh was held in Carlisle gaol after prophesying 'against all deceit and ungodly practice' in the marketplace, a scold's
bridle was placed on her to make her 'an example to all': 'so I stood their
time with my hands bound behind me with the stone weight of iron upon
my head, and the bit in my mouth to keep me from speaking'. Waugh's
account suggests that, far from this spectacle undermining her position as
a prophet of God's truth, it instead confirmed it, as 'the people to see me
so violently abused were broken into tears'.[21] Rather than witnessing the
proper civic correction of a disorderly woman, Waugh's words imply that
her witnesses saw this as a sorry instance of a prophet being 'not without
honour, save in his own country' (Matthew 13:57). A punishment intended
to discredit her prophetic claims was appropriated as a further authorizing
sign of her godly credentials.

Authorization of the prophet's activities is a recurrent concern in these
writings: how is the female author, whose reputation was dependent on a
modesty compromised by engaging in public discourse, to secure for her
words the respect and authority she seeks? One key way is through the
invocation of the Bible, citations from which not only endorse the prophecy, but endow it with a Scriptural vocabulary, rhythm and gravitas, and
thereby a mode of legitimization rooted in the culture's most authoritative
text. Margaret Fell's *Women's Speaking Justified* (1666) is one text whose

polemical purpose (to defend the Quaker practice of allowing women Friends to speak in religious meetings) is undertaken through the explication of biblical texts that together might be understood to rewrite St Paul's prohibition of women speaking in church.

In addition to this habitual Scriptural citation, the body and identity of the prophet herself – both her social identity and her identity as the author of the text – are frequently invoked within the process of authorization. For Waugh, her body's capacity to confirm her prophetic status as a conduit of the word and will of God figures as a key signifying element. Similarly, in *The Cry of a Stone*, Trapnel's 'relator', who transcribed her words during her trance, frequently returns to her startling capacity to prophesy 'without any sustenance at all for the first five days, and with only a little toast in small beer once in twenty-four hours for the rest of the time' (*Cry of a Stone*, p. 79). Trapnel too makes her ability to thrive on such a regimen a prophetic element in itself, foreseeing that, 'Father, when thou withdrawest thy glory from thy handmaid, thou shalt leave so much heat as shall refresh the body, and her health shall return again from thee to her' (*Cry of a Stone*, p. 54). And so, the text assures us, it transpired: when Trapnel emerged from her trance, after some twelve days, 'she rose up in the morning, and the same day travelled on foot from Whitehall to Hackney and back to Mark Lane in London, in health and strength' (*Cry of a Stone*, p. 79). Her capacity to walk these ten miles is the final authorizing gesture of the prophecy, confirmatory of the interpretation of her bodily state previously offered. The insistence on the prophetic body as itself an authorizing sign of godly intervention and a guarantee of the authenticity of the prophet's words suggests the vulnerability of those words, and of the whole prophetic performance, to misconstruction.

It is not only the miraculous capacity of the prophetic body to withstand deprivation that marks it out as divinely significant. The form of the sign is itself important: the temporary abeyance of the prophetic body, its capacity to thrive in defiance of its human needs, is also invoked as a portent of the prophetic words: 'Vision! The body crumbles before it, and becomes weak; men are mistaken when they think that the great things of God will puff up ... they that have the flowings of thee, are self-denying' (*Cry of a Stone*, p. 77). Here the body serves as an adjunct to, or metonym of, the 'self', that faulty fallen sign of humanity whose frail carnality habitually limits the apprehension of God's grace. For the prophet, body and self dissolve, however temporarily, allowing divine 'flowings' to find a channel through the now less-than-human – and hence more-than-human – prophet. 'Oh Lord', Trapnel observes, 'there is no self in this thing' (*Cry of a Stone*, p. 45).

Anne Wentworth's prophecy, *A Vindication of Anne Wentworth* (1677), published over twenty years later, seems to promise a different strategy with regard to the 'self' of the author: if the text's declared mission is self-vindication, then self-erasure in the face of what Trapnel called God's 'flowings' would appear counterproductive. However, this text also calls on the dissolution of the self of the prophet in the service of her self-vindication, which, in turn, is in the service of God. Wary, like all prophets, of accusations of either delusion or self-interest (she notes 'how dangerous and desperate an attempt it is to put the *commission* and *authority* of God upon the *dreams* and *visions* of my own heart'), Wentworth records how such deluded self-centredness is rendered impossible: 'my God who has been so many years *emptying* me from vessel to vessel, *breaking* me all to pieces in myself, and making me to become as *nothing* before him … has thereby called and commanded me into this work, when I was a thing that *is not* [1 Corinthians 1:28] in my own eyes'.[22] Wentworth's allegiance to her 'heavenly bridegroom', Christ, necessarily outweighs that owing to her earthly husband, and since the actions of the latter threatened the former, she 'was forced to fly to preserve a life more precious than this natural one … in obedience to my heavenly bridegroom … to undertake and finish a work which my earthly husband in a most cruel manner hindered me from performing' (*A Vindication*, pp. 186–7). Thereafter, God revealed 'what I did not then know, that my oppressions and deliverance had a public ministry and meaning wrapped up in them' – namely, that 'wrath shall fall upon the *same spirit* throughout the nation, which everywhere oppresses the true seed as I have been oppressed by it' (*A Vindication*, pp. 193, 194). The divine erasure of her carnal self lends an authority to her later prophetic interpretation of her earlier sufferings and actions. Where Trapnel had looked to her own life to underwrite her visionary prophecies, Wentworth finds her own life a living prophecy, the nation figured in the home, her carnal self erased only to be resurrected, transfigured, as a player in a new, portentous, divinely directed drama.

The culture of the 1670s, when Wentworth was writing, was, as we have seen, hostile to prophetic discourse in a way that that of the 1640s and 1650s was not. Where the women prophets of the 1640s and 1650s had expanded their sphere of activity beyond the domestic by taking up their place in religio-political discourse, Wentworth took public discourse back into the home, rereading those 'private' familial events through the conventions of prophecy. The desires driving their prophecies are in one sense quite distinct: women of the 1640s and 1650s claim their place in public debate in a forum amenable to providentialist intervention and prophetic signs, while Wentworth must refute charges of madness before she can seek to persuade her readers of the immanence of the public within the personal. In both cases, however, prophecy, through its contradictory reliance on and erasure of the figure of the female author, produced a space, however temporary and vulnerable, in which those desires might be textualized. In other words, it is its discursive form, as well as its articulation of desire, that marks prophecy out as such a significant and ground-breaking mode within the history of women's writing.

NOTES

1. Mary Cary, *A New and More Exact Mappe; or, Description of New Jerusalems Glory* (London, 1651), p. 238.
2. *Areopagitica*, in *The Complete Prose Works of John Milton*, volume II, ed. Ernest Sirluck (New Haven, CT: Yale University Press, 1959), pp. 480–570 (555–6).
3. See 1 Corinthians 14: 34: 'Let your women keep silence in the churches: for it is not permitted unto them to speak.' Many women sectaries sought to refute this prohibition in their writings. All biblical citations are taken from the King James (Authorised) version.
4. Francis Higginson, *The Irreligion of the Northern Quakers* (London, 1653), p. 12.
5. Diane Purkiss, 'Producing the Voice, Consuming the Body: Women Prophets of the Seventeenth Century', in Isobel Grundy and Susan Wiseman (eds.), *Women, Writing, History 1640–1740* (London: Batsford, 1992), pp. 139–58 (139).
6. Geoffrey F. Nuttall, *The Holy Spirit in Puritan Faith and Experience* (Oxford: Basil Blackwell, 1947), p. 75; Cary, *Mappe*, p. 237.
7. Anna Trapnel, *The Cry of a Stone* (London, 1654), ed. Hilary Hinds (Tempe: Arizona Center for Medieval and Renaissance Studies, 2000), p. 45.
8. Marcus Nevitt, *Women and the Pamphlet Culture of Revolutionary England* (Aldershot: Ashgate, 2006), p. 37; see too Susan Wiseman, *Conspiracy and Virtue: Women, Writing and Politics in Seventeenth-Century England* (Oxford: Oxford University Press, 2006), pp. 129–32.
9. Susanna Parr, *Susanna's Apology Against the Elders* (London, 1659). Quotation taken from Elspeth Graham, Hilary Hinds, Elaine Hobby and Helen Wilcox (eds.), *Her Own Life: Autobiographical Writings by Seventeenth-Century Englishwomen* (London: Routledge, 1989), p. 110.
10. Joad Raymond, *Pamphlets and Pamphleteering in Early Modern Britain* (Cambridge: Cambridge University Press, 2003), pp. 299, 300.
11. Phyllis Mack, 'The Prophet and her Audience: Gender and Knowledge in the World Turned Upside Down', in Geoff Eley and William Hunt (eds.), *Reviving the English Revolution: Reflections and Elaborations on the Work of Christopher Hill* (London: Verso, 1988), p. 150 n.1.
12. On the political implications of Wight's writings, see Wiseman, *Conspiracy and Virtue*, pp. 97–142.
13. Bertrand Taithe and Tim Thornton, 'The Language of History: Past and Future in Prophecy', in Bertrand Taithe and Tim Thornton (eds.), *Prophecy: The Power of Inspired Language in History 1300–2000* (Stroud, Gloucestershire: Sutton Publishing, 1997), p. 11.
14. Milton, *Areopagitica*, p. 553.

15. Raymond Williams, *The Long Revolution* (London: Chatto and Windus, 1961), p. 47.
16. T. E. [Thomas Edgar], *The Lawes Resolutions of Womens Rights* (London, 1632), pp. 124–5; my emphasis.
17. Phyllis Mack, 'Women as Prophets during the English Civil War', in Margaret Jacob and James Jacob (eds.), *The Origins of Anglo-American Radicalism* (London: George Allen and Unwin, 1984), p. 225.
18. Anna Trapnel, *Anna Trapnel's Report and Plea* (London, 1654). Quotations taken from Graham *et al.*, *Her Own Life*, pp. 77, 84.
19. Joseph Glanvill, *An Essay Concerning Preaching* (London, 1678), pp. 19–20.
20. Julie Crawford, *Marvelous Protestantism: Monstrous Births in Post-Reformation England* (Baltimore, MD: Johns Hopkins University Press, 2005), p. 172.
21. Dorothy Waugh, 'A Relation Concerning Dorothy Waugh's Cruel Usage by the Mayor of Carlisle', in *The Lambs Defence Against Lyes* (London, 1656); reproduced in Hilary Hinds, *God's Englishwomen: Seventeenth-Century Radical Sectarian Writing and Feminist Criticism* (Manchester: Manchester University Press, 1996), pp. 227–8.
22. Anne Wentworth, *A Vindication of Anne Wentworth* (London, 1677). Quotation taken from Graham *et al.*, *Her Own Life*, p. 185; original emphasis.

READING LIST

Brown, Sylvia (ed.). *Women, Gender and Radical Religion in Early Modern Europe.* Leiden and Boston: Brill, 2007.
Gillespie, Katharine. *Domesticity and Dissent in the Seventeenth Century: English Women Writers and the Public Sphere.* Cambridge: Cambridge University Press, 2004.
Hinds, Hilary. *God's Englishwomen: Seventeenth-Century Radical Sectarian Writing and Feminist Criticism.* Manchester: Manchester University Press, 1996.
Holstun, James. *Ehud's Dagger: Class Struggle in the English Revolution.* London: Verso, 2000.
Longfellow, Erica. *Women and Religious Writing in Early Modern England.* Cambridge: Cambridge University Press, 2004.
Mack, Phyllis. *Visionary Women: Ecstatic Prophecy in Seventeenth-Century England.* Berkeley: University of California Press, 1992.
Smith, Nigel. *Perfection Proclaimed: Language and Literature in English Radical Religion 1640–1660.* Oxford: Clarendon Press, 1989.
Watt, Diane. *Secretaries of God: Women Prophets in Late Medieval and Early Modern England.* Cambridge: D. S. Brewer, 1997.
Wiseman, Susan. *Conspiracy and Virtue: Women, Writing and Politics in Seventeenth-Century England.* Oxford: Oxford University Press, 2006.

17

MARTA STRAZNICKY

Private drama

Early modern England was less than hospitable to women playwrights. Although there is no known formal prohibition against women writing for the stage, not a single play from the theatre of Shakespeare's time was written by a woman. Scholars have not yet fully accounted for this strikingly overt bias, but there is enough evidence in anti-theatrical and moral writings of the time to suggest that the secular, public nature of commercial theatre was fundamentally incompatible with the conception of female virtue as domestic: the ideals of godliness, chastity and good housewifery were invariably imagined as achievable only within the space of the home. Ideological constraints of this kind are, of course, always open to violation, and indeed we have enough records of women transgressing domestic boundaries with impunity to suggest that, in terms of women's lived reality, female virtue and the public sphere were not categorically opposed. And yet women did not write public stage plays until the early 1660s. What they did write is variously identified as domestic, household or closet drama, all three terms signalling a perceived distinction between plays written for a paying, public spectatorship and plays written for a private audience of family and friends.

This dichotomy of public (male) stage and private (female) household drama is a useful framework for understanding the nature of women's playwrighting in the early modern period until the 1660s, but it also has conceptual and rhetorical limitations. As the following outline of women's 'private' drama will show, these plays could and did engage important political debates, were co-authored with or addressed to men, were released to the public in print or circulated beyond the author's family in manuscript and in many instances were written for performance. Furthermore, the early modern professional theatre itself developed what we might call a rhetoric of privacy that stratified theatrical culture in terms of class, education and taste. 'Private' theatres such as the Blackfriars were and were perceived to be far more upmarket than public theatres such as the Globe, and according to comments made by playwrights, officials and spectators, the distinction was in the social status of the audience, the verbal sophistication of the repertory and – not least – the indoor playing space. Except for the paying spectators, these characteristics could well describe early modern women's plays. Thus, when we speak of women's private drama, we should bear in mind that these plays belong to a larger theatrical culture in which the terms 'public' and 'private' were fraught with historical, professional and ideological significance. While early modern women playwrights did not write for the commercial theatres until the 1660s, they were nevertheless members of a social and literary élite whose long-standing patronage of private drama continued to influence theatrical discourse and practice throughout the seventeenth century.

Women's drama and humanist education

The earliest surviving English drama by women is translated from classical playwrights who were standard texts in the humanist curriculum. Although the humanist educational programme, geared as it was to public service, formally excluded women, a number of aristocratic families hired private tutors who delivered the humanist curriculum to sons and daughters alike. This was certainly the case in the Tudor royal family, where Princess Elizabeth's personal tutor, Roger Ascham, was a leading proponent of humanist pedagogy, and also in the family of Lady Jane Lumley, whose father Henry Fitzalan, 12th Earl of Arundel, employed a tutor for his daughters and made available to them the full resources of his vast library. That library had well over 1,000 volumes and included the major humanist pedagogical writings, reference works and standard teaching editions of the Greek and Latin classics. Princess Elizabeth would have had an even richer library at her disposal. That these two women produced our earliest examples of English dramatic writing, and that their work was in translation rather than original composition, is directly attributable to the education they received.

In the humanist programme, the study of Greek and Latin drama was a core pedagogical activity. Reading, translating and reciting classical plays was considered an excellent method of teaching grammar, style and – more dubiously – ethics. The rhetorical and moral objectives of academic play-reading meant that the dramatic text was approached as an object of linguistic and literary instruction rather than as a script for performance. Even when pupils were required to recite passages from classical plays, the pedagogical aim was improvement in language facility, speech and conduct. Given these aims, it is not surprising that academic translation was governed by the twin ideals of imitation and invention: above all, to be faithful to the sense of the original, but also to render the original in an elegant, lively vernacular.

It is interesting, then, that Lady Jane Lumley's translation of Euripides's *Iphigeneia at Aulis*, the earliest complete play in English by a woman *and* the earliest English translation of Euripides, plainly departs from the academic ideal. A spin-off of the Trojan War narrative, the play is set at the port of Aulis, where a calm sea prevents the Greek army from launching the recovery of Helena. Seeking the advice of a prophet, the Greek general Agamemnon is told that the winds will return only if he sacrifices his daughter Iphigeneia to the goddess Artemis. The plot then turns on this conflict of Agamemnon's as father and general, with a predictably dire result for his daughter. Iphigeneia, however, is transformed in the play from a pitiful young woman to a self-proclaimed saviour of her nation. At the stroke of death, she disappears and is replaced by a stag, much to the fear and confusion of the Greek soldiers. It is a story of family loyalty, public service, self-sacrifice and female heroism; clearly it had some special appeal to a teenaged Lumley when she undertook the translation in the early 1550s.

The play survives in a manuscript volume that also contains Lumley's translations from Greek into Latin of four orations of Isocrates; other volumes at the British Library of seemingly academic translations by Lumley, her sister, brother and stepbrother indicate that the home schooling she received followed the humanist curriculum in its emphasis on the classical languages. This pedagogical context for Lumley's *Iphigeneia*, however, fails to explain why her translation departs so strikingly from the humanist norm: substantial sections of the original are simply cut, including most of the metrically complex choruses, while sequences of dialogue are compressed into single speeches and – most unusually – the play is rendered from verse into prose, a much-debated and largely discouraged form of translation. The overall effect of these changes is to enhance the dramatic coherence of the play. Where Euripides has extended laments or passages that slow down the action, Lumley scales back on rhetorical dilation, eliminates indirect speech, minimizes descriptions of offstage events and generally keeps up a steady momentum. From the frequency and consistency of these changes, it would seem that Lumley's *Iphigeneia* was written with an eye to performance, a translation 'exercise' – if such it be – that falls well outside the parameters of the humanist schoolroom.

As for the narrative itself, Lumley concentrates the story on Iphigeneia and her parents, downplaying the abduction of Helena and the subject of brotherhood that are prominent in Euripides's original. An interest in the domestic angle of the tragedy might be expected of a young female writer, but given her family and class status there is no reason to think that Lumley could not have been equally drawn to the play's political theme. And indeed, there is good evidence that at the time of writing Lumley's father was deeply implicated in the succession crisis involving another young girl destined to be sacrificed for the good of the state, Lumley's own cousin Lady Jane Grey. In this context, Lumley's narrative and stylistic departures from Euripides could well be evidence of an intended household performance. One intriguing feature of Lumley's manuscript is her use of graphic distinctions such as flourishes and marginal speech prefixes to distinguish between speakers, a convention that is otherwise found only in theatrical play scripts. In Lumley's hand, the dramatic text achieves a striking orchestration of voices. Whether this orchestration was ever realized is not known, but there is enough evidence of theatrical activity at Nonsuch, the country estate where Lumley lived when she wrote the play, to make this a real possibility. While Lumley's *Iphigeneia* clearly originated in the context of humanist education, its execution, its graphic design, and the personal and political resonance of its story point towards a function quite other than a schoolroom exercise.

Household drama

The domestic origins, thematic focus and conceivable performance of Lumley's play place it within a well-established tradition of household drama. For at least a century before the opening of public theatres in Elizabethan London, the country homes of England's nobility were the scene of a wide range of theatrical activities, from full-scale dramas produced by troupes of travelling professional players to performances by household members and staff. There is a bewildering diversity of such entertainments, but despite the absence of a unifying conceptual model for this practice scholars are agreed that it forms a distinct branch of early modern theatre history. Distinguished from London theatre primarily by its non-commercial nature, private household drama was a more communal, self-reflexive and experimental theatrical tradition than the drama developed on fixed stages for a public, paying audience towards the end of the sixteenth century.

One of the areas in which household theatre was more advanced than the professional stage was in the involvement of women as patrons, performers and writers. To take some significant but little-known examples, Lady Elizabeth Russell wrote an entertainment, in which her daughters performed, for the Queen's visit to her estate at Bisham in 1592; Mary Sidney Herbert, Countess of Pembroke, wrote a pastoral dialogue intended for performance also before Queen Elizabeth at her planned visit to Wilton in 1599; Lady Alice Egerton, Dowager Countess of Derby, wrote an entertainment for performance at Harefield in 1602; and Rachael Fane, who grew up in a household in which she was part of the third generation of educated women, wrote numerous pastoral and masque-like entertainments for presentation at the family estate of Apethorpe. It is not insignificant that Rachael's brother Mildmay Fane is well known as the author of at least six plays and entertainments that were also written for presentation at Apethorpe by the family, servants and friends. Similarly, Lady Alice Egerton belonged to a family that had a long tradition of sponsoring coterie drama, and Mary Sidney Herbert's brother, husband and sons were all variously involved in amateur and professional drama, culminating perhaps in her two sons being selected as the dedicatees of Shakespeare's collected plays in 1623. In short, like Jane Lumley, these women not only produced dramatic writing but did so as members of families and households where theatrical activities were a familiar form of entertainment.

Two of the period's best-known women's plays are products of just this context. Lady Mary Wroth's *Love's Victory*, written around 1620, is a fully fledged pastoral drama portraying several sets of shepherds and shepherdesses whose romantic pursuits are impeded by jealousy, misunderstanding or malice. Much of the play's structural design and linguistic texture is drawn from pastoral conventions that had become voguish at the Jacobean court in the preceding two decades and are exemplified in such plays as Samuel Daniel's *Queen's Arcadia* (1606) and John Fletcher's *The Faithful Shepherdess* (1610). The pastoral mode was also a staple of the court masques of the early seventeenth century in which Wroth herself had performed, and of Queen Anna's court in particular, where Wroth continued as lady in waiting even after her marriage in 1603.

Despite the popularity of pastoral among aristocratic audiences, the failure of Fletcher's play at the Blackfriars theatre suggests that there is something inherently closed or private about the genre, its meanings limited to the particular interpretive community whose concerns and values are being depicted allegorically. Philip Sidney, Wroth's uncle and a leading literary figure for a generation of writers, noted that 'under the pretty tales of wolves and sheep', pastoral could usefully engage 'whole considerations of wrong-doing and patience'.[1] Scholars have identified such moral and political registers in much pastoral writing of the early modern period: Elizabethan court poets, for example, used pastoral to negotiate the complexities of courtiership under a female monarch, and the predominance of pastoral at the Stuart court in Wroth's own time functioned as a vehicle for the mythological founding of a new dynasty. Recent critics have suggested that Wroth's play is similarly coded, its range of reference extending from family to court politics and engaging at both levels 'considerations of wrong-doing' such as arranged marriages, insincere courtship and jealousy. Prevailing over these and possibly other allegorical meanings is, as Barbara Lewalski has shown, a strikingly non-conventional emphasis on female agency: Venus rather than Cupid is the central agent, a mother rather than a father orchestrates the arranged marriage, and women rather than men act to resolve problems.[2] Unique to Wroth, this consistently feminist adaptation of pastoral seems to suggest that hermeneutically restricted genres are not only available but perhaps also particularly amenable to female playwrights in this period. It also raises the important question of the play's intended audience and performance venue.

Whether Wroth wrote for a courtly or more limited familial audience cannot be known, although these would in any case have been overlapping communities for her. Certainly there are enough discernible allusions in the names and situations of some of her characters to suggest a fairly straightforward shadowing of immediate family members, and the design of the play as a whole would make it suitable for a household production or group recitation at one of Wroth's several residences. Alison Findlay's recent work on garden theatre is also suggestive for imagining a possible venue for *Love's Victory*: the play's settings in fields and groves, its controlled movement of groups of characters from one vignette to another and its extensive use of lyrical songs and musical set pieces would make it ideal for performance in a formal Renaissance garden such as still survives at the Sidney family estate of Penshurst.[3] One can imagine the audience moving from one garden room to another as the play changed locations, each room providing a fresh change of scene both for the fiction and the guests. The location itself at a Sidney or Wroth estate would have anchored the play's range of meanings in a specific architectural site that would presumably have some resonance for the intended audience. Imagining a performance such as this, however speculative, is necessary if *Love's Victory* is to be understood as more than a female version of pastoral or coded autobiographical writing. One can praise the elegance of its design, its innovative structural features, its experimental metrical forms and its overtly feminist handling of character and theme, but even so the play often fails to engage contemporary readers who are perforce excluded from the interpretive community for which it was written. Interestingly, there is some evidence that the play was not only known but also performed outside Wroth's immediate family circle, and the survival of two substantially different manuscripts in Wroth's hand indicates that she spent a considerable amount of time and effort revising and preparing a formal copy of the play. *Love's Victory* could and apparently did engage not only the author but also her close friends and acquaintances, so its relatively lifeless character on the page is, if not beside the point, then the very thing that should prompt us to look to the tradition of household theatre as a context in which the play might be imaginatively revived.

Some twenty years after Wroth wrote *Love's Victory*, when England was in the midst of civil war and aristocratic households throughout the country were under siege by parliamentary forces, two young women of the prominent Royalist Cavendish family wrote a remarkable comedy in which gender and state politics are openly debated by a cast of characters resembling many a stage play from the commercial theatre of the 1630s. Dating from about 1645, *The Concealed Fancies* was written by the sisters Jane Cavendish (1621–69) and Elizabeth Brackley (1626–63), daughters of William Cavendish, a Royalist general and leading patron of the professional stage. Cavendish's army suffered a brutal defeat in 1643, following which he went into exile in Paris and Antwerp and left the management of his estates to his daughters. *The Concealed Fancies* appears to have been written during Cavendish's exile, for it depicts not one but two sets of sisters living without male supervision in country homes whose architectural features allude to Bolsover Castle and Welbeck Abbey, two of Cavendish's estates. Interestingly, both estates had in happier times been the sites of extravagant household theatricals.

The central dramatic concern of *The Concealed Fancies* is romantic, with two sisters at one estate and three at another seeking marriage arrangements that will permit continued sovereignty of the kind they enjoy as unwed guardians of their fathers' estates. The gender politics of the play are remarkably complex, as Catherine Burroughs has shown, involving the women's control not only of land and property, but also of their sexuality.[4] The play is laced with comedy that takes some cutting swipes at the besotted young men, at the household servants and at 'Lady Tranquillity', a figure who seems to represent Cavendish's young bride Margaret Lucas (whose own plays are discussed later in this chapter). And other than a single masque-like scene in which the betrothals are concluded, the situation and tone of the play do not move far outside what might be expected of a seventeenth-century comedy of manners. This is, in other words, a strikingly assured piece of writing that adopts but is not restrained by contemporary playwriting conventions, including moral conventions for handling female wit and behaviour.

The Concealed Fancies is also remarkable for the extent to which it indulges a self-reflexive conception of its own performance. In addition to thematizing performativity and self-display as the very condition of courtship, the play opens and ends with multiple prologues and epilogues that articulate a very clear expectation that it will be both read by Cavendish and performed in front of him and others. While evidence of an actual performance does not survive, the manuscript volume in which the play is found reveals that Cavendish and Brackley saw themselves as members of an extended literary coterie who would presumably have been their primary audience.[5] Designed for if not actually realized in a domestic performance, *The Concealed Fancies* reveals that in this context women writers could manipulate dramatic and moral conventions not only with impunity but with the positive support of their families and associates.

Women's plays in print

Although manuscript circulation in the early modern period was understood as a form of publication, none of the plays written by women in the context of humanist education or household entertainment were printed. This may have to do more with the authors' decision to restrict the circulation of their work to a controlled readership than the systemic exclusion of women writers from the book trade, but it is all the more striking that of the roughly 1,000 plays printed between 1580 and the Restoration in 1660 only two were written by women. Moreover, these two plays, Mary Sidney's *Antonius: A Tragedie* (1592, reprinted as *The Tragedie of Antonie* in 1595) and Elizabeth Cary's *Tragedie of Mariam* (1613), belong to a group of classical dramas written by a small coterie connected in various ways with the Sidney family. Mary Sidney's position at the centre of this coterie goes a long way to explaining the publication of two plays by women from the group, but it is also important to know that both Sidney and Cary published work other than drama in their lifetimes and that they were both active participants in religious controversies that were playing out in the early modern public sphere. The appearance of their plays in print should, then, be seen in the context not only of the male-dominated field of play publication but also of each individual author's fashioning of a public identity that extended beyond theatrical culture.

The printed text of Mary Sidney's *Antonius: A Tragedie*, a translation from a French play by the avant-garde writer Robert Garnier, was originally issued together with Sidney's translation of Philippe de Mornay's moral and philosophical tract *A Discourse of Life and Death*. The publication of these two works together suggests that they bear some relation to one another, and indeed the handling of the story of Antony and Cleopatra in Garnier's play foregrounds the conflict between private passion and public duty that is also the subject of de Mornay's treatise. Moreover, both of these works are products of the French religious wars in which Philip Sidney himself had been involved. Philippe de Mornay, in fact, had been a close friend of Sidney's and considered him one of his closest allies. It seems likely, then, that the co-publication of Mary Sidney's play with de Mornay's treatise in 1592 was part of a larger effort to promote continental Protestant intellectual culture in England.

The play itself was reprinted singly in a smaller format in 1595, the text substantially unchanged but the title altered to *The Tragedie of Antonie*. Just a year earlier, two other plays on stoical themes by writers associated with Sidney had appeared in print (Samuel Daniel's *Cleopatra* and Thomas Kyd's *Cornelia*), and another would follow several years later (Samuel Brandon's *Octavia*). Significantly, all three are dedicated to women readers, most notably Daniel's to Mary Sidney herself, and all three obviously concern themselves primarily with the trials of women powerless to control their own destinies. In their form, too, these plays imitate Sidney's *Antonius*: they have very little stage action, the drama being focused instead on the conflicting perspectives of characters who speak largely in monologues. For many years, these plays were disparaged as 'closet drama', anti-theatrical in nature, overly intellectual and unrelentingly serious and thus running counter to the brilliant accomplishments of London public theatre. More recently, feminist critics have reassessed closet plays in the context of early modern public discourse and found them to be participating in debates on pressing and frequently dangerous political matters. That they were written primarily for reading or private recitation rather than for performance in the public theatre now seems less an aesthetic deficiency than an indication of their belonging to a different public sphere than that engaged by London's commercial theatres.

Elizabeth Cary's *Tragedie of Mariam* deals with many of the same questions of women's moral and political agency as Sidney's *Antonius* and is in its printed form clearly modelled on the literary drama. While there is no known personal relationship between Cary and members of Sidney's circle, there is enough circumstantial evidence to suggest that she was aware of and influenced by their literary projects from an early age, chief among which was the use of narratives drawn from classical history to engage in a critique of tyranny. Beyond the biographical evidence, though, *Mariam* itself conforms to the dramatic mode of the Sidney writers: its extended monologic speeches, its emphasis on verbal rather than physical action, its choral commentaries and the sententious quality of its thought are all hallmarks of Sidnean 'closet' dramas. Like those plays, too, Cary's seems designed for a closed interpretive community even though its issue in print means it could potentially reach a limitless public readership. The evidence for the deliberate marketing of *The Tragedie of Mariam* to a 'private' audience is chiefly on the title page, where the play is said to have been 'Written by that learned, vertuous, and truly noble Ladie, E.C.' A limited or private readership does not, however, mean that the publishers are trying to protect

Cary, as a female writer, from public view. The prominence given to Cary's 'learning' on the title page suggests that, rather than trying to conceal her authorship, the play is in fact appealing to a specific segment of the play-reading public, the better-educated readers for whom an author's learning would presumably be a guarantee of a better quality literary product. Similarly, the publication of the play in two issues – one of which includes a dedicatory sonnet to Cary's sister-in-law – may be designed more to differentiate general from select readerships than to conceal the author's identity. The dedication does not, in fact, reveal the author's identity at all, but what it does do is show that the play was rooted in a private literary coterie which included Cary, her husband and her sister-in-law. The selective inclusion of the sonnet thus produces two versions of the play, each of which is 'private' in a different sense: one of these is targeted to an educated public of play-readers, the other to an exclusive group of personal acquaintances. The first locates the play in the tradition of élite drama, the second within a domestic literary circle, but both versions place the play in a culture of private play-reading rather than public performance.

The plays of Margaret Cavendish, published in two large folio collections some fifty years after *The Tragedie of Mariam*, are the first female-authored plays of the seventeenth century confidently to lay claim to public space. Margaret Lucas was the second wife of William Cavendish and appears to have benefited, as did his daughters Jane and Elizabeth, from belonging to a household in which playwriting and theatrical activities were regular forms of entertainment. Certainly it is clear from Cavendish's many prefaces that her husband actively supported her writing, and she makes no attempt to conceal or excuse the domestic conditions that gave rise to her plays. Furthermore, there is no sense in Cavendish's works that any effort was made to differentiate readerships along the lines of education or status, nor is there any desire for the plays to be associated with a specifically literary culture. What sets her apart from all earlier women playwrights is that she seeks to be read by as broad a public as possible.

In an age when civic and heroic action is an exclusively masculine domain, says Cavendish, print is the only possible means for women to gain public recognition. She expects that 'Contemplating and Writing' will earn her a place in the historical record just as surely as will her husband's actions of 'War and Fighting', even though his are 'performed publickly in the Field' and 'mine privately in my Closet'.[6] Cavendish's confident claim to fame may initially strike us as sheer vanity, but the numerous prefaces to her plays reveal that she also understands herself as a public figure with responsibility for the moral improvement of her audience. Interestingly, many of Cavendish's heroines can be seen as surrogate playwrights putting just this idea into action. In a play called *The Female Academy*, for example (published in Cavendish's earlier collection of 1662), the major character is simply called 'Lady Speaker' and her sole function is to deliver lengthy public addresses, seated on a chair, on questions of female behaviour. Predictably, both male and female auditors are swayed by Lady Speaker's largely conservative opinions, and she having had her say, the play concludes with a number of gentlemen fawning on the Matron who promises to bring them into the company of the Academy's virginal students. Not all of Cavendish's plays reach quite this unproblematic a resolution, but her nearly ubiquitous depictions of female oratory as 'profitable to the Life'[7] reinforce what she says in her prefaces about drama having a serious social purpose.

An extension of this idea may also be found in the many meta-theatrical scenes in Cavendish's plays. In *The Convent of Pleasure*, for example, a sequence of female plays, masques and songs forms the structural framework through which the play's central ethical debate is orchestrated. Centred around a group of women who remove themselves from male society, this play poses some hard-hitting questions about whether women are better off in all-female fellowships or in traditional marriages. The convent is infiltrated by a man disguised as a foreign princess, and his developing love for the convent's founder Lady Happy gradually undermines, for the audience if not for the unwitting Lady Happy, the anti-marital ideology of the play. The emerging conflict is deftly handled by Cavendish in a series of scenes in which the 'Princess' and Lady Happy either observe or act in spectacles that comment directly on the same concerns about women's emotional and sexual fulfilment that are enacted by these characters themselves. Like Lady Speaker's auditors in *The Female Academy*, Lady Happy is 'schooled' through performance to both accept and rejoice in her heteronormative sexuality. At the same time, the lesbian resonance created in the pastoral masque in which Lady Happy and the 'Princess' 'imbrace and kiss, and hold each other in their Arms' (later described by Lady Mediator as 'a kind of Titillation, and more Vigorous' than is normal for female embraces), is not fully extinguished.[8] The layering of perspectives made possible by metatheatrical representation thus creates a wonderfully sophisticated treatment of the play's central issues, rendering Cavendish's underlying educational mission here much more complex than in the plays featuring ethically one-dimensional female orators.

The conjunction of ideas about the ethics of playwriting and the representation of female performance in Cavendish's plays raises the question of why her own work was never staged. The plays were, after all, published in the same decade when women began acting and writing for the commercial theatre, and we know that Cavendish herself was an avid playgoer. It may thus come as a surprise that much of what Cavendish says about the actual theatre reveals a deep ambivalence about this particular form of public exposure for her works. Although the plays were written in the 1650s while Cavendish and her husband were in exile in Paris and Antwerp, she is acutely aware that the possibility of stage production is likely to arise in the minds of her readers. She almost obsessively disavows theatrical performance as the intended mode of publication for her plays, conceding that their prior appearance in print and their excessive length would make them boring to spectators. In contrast, she takes comfort knowing that as books the plays are not exposed to the harsh censure of a theatrical audience. The contradiction between Cavendish's stated commitment to drama as an art of public engagement and her rejection of performance strongly suggests that the publication of her plays was strategic rather than fully voluntary.

Even for Cavendish, then, who was remarkably prolific and an unabashed self-promoter, the public sphere of commercial theatre is not unambiguously available for the presentation of a woman writer's plays. Instead, as we have seen, women playwrights of the early modern period turn to other contexts, both textual and theatrical, in which to explore the intellectual possibilities of drama. These alternative traditions, whether in academic settings, households, or print, were by no means exclusively female, but they were traditions that, precisely because of their differentiation from public theatre, were open to women writers.

NOTES

1. Philip Sidney, *A Defence of Poetry*, ed. Jan Van Dorsten (Oxford: Oxford University Press, 1988), p. 43.
2. Barbara Lewalski, *Writing Women in Jacobean England* (Cambridge, MA: Harvard University Press, 1993), pp. 91–5.
3. Alison Findlay, *Playing Spaces in Early Women's Drama* (Cambridge: Cambridge University Press, 2006), pp. 66–109.
4. Catherine B. Burroughs, ' "Hymen's Monkey Love": *The Concealed Fancies* and Female Sexual Initiation', *Theatre Journal* 51 (1999), 21–31.
5. Margaret J. M. Ezell, ' "To Be Your Daughter in Your Pen": The Social Functions of Literature in the Writings of Lady Elizabeth Brackley and Lady Jane Cavendish', *Huntington Library Quarterly* 51 (1988), 281–96.
6. Margaret Cavendish, 'To His Grace The Duke of Newcastle', in *The Life of the Thrice Noble, High, and Puissant Prince William Cavendish* (London, 1667), b1.
7. Margaret Cavendish, 'To the Readers', in *Playes* (London, 1662), A4.
8. *Paper Bodies: A Margaret Cavendish Reader*, ed. Sylvia Bowerbank and Sara Mendelson (Peterborough, ON: Broadview, 2000), 118, 130.

READING LIST

Brown, Pamela Allen and Peter Parolin (eds.). *Women Players in England, 1500–1660*. Aldershot: Ashgate, 2005.

Cerasano, S. P. and Marion Wynne-Davies (eds.). *Readings in Renaissance Women's Drama: Criticism, History, and Performance 1594–1998*. London: Routledge, 1998.

Renaissance Drama by Women: Texts and Documents. London: Routledge, 1996.

Findlay, Alison. *Playing Spaces in Early Women's Drama*. Cambridge: Cambridge University Press, 2006.

Findlay, Alison and Stephanie Hodgson-Wright, with Gweno Williams. *Women and Dramatic Production 1550–1700*. Harlow: Pearson Education Ltd, 2000.

Purkiss, Diane (ed.). *Three Tragedies by Renaissance Women*. London: Penguin, 1998.

Romack, Katherine and James Fitzmaurice (eds.). *Cavendish and Shakespeare: Interconnections*. Aldershot: Ashgate, 2006.

Shaver, Anne (ed.). *The Convent of Pleasure and Other Plays by Margaret Cavendish*. Baltimore, MD: Johns Hopkins University Press, 1999.

Straznicky, Marta. *Privacy, Playreading, and Women's Closet Drama, 1550–1700*. Cambridge: Cambridge University Press, 2004.

'Reading through the Body: Women and Printed Drama'. In Straznicky (ed.), *The Book of the Play: Playwrights, Stationers, and Readers in Early Modern England*. Amherst: University of Massachusetts Press, 2006, pp. 59–79.

18

DEREK HUGHES

Public drama

In 1660, following the restoration of the monarchy, public theatre became legal for the first time since 1642: patents were issued to two companies, the King's and the Duke's, and illicit rivals were suppressed. The circumstances of performance in the post-Restoration theatre, however, differed significantly from those in the earlier period: for example, outdoor theatres were quickly abandoned, and changeable scenery was introduced. Moreover, whereas women's roles had before the Restoration been played by men, actresses now appeared: a performance by the King's Company on 8 December 1660 featured a special prologue by Thomas Jordan, 'to introduce the first Woman that came to Act on the Stage'.[1] The play was *Othello*; the actress is unknown. Less than a month later, the new phenomenon had been witnessed, without much comment, by Samuel Pepys: 'I to the Theatre, where was acted *Beggars bush* – it being very well done; and here the first time that ever I saw Women come upon the stage.'[2] Pepys certainly enjoyed the new opportunity to admire female beauty: on 28 October 1661 he 'saw *Argalus and Parthenia*, where a woman acted Parthenia, and came afterwards on the Stage in man's clothes, and had the best legs that ever I saw; and I was very well pleas'd with it'. Pepys's theatre-going was not, however, confined to mere ogling, as his variable reactions to Nell Gwyn show. When she acted in Dryden's *Secret Love*, his admiration was unbounded: 'there is a comical part done by Nell, which is Florimell, that I never can hope ever to see the like done again, by man or woman ... but so great performance of a comical part was never, I believe, in the world before as Nell do this' (2 March 1667). Pepys exercised his critical faculties in a contrary way, however, when he saw Nell in serious roles, in which she tended to disappoint him (22 August and 26 December 1667). He did not go to the theatre just to look at legs.

Women were displayed in other ways at the theatres, more simply appealing to Pepys's appetite for beauty, for the King appeared there with his mistresses: 'I went to the Theatre and saw *Breneralt*;[3] I never saw it before. It seemed a good play, but ill acted; only, I sat before Mrs Palmer, the King's mistress, and filled my eyes with her, which much pleased me' (23 July 1661). Like the actresses on the stage, the royal mistresses on display in the audience reveal that women were gaining a public presence that they did not previously possess: the 1660s were the first decade in which it was possible for a woman to become a star. Women gained more substantial forms of prominence as well. By the end of the 1660s, one of the two London theatre companies – the Duke's – was managed by a woman; for Sir William Davenant, the founder of the company, died in 1668, and during the minority of his sons the company was managed by his widow, Mary. She left artistic matters to the two senior actors, Betterton and Harris, but appears to have been a capable businesswoman. In the same decade, we also witness the appearance of the professional woman playwright.

While in Ireland in 1662–3, the poet Katherine Philips (1632–64) was encouraged by the politician and playwright, Roger Boyle, Earl of Orrery, to translate Pierre Corneille's *La Mort de Pompée* (*The Death of Pompey*) into English verse. The play was performed in Dublin in February 1663 and published the same year. The following year the poems which Philips had, for more than a decade, written for – and about – her coterie of friends were published, ostensibly – and perhaps genuinely – without her knowledge. Philips died of smallpox the same year, leaving the greater part of a second Corneille translation (of *Horace*), which was completed by Sir John Denham, and performed in 1668 and 1669, firstly at court and then at the Theatre Royal, Bridges Street. In common with most plays of the 1660s, these plays are politically resonant, despite their importation from a foreign theatrical culture: *Pompée* concerns a virtuous political leader, treacherously beheaded after defeat in a civil war – just like Charles I. So topical was the play that another translation was staged in London in 1664. *Horace* is also a politically pertinent play, since it portrays personal loyalties tragically defeated and frustrated by the conflicts of what is essentially a civil war. A Roman warrior kills his sister's betrothed and his two brothers in combat, and then kills her in outrage at her protests. The choice of subjects reveal a backward-looking mind, haunted by the horrors of the preceding two decades.

Under her coterie name of Orinda, Philips became an archetype of the virtuous female muse, paired (but also contrasted) with the looser muse of Aphra Behn. The pair were commonly evoked by the second generation of women writers that emerged in the 1690s:

> Thus like the Morning Star Orinda rose
> A Champion for her Sex, and wisely chose,
> Conscious of Female weakness, humble wais

T' insinuate for applause, not storm the Bays.
Next gay Astrea briskly won the Prize,
Yet left a spacious room to Criticise.[4]

The woman writer of the 1660s who came closest to celebrity (or, at any rate, the celebrity of notoriety) was not, however, a professional but a noblewoman: Margaret Cavendish, Duchess of Newcastle, whose thick folios, published at her own expense, included poetic, scientific, and many dramatic works. On 30 May 1667, Cavendish was an honoured visitor to the Royal Society. On the first of that month, Pepys went to the Park, eager to see this further version of the female star: 'That which we and almost all went for was to see my Lady Newcastle: which we could not ... When we had spent half an hour in the park, we went out again, weary of the dust and despairing of seeing my Lady Newcastle.' In contrast to Philips's modest output of two translations, Cavendish published over twenty plays, though these were not performed in her lifetime, and indeed until recently were thought to be unperformable (on Cavendish, see Marta Straznicky in this volume).

It was not, however, long before women's drama was acted on the London stage. It made its debut in performances by the court (February 1668) and by the King's Company (January 1669) of Katherine Philips's translation of *Horace*. As mentioned above, this translation seems to look back to the agonizingly divided family loyalties of the civil war, as *Pompée* clearly looks back to the execution of Charles I. When Philips's *Horace* finally reached the stage, however, the performances seemed to reflect a trivializing reaction against earlier traumas. The court performance featured the King's mistress, the Countess of Castlemaine: the 'Mrs Palmer' whom Pepys so often admired in the public theatre. She was clad in jewels (including the crown jewels) to the immense value of £200,000. If this is further testimony to the parallel rise of the actress and royal mistress, this extravagant and decadent spectacle contrasts grossly with a play in which the personal and sexual are savagely sacrificed to national interest. The public performance the following year (attended by Pepys) furnished an incongruity of another kind: an interlude in which some Dutchmen climbed through the mouth and fundament of a giant sow (19 January 1669).

It was in this more complex climate that the first women authors of original plays arrived on the stage; a climate which reveals the rapid dissipation of the idealism and optimism that had accompanied the King's restoration. The first of all was the mysterious Frances Boothby, possibly the daughter of Walter Boothby of Tottenham. Her *Marcelia* was performed by the King's Company, probably in August 1669. Unlike Philips's translations, *Marcelia* is a play that is rooted in the disillusionment of the post-Restoration world, and – albeit timidly – participates in the tactful and restrained reproof of the King's sexual inconstancy that had sporadically appeared on the stage since the middle of the decade. Here, a king marries his fiancée after having been tempted to throw her over for another woman: an altogether more decorous temptation than those to which Charles II was nightly yielding. More pointedly topical is the plot line in which a corrupt courtier is banished after attempting to marry a kinswoman to the king. Growing divisions among the King's former supporters had, the previous year, resulted in the banishment of the Lord Chancellor, Edward Hyde, Earl of Clarendon, who had been a mentor of the young King during his exile. One charge against him was that he had married a kinswoman into the royal line; for, in 1660, Charles II's brother James had been shamed into marrying Clarendon's daughter, Anne, whom he had made pregnant. That which is prevented in the play had happened in fact.

Another early woman playwright was the still more mysterious figure of Elizabeth Polwhele, whose tragedy 'The Faithfull Virgins' (unpublished, but surviving in manuscript) was licensed for production – and probably performed – by the Duke's Company in 1670. In contrast to the muted criticism advanced in *Marcelia*, this is the most spectacularly forthright play yet produced in the period. It is a description of a decadent and lecherous court which is eventually purged by the murder of the ruler: 'for it is fitt / all that so sinn, should punisht be for itt' the play asserts, in lines that were understandably censored by the Master of the Revels, Sir Henry Herbert.[5] Polwhele's other play, also unpublished (until 1977), is a comedy called *The Frolicks* (1671), which may well have been performed, though no performance record survives. Like 'The Faithfull Virgins', it is unusually bold and critical in its (anti-male) sexual attitudes. At the start of the 1670s, comedy was not nearly as sexually frank as it was to become by the mid decade, and the play is unusual for its period in containing a seduction (though the seducer is treated with great severity). Conversely, there is sympathy for a wife tempted to infidelity, though the infidelity is not explicitly consummated. Though not – on the evidence of these plays – a major talent, Polwhele is certainly an adventurous dramatist, and it is a pity that we hear no more of her.

By the end of 1670, however, a major woman talent had reached the stage. In September the Duke's Company performed Aphra Behn's tragicomedy *The Forc'd Marriage*, which was the first of her plays to reach the stage, though the second to be written. With four women having plays on the London stage within two years, it might seem that the floodgates had opened. Yet, in fact, only Aphra Behn went on to make a career as a playwright. From 1671 to 1695, she was the only woman playwright known to have been active in the professional theatre. Some anonymous plays may be by women (indeed, some of Behn's plays were at first published anonymously), but there is no overwhelming reason to assume that they were.

Behn, however, was a considerable talent – one of the most important British writers of her period – and her talent was not confined to the theatre. She was a major innovator in prose fiction, for example, and can claim to be the author of the first English novel: the three-volume *Love-Letters between a Nobleman and his Sister* (1684–7), based on a contemporary intertwining of political conspiracy and sexual scandal. It is often automatically assumed that Behn must have been a marginal and rather vulnerable figure, and there is no doubt that she did encounter anti-feminist prejudice. She records, for example, that a man at the first night of her third play, *The Dutch Lover* (February 1673), announced to those around him 'that they were to expect a woful Play, God damn him, for it was a womans'.[6] After her death, she was satirized by the poetaster Robert Gould as little better than a prostitute: 'For *Punk* and *Poesie* agree so pat, / You cannot well be *this*, and not be *that*'.[7] Gould's lines have been taken to typify a blanket and near-universal Restoration prejudice against the woman writer. It is, however, less often mentioned that even Gould warmly admired that other and more chaste early woman writer, Katherine Philips; indeed, the lines just quoted immediately precede a tribute to Philips. Gould objected to women who wrote bawdy plays; he did not object to women who wrote.

Surveying the larger picture, indeed, one is impressed at how open the stage was to Behn. Although she did not emerge as a playwright until ten years after the reopening of the theatres, she was in fact only the third full-time professional dramatist to emerge since the Restoration, her predecessors being John Dryden and Thomas Shadwell. The suspension of theatrical activity between 1642 and 1660 meant that there was not a cadre of trained dramatists when the theatres reopened, and many of the early Restoration plays were by aristocratic or gentlemanly amateurs. Dryden and Shadwell were themselves gentleman professionals, both educated at Cambridge, and Frances Boothby had connections with the gentry, dedicating *Marcelia* to her kinswoman Lady Yate of Harvington Hall, Worcestershire. All the evidence suggests, by contrast, that Aphra Behn was the daughter of a Kent barber. She may have had access to the library of the Sidney family, but she remains – like Charles Dickens – an extraordinary example of genius manifesting itself without any of the then usual supports of birth or education.

The stereotyped image of Restoration comedy was for a long time that of a witty, urbane, London-based comedy, probably containing illicit sex: a comedy reflecting the lifestyle of the witty, urbane and libertine Charles II. An archetypal example is often taken to be William Wycherley's *The*

Country-Wife (January 1675), whose hero manages to sleep with a succession of women by pretending that he is a eunuch, and therefore no threat to the guardians of their chastity. In fact, such sexually explicit comedy took a long time to develop, *The Country-Wife*, which appeared fifteen years after Charles II's restoration, being the first fully fledged example. Thereafter, it is a sporadic phenomenon, occurring in short and isolated pockets, each different in character from the others. For the character of the Restoration theatre changed almost year by year, and Behn's career responded to its changes.

In the decade after 1660, Restoration drama looked rather different from its now stereotyped image, for dramatists repeatedly wrote plays which, with greater or lesser closeness and moral solemnity, allegorized the events of 1660: the defeat of usurping power, and the providential restoration of authority. The principal dramatic genre was tragicomedy: appropriate for portraying the emergence of triumph from disaster.[8] Although comedy could contain sexually daring conversations, its writers did not at this stage dare to engage their principal characters in consummated sex.

Behn's first three plays followed the early Restoration trend for tragicomedy: these were *The Young King* (not performed until, probably, 1679), *The Forc'd Marriage* (September 1670) and *The Amorous Prince* (February 1671). *The Young King* is an ambivalent treatment of the theme of restoration: a king is excluded from the throne in favour of his sister, but this attempt at female rule yields to the restoration of patriarchy, when an initially sexually aggressive (and potentially rapist) prince is tamed into kingship and monogamy. *The Amorous Prince* again takes up the delicate theme of royal sexuality, portraying the reform of a ruler who is initially a cynical and unscrupulous seducer. Amidst the increasing conflicts of Charles II's and James II's reigns, Behn was unwaveringly to support the royal cause, yet these early plays introduce an ambiguity that was always to characterize her work. The cause which she supports at the level of national politics is, at the domestic level, inseparable from high-handed mistreatment of women. The patriarchal impulses that stabilize the state produce oppression in the home.

After the failure of *The Dutch Lover*, the play which followed *The Amorous Prince*, Behn was silent for three years, before producing her one venture into pure tragedy, *Abdelazer* (June/July 1676), based on the early seventeenth-century play *Lust's Dominion*. She really found herself, however, once Wycherley's *The Country-Wife* had opened the way to a very explicit stage treatment of human sexuality. Though often treated as the archetypal Restoration comedy, this is in fact a quite exceptional play. It portrays sex without painful complications, and its influence lies not in inspiring direct imitations but in breaking the taboos on the representation of sex and opening the way for a more emotionally and psychologically searching portrayal of sexual experience. This came in a play of fourteen months later: Sir George Etherege's *The Man of Mode* (March 1676), which *does* portray the emotional complexity of sex. Its hero, Dorimant, is a charming, dispassionately observed seducer, who enjoys giving pain to women, and succeeds. In contrast to *The Country-Wife*, this play had an immense impact, though mainly in provoking reaction. Comedy grew darker, and there was a sequence of plays featuring Dorimant-like seducers, who (unlike their original) are portrayed with unambiguous severity; the playwrights' sympathies are always with the women on whom the seducer preys. It is in the aftermath of *The Man of Mode* that Behn wrote her first unmixed comedy of sex, *The Rover* (March 1677), whose hero, Willmore, is a woman's-eye view of the Dorimant-figure. It is important, however, to remember that male writers were creating more unambiguously hostile versions of the charming seducer. It is easy to make false assumptions about the nature of Behn's originality if her plays are viewed in isolation from those of her male contemporaries.

As already indicated, however, sex comedy was a genre of fluctuating fortunes. Within three years of the first performance of Wycherley's *The Country-Wife*, audiences seem to have turned against the growing trend for sexual frankness, for there were many failures in the season of 1677–8, including Behn's excellent cuckolding comedy *Sir Patient Fancy* (by January 1678). Behn's responsiveness to audience mood is shown in her next comedy, *The Feign'd Curtizans* (by March 1679), which – while risqué enough – avoids consummated sex. Her next two plays were not comedies at all but tragicomedies. When she did return to comedy, with *The Second Part of The Rover* (*c.* January 1681), it was only the second new sex comedy in three years, its predecessor being Otway's *The Souldiers Fortune* (June 1680). Both these plays are darker than previous sex comedies – far darker than *The Country-Wife* or the first part of *The Rover* – their emphasis being on betrayal and the humiliating compulsiveness of desire. Even after its short period of hibernation, sex comedy returned in changed form.

One factor in the changing character of drama was the tense political climate at the end of the 1670s. Late in 1678, a shady ex-clergyman named Titus Oates made allegations of a Popish plot to murder the King and initiate a general Catholic rebellion. The allegations – at first, widely believed – led to the execution of several innocent people and provoked a series of parliamentary attempts to exclude the King's brother James from succession to the throne, on the grounds that he was a Catholic. This crisis prompted the first formation of political parties: the Tories, who supported the succession of James, and the Whigs, who opposed it. While many dramatists wavered during the course of the crisis, Behn remained consistently loyal to James, though her loyalty was, as usual, gloomy as well as absolute. By mid 1681, however, it was clear that the Exclusion movement had been defeated, and most dramatists sided with the winners. Comedy, which had rather languished during the years of crisis, revived as dramatists jumped on the bandwagon to satirize Whigs as impotent, grasping dotards, triumphantly cuckolded by vigorous young Tory blades. It is a further sign of Behn's prominence that, of the eight new comedies performed in the 1681–2 season, four were by her. Her best comedy of this season – one of the best comedies of the Restoration – is *The City-Heiress* (April 1682), which follows the trend by showing the humiliation of a grasping and elderly Whig: the Tory heroes infiltrate his house in the guise of Polish aristocrats, tie him up and burgle his house, in the process discovering treasonable correspondence. Yet the virile energy which is expressed in this triumph over political villainy is equally expressed in the seduction and harassment of women; interwoven with the burglary is the seduction of a respectable widow, Lady Galliard, by two of the burglar-heroes, the manhandling of the elderly villain being uncomfortably replicated in their pulling and manhandling of her body. The very forces that save the political kingdom produce injustice in the domestic sphere.

After the four new plays of 1681–2, Behn only saw another two new plays staged during the remaining seven years of her life, with her tragicomedy, *The Widdow Ranter, or, The History of Bacon in Virginia*, appearing a few months after her death in 1689. The reasons for this decline were quite beyond her control. Late in 1682 the two London theatre companies merged, because the badly managed King's Company was no longer viable. The disappearance of competition meant that there was little inducement for management to take the risk of putting on new plays, and the number of premières plummeted alarmingly. All dramatists felt the pinch, and Aphra Behn's friend Otway may even have died as a result of malnutrition. Dryden, whose output had for many years been primarily for the theatre, now started to produce some of his noblest translations and original poems. And Behn diversified enormously, becoming a competent poet and a trail-blazer in the spheres of the novel and short fiction.

The blight eased somewhat after the Revolution of 1688, which deposed James II and put William of Orange and his wife Mary (James II's daughter) on the throne, but the theatrical marketplace really opened up again in 1695, six years after Behn's death, when the tyrannical and cheese-paring practices of the manager of the United Company, Christopher Rich, led to a breakaway by senior actors and actresses, including Thomas Betterton, the greatest actor of the period, and Elizabeth Barry, for whom Behn had written some of her most complex and searching roles. Suddenly, there was a demand for new plays again: a demand that rather exceeded the supply of capable writers, since many of the playwrights who had appeared in the early years of the Restoration were now either dead, retired or in decline. This situation provided a new opening for the woman dramatist. Indeed, the opening night of the new company – with the first performance of Congreve's masterpiece *Love for Love* – was countered by Rich's company with a performance of Behn's tragedy *Abdelazer*. In 1696 her hitherto unperformed comedy *The Younger Brother* was tidied up by Charles Gildon and unsuccessfully brought to the stage. One of the great hits of the 1695–6 season, Thomas Southerne's *Oroonoko*, was an adaptation of Behn's novel of the same name (his third adaptation of her fiction), and its success seems to have produced heightened interest in Behn. In 1698–1700 a number of stories allegedly by Behn were published for the first time. Their authenticity is a matter of some doubt, but they testify to her drawing power.

Between 1695 and 1700, moreover, six further women had plays staged. Susannah Centlivre, the most productive and talented of Behn's immediate successors, made her debut in October 1700 with a rather uncharacteristic tragedy, *The Perjur'd Husband*. The season of 1695–6 alone witnessed the first performance not only of Behn's *The Younger Brother* but of no fewer than six plays by five women dramatists. These were the anonymous *She Ventures and He Wins* (by 'Ariadne'), Catharine Trotter's Behn adaptation *Agnes de Castro*, Delarivier Manley's *The Lost Lover* and two plays by Mary Pix, *Ibrahim, the Thirteenth Emperor of the Turks* and *The Spanish Wives*.

All these plays belong to a dramatic and political culture that was quite different from the one in which Behn had written. Sex comedies still occasionally succeeded, but those that did (such as Vanbrugh's *The Relapse* (November 1696)) tended to be cheerful and festive. Dark explorations of infidelity and marital unhappiness, such as Congreve's *The Double-Dealer* (October 1693), tended to fail. Behn had spent her life defending the right of the Lord's anointed to rule the kingdom; in contrast, many plays since the Revolution celebrated the removal (by flight or abdication) of a tyrannical king, and by the mid-nineties dramatists started to suggest what had been anathema during the previous two reigns: that it was right to kill a tyrant, even when he had a hereditary right to the throne. There is also a very slight increase in sympathy for the bourgeoisie, whose sexless acquisitiveness had so often been the butt of Behn's satire. Both new trends are evident in Pix's *Ibrahim*, in which the eponymous tyrant is justly killed after plundering merchants' property to clothe his mistresses and raping the daughter of the man who had saved his life. Sympathy for the middle classes is also evident in Pix's comedy *The Beau Defeated* (March 1700). In one of its plots, a rich bourgeois woman is taken in by fake aristocrats and finally marries a genteel fool for the sake of his title, mistakenly thinking that his boorishness is a witty pose. The final speech asserts the 'greater Power' of bourgeois wealth in comparison with 'empty Scutcheons' of the nobility: 'Mixt with their Coin, the Title sweetly sounds, / No such Allay as Twenty Thousand Pounds'.[9]

Writers of comedy celebrated the Revolution by re-enacting its events on a domestic scale, portraying the expulsion or neutralization of a household tyrant. Congreve's *The Way of the World* (March 1700) is the best-known comedy of this kind. Replicating the events of the Revolution at a household level, however, led easily to one awkward question: if subjects could get rid of an unsatisfactory king, why could wives not get rid of an unsatisfactory husband? Divorce was rare and ruinously expensive, and no woman was granted a divorce until 1801. In Restoration comedy, unhappy marriage was an excuse for a cuckolding plot. In comedy of the 1690s, an unhappy marriage could be the main problem of the play.

As a result, dramatists – both men and women – write comedies in which heroines test the character of prospective husbands, aware that mistakes cannot be rectified after marriage. In another plot in *The Beau Defeated*, Lady Landsworth tests her lover by posing as a prostitute. In *She Ventures and He Wins*, one of the women's plays of the 1695–6 season, a woman also tests her lover (though, imprudently, she does so after marriage): having married the penniless Lovewell, the heiress Charlot pretends to be an impostor, getting a beautiful friend to pretend to be the real Charlot, and to feign love for him.

Behn had portrayed a clash between the political system, which she defended, and the individual lives which were lived within its limits, and often in conflict with its demands. These she also defended. On the whole, post-Revolution dramatists envisage the attainment of a just system, in which individual lives can be harmoniously lived. At the end of Congreve's *The Way of the World*, for example, the rights of the principal characters are protected by contract, no longer subject to the tyrannical whim of the senior family member: a transformation which mirrors the political change in the kingdom. There are, of course, exceptions: for example, the portrayal of an incurably unhappy marriage in Vanbrugh's *The Provoked Wife* (April 1697). The woman's play that perhaps comes closest to preserving Behn's sense of a social system incurably weighted against women is Catharine Trotter's comedy *Love at a Loss* (November 1700). In one of its plots a woman is torn between the respectable option of marriage to her seducer and marriage to the man she loves, and who is prepared to marry her in full knowledge of her history. At the end of the play, the question is decided by a vote of the characters, and they elevate respectability over the needs of the heart: they decree that the heroine is to be made an honest woman by her seducer. The ending varies from that of *The Rover*, where the characters also vote on the marriage of the hero and heroine. There, the vote supports a love-match, but there is nevertheless a sense of something unresolved, for the courtesan who also loves the hero is excluded from the final harmony. In both cases, the demands of social morality cannot be fully adapted to the needs of the personal life.

This unresolved conflict also survives in another woman's play, Delarivier Manley's notorious tragedy *The Royal Mischief* (April 1696). This play portrays the double standards of a world whose moral codes are constituted in the image of male desire: Prince Levan Dadian of Colchis sleeps with his uncle's wife, Homais, while savagely protecting the chastity of his own wife, Bassima. She in turn loves another man, the Vizier Osman, but virtuously refrains from consummating her passion. Selima, Osman's jealous wife, persuades Levan Dadian that the pair are guilty of adultery, and he consequently executes Osman by having him shot from the mouth of a cannon. The penitent Selima then gathers and pieces together Osman's fragments, so that his body is taken over and reshaped by the woman whose jealousy had destroyed him. The fragmentation of Osman's body symbolizes the hostility of the moral system to the integrity of individual life. Its reassembly by his wife is an extreme example of the nature of sexual possession: the creation and worship of an imaginary replica of the loved one, with no interior autonomy or consciousness. Love in this play is, indeed, repeatedly excited by pictures rather than living human beings.

Yet such complex pessimism was no longer the mode, and women playwrights could sometimes display a most un-Behn-like quiescence. An extreme example is Mary Pix's *The Spanish Wives* (August 1696). In one of its plots, a wife is released from an unhappy marriage because it is found to be illegal; there is no clash between personal happiness and social regulation here. In the other plot, a good-humoured and elderly Governor (referred to only by his title of authority) trusts and allows freedom to his young and attractive wife. We expect this trust to be repaid, but the wife is in fact exposed while about to commit adultery. By the end of the play, the Governor has decided that his wife, having learned her lesson, can safely be trusted again, but the trust which he bestows is inevitably more sober and watchful.

None of these dramatists has the stature or inexhaustible originality of Behn; the most talented dramatist of the next generation, Susannah Centlivre, was just setting out on her career as the century ended. The really remarkable thing about the seasons after 1695 is the number of women playwrights who swarmed to the stage once the marketplace reopened. After the brief burst of women's playwriting round about 1670, only Aphra Behn (for whatever reason) went on to forge a full-time career in the theatre. As women writers repeatedly acknowledge in the years after Behn's death, however, she opened the door for them. And, when the time came, they pressed through it.

NOTES

1. Tho[mas] Jordan, *A Nursery of Novelties* (London, 1665?), pp. 21–2.
2. *The Diary of Samuel Pepys*, ed. Robert Latham and William Matthews, 11 vols. (London, 1970–83), 3 January 1661.
3. Sir John Suckling, *Brennoralt, or The Discontented Colonel* (1639; printed 1646).
4. S[arah] Pierse, 'To the Excellent Mrs Catherine Trotter', in Catharine Trotter, *The Unhappy Penitent* (London, 1701), italics reversed.
5. Elizabeth Polwhele, 'The Faithfull Virgins' (1670), Bodleian Library, MS Rawl. Poet. 195, fols. 49–78 (fol. 76).
6. *The Works of Aphra Behn*, ed. Janet Todd, 7 vols. (London: Pickering; Columbus: Ohio State University Press, 1992–6), V: 162.
7. Robert Gould, *A Satyrical Epistle to the Female Author of a Poem call'd Silvia's Revenge &c.* (London, 1691).
8. See Nancy Klein Maguire, *Regicide and Restoration: English Tragicomedy, 1660–1671* (Cambridge: Cambridge University Press, 1992).
9. Mary Pix, *The Beau Defeated; or, The Lucky Younger Brother* (London, 1700), Act V, p. 47.

READING LIST

Chalmers, Hero. *Royalist Women Writers, 1650–1689*. Oxford: Oxford University Press, 2004.
Copeland, Nancy. *Staging Gender in Behn and Centlivre: Women's Comedy and the Theatre*. Aldershot and Burlington, VT: Ashgate, 2004.
Frank, Marcie. *Gender, Theatre, and the Origins of Criticism from Dryden to Manley*. Cambridge: Cambridge University Press, 2002.
Howe, Elizabeth. *The First English Actresses: Women and Drama 1660–1700*. Cambridge: Cambridge University Press, 1992.
Hughes, Derek. *English Drama, 1660–1700*. Oxford: Clarendon Press, 1996.
  The Theatre of Aphra Behn. Basingstoke: Palgrave, 2001.
Hughes, Derek, and Janet Todd (eds.). *The Cambridge Companion to Aphra Behn*. Cambridge: Cambridge University Press, 2004.
Hutner, Heidi (ed.). *Rereading Aphra Behn: History, Theory, and Criticism*. Charlottesville and London: University of Virginia Press, 1993.
Kelley, Anne. *Catharine Trotter: An Early Modern Writer in the Vanguard of Feminism*. Aldershot and Burlington, VT: Ashgate, 2002.
Todd, Janet. *The Secret Life of Aphra Behn*. London: André Deutsch, 1996.
Todd, Janet (ed.). *Aphra Behn Studies*. Cambridge: Cambridge University Press, 1996.

19

LORI HUMPHREY NEWCOMB

Prose fiction

'It is impossible to say when women began to write fiction', Elaine Showalter mused in 1977, then proposed that a novelistic 'literature of their own' could be traced 'from about 1750 on'. Even as Showalter cautioned against generalizing from the 'covert solidarity' of Victorian women novelists to a long feminine literary tradition, she assumed that women's fiction writing must have begun with the novel.[1] Since 1977, the recovery of early modern women writers has led us all to rewrite our literary histories, but prose fiction still remains the genre of early modern writing in which women's share seems most surprisingly sparse. I would like to recover a fuller sense of early women's participation in fiction writing by offering generous definitions of every term in Showalter's early comment. As recent work has shown, we now count as *women* writers those who pen in manuscript or anonymously or collaboratively, as well as those who publish in their own names. *Writing* now includes translation, continuation and imitation as well as original creation. We should also define *fiction* inclusively, since in this period before the novel coalesced as a genre, the variety of imaginative prose writing exceeded any extant generic vocabulary. These more comprehensive definitions embrace literary strategies and practices that were not unique to women-authored fiction, but were the conditions of production of all early modern fiction. Indeed, women-authored fiction, although statistically rare, was crucial in enlarging the scope of a genre the period considered marginal. Precisely because women had to approach writing fiction with double caution, both gendered and generic, they articulated unusually subtle claims for the artistic, ethical and political seriousness of imaginative prose. This chapter, then, addresses both the various justifications women found for writing prose fiction and the inventive uses they made of this emerging genre.

Western culture has tended to imagine women as the primary readers of imaginative prose at least since the late classical period, an association that has served to derogate both fiction and women readers. Classical literary theory did not define prose fiction; a genre only by default, it was seen as shapeless and directionless, writing by and for the untrained speaker and the idle listener. A series of European intellectual traditions – classical, patristic, humanist, Protestant – charged women with producing and consuming oral fictions for their sins; writing fiction was thought to feminize a male writer. Suspicions of fiction persisted more strongly in England than on the Continent, even as its growing popularity and cultural utility grew. In the salons of seventeenth-century France, élite women developed new fiction sub-genres that allowed decorous comment on gender and political conflict. The Francophile English élite snapped up these pseudonymous and anonymous fictions, apparently with little awareness that their female authorship was an open secret in France. With the French precedent for female authorship of fiction so veiled, Englishwomen seem to have written fiction in literal exile or as a kind of symbolic exile. Fiction could empower women, insofar as it was a field slightly outside the English literary commonwealth. Still, it is not surprising that the road from these exilic women's fictions to that quintessential English literary instrument, the classic English novel, was indirect.

As Showalter might have predicted, early modern women fiction writers do not articulate gender solidarity, but individuals recurrently developed gendered tropes, drawing on women's familiar roles as story-tellers or story-readers to justify some form of public authorship. Through the early modern era, women writers grew more bold in turning fiction consumption into fiction production. Under the coterie formation of élite romance-reading, women of privileged households circulated fiction privately and mostly orally, but by the end of the period, it was possible for a middling-class woman author to market fiction titles in her own name. The extension of women's fiction reading into women's fiction writing, almost unthinkable at the start of the early modern period, began to seem inevitable by the eighteenth century, although the career of lady novelist would not be a commonplace until the nineteenth century. This chapter draws on the close ties between Englishwomen's reading and writing of fiction. As women claimed authority over and through fiction, each writer negotiated her way between indulgence of women's reading and hostility to women's writing; between the diffuse international romance tradition and an equally diffuse impulse towards history, not necessarily factual; between coterie practices of romance-spinning and an emergent popular audience for print entertainment; between the safe stance of escapism and riskier claims to topicality or autobiography; between a discursive community in England and a sense of fiction as a world elsewhere. Such negotiations are recurring themes as early modern women begin writing prose fiction.

Insofar as fiction was theorized in the Renaissance, it fell into the mode of romance, ambivalently seen as feminine.[2] The gendered anxiety about romance is especially explicit in Robert Greene's *Penelopes Web* (1587). Greene gathered three romance tales about faultless virgins and wives within the framing narrative of Penelope's daily weaving and nightly unweaving. Because the virtue of Penelope's web is in its unmaking, this frame actually defuses women's capacity to weave texts. Even within humanist debate about women's potential, *Penelopes Web* was conservative: its trilogy of feminine virtues is the memorable (and now much-cited) phrase 'chaste, silent, and obedient'.³ Yet despite the explicit anti-feminism of *Penelopes Web*, such was the bias against romance that another male 'university wit' mocked Greene as 'the Homer of women'.⁴

The pejorative feminization of romance-spinning did not deter women, but certainly it made fiction a field of production in which women writers worked with special self-consciousness. Even writing a translation to or a sequel of a romance could require careful defence, as seen in the examples of Margaret Tyler and Anne Weamys, discussed later in this chapter. Yet despite explicit disavowals of topicality, the correlation of political or linguistic exile on the part of the woman writer or translator with the prominence of exile as a romance plot motif suggests that the claimed purposelessness of romance veiled a very real capacity for political reference.

The early modern period's other term for prose fiction, confusingly, was 'history'. As the *Oxford English Dictionary*'s definitions attest, the separation of factual 'history' from the looser use of 'histories' recapitulated the separation of 'history' from 'story': slowly, forms with more rigorous truth claims split off into a coherent discipline of historiography, leaving an indistinct fictive residue. Still, the period never distinguished 'history' from 'romance' as systematically as it insisted that women read of love and men of war. Women writers as well as men insisted that works we would now call romance were nothing of the kind, even claiming that their productions recounted outré real events in a narrative cloak. The only woman writer who made no bones about inventing her plots was the fearless Margaret Cavendish, and even she explicitly rejected the term 'romance', as we will see. Other early women fiction writers, from Mary Wroth to Aphra Behn to Delarivier Manley, may have insisted on the real-life basis of their stories in part to distance themselves from charges of 'feminine' mendacity or credulity, even as they made feminine affect, and especially the affect of misused women, their central concern. However, to announce that one was passing on fictionalized scandals was by no means to preserve one's modesty or deny political purpose, and indeed Wroth, Behn and Manley all faced sexual innuendo and charges of slander. While Rosalind Ballaster has proposed that woman-authored 'Romance ... absorbs the master narrative of "history" into the privatized discourse of "love"', I would argue that women could also invoke that dynamic as a feint, then use the apparently apolitical discourse of love to do political work.[5] Of course throughout the seventeenth century both men and women mixed fiction and topicality in politicized romances, secret histories, scandal histories, epistolary and key histories, novels and novellas. In France, many of these fiction forms emerged in coteries where women enjoyed substantial power or family protection; they were first imported to England by men, and after the Restoration by women who thrived in their own and in fiction's marginality. Variously questioning political or gender mores, so-called amatory fiction held sway through the seventeenth century and beyond. Its values only seemed a dead end in the hindsight of the eighteenth-century novel, with its theory that verisimilitude should mask imaginary events rather than the reverse. There are still further continuities among romance, amatory fiction and the classic novel to be recovered by attention to their male and female readers and writers.

As in many other genres of English writing, the first work of fiction that a woman published under her own name is a translation. Early modern women recognized that a translator enjoyed protections that an author did not: as long as her translation was reasonably accurate, she could portray herself as mere handmaiden rather than creator, and her efforts were further justified by the value already accorded to the foreign-language original.[6] Margaret Tyler's *The Mirrour of Princely Deedes and Knighthood* (1578) fits this pattern broadly, but its remarkable preface proclaims how self-consciously she innovated in producing this, the first Spanish chivalric romance to be translated into English. Tyler announced that while most women translators tackled religious or didactic subjects, she would risk pleasure reading and even military matters sometimes seen as 'more man-like than becometh my sex'.[7] Tyler staked her freedom to produce fiction on women's being allowed to consume fiction, claiming that 'it is all one for a woman to pen a story as for a man to address his story to a woman' (*Mirrour of Princely Deedes*, A4v). Her syntax may imply that women's writing for themselves is less sexually charged than their listening to male blandishments. Tyler's second justification is more immediate: she claims she was commanded to write the translation by her employer, the Duchess of Norfolk. That detail situates the translation in what Louise Schleiner has called 'an international reading formation' in which aristocratic women employ female attendants to read aloud or sight-translate texts that appropriately 'idealize possible situations of female power and gratification'.[8] Tyler's knowledge of Spanish is unusual in a woman of the period of any rank; her husband was apparently a trade factor for the Norfolk household. Her decision to publish her translation, apparently after leaving the Norfolk household, moves romance production from a privatized multilingual élite into a specifically

English commercial context, and from a circle of primarily female listeners to a mixed reading audience. Thus, Tyler was ahead of any male writer in introducing chivalric romances into English translation, opening up a large readership of the middling sort (including men). She was also ahead of her own gender in translating fiction: oddly, even later in the seventeenth century, when fashionable Englishwomen were very likely to have French as a second language, given the increasingly Francophile culture of the Stuart court, no record survives of an English woman publishing a translation of a French work of fiction.

The popular market for chivalric romance flourished through the seventeenth century in England, even after chivalric romances went out of vogue on the Continent and in court circles. The remaining English translations of Peninsular romances were made by frankly commercial male writers, such as Anthony Munday and Francis Kirkman. Still, Tyler's innovation may have fed the ongoing feminization of chivalric romance in England, for better and for worse. Lady Mary Wroth's unpublished second volume of her *Urania* (after 1621) contains an episode alluding intertextually to the *Mirrour*.[9] Wroth scholar Josephine Roberts has speculated that Wroth may have known Tyler's preface and been inspired to take the next step from translation to original composition.[10] Meanwhile, when male satirists in the Jacobean élite mocked lower-class women readers of chivalric fiction, they named the *Mirrour* as often as the more pervasive *Amadis* cycle. For instance, a 1613 satire portrays a maidservant 'run out of her selfe, and become a Ladie Errant' because she is 'so carried away with the *Myrrour of Knighthood*'.[11] Perhaps the satirists were right to single out the *Mirrour*: scholars have detected a greater emphasis on self-assertive female characters in Tyler's first volume than in its sequels, the *Amadis* cycle, or the randy imitations by Jacobean writers Richard Johnson and Emanuel Forde.

Certainly women's reading experiences were essential to the second romance sensation of the Elizabethan era, the Arcadian fictions that arose from the Sidney family's multi-generational coterie. During the 1580s, the young Philip Sidney began composing a romance on his travels, sent in instalments to his prosperously married sister, Mary Sidney, Countess of Pembroke. *The Countess of Pembroke's Arcadia* was a serial gift from mobile brother to relatively confined sister. Its titular tie between author and reader was a personalized intensification of a culture of patronage surrounding Mary Sidney: she and her husband were the dedicatees of many works, and several of the impecunious authors she brought to Wilton incorporated her name in the titles of works they published. Although Sidney never intended commercial publication of his gift, the circulation of several copies of his incompletely revised *New Arcadia* meant that upon his premature death in the Continental wars, unauthorized publication was perhaps inevitable. The authorized publication of a reasonably complete narrative clearly turned on the Countess's release of the so-called *Old Arcadia*, although scholars have disagreed about how actively she assisted in preparing the composite edition that appeared in 1593. Gavin Alexander describes Mary Sidney's 'stewardship' and 'editing' of the *Arcadia*, while noting that the various paratexts by Philip, Mary, Fulke Greville and Hugh Sanford figure the author's sister as both 'mother' and 'adoptive mother' of his work.[12] While Sanford signed the familiar preface to the composite 1593 edition, the 1613 edition uniquely contains an unsigned leaf (at the break between the revised and unrevised sections) – which helpfully explains that the work drew on 'severall loose sheets' that Philip had 'never after reviewed, nor so much as seene all together by himself'. The printed editions, it continues, offer the 'best coherences, that could be gathered out of those scattered papers, made, and afterwards printed as now it is, only by hir Noble care to whose deare hand they were first committed, and for whose delight and intertayne-ment only undertaken'.[13] Alexander apart, most scholars have assumed, cautiously, that 'care' implies that the Countess delegated editorial work to Sanford and Fulke Greville rather than performing it herself, yet this leaf's emotive details focus on her experience. It is Mary Sidney's readerly delight that authorizes her editorial care, along with the material possession that 'first committed' the 'loose sheets' to her 'hand' and the title to her name. This leaf, whether or not authored by Sidney, locates her authority over the romance in her role as titular first reader. Still, Mary Sidney was more circumspect about her collaborative hand in the 1593 *Arcadia* than about her share in the siblings' (incomplete and unpublished) metaphrase of the Psalms, which posed its own doctrinal dangers. When male coterie writers praised Mary Sidney's literary skills, they mentioned the Psalms, not the shaping of *Arcadia*.

If Mary Sidney could not express pride in helping to bring *Arcadia* from coterie circulation to the press, her role was undoubtedly crucial in the next generation, when her niece Lady Mary Wroth debuted the astonishing *Countesse of Mountgomeries Urania* in 1621. The title page makes the most of Wroth's relation to both uncle and aunt: 'The Countesse of Mountgomeries Urania. Written by the right honorable the Lady MARY WROATH ... Neece to the ever famous, and renowned Sr. Phillips Sidney knight. And to the most excellent Lady Mary Countesse of Pembroke late deceased.' Philip Sidney and Fulke Greville portrayed Mary Sidney as mere midwife, but Mary Wroth claimed her as a progenitor. *Urania* is as bold an achievement among women-authored works as Tyler's had been among translations. It embraced many of the literary influences seen in Wroth's uncle's romance, but on a much larger scale and with a clear intent to publish. Unlike Philip Sidney, Wroth herself apparently arranged publication, in folio no less, and commissioned an elaborate title page by the noted engraver Crispin de Passe. The engraving's allegory of the Throne of Love anticipates the ambitious coordination of geographic and amatory politics by French heroic romance, as in Madame de Scudéry's map of love, the *Carte de Tendre* from *Clélie, Histoire Romaine* (1654).

Wroth's 1621 volume redefines Sidnean tropes of authorship by multiplying instances of women's production of poetry, narration, prophecy and adjudication, and thus widens period expectations for women's literary and political roles. Rather than the isolated heroine of male-authored romance, Wroth creates multiple and distinct female characters and story-tellers. Two of these are clearly versions of a woman writer: the superlative and omni-competent central figure Pamphilia, and the near-mad Antissia, who may discharge certain anxieties about fiction-making. In Philip Sidney's romance, the heroes took political initiative by penetrating their king's rural retreat, won love by learning to emulate the heroines' unquestionable chastity and then escorted daughters and king back to a reformed society. Wroth's many heroines, however, remain partnerless and variously exiled at their narratives' ends. Her plots demand that each woman character not just win a noble lover, but remain constant when he abandons her for political, martial, romantic or marital rivals – or fails to notice her existence. Wroth rewrites female ideals notably, altering Greene's triad of chastity, silence and obedience to an unbreakable but outspoken constancy to a freely chosen (if absent) love object. *Urania* does include a Utopian vision of women and men together occupying the Throne of Love, which suggests that when women's constancy is matched by men's, those lovers enter into a privileged space of emotional and geo-political peace. However, this vision of order quickly collapses and conflict ensues again, with the implication that in Wroth's view, men's military Stoicism cannot match women's emotional Stoicism.

Urania is also remarkable as the first English novel that can be fully keyed to real-life events: the first English *roman-à-clef*. As such, it excited such strong objections from one of the families portrayed that Parliament ordered the book's recall and Wroth's apology. Only partially deterred, Wroth wrote a massive second volume, never published, which confirms that her formal ambitions for participation in the international romance tradition went even beyond the innovation of a key novel.[14] As this continuation explores the protracted travels of Pamphilia and Amphilanthus, the fate of Pamphilia's mixed-race 'natural' son and the conflict between Christianity and Islam, it engages romance internationalism on the largest scale. The temporal sweep of the second volume prefigures the Interregnum's use of prose romance as political allegory: in the 1650s a number of male Royalist writers wrote romances (mostly unpublished) to describe the crisis of monarchic politics and to defuse their sense of exile.

One more Sidneian work by a woman dates from the Interregnum, although its politics are relatively subdued: the *Continuation of Sir Philip Sidney's 'Arcadia'* published in 1651 by a 'young lady, A.W.', now identified as Anne (or Anna) Weamys. While Mary Wroth and Mary Sidney were aristocrats who could directly assert family privilege, Weamys was apparently a clergyman's daughter with ties to leading Royalists who had accommodated themselves to parliamentary rule. Weamys's title announces that unlike Mary Wroth and Mary Sidney, she places a man as the prevailing intelligence of the romance series. Her continuation is also respectful in tackling only those stories that Philip's *New Arcadia* had listed as loose ends (with one exception), but confident in using selective synopses to refocus those stories and characterizations. The exception is the tale of the rural servant Mopsa, which Sidney's Philoclea, but not his narrator, had promised to finish. Weamys develops Mopsa's tale into new material for a woman writer, a parody of a folk tale or ballad, complete with frank sexuality. Weamys makes all the other plots culminate in marriages, neatly stacked in a bravura ending. The extravagant marital closure seems to anticipate the Victorian marriage plot, but in an Interregnum context may gesture towards a fantasy of reconstituting the national status quo. Certainly the toll of political conflict is evident in the wistful concluding remark that when all these lovers return from their exile to rule their home countries, they rule happily – and then yield neatly to the next generation of royals. A consciousness of Royalist romance as a vehicle of loss also haunts the last page, with the unanticipated deaths of the elder shepherd Claius, and of Philisides, the Philip Sidney figure, atop a 'famous Monument' to his never-named love.

Other Royalist women draw on romance to frame their life narratives in the Interregnum's literal or symbolic exile from unified identity. The Frenchness of romance somehow comforted the Royalist Dorothy Osborne as she endured the war at home. Barred by her family from engagement to the less wealthy William Temple, she writes to him regularly, quoting the French romances they both are reading as vicarious substitutes for intimacy and as alternatives to the distressing political upheaval. And most extensively, Margaret Cavendish, Duchess of Newcastle, engaged with romance during and after her exile from England, as she formulated her own unique literary citizenship. Cavendish published her first volume during a brief visit to England in 1652–3. Returning to Antwerp and continuing to publish with her husband's encouragement, she included two prose fiction works in her 1656 volume, *Natures Pictures drawn by Fancies Pencil*. Cavendish explicitly denies that these are romances or are even influenced by romances: 'Though some of these Stories be Romancical, I would not be thought to delight in Romances, having never read a whole one in my life.' Cavendish claims that she would never have allowed her stories 'to be printed' if she thought that 'they could create Amorous thoughts in idle brains'. Instead her 'Tales' are meant to 'benefit the Life' and 'please the Mind'.[15] Despite these denials, one of these two fictions, 'Assaulted and Pursued Chastity', still dallies with romance. Its opening echoes the Greek romance convention of attributing troubles to arbitrary Fortune, for instance. The tale then winds through other conventions, some explicitly anti-romantic – scandal history, Shakespearean comedy, utopian speculation, military history – with the generic twists marked by the heroine's chameleonic name changes. A virtuous gentlewoman, trying to return to her homeland after its civil war, is shipwrecked in the Land of Sensuality, where a bawd tries to sell her virginity to a prince. 'Miseria' protests the Prince's tyranny like a sixteenth-century assaulted virgin, but in a civil war twist, rather than putting a knife to her own breast, she points a pistol (a small one) at the Prince. The Prince parks the redoubtable young woman with his aunt, who offers her leisure reading. Miseria – despite now calling herself Affectionata – categorically refuses romances and requests more 'useful' items: 'mathematical books' and 'stage plays'. The latter genre indeed proves useful as our heroine, cross-dressed as a page, 'Travellia', escapes by ship. But Fortune frowning again as in Greek romance, our heroine is shipwrecked on an island, and the romance narrative becomes colonial. The ever-resourceful Travellia avoids ritual sacrifice to the cannibalistic fish-men islanders by firing another handy pistol; able to speak their language, the exile and prisoner becomes goddess and ruler. Still pursued by the Prince into the Land of Amour, she serves as general and military technician to the Queen of Amity – until she wins the Prince. Never returning to her homeland, they live in Amity as Viceroy and 'Viceregency'. In short, 'Assaulted and Pursued Chastity' is as changeable in its genre as Miseria/Affectionata/Travellia is in his/her gender. Although the tale echoes hopeful Royalist readings of the Interregnum as a series of romance reversals, it ultimately rejects political restoration to place its heroine in permanent colonial leadership.[16]

The Blazing World (1666), written after Cavendish had returned to England, more fully breaks away from romance towards a unique form of speculative fiction, appended to her *Observations upon Experimental Philosophy*. Like Cavendish's romance-based fictions of 1656, it explores the difficulty of reconciling self-assertion with modesty, marriage with free travel, and exile with homeland, but with a greater confidence enabled by the restoration of the English court. *The Blazing World* is another exotic land that comes to be ruled by a European outcast, but extraordinarily, this romance heroine-turned-Empress also hires an English amanuensis, a very recognizably eccentric Duchess of Newcastle, to help write her cabbala. As the exiled Empress, the native Emperor and the visiting Duchess live in a happy ménage of minds, authorial fiction-making, not romantic or political success, becomes the ultimate form of self-assertion and social order. Thus, in *Blazing World*, Cavendish moves beyond merely distinguishing her tales from romance conventions to inventing a fully fledged conceptual utopia. Her 1666 epistle 'To the Reader' charmingly asserts that this fiction has 'made a world of her own: for which no body, I hope, will blame me, since it is in every one's power to do the like'.[17] Of course Cavendish's 'world of her own' draws on her personal notoriety to ground her public authorship, and on her correspondence with scientists to build its parody of the fledgling empiricism of the Royal Society. It was a long time before another woman writer could 'do the like' and publish a utopia, but the defence of authorial idiosyncrasy was a breakthrough for women writers.

Yet after the Restoration, the femininity of romance was devalued further; in extreme cases, women's self-fictionalizing pretensions were associated with insanity or crime. In the 1660s, when Mary Evelyn marvelled that Cavendish's 'mien surpasses ... the descriptions of a romance heroine's greatness', her larger point was that Cavendish should be 'confined within four walls'.[18] In Restoration England, the reading of one's life narrative as a romance was, at best, a persistent fantasy of the upwardly mobile. That fantasy was exploited by the ambitious middling-class author and publisher Francis Kirkman in his efforts to interest a new generation of readers, men and women, in pre-war romances and his own aspiring imitations.[19] Romance fantasy was also echoed, infamously, in the life-writings of two notorious women, the alleged Catholic plotter Elizabeth Cellier and the imposter Mary Carleton. Both of these women were quixotic to disastrous political effect, their fantasies of romance heroism working to betray their class and national identities. When Mary Elizabeth, the so-called 'Popish midwife' of the Meal Tub Plot, wrote an account of her arrest and trial, *Malice Defeated; or, A Brief Relation of the Accusation and Deliverance of Elizabeth Cellier* (1680), she portrayed herself as a 'Distressed She' with no knight to rescue her. Frances Dolan proposes that Cellier resorted to familiar chivalric romance tropes in hopes that this 'safely remote, fairytale past' might 'justify her presence in the public sphere'. But since the era also associated romance with Catholicism and with quixotic self-deception, Cellier's *Malice Defeated* failed to vindicate her. Indeed, its 'heroina' Cellier, who had been selling the pamphlet from her home, was charged with libel.[20]

Mary Carleton, the provincial tinker's daughter who posed as a German princess to hoodwink a wealthy suitor, was similarly depicted as a romance heroine gone wrong in several life narratives. One of these, *The Case of Mary Carleton* (1688), is now often taken as genuinely autobiographical; it appealingly sketches a woman's desire for self-discovery through courtship, and her manipulation of romance conventions to fool men. Mary Carleton's self-romanticization apparently inspired Daniel Defoe's 1722 *Moll Flanders*, which took her criminal self-fictionalizing as a characteristic subject for what we now call the realist novel.

Restoration England's most successful playwright, Aphra Behn, seems to have turned to fiction as a political exile from the stage: apparently she was blacklisted in the theatres after she wrote a preface critical of the pretender James, Duke of Monmouth. In her prose romances, too, Behn played with topicality on the voyeuristic border between 'secret' and 'history'. Her romances always carry the claim to be shocking but true, an excuse that of course flaunts the material's licentiousness. The three-part *Love-Letters between a Nobleman and his Sister* (1684–7), her first and longest venture into prose romance, was also the most riskily identifiable. The tale of one of Monmouth's supporters, an aristocrat who ran off with his sister-in-law, is resituated in a French setting, but with enough telling details to do political damage. Its two volumes exhibit some sympathy for the lovers while arguing that incest and regicide are parallel refusals to obey the law of nature. Prose romance made this work only superficially less dangerous in print than lines spoken on the public stage, and Behn's remaining prose novellas are less overt about their factual bases, if there are any. Her later, shorter prose romances defend certain kinds of libertine behaviour as resistance to tyranny – with the resister being a female with enough sexual savvy to outwit a predatory male. For instance, 'The Unfortunate Happy Lady' of Behn's 1689 novella escapes her brother's scheme to sell her virginity, then reduces him to begging for a share of the wealth she has generated through profitable marriages.

Behn's most reprinted work, *Oroonoko, or the Royal Slave* (1688), tests the position of women at two margins of fiction production, epistemological and imperial. Setting the story in Surinam, which she apparently had visited, Behn positions herself beyond the national where her authority cannot be disputed. Surinam, a slave-holding Dutch colony at this time, is both radically other and yet at some level a comparand for English social values. Behn produces the narrator as a version of herself in colonial exile: white, English, female, middle class, a playwright. The novella's eyewitness claims are sometimes observed scrupulously, but in the end extend where no eyewitness could have gone. Oroonoko, an African prince sold as a slave and brought to Surinam, must protect the virtue of his similarly enslaved consort Imoinda and secure the freedom of his unborn child. When Oroonoko's attempt to lead a slave revolt fails, he kills the pregnant Imoinda and is himself brutally executed. The narrator's fascinated descriptions of the lovers' deaths (only one of which she could have witnessed) are riven by deep racial ambivalence: Oroonoko and Imoinda are regal but exoticized. Most scholars agree that the narrator extends sympathy to Oroonoko for his aristocratic birth not his race, and that his execution echoes Royalist accounts of the martyrdom of Charles I. The startling added detail that Oroonoko beheads Imoinda may redouble that effect. At the same time, Oroonoko is himself feminized like a long-suffering romance heroine, a strategy that defuses his revolt.[21] Behn may even project her own obscure birth and cosmopolitan achievements on to the enslaved prince, linking his trajectory to her own romance-heroine ambitions.

The professionalization of English women's fiction authorship gained momentum when another dramatist, Catharine Trotter, published her first work of fiction: an epistolary novella, *The Adventures of a Young Lady. Written by her self, in several Letters to a Gentleman in the Country* (1693). The young female narrator mocks her current suitors, then describes her barely chaste involvement with a distinguished married man in incriminating detail. 'Olinda' encourages the general's assault on her virtue without concern for moral or political consequences, unlike Cavendish's 'Assaulted and Pursued' heroine, who even when disguised as a male, cringes from the unlawful advances of the Prince she secretly loves. Trotter's titillating 'adventures' debuted anonymously as the first volume of *Letters of Love and Gallantry*, published in 1693. Its publisher Samuel Briscoe then brought out a second volume of letters, comprised of, he claimed, the spontaneous, collective responses of female readers to the first volume: 'The Report of my going to Print the Adventure of *Olinda*, written by her self ... having Rais'd an Emulation in some other Ladies, several others were sent me by the Penny Post in unknown Hands, while the first were in the Press, with a desire to have them also publish'd. I joyfully embrac'd the Proposition.'[22] Even when these submissions are translations, Briscoe's preface leered, they are 'still by Ladies, and done after the best Hands'. The preface closed by inviting other female readers to contribute to the next instalment: 'Such Ladies as are desirous to promote this Undertaking, and to favor the World with any Letters in Prose or Verse ... to be incerted [sic] in the next Volume, are desired to direct them to my Shop ... and I engage to Comply with their Desires' (*Letters of Love and Gallantry*, A3r–A3v). Thus Briscoe played on the 'Desires' of 'Ladies' (and presumably male readers as well), teasing them to join, authorially or vicariously, in an anonymous fling in print.

Trotter's novella itself was first attributed to 'Mrs Trotter' when it appeared, under a slightly different title, in a 1718 expansion of the miscellany (the added letters being by famous men). It was also translated into French as 'Les Amours d'une belle Angloise', extending the cycle that had brought scandal fiction from France to England.[23] In the 1690s, then, a sophisticated cultural formation encouraged some women to play collaboratively with sexual mores in the scandalous borderlands between English and French culture, gossip and personal memoir, fiction and truth, authorship and readership. In the next decade, Delarivier Manley would push the boundary of scandal ever further: her own letters published in 1695 were only mildly self-revelatory, but her *Secret History of Queen Zarah* (1705) was a full-throttle if fictionalized attack on one of the most powerful noblewomen of her era, and tales from *New Atalantis* (2 volumes, 1709) attributed even more salacious activities to her thinly disguised Whig opponents. Only the title page claim that these works were translated protected Manley from charges of libel, especially when the works were republished with keys. Within a few decades, partisan writing like Manley's would be repudiated: the scandal chronicle's expansive web of self-dramatization and topicality could not survive new forms of moralism that again narrowed women's political and literary expression in the writing of prose fiction.

NOTES

1. Elaine Showalter, *A Literature of Their Own: British Women Novelists from Brontë to Lessing* (Princeton, NJ: Princeton University Press, 1977), pp. 16, 15. Showalter's assumption comes despite her citation of Germaine Greer's famous 1974 insight that 'since the Interregnum, a small group of women have enjoyed dazzling literary prestige during their own lifetimes, only to vanish without trace from the records of posterity' (quoted p. 11).
2. Patricia Parker has extensively explored male ambivalence about the femininity of romance; see, for instance, her *Inescapable Romance: Studies in the Poetics of a Mode* (Princeton, NJ: Princeton University Press, 1979).
3. Hence the title of Suzanne Hull's pioneering bibliography of writing directed to a female readership, *Chaste, Silent & Obedient: English Books for Women, 1475–1640* (Pasadena, CA: Huntington Library, 1981).
4. Thomas Nashe, *The Anatomie of Absurditie* (London, 1589).
5. Rosalind Ballaster, *Seductive Forms: Women's Amatory Fiction from 1684 to 1740* (Oxford: Clarendon Press, 1992), p. 47.
6. On the complexities of women's translations, see Danielle Clarke's chapter in this volume.
7. Margaret Tyler, *The Mirrour of Princely Deedes and Knighthood* (London, 1578), A4v.

8. Louise Schleiner, *Tudor and Stuart Women Writers* (Bloomington: Indiana University Press, 1994), p. 21.

9. Helen Hackett, *Women and Romance Fiction in the English Renaissance* (Cambridge: Cambridge University Press, 2000), p. 164.

10. *The Second Part of 'The Countess of Montgomery's Urania'*, ed. Josephine A. Roberts, Suzanne Gossett and Janel Mueller (Tempe, AZ: Renaissance English Text Society, 1999), p. xxxix.

11. Quoted in Hackett, *Women and Romance Fiction*, p. 4.

12. Gavin Alexander, *Writing after Sidney: The Literary Response to Sir Philip Sidney, 1586–1640* (Oxford: Oxford University Press, 2006), pp. xxiii, 84 and 86–7.

13. *The Countess of Pembroke's Arcadia* (London, 1613 edition), cited in *ibid.*, pp. xxvi–xxvii.

14. The continuation is preserved in holograph, with authorial emendations, at the Newberry Library in Chicago. For the scholarly edition prepared by Roberts, Gossett and Mueller, see note 10.

15. Margaret Cavendish, *Natures Pictures* (London, 1656), 'The Preface' (b2v). In his 1656 prefatory poem, 'To the Lady Marchioness of Newcastle, on her book of Tales', Cavendish's husband William describes the volume as containing 'romancies' but similarly insists that they are 'innocent' (b1r).

16. See Annabel Patterson, ch. 5: 'The Royal Romance', in *Censorship and Interpretation: The Conditions of Writing and Reading in Early Modern England* (Madison: University of Wisconsin, 1984); Lois Potter, *Secret Rites and Secret Writing: Royalist Literature, 1641–1660* (Cambridge: Cambridge University Press, 1989); Elizabeth Sauer, 'Emasculating Romance: Historical Fiction in the Protectorate', in Constance C. Relihan and Goran V. Stanivukovic (eds.), *Prose Fiction and Early Modern Sexuality in England, 1570–1640* (New York and Basingstoke: Palgrave, 2003), pp. 195–213. On Margaret Cavendish's life as a 'series of exiles' offering a 'privileged literary stance', see Anna Battigelli, *Margaret Cavendish and the Exiles of the Mind* (Lexington: University Press of Kentucky, 1999), p. 7.

17. Margaret Cavendish, *The Description of a New World, Called the Blazing World* (London, 1666), b*2r.

18. Quoted in Emma L. E. Rees, *Margaret Cavendish: Gender, Genre, Exile* (Manchester: Manchester University Press, 2003), p. 12.

19. On Kirkman's fiction publishing, see Lori Humphrey Newcomb, 'Literary Restoration: Francis Kirkman and the Canons of Pre-War Drama and Romance', *Analytical and Enumerative Bibliography* 12.3–4 (Spring 2002), 229–40.

20. Frances E. Dolan, *Whores of Babylon: Catholicism, Gender and Seventeenth-Century Print Culture* (Ithaca, NY: Cornell University Press, 1999), pp. 183, 185.

21. Charlotte Sussman, 'The Other Problem with Women: Reproduction and Slave Culture in Aphra Behn's *Oroonoko*', in Heidi Hutner (ed.), *Rereading Aphra Behn: History, Theory, and Criticism* (Charlottesville: University Press of Virginia), pp. 212–33.

22. Catharine Trotter, *Letters of Love and Gallantry and Several Other Subjects, All Written by Ladies* (London, 1693), A2r–A2v.

23. Catharine Trotter, *'The Adventures of a Young Lady' and Other Works*, selected and introduced by Anne Kelley (Aldershot: Ashgate, 2006), p. ix.

READING LIST

Ballaster, Rosalind. *Seductive Forms: Women's Amatory Fiction from 1684 to 1740.* Oxford: Clarendon Press, 1992.

Cooper, Helen. *The English Romance in Time.* Oxford: Oxford University Press, 2004.

Fuchs, Barbara. *Romance: The New Critical Idiom.* New York and Oxford: Routledge, 2004.

Hackett, Helen. *Women and Romance Fiction in the English Renaissance.* Cambridge: Cambridge University Press, 2000.

Salzman, Paul. *English Prose Fiction 1558–1700: A Critical History.* Oxford: Clarendon Press, 1985.

Todd, Janet. *The Sign of Angelica: Women, Writing and Fiction, 1660–1800.* New York: Columbia University Press, 1989.

INDEX

Note: text illustrations are denoted by italic page numbers.

Cambridge Companions to …

AUTHORS